Building the Agile Enterprise

Building the Agile Enterprise
With Capabilities, Collaborations and Values

Second Edition

Fred A. Cummins

AMSTERDAM • BOSTON • HEIDELBERG • LONDON
NEW YORK • OXFORD • PARIS • SAN DIEGO
SAN FRANCISCO • SINGAPORE • SYDNEY • TOKYO

Morgan Kaufmann is an imprint of Elsevier

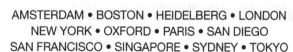

Morgan Kaufmann is an imprint of Elsevier
50 Hampshire Street, 5th Floor, Cambridge, MA 02139, United States

Notices
Knowledge and best practice in this field are constantly changing. As new research and
experience broaden our understanding, changes in research methods, professional practices,
or medical treatment may become necessary.

Practitioners and researchers must always rely on their own experience and knowledge in
evaluating and using any information, methods, compounds, or experiments described herein.
In using such information or methods they should be mindful of their own safety and the safety
of others, including parties for whom they have a professional responsibility.

To the fullest extent of the law, neither the Publisher nor the authors, contributors, or editors,
assume any liability for any injury and/or damage to persons or property as a matter of
products liability, negligence or otherwise, or from any use or operation of any methods,
products, instructions, or ideas contained in the material herein.

Library of Congress Cataloging-in-Publication Data
A catalog record for this book is available from the Library of Congress

British Library Cataloguing-in-Publication Data
A catalogue record for this book is available from the British Library

ISBN: 978-0-12-805160-3

Publisher: Todd Green
Acquisition Editor: Todd Green
Editorial Project Manager: Lindsay Lawrence
Production Project Manager: Priya Kumaraguruparan
Cover Designer: Mark Rogers

Typeset by SPi Global, India

Contents

List of Figures

Preface

The first edition of this book was focused on service-oriented architecture (SOA), business process management (BPM), and model-based management (MBM). At that time, I was a fellow at EDS and was engaged in advancing technology for better business solutions, improving application development methods, and developing industry standards related to SOA, BPM, and MBM.

The first edition was the culmination of a many years of technical and business consulting along with work on industry standards as the EDS representative to the Object Management Group (OMG). Throughout my career, I have had the opportunity to be on the forefront of emerging technologies and participated in applying the technology to business solutions. My experience and insights grew further through collaboration with industry leaders in my role as cochair of the OMG task force that is currently the Business Modeling and Integration Domain Task Force (after several name changes as it has evolved over the last 17 years).

When I undertook writing of the first edition, it was clear to me that SOA could help better align information technology to business needs for business systems since businesses have used shared services for accounting, purchasing, human resource management, and other shared capabilities for many years before computers—it is a basic business pattern. I participated in the development of SoaML, a modeling language for specification of computer-based services and component-oriented design of business systems. During this time, I also participated in a joint effort of EDS and Oracle to develop a SOA maturity model that defined the typical five levels of maturity for business and technology to implement a service-oriented business/enterprise architecture.

During the same years, BPM had become an established business practice that was becoming strongly influenced by business process management systems (BPMS). This was important for putting business people more directly in charge of their business processes, whereas earlier systems embedded business processes in large applications where only computer programmers could understand and adapt the processes to business needs and changes. I participated in the development of early specifications for automation of workflow management and later specifications for modeling business processes. The end result was the OMG specification, BPMN (business process model and notation) that brought together business process modeling efforts of OMG, and business process modeling graphics of the Business Process Management Initiative (BPMI) after BPMI merged with OMG.

Finally, modeling tools emerged to assist business leaders in support of strategic planning (the OMG business motivation model—BMM) and the capture of business rules along with associated terminology and semantics (semantics of business vocabulary and rules—SBVR). BMM came to OMG as a draft specification developed by collaboration of a number of consultants who had supported strategic planning and had developed a shared framework. SBVR was developed through the OMG process involving a diverse group of consultants, academics, and industry experts driven by a desire to provide business people and consultants with a robust capability to capture and express business rules with consistent, well-defined business concepts.

My goal with the first edition was to bring together business people and information technology people with an understanding of how information technology should serve business and how a number of information technology standards can come together to meet business needs. I believe it reflected the then current state of business and technology.

I recently undertook writing of this second edition to reflect more recent advances. I expected to make some refinements to some of the chapters and add the impact of CMMN (case management model and notation) and VDML (value delivery modeling language). However, as I got into the detail, I realized the full significance of these new standards and other industry advances, and this second edition was a lot more work than I anticipated.

Essentially, the current potential for enterprise agility has evolved. Beyond the advances in modeling, smart phones have connected hand-held computers and personal interactions to the Internet. Social media have engaged people everywhere, driven changes in awareness and attitudes, and extended the reach and exposure of business information systems. The Internet is being connected to a wide range of sensors, devices, appliances, and vehicles—the Internet of Things. Cloud computing is gaining tractions as a computing and communications utility, and distributed computing developed for Internet searches and the cloud have enabled massively parallel, distributed computing applied to "big data" for "analytics," the analysis of correlations, events, and emerging trends.

In Chapter 1, I expand on the evolution of technology, where we have been and where we are today with an introduction to a new way of thinking about how the enterprise should work.

In Chapter 2, I introduce VDML as a modeling language to bridge the gap between strategic plans, business requirements, the transformation of business operations, and design of operational systems of an agile enterprise. VDML brings a focus on creation of value in the enterprise as a network of collaborations applying capabilities to create value and delivery of values in customer value propositions. VDML provides an abstraction of the business that is more suitable for consideration by business leaders and analysis of operating performance from an enterprise perspective.

In Chapter 3, I describe a business architecture composed of capability building blocks and present some techniques for analysis of an existing enterprise to discover the inherent capability building blocks. The building blocks can be configured to consolidate capabilities shared by multiple value streams that deliver different products and value propositions to different market segments as well as internal consumers. The sharing of capabilities drives information technology infrastructure requirements as well as organizational change, discussed later. VDML provides the modeling structure to configure, analyze, and optimize the implementations of shared capabilities from an enterprise perspective. The chapter then expands on requirements for service units (introduced in the first edition) that are the operational implementation of sharable capabilities.

In Chapter 4, I go deeper into business design with a focus on business processes. It provides an overview of BPMN and CMMN modeling languages. In the first edition, the business process focus was on prescriptive, repeatable processes of BPMN. CMMN brings automation support for adaptive processes that are defined and adjusted by the participating knowledge workers as the situation evolves, and it supports collaboration, coordination, and adaptation that were not automated when the business processes were predefined by BPMN. CMMN brings the potential for automation support to the work of knowledge workers and managers to support collaboration, coordination, and timely response to changing circumstances. In this chapter, we propose a discipline that goes beyond current BPM practices to address the integration and support of the network of collaborations by which the enterprise actually works.

In Chapter 5, I focus on business rules. Rules define required relationships, actions, and constraints and are of particular concern where they implement policies that may express management intent or government regulations. Rules are also important to support decision making and analysis, including rule-based systems that may support complex planning, configuration, search, and diagnosis.

In Chapter 6, I describe a data management architecture to support the agile enterprise. The chapter begins with some general patterns and principles and then discusses the architectural components that include the distributed management of master data (the enterprise records), the capture of performance data, the capture and management of business knowledge, the coordination of data updates, and support of business intelligence and analytics. The chapter concludes with an overview of data modeling and highlights of implementation of the data management architecture in the context of the Value Delivery Maturity Model of Appendix A.

In Chapter 7, I discuss information security issues and technology. Information security is essentially about mitigation of risk. Exposure of data and systems is a major concern for business leaders both with global exposure through the Internet, and the integration of capabilities of the agile enterprise that requires increased accessibility across organizational and enterprise boundaries. This chapter begins with perspectives on the risks of information security and then provides an introduction to key security technologies and management of authorization.

Chapter 8 is about identification and response to events that drive the operation of the enterprise. These are identified as exceptions or controls in formal business processes, changes of business state that are relevant to oversight or corrective action, and other less predictable and more disruptive events that may cause operational failures. The chapter discusses the various forms, sources, consequences of events, and mitigation of failures and describes the required notification service of the information infrastructure.

In Chapter 9, I focus on sensing and responding to events and circumstances that may require changes to the enterprise. An agile enterprise must recognize and respond to relevant events, particularly events in the ecosystem as well as internal insights or innovations. These events are primarily recognized in business intelligence and analytics, or by observations of individuals. The chapter proposes a sense and respond directory to record events, resolve duplication of alerts, alert appropriate responders, and track efforts for resolution. It also recommends escalation of responses based on the scope and severity of impact. The chapter then turns to consideration of transformation planning and management and product lifecycle management that are driven by strategic planning and supported by services for business development and transformation.

In Chapter 10, I focus on a management hierarchy for the agile enterprise. This begins with the general design requirements of service units—the operational equivalent of sharable capabilities and the organizational grouping and management hierarchy for management of shared services. Next, we consider governing board support services, executive staff services, administrative support services, and business operations services that are divided between line of business capabilities and shared capabilities. The chapter closes with a brief discussion of the organizational transition as it increases in levels of maturity (Appendix A).

Chapter 11 concludes the book with a focus on enterprise leadership. It starts with consideration of the supports that should be available to business leaders. It then examines leadership roles in four categories: the governing board, top management, capability management, and knowledge workers.

There are several themes. The governing board should be more involved in ensuring that the enterprise is doing the right thing and doing it well from an investor's perspective, it should ensure objective risk assessment and an acceptable level of risk, and it should monitor performance for business transformation and customer expectations of values. The top management must provide industry leadership, conduct continuous strategic planning, drive the sharing of capabilities that are optimized from an enterprise perspective, and provide the cultural environment that inspires and empowers employees to contribute beyond routine responsibilities—a conceptual model of culture is discussed in Appendix B. The capability managers, within the scope of their responsibility, must contribute to risk assessment and mitigation, optimize capability performance, manage and protect enterprise master data, and enable and provide incentives to empower and inspire knowledge workers. Knowledge workers should be a key source of alerts and solutions for sense and respond, they should contribute to optimization of their capability units, and they should contribute to innovations and collaborations across organizational boundaries to bring solutions and new ideas, bottom-up.

The chapter then turns to the challenge of making the enterprise an industry leader through strategic initiatives, industry advances, influencing government regulations, and development of industry standards. A list of potential industry standards is outlined as opportunities to further improve business agility as well as efficiency and customer value.

This book is not a product of research, per se, because it is about how things could be done, not how they are done. It is the product of many years of systems development, technology transfer, business and technology consulting, and collaboration on industry standards that change the state of the art. There will be new ideas, but the inherent conceptual model of this book is based on industry standards, successful business practices as well as challenges and opportunities that call for both a better understanding of the way the enterprise actually works, and the means to formulate and implement better solutions. I hope it will help business leaders appreciate the potential of the technology and the value of industry standards, and encourage participation in the development of future industry standards as well as government regulations to bring greater value to customers and opportunities for the enterprise.

Acknowledgments

I want to thank my wife, Hope, for her encouragement, patience, and tolerance during all the time I spent working on both the first and second editions of this book as well as the personal time I devoted to OMG participation.

This second edition "stands on the shoulders" of the first edition, and, therefore, those who I acknowledged for the first edition have indirectly contributed to my efforts on this second edition. Tom Hill, lead EDS fellow, gave me time and encouragement to write the first edition. I owe many coworkers at EDS for insights I have gained over the years—in particular, at EDS, Jef Meerts, Wafa Khorsheed, Carleen Christner, Ivan Lomelli, and the EDS fellows community. At OMG, Cory Casanave, Antoine Lonjon, Conrad Bock, Donald Chapin, John Hall, Manfred Koethe, Karl Frank, Jim Amsden, Henk de Man, and many other industry experts from whom I gained the benefit of their insights and experiences in our collaborative activities.

For this second edition, I have gained from additional collaborations, working on OMG, industry standards, particularly the work on VDML and CMMN. Henk de Man worked closely with me on the development of the VDML RFP and through the finalization of the specification. In addition, Arne Berre brought the insights of the NEFFICS project of the EU and several industry experts from that effort including Verna Allee, Peter Lindgren, and Pavel Hruby. In addition, Pete Rivett, Larry Hines, and Alain Picard contributed directly to refinement of the details of the specification. For the development of CMMN, Henk de Man brought attention to the need and opportunity for a standard. We worked together to develop the RFP and an initial submission that established the core concepts of CMMN. The final specification was developed through the additional efforts of Henk de Man, Ralf Mueller, Mike Marin, Denis Gagne, Ivana Trickovic, and a number of others who developed the refined and robust specification.

I also want to thank Henk de Man for his thoughtful reviews of the manuscript for this edition, Steven Witkop for his feedback on Chapter 1, Willem Jan Gerritsen for his feedback on the security chapter, and Mark von Rosing for the perspective he brings from the Global University Alliance and LEADing Practice.

The Agile Enterprise

An agile enterprise rapidly adapts to changing business challenges and opportunities. Agility has always been important for an enterprise to achieve and maintain competitive advantage. However, the threshold for competitive agility is constantly changing.

Fifty years ago, General Motors required 5 years to develop and launch a new vehicle line. This was a competitive disadvantage, and the goal was to reduce that to 3 years. In today's world, an enterprise that takes 5 years to introduce a competitive product will probably be out of business before the product can go to market or the target market is likely to have changed.

There are many factors involved in enterprise agility. An enterprise may need to respond to changes in financial markets; changes in the cost or availability of resources or commodities; changes in critical personnel skills and methods; changes in required facilities and infrastructure; changes in economic, social, or political conditions; and so on. However, these are beyond the scope of this book.

Here, we are concerned with agility in the operation of the enterprise. The enterprise is effectively a system of people and machines, working together in harmony to achieve enterprise objectives. Information technology supports these systems with automation to improve efficiency and accuracy.

At the same time, information technology is also a principle barrier to agility. Legacy systems have been built to automate current business operations that are now obsolete and may be poorly understood. The information technology of these systems is also obsolete, so the people who have the necessary skills are in short supply. In addition, these systems were not designed for change, but rather to automate the best practices of the time.

Nevertheless, information technology is needed to enable agility, and advances in information technology continue to raise the threshold for competitive agility. Enterprise agility involves not only the ability to change the enterprise business systems but also the ability to sense and respond to threats and opportunities, and the ability to innovate to create new opportunities.

Building the Agile Enterprise. http://dx.doi.org/10.1016/B978-0-12-805160-3.00001-6
Copyright © 2017 Elsevier Inc. All rights reserved.

Today's agility must reflect the fact that business systems have become increasingly complex in order to optimize cost, quality, and timeliness of results and comply with variations in regulations in a global marketplace. Some of this complexity is also the result of inconsistency of information systems and infrastructure developed at different times to solve different problems, or developed or acquired with a new line of business (LOB). This inconsistency is a handicap for agility. However, as we will see, business systems are also becoming increasingly complex to optimize customer value, control, and performance while increasing agility. Computer-based modeling is essential to manage the complexity; reconfigure business systems; support analysis; and provide a context for strategic planning, transformation, and continuous improvement.

A critical aspect of reducing time-to-market for General Motors was the use of information technology to reduce the time and improve the efficiency of product development. This not only reduced the time to market but also enabled the development of much more sophisticated products with improved quality, along with the ability to configure individual automobiles to address individual customer preferences. Of course, this only maintained the competitive position in an evolving industry.

While becoming more complex, the agile enterprise must be highly configurable to meet changing business challenges and opportunities. This requires consistency and synergy in the design of the business systems and the information systems to support the design, implementation, and operation of the business.

The changes to business systems also involve changes to the business culture—the attitudes, priorities, and roles of people working together to achieve enterprise objectives. The following are some key cultural objectives:

- *Knowledge worker empowerment.* Knowledge workers must be empowered and supported to apply their knowledge and experience for appropriate actions that may evolve as a result of innovation and business changes. They must not be constrained by prescriptive processes designed for the typical situation.
- *Model-based decisions.* While the structure of the enterprise and its systems may be amenable to change—continuous change, optimization, and adaptive configuration require more complex analysis. This analysis calls for the use of computer-based business models for effective management of the complexity and planning for transformation.
- *Commitment to change.* Employees and other stakeholders must accept that change is now a normal part of sustaining the enterprise. They must

welcome and contribute to change as an opportunity to innovate, excel, and collaborate for orderly transformation.

- *Continuous strategic planning and transformation.* It is impossible neither to predict all the forces that will require business change nor to anticipate the enterprise-level need for strategic planning. Leaders throughout the organization must be sensitive to the need for change and responsive to innovative ideas. A significant transformation will likely be incomplete when the next transformation is initiated.
- *Think global.* Many large enterprises have business operations in multiple countries, but even small companies may serve international markets. Companies must be always on-line and should consider accessibility by people in different cultures speaking different languages. In addition, their products, if not their operations, must be sensitive to laws, regulations and, possibly, customs in other countries.
- *Sense and respond.* All employees should be the eyes and ears of the enterprise to sense threats and opportunities, while others in the enterprise must be prepared to respond to mitigate the threat or exploit the opportunity.
- *Focus on customer value.* Maintaining and improving customer value, from and enterprise perspective, should be the basis for evaluation of all efforts.
- *Shared enterprise purpose.* People of the enterprise should commit to a long-term purpose for the enterprise that is a key factor in the good will of the enterprise and a guide to long-term strategy.

This book is about the design of an enterprise, exploiting information technology, to achieve and maintain competitive agility while optimizing customer value and meeting the needs of other stakeholders.

In this chapter, we will begin by highlighting changes that have occurred since the first edition of this book. We will then review the evolution of the application of information technology in business systems and its impact on the current state of enterprise business systems. Next we will provide an overview of a new way of thinking about the design of the enterprise as an introduction to the rest of this book and its themes of capabilities, collaborations, and values. Finally, we will highlight the impact of value delivery management (VDM) on major strategic initiatives, followed by some critical success factors (CSFs) on the journey to competitive agility.

RECENT ADVANCES

The first edition of this book focused on SOA (service-oriented architecture), BPM (business process management), and MBM (model-based management). Information technology readers are probably familiar with the information technology notions of SOA, business process management systems (BPMS) for business process automation, and model-driven architecture (MDA) for model-based development because most IT organizations have heard of these technologies and most have explored them.

SOA technology has enabled rapid and flexible integration of systems across organizational boundaries. BPMS technology is improving flexibility and optimization of business processes. MDA technology has enabled business modeling. MDA introduced standards for exchange of models between different modeling tools and for generating applications from models. More recently, MDA has been applied to the development of business modeling languages.

The current awareness of and experience with these technologies is a good thing, for two reasons. First, it means that IT organizations are familiar with the basic concepts as well as the business reasons behind applying them (reuse, consistency, economies of scale), for IT cost reductions, and for systems flexibility.

The second reason is that IT organizations are beginning to understand that realization of the full business value of these technologies requires changes in the operation of the business, and they should be better prepared to support the agile enterprise described in this book. The traditional delivery of information technology is bottom-up, opportunistically introducing automation and integration but leaving the design of the business fundamentally the same. The new economies of scale and flexibility are not just in the use of shared code and component software architecture but in consolidation of business functions and an adaptive business architecture.

In this edition, these technical foundations have been further developed from a business perspective. SOA defines a component-based architecture. While SOA remains a valid design pattern, it has been driven by information technology as a systems design architecture. In this edition, we will focus on a business perspective where the components are aligned with business capabilities in a capability-based architecture (CBA). A CBA is focused on the design of the business, building on SOA and current information technology, sharing business capabilities across lines of business (LOB), and aligning the organization structure for effective management of shared capabilities. The basic concepts of CBA are not new to business; they are the basis for shared services of accounting, purchasing, and human resource management. The difference is the discipline, scope, and IT support of shared business services. CBA and SOA will be discussed further in Chapter 3.

BPM is rooted in the design and optimization of repeatable business processes. While it comprehends manual processes, the emphasis has been on automated business processes implemented with BPMS typically designed with the BPMN (Business Process Model and Notation) language. Today, technology is emerging to support processes that are directed, ad hoc, by knowledge workers and support collaboration of teams to address diverse circumstances characterized by legal cases and medical care. CMMN (case management model and notation), adopted by the OMG, defines a language for specification of computer support of adaptive processes. In addition, organizations are no longer described by the traditional management hierarchy, but, instead, essential business operations involve people from different organizations collaborating in various ways to solve problems, coordinate changes, and respond to events. Consequently, we define BCM (business collaboration management) to expand the scope of BPM to include various forms of collaboration, including adaptive processes, ad hoc teams, and professional interest groups. BCM will be discussed in further detail in Chapter 4.

Finally, the first edition recognized the need for computer-based models for top management. It discussed BMM (business motivation model) that supports strategic planning, and SBVR (semantics of business vocabularies and business rules) that supports the clarification of business terminology and the capture of business rules. However, for the most part, business analysis and design have been done with a fragmented collection of graphical drawings and spreadsheets. In the last several years, there has been a growing interest in Business Architecture as a discipline to drive the design and transformation of the business from executive-level strategic planning and business requirements.

At the same time, VDML (value delivery modeling language) has been developed and adopted by OMG. VDML enables business architects to fill the gap between strategic planning and the operational design of the business. It supports a conceptual model that integrates multiple views of the business to represent the current or future state of the enterprise at a business leader level of abstraction. VDML supports analysis of the creation of value to drive business analysis and design based on delivery of values to customers and other stakeholders. Thus, in this edition, we will focus on VDM (value delivery management) as the central theme of business modeling. Chapter 2 will provide a more detailed description of the VDML language and the nature of VDML models. VDML supports VDM incorporating CBA and supporting BCM at a management level of abstraction.

These concepts and relationships are applicable across all industries. Manufacturing represents a rich diversity of business functions and challenges, and it touches on most other industries. In financial services, much of the ability to develop and deliver new products depends on supporting information technology. Telecommunications and financial services typically have great opportunities to exploit CBA, since many of these companies have experienced unresolved mergers and acquisitions.

All industries are affected by expanded use of the Internet. Wireless technology and mobile computing with smart phones and tablets have expanded the potential for education and entertainment, on-line business communications, and social networking. The Internet, through a global, fiber-optic network, has enabled instant communication between individuals and systems, anywhere in the world. Cloud computing networks are emerging as global, computing utilities. The Internet is increasingly connected to sensors, appliances, and other devices that are sources of large volumes of data that can be analyzed to gain insights on relevant events and trends.

Regardless of the industry, top management must understand the potential of the technology, recognize the competitive necessity of enterprise agility, assess the current state of the enterprise, and commit to a transformation to an agile, value-driven architecture that may take a number of years. Applying VDM, CBA, and BCM requires a transition to a business-oriented approach that puts bottom-up automation, integration, and optimization in a proper business context.

This chapter provides a foundation for later chapters. First, we position technical support for the agile enterprise in the evolution of information technology. Next, we outline the new way of thinking that is needed to realize the agile enterprise, and we highlight the agile enterprise business value. Finally, we suggest several CSFs to drive the transformation to competitive agility.

HOW WE GOT HERE

Agility is a moving target enabled primarily by advances in technology. It is useful to consider the evolution of the business use of information technology to understand how the current "hairball" of systems and communications developed over time and why the time to focus on the agile enterprise has come. This mish-mash is the legacy that we must transform to realize the agile enterprise.

Long before business process automation, business processes were recognized as fundamental to making business operations efficient and reliable. BPM focused on design of business processes as fundamental to effective operation and transformation of the business. Other techniques focused on optimization from particular business perspectives. These techniques used various graphical representations; points of view; and analytical techniques to abstract, depict, and optimize business processes. However, these techniques each focused on a particular theme for process improvement leaving other aspects to be worked out in the implementation. The techniques are still relevant, but analysts were limited by the available business design tools.

The optimal design and implementation of business processes is a complex, expensive, and time-consuming undertaking. During implementation, problems would be revealed that could be disruptive to resolve. After implementation, the processes were difficult to adapt to new business requirements. As processes became automated and embedded in computer applications, they became less visible and more difficult to change.

Task Automation

The first phase of computer technology adoption was task automation. Seventy years ago, business, for the most part, was driven by the flow of paper. Business processes were prescribed in procedure manuals to be implemented through training people. Substantial changes to business operations could take years for full realization.

Early, widespread applications of the computer were for task automation. The computer could do monotonous, repetitive tasks faster, cheaper, and more reliably than people could. Computers were kept in controlled environments, and people brought the work to the computer and picked up the results when processing was done.

As more tasks were automated, they were bundled together into increasingly large applications. People interacted with the applications online, so the data stayed with the applications and were eventually stored in departmental databases. Some workflow management systems emerged to direct the flow of records between tasks performed by people. But, most of the flow of work between the tasks was built into the systems, embedded in program code.

Business leaders started to focus on business processes for incremental improvement and business process reengineering for significant restructuring of business operations. Typically, work flowed from department to department, order to cash, to produce and deliver the end product or service.

Large applications grew within departments to streamline their operations, and files were transferred between departments, initially on magnetic tapes and later through electronic transfer of files. The movement of files between applications was automated for efficiency and control. Within large applications, embedded business processes could move transactions between tasks as they occurred, but records were still batched for transfer to the applications of other organizations.

The transfer of files between applications extended outside the enterprise, to suppliers, large customers, health care insurers, and financial institutions. Industry standards were developed for electronic data interchange (EDI). File transfers were typically a daily occurrence—batches of records from the day's business activity. This movement of files between applications was generally point-to-point communications, as depicted in Fig. 1.1A. For remote locations, the communications occurred over dedicated telephone lines.

The development of interactive applications and personal computers enabled widespread, computer-based modeling. Business process models emerged as a method of designing and analyzing business processes and business process modeling systems emerged to transform the models into automated process control systems, coordinating the work of people and machines. As the scope of computer applications expanded, the scope of automated business process models expanded as well.

Commercial off-the-shelf (COTS) systems offered industry-best-practice solutions and process automation, but widespread adoption limited the ability of a company to differentiate and gain competitive advantage. Implementation of these systems took years and locked adopters into a particular stage of evolution of the technology, thus requiring major investment of time and money to exploit further advances. More recent enterprise applications have incorporated business process modeling to enable adaptation of business processes.

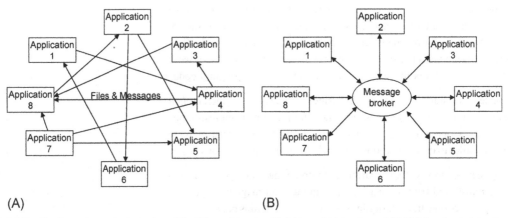

(A)   (B)

■ **FIG. 1.1** Transition from point-to-point integration to EAI middleware integration. (A) Point-to-point integration and (B) EAI hub and spoke integration.

Enterprise Application Integration

Enterprise application integration (EAI) middleware emerged in the marketplace to streamline the transfer of data between systems. It brought the hub-and-spoke communication model depicted in Fig. 1.1B. Within an enterprise, the middleware could route messages from many sources to many destinations, reducing the number of communication links and improving control. In addition, there was no longer the need to send records in batches, but individual records could be sent as messages as they became available thus reducing delays.

EAI middleware enabled a transition from batch-oriented enterprise integration to transaction-driven integration. The EAI middleware provides a buffer so that a message can be sent when a receiver is not yet ready to receive—*store-and-forward* mode. It can also provide a buffer between legacy batch processing systems and those systems that process and send transactions as they occur. EAI middleware products provide adapter software to integrate systems implemented with diverse technologies and message transformation services, to make the data structures compatible between applications. Transaction-driven systems accelerate the delivery of results; for example, a customer order for stock items might be processed and the order shipped the same day.

Of course, the hub-and-spoke configuration relies on the use of shared middleware. Unfortunately, incompatibility of EAI products was a barrier to integration between enterprises and sometimes within a large enterprise, particularly in the absence of interoperability standards for message exchange.

The Internet

As EAI was gaining widespread adoption, the Internet and the World Wide Web were gaining momentum. The Internet opened the door to many-to-many communications in a different way as depicted in Fig. 1.2. The public Internet was the global hub through which messages could be directed from any Internet subscriber to any other Internet subscriber. Dedicated telephone lines were no longer needed between business partners.

There was no industry, technology-independent standard for message exchange using EAI middleware, so a standard format was required for communicating between diverse systems over the Internet. Web pages were already being communicated between diverse systems, so this technology was adapted to communication of messages between business systems.

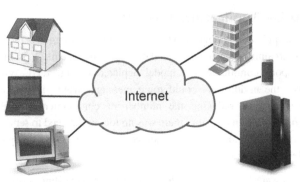

■ **FIG. 1.2** The Internet as the global communication hub.

Hyper Text Transport Protocol (HTTP) from the Internet Engineering Task Force (IETF) and the World Wide Web Consortium (W3C) became the accepted messaging protocol, and HyperText Markup Language (HTML) from W3C became a basis for exchange of content; it was already allowed to pass through corporate firewalls for Web access. Since business messages were not intended for graphical display, HTML per se was not appropriate for application integration, but eXtensible Markup Language (XML), also from W3C, shares the underlying technology of HTML that enables interpretation by diverse computer systems, and it also provides greater flexibility for content specification and transformation. XML is discussed further in Chapter 6.

The Internet became the medium of exchange for business-to-business communications. IT industry leaders recognized a potential for ad hoc relationships between businesses to be established automatically, at a moment's notice, if only there were industry standards by which these relationships could be discovered and specified.

Web Services and SOA

The concept of "Web services" emerged. Fig. 1.3 illustrates the vision. The arrows depict request-response relationships. In concept, an enterprise posts a service offering on a public registry. Another enterprise in need of a service queries the registry to obtain information on available services. The registry includes information about the service and the protocol for using the service. The service user then sends a message to the service provider, initiating the exchange. All this is expected to be performed automatically by applications of the participating enterprises. Within the enterprises, the exchanges are mediated by automated business processes.

Standards for Web services have been developed, but the ad hoc, automated selection of services has not caught on. Business leaders are not ready to

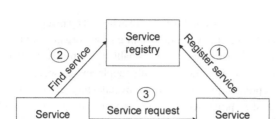

■ **FIG. 1.3** Web services vision.

trust computer systems to establish and manage trusted business relationships, not least because the current abilities to express the actual semantics of a given service offering leaves a lot to be desired. However, much of the technology has been adopted, and relationships established by humans can be quickly automated for exchange of business transactions over the Internet. Web access by humans is still the primary mechanism for ad hoc access to services on the Internet.

The concept of business systems interacting over the Internet is well established. Development of standards for interactions with prescribed services led to the SOA. Internet-based technologies support the integration of systems offering services and using services. This greatly expanded the market for a new breed of middleware to perform Internet-based communications and drive interactions with automated business processes.

Within the enterprise, SOA has been viewed as a way to implement shared application components. Functionality used in different areas of the business can be implemented as shared services and invoked by other applications. The concept of the enterprise service bus (ESB) emerged as middleware that enabled applications to be connected using Internet technology. Essentially, an ESB is decentralized EAI middleware with standards-based communications.

However, the major impact of SOA will be realized by a business architecture rather than just an IT architecture—the CBA. CBA defines services based on business capabilities that are the building blocks of the enterprise discussed further in Chapter 3.

CBA builds on the following benefits enabled by SOA:

- Economies of scale are realized through shared services.
- Quality and productivity are improved by enabling the development of special skills and methods for shared services that would not be justified for multiple, smaller operating activities.

- Improved consistency and control are achieved by placing responsibility for management of key operations in a single organization.
- Distributed operations are enabled through Internet-based communication of interactions with people and between services.
- Process optimization is enhanced by enabling each service unit to optimize the processes of the services it provides within the constraints of its interfaces.
- Greater assurance of regulatory compliance can be achieved through consolidation of regulated processes and related business functions.
- The enterprise gains the ability to utilize the most effective alternative sources of services such as outsourcing or operations in other countries.
- The scope of changes is more focused because sharable service interfaces conceal changes that only affect the service implementation and do not adversely affect performance.

CBA extends SOA with the business concepts and relationships for the specification, integration, and management of shared business services as components of value streams and business exchanges.

The Evolving Internet

Web access to services opened the door to new relationships with customers. The Internet is now a major vehicle for retail sales. Customers also access product information and support services. Web services for customers expanded to portals for various stakeholders, particularly employees and suppliers. These interactive services require automated processes to guide the interactions with users and respond to their requests.

The Internet has changed the marketplace—the scope, diversity, sales channels, and products, as well as customer expectations. Customers expect fast response—including product delivery, access to information, access to competitive offerings, and product evaluations/reviews. Furthermore, "social computing" has emerged from consumer services such as Facebook, Twitter, and LinkedIn with voice and video communications in addition to email. These services have created new mechanisms for collaboration as well as marketing and analytics.

Smart phones have connected everybody to the Internet, everywhere, and have put computing resources in their hands to perform personal applications and engage them with Internet service offerings. The Internet has been extended with cellular networks and wireless hot spots. The "Internet of Things" is an emerging Internet phenomenon. Sensors and computers embedded in all forms of devices are being connected to the Internet. The volume of data exchanged over the Internet has exploded and continues to explode.

The Internet has become the new, distributed computing platform for cloud computing—making the Internet the basis for a computing utility. Cloud computing supports the configuration of applications as massively parallel computations, greatly increasing the speed and reducing the cost of computationally intensive applications. Analytics has emerged as an approach to utilizing this computational power for analysis of the large volumes of data—"big data"—generated from the expanding scope of computations and interactions occurring over the Internet and within the enterprise.

The continued expansion of applications of the Internet will continue to create new challenges and opportunities for business.

VDM: A NEW WAY OF THINKING

The design and management of an agile enterprise and the tools and methods to support that design and management require a new way of thinking about the operation of the enterprise. This edition of this book builds on the first edition to describe the next-generation agile enterprise based on VDM, CBA, and BCM along with other related developments. In this section, we examine how these three disciplines are the basis for a new way of thinking about the design and management of an enterprise. We will describe the relationships between these disciplines in the context of a business design hierarchy.

The Business Design Hierarchy

Fig. 1.4 depicts a business design hierarchy. Strategic planning is the most abstract and furthest removed from the actual operation of the business. It focuses on the characteristics of the enterprise inspired by its mission and vision. It considers strengths, weaknesses, opportunities, and threats; the evolving ecosystem; and innovations that will strengthen the business and exploit its opportunities.

The Conceptual Design is an abstraction of the business design like a blueprint is the conceptual design of a home. It presents the design in terms that management understands with enough detail to be clear about what the people, organizations, systems, and processes do without getting into all the details of exceptions and optimization. This layer has not been well supported but is the domain of VDML and the focus of VDM. VDM includes modeling of both the internal business design and the relationships with

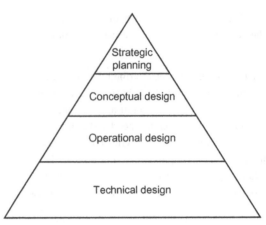

■ **FIG. 1.4** Business design hierarchy.

external entities. It includes conceptual models for both CBA and BCM. For CBA, it defines the capabilities and their configuration and relationships as sharable services. For BCM, it defines the collaborations that do the work of the enterprise including the organization units and the activity networks that describe the work of capabilities. It defines organizational responsibilities, including capability units responsible for management of bundles of capability methods, personnel, and other resources that provide a general, sharable capability. It includes the statistical measurements of performance and customer value to optimize multiple value streams from an enterprise perspective.

The Operational Design develops the detailed models for how the business works. This is the domain of the design of service interfaces and service level specifications along with process design in the context of services, and the application of rules to implement policies, controls, and guidance. Service units at the Operational Design level are the counterparts of capability units at the Conceptual Design level. Capability methods are implemented as services. Automated business processes can be designed at the Operational Design level with tools that implement BPMN and CMMN, discussed in Chapter 4, and DMN (decision model and notation) discussed in Chapter 5.

At the Technical Design level, we are concerned with information technologies. Other technologies such as physical machines, plant layout, buildings, vehicles, and so on are out of scope. Subsequent chapters of this book will clarify the nature of the relevant information technologies and their importance to the business.

All of these models together align the design and implementation of the enterprise to deliver value to customers as well as other stakeholders. This delivery of value is fundamental to the viability and success of the enterprise.

Capability-Based Architecture

In this section, we will start by developing an understanding of CBA as a fundamental aspect of VDM that builds on current practices of capability analysis and mapping. We will then examine BCM that addresses the network of collaborations where people, machines, and other participants interact to do the work of the enterprise. Finally, we will briefly describe how VDM brings these together with the creation and delivery of value, to describe a robust representation of how the business works.

Capabilities determine the purpose and scope of building blocks of the agile enterprise. We will consider the design of these building blocks and configuration of the enterprise in detail in Chapter 3. Here, we examine the general characteristics of capabilities as enterprise components.

A *capability* consists of the knowledge, skills, resources, facilities, and organizational structure to perform certain activities and produce a desired result. A *capability method* defines the activities, interactions, deliverables, and roles of participants to deliver a particular result from a capability. A *capability unit* is the organizational unit that manages the capability methods, personnel, other resources, and facilities that provide a particular capability. A capability unit may be an organization unit that is parent to multiple organization units that offer capability methods for more specific capabilities. A capability unit may have multiple capability methods to address different service needs or local circumstances.

CBA is an approach to the design of an enterprise in which distinct business capabilities are offered through well-defined interfaces and media of exchange so that the capabilities can be shared by multiple business endeavors now and in the future. Shared capabilities can be managed for performance, consistency, control, and economies of scale and can be used to configure a new LOB incorporating shareable capabilities. We return to these concepts in the discussion of CBA in Chapter 3.

The concept of CBA as a business architecture is beginning to emerge in the industry. Unfortunately, though the potential benefits are great, the challenges are also great.

Traditional businesses are typically organized around LOB. Each business silo manages all of the capabilities needed to deliver the end product or service. Many duplicated capabilities are embedded in the processes of multiple silos. These represent opportunities for sharing of capabilities to realize economies of scale, achieve consistent control over that aspect of the business, implement improvements more quickly, and develop higher levels of expertise.

Capability Mapping

"Capability mapping" has become a fairly popular technique where capability types are organized in a graphical taxonomy to abstract the capabilities away from the organizations that manage them, see Fig. 1.5 for a simplistic illustration. It helps remove the analysis from more political discussions. This helps clarify the nature of each capability for consideration of where there is a need to invest in development or improvement of certain capabilities. A "capability heat map" is a capability map where capabilities that require attention are highlighted.

The capability map should be supported by information on the associated resources, facilities, and intellectual property. With links to the various capability organization units, the capability map can help identify capabilities that may be consolidated. However, current methods are weak on linking capabilities to organization units, evaluating the potential for consolidation, and determining priorities for investment in capability improvements.

Shared Capabilities

A capability provided by multiple organizations is a candidate for consolidation to be shared by the multiple capability consumers. The sharing of capabilities brings a fundamental change to the architecture of the enterprise.

Traditionally, an enterprise operates as a number of distinct LOB or divisions, each with its own systems and business operations in its own silo, as depicted in Fig. 1.6. In the diagram, A and B might be different divisions or product-line organizations. Each division has its own specialized business units, contributing capabilities to the divisional efforts. Boxes with the same

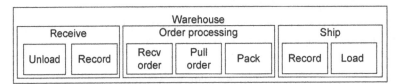

■ **FIG. 1.5** Characterization of a capability map.

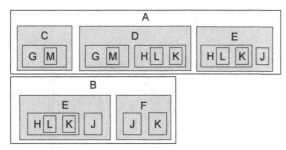

■ **FIG. 1.6** Capabilities of conventional business unit silos.

letter are the same capability, performed by different teams. Some of the capabilities are duplicated between business units within a division, but this may not be apparent in the actual operations since they are embedded in the mainstream processes. Some of the capabilities are duplicated across the divisions as indicated by the duplicated boxed letters. Each division has its own computer applications used by people within the division. Interactions with customers and suppliers are through channels that may be different for each division. Access to the internal capabilities is restricted by locked doors and passwords that control access to each division's operations.

Typically, the transfer of business transaction data from one business activity to another also transfers responsibility and control for the transaction. The business units in a division may be using the same system with a single database, or the sending business activity is trusted to send valid records, so the receiving business activity accepts responsibility for the subsequent action. The sources and destinations of these data transfers are well known and persistent. Changes to business processes are restricted by the flow between activities, and the hardcoded processes that define and integrate capabilities.

CBA opens up these silos and makes capabilities within them available for use as sharable services. Similar capabilities can be consolidated for economies of scale and to achieve consistency and control across the enterprise. A single capability may be applied with alternative capability methods depending on specific consumer requirements, but each method should provide a sharable service.

As a result, a CBA has interorganizational interactions and sharing of capabilities at a lower level of granularity. Fig. 1.7 represents a transformation from Fig. 1.6. Each of these boxes, except the top-level A and B, represents a sharable capability although not all of them are shared in the example.

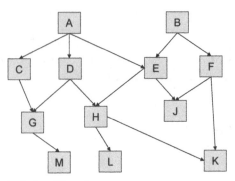

■ **FIG. 1.7** CBA network of capability services.

Effectively, this transformation replaces product delivery silos with value streams: one driven by capability A and the other driven by capability B. More about value streams, later.

Each of the shared capabilities addresses similar needs in different contexts. The divisions or product lines, A and B, still exist from a mainstream perspective, and they may have capabilities unique to their LOB, such as C and D in business A, and F in business B, but they share services of the common capabilities.

Capabilities, or more specifically, capability methods, become the building blocks for producing new products or services. The services that implement each capability method must have a well-defined interface, so they can be engaged in different contexts.

A capability method may be a consumer of other capability methods. Consequently, a request for one capability method may propagate to many other capability methods. Smaller granularity of capability methods enables them to be more stable and usable in different contexts, both as the enterprise currently operates and in future business endeavors.

Business Collaboration Management

A *collaboration* is interactions of a group of people (or other collaborations) to achieve a desired result. A collaboration may specify the roles of participants, the activities they perform, and the deliverables they exchange. A collaboration may employ technology for coordination of performance or certain functions, and it may engage other collaborations to obtain supporting services. BCM expands the scope of BPM, a management discipline traditionally focused on management of prescriptive, repeatable business processes. A traditional business process is effectively a collaboration with prescribed activities and flow of control.

Scope of BCM

The scope of BCM extends from the interactions of independent business entities in the business ecosystem to the interactions of managers and knowledge workers, and to the ad hoc work groups and informal exchanges of information that are a necessary part of successful business operations. A collaboration engages participants to achieve a shared objective. The enterprise is a network of collaborations.

Thus BCM includes adaptive processes and ad hoc activities of people working together in joint efforts. So, a collaboration to fulfill an order may have an application to receive and validate orders, persons to resolve errors, authorize credit, accept changes, and resolve customer questions, along with delegations to other collaborations that manage production, manage packaging and shipping, and perform billing and collections. As we dive down into these delegations, the collaborations will involve more people and collaborations. The operational design of these collaborations may be modeled as business processes where each may be prescribed, adaptive or ad hoc.

In addition to such production collaborations, the management hierarchy is essentially a hierarchy of collaborations, projects are collaborations of project team members, committees are collaborations, interactions with business partners or customers are collaborations, and professional groups are collaborations. The collaboration concept is a consistent basis for modeling all business activities and interactions.

BCM expands the scope of BPM to potentially address all forms of collaboration, i.e., ways people, groups of people, and machines work together to achieve a shared purpose. This expands the ability of practitioners to consider all roles, interactions, and working relationships that are essential to the operation of the business but may be outside the scope of the management hierarchy and prescriptive processes.

Collaboration Network

In a traditional business organization, people are assigned roles in the management hierarchy. To implement substantial changes or solve business problems, ad hoc project teams or task forces may be assembled bringing people with complementary skills together. These teams and task forces often do not appear in any organization charts. In addition, there are many less formal working relationships that are essential to the operation of the business. The full operating structure of the business is not visible from the typical organization chart.

These cross-organizational, ad hoc, and informal relationships have become more pervasive and are often essential to the delivery of customer value. This change in organizational patterns is, at least in part, a result of automation of rote business operations leaving the remaining work as that of knowledge workers who must take actions based on their expertise rather than prescribed repetitive processes. In order to understand the full operation of the business and the contributions of individual employees, the organization must be represented as a network of collaborations. These interactions may be face to face or by telephone, fax machines, email, text messages, computer applications, or even social media. Important business activities may include essential, informal exchanges that result in intangible, informal artifacts or communications.

Management Hierarchy

As noted above, the management hierarchy is a hierarchy of collaborations. These collaborations are distinct from other collaborations because they are responsible for the management of assets, including money, personnel, facilities, intellectual property, and resources that are used or consumed, as well as the use of services engaged to support or maintain capabilities.

The manager of an organization unit is a participant in the organization unit collaboration as well as a participant in the parent organization-unit collaboration. There may be a variety of informal collaborations among members of an organization unit, and there may be formal processes specified as capability methods in a business conceptual design model. The organization unit assigns personnel and provides other resources to collaborations to do work.

Knowledge Workers and Managers

Today's business organizations involve many knowledge workers—workers whose activities are relatively self-directed and rely on their knowledge and experience. This is a result of automation of most rote activities. Managers are also knowledge workers. These self-directed employees engage in collaborations to develop plans, solve problems, and coordinate work. Technology is now available to support the planning and coordination of these collaborations. CMMN, a specification for modeling this support, is discussed in Chapter 4.

Business Network

The enterprise also collaborates with its business partners, customers, and other external entities. These interactions are modeled as *business networks* where the different business entities are participants in defined roles, and they interact based on cooperative process specifications—defined as Choreography in BPMN. These processes are not controlled by a shared system but depend on each participating entity following the prescriptions of the choreography.

These collaborations link the enterprise and its internal processes to the external business entities for exchange of deliverables and values. The value exchange specifications support analysis of the viability of these relationships.

Value Delivery Management

VDM builds on CBA and BCM as core design concepts to define an integrated business design that adds the creation, aggregation, and exchange of business value. VDML is the computer-based modeling language to model this integration of VDM, CBM, and BCM that supports the development, analysis, refinement, and transformation of business design.

VDML was recently adopted by the Object Management Group (OMG). It provides integration of multiple dimensions of enterprise design that fills the conceptual modeling gap between strategic planning and operational business design. VDML is discussed in some detail in Chapter 2 and Chapter 3 will describe the details of the integration of capabilities, collaborations, and value streams.

The following paragraphs describe four ways VDM significantly improves strategic planning and transformation.

Strategy Validation

VDM supports strategic planning with the development of an integrated and robust model of a proposed business with a focus on the creation and delivery of value both internally and in exchanges with customers and business partners. The model supports reasonable estimates of value creation and performance based on current measurements of existing capability services and careful analysis of new or significantly changed capability services. The model can support computations of values for value propositions of multiple market segments. Consequently, management can obtain a reasonable assessment of the competitive value of the proposal and the cost of implementation.

Extended Enterprise Modeling

The enterprise does not exist in isolation. Relationships with business partners, suppliers, regulators, and markets are important at all levels. VDM addresses these relationships in various ways. Relationships of the extended enterprise are addressed by VDML modeling of exchanges of deliverables and value propositions as pioneered by Allee (2008) in Value Networks. VDML provides supporting detail and can support the graphical displays for Lindgren's Business Model Cube and Osterwalder's Business Model Canvas for multiple dimensions of analysis of viability of a business venture. These VDML viewpoints are discussed further in Chapter 2.

Value Optimization

A *value stream* defines the capabilities involved in the delivery of a product or service and the associated value proposition. A value stream may have multiple tributaries leading to the end product. A shared capability method contributes values to multiple value streams, and a value stream may serve multiple market segments with different value propositions that reflect different value priorities. So, a capability method can be considered in the context of all the value streams and markets to which it contributes. A change to a capability method may enhance some value propositions and diminish others. It may change the flow of deliverables that lead to delivery of a product or service, and the value contributions of capabilities and their activities to the customer value proposition.

This provides the basis for optimal allocation of investments to improve value delivery at the enterprise level. A proposed improvement for a capability can be considered in terms of the investment required and the impact on customer values in all the LOB to which the capability contributes. This can be compared to the impact on customer value of alternative investments.

Shared Future State

The traditional model for strategic planning and transformation involves top management development of vision, mission, goals, and objectives along with analysis of strengths, weaknesses, opportunities, and threats. Strategic plans reflect consideration of any significant changes needed to the operation of the business, but requirements for these changes lack detail.

Implementation of the strategic plans is delegated to business leaders. The business leaders interpret these plans in ways that best fit their individual LOB or functional responsibility. This interpretation of the strategic plans may occur repeatedly for different functional areas and at several levels of management. As a result, the intent of top management may be misinterpreted or implemented in a suboptimal way. Many transformation efforts fail to meet management expectations.

The Balanced Scorecard and Strategy Maps are techniques for defining top management objectives to guide implementation of strategic plans. These techniques are useful, but they are still focused on a high-level view of the operation of the business and don't resolve inconsistent interpretations.

The adverse consequences of this approach are more severe when the enterprise has implemented shared capabilities that must be optimized for their effects on multiple LOB. This requires enterprise level planning and design that reflects a deeper level of understanding of the operation and interdependencies of the business operation and will likely require trade-offs with the suboptimized objectives of individual LOB.

To avoid this fragmentation of efforts, VDM, supported by VDML, provides a shared, robust representation of the desired future state of the enterprise. Then there is a need to define incremental, "bite sized" changes that maintain effective operation of the business while realizing business benefits along the way. This avoids the risks and delays of a big-bang implementation where all the pieces of a future state of the business must come together for a successful transition. This planned and managed transformation is discussed further in Chapter 9.

VDM FOR MAJOR CHANGES

This section identifies a number of major business changes faced by many enterprises that will benefit from VDM. An agile enterprise is prepared to face these challenges, mitigating the risks, realizing the opportunities, and optimizing the values.

Performance Management and Corrective Action

VDM provides an abstraction of the operation of the business that is meaningful to top management and aligns with the detailed, operational design. Consequently, VDM can put operating measurements into a meaningful context both for consideration of the impact of performance variations and disruptions, and support drill-down into the business design to understand sources of variation or poor results.

Business Relationships

The relationships between the enterprise of interest and other business entities can be modeled as business networks, along with the exchanges of value propositions or deliverables to provide an understanding of how the enterprise fits into the ecosystem, and to support assessment of the importance and viability of relationships with other entities. Analysis of the exchange of value propositions will reveal if each participant experiences a net gain that is necessary to sustain the relationship. Business leaders need to consider if these relationships can be abandoned or if steps must be taken to strengthen the relationships.

Innovation

In today's world, competitive advantages are temporary. Every enterprise must realize innovations to maintain and improve its competitive position. It is not enough for somebody to have an innovative idea, and the ideas must be validated and implemented in a timely and effective manner.

The value-driven, agile enterprise has several advantages. CBA provides a business design that can be reconfigured to address new requirements, and a shared understanding of the impact of change of a capability method on the consumers of that service. BCM provides model-based and adaptive processes that can rapidly implement new methods as well as an understanding of other collaboration relationships required by the enterprise. VDM provides a conceptual business design that integrates CBA and BCM and supports analysis of the impact of change on customer values and enterprise performance.

VDM also provides an innovator with an ability to explore an innovation in the business context in which an innovation must be implemented. The conceptual design also helps identify other knowledge workers for collaboration on feasibility and implementation issues.

Capability managers should have the funding discretion to implement some innovations, and the support of an innovation assessment process to quickly determine if more substantial funding is justified and is an appropriate investment.

Mergers and Acquisitions

Mergers and acquisitions bring together formerly independent business organizations. In general, it is expected that at least one and potentially both businesses should be improved through access to needed capabilities, synergy between capabilities or economies of scale in addition to potential increase in market share and new business. These all depend on the compatibility of the capabilities.

Typically, the combined enterprise organization reflects aggregation without consolidation. This is common in financial services companies, telecommunications companies, and information technology companies. The synergy and economies of scale that might have been envisioned are typically not achieved, because each organization continues to operate in its own silo, each with its own methods and computer applications. Large corporations with decentralized divisions or product-line organizations typically have similar opportunities for consolidations.

With considerable effort, some consolidation of operations may occur over a period of years. But because mergers and acquisitions occur frequently, especially in the industries noted, it is difficult for operational consolidation efforts to keep up.

In contrast to the norm, an agile enterprise should be able to assess the benefits and define a plan for merger in a fraction of the time and cost experienced by a conventional enterprise. If each of the original companies has implemented CBA, this consolidation can be faster. Even if similar capabilities employ different methods, organizational consolidation of responsibility for similar methods creates the opportunity for reconciliation and economies of scale.

In due diligence, value delivery models of the potentially combined organizations should be developed to clearly identify the capabilities, the contexts in which they are used, and the values they contribute to value streams. The potential consolidation of each of the capabilities, particularly those that are core competencies (providing competitive advantage), must be evaluated to determine the feasibility of consolidation—or the capacity expansion of one capability to replace the other—to fulfill the requirements of all the capability consumers.

From this analysis, top management should realize a reasonable assessment of feasibility, cost, duration, and risk of the merger or acquisition and subsequent transformation.

Divestitures

Divestiture requires the separation of an existing, potentially integrated enterprise into two (or more) viable organizations. If the organization has a CBA structure and model, then the shared capabilities and their resources can be easily identified. In addition, it should be quite easy to configure the business designs of the new organizations.

Conventional shared services (eg, accounting, purchasing, etc.) are, by definition, shared capabilities. The challenge is then to either partition each of the shared capabilities into implementations for each of the new organizations, or create, or acquire equivalent capabilities. Each of the new organizations will have smaller scale requirements for the formerly shared services, so the loss of economy of scale will result in a net increase in cost for the remaining value streams.

There are various solutions to be considered such as (1) partition the shared capabilities and acquire the necessary personnel and facilities to meet the increased needs from reduced economies of scale, (2) outsource shared capabilities for one new organization and scale back for the other, (3) sell the divested organization to another organization that can provide the shared services (scaling up), and scale back the retained organization.

Consolidations

Consolidation is the primary source of benefits in the early stages of CBA adoption. Table 1.1 outlines benefits of consolidation that were claimed by several participants in the SOA Consortium. These examples highlight actual projects in various industries.

These examples are typical of early stages of implementation of CBA. At an early stage, it is not very difficult to recognize some key capabilities that are candidates for consolidation—the "low-hanging fruit."

In the short term, as an enterprise is moving toward agility, consolidation of redundant capabilities is a major source of value, even when the enterprise is still in the early stages of transformation. These consolidations will often have an IT focus, but the objective is to involve the consolidation of the associated business organizations. This will demonstrate the business value of shared business capabilities and is representative of the current level of transformation of most early adopters. Other benefits of the value-driven agile enterprise are not as apparent in the early stages.

An initial consolidation should have potential for substantial business value because initial implementations bear the burden of implementation of supporting infrastructure, development of the skills and methods for defining and integrating well-defined service interfaces and level of service agreements, and development of the working relationships between capability provider and capability consumer organizations.

Typically, these shared capabilities are fairly large and complex business functions. It is useful, but not necessary, to consider that there are sharable capabilities embedded within the consolidated capabilities. In the long term, these should be factored out and implemented as sharable capabilities as well. In the short term, it will be expedient to develop well-defined interfaces that hide the technology implementation of the legacy system.

In the long term, value stream modeling supports identification of redundant or similar capabilities as candidates for consolidation and defines the contexts in which the shared capabilities will be used. It also supports the impact of value contributions to the value propositions of the affected value streams—there may be competing values that must be resolved by

Table 1.1 Examples of SOA Benefits Through Consolidation by Industry

Industry	Realized Benefits
Automobile	Improved customer satisfaction
	Reduced duplication of customer data and near-real-time access to vehicle information
	Increased agility through a governance focus
	Easier integration with partners
Energy	Flexibility and speed in changing business processes
	Business optimization and risk mitigation: accurate real-time commercial, financial, and profitability data across the value chain
	System reliability: simplification of interfaces by duplicate master data reduction
Pharmaceutical	Improved visibility into product line
	Increased agility in taking pharmaceutical products to market
	Cost savings and reduced headcount
	Better use of core architecture, providing improved data integration, management, and reusability
	Achieving 99.999% uptime on a stable platform
Telecommunications	Elimination of network outages
	Stronger focus on strategic initiatives while reducing cost of IT operations to 30% of previous level
	More transparency by masking systems complexity from users
	$80 million in value over 2 years from improved efficiency, responsiveness, and adaptability of the organization
	67% reduction in mobile phone provisioning costs
	50% reduction in cost of third-party development bids, and faster development times (hours vs weeks) due to SOA environment and automated tools
	Faster time-to-market for new services
	Seamless migration to a convergent system of prepaid and post-paid customers
	Lower maintenance costs
	Improved scalability
Transportation	Flexibility and speed in providing new services to customers
	Ability to grow higher-margin businesses in the United States and overseas
	Reduced cost of supporting infrastructure for internal/external customers
	Easier integration of acquisitions though a common core set of services
	Rapid transformation and reuse of processes and services
	Elimination of errors and shortening of response cycle through automated processes
	Significantly scaled-up usage of self services and end-to-end process integration
Entertainment	Consolidation of multiple content rights systems into one
	50% decrease in time needed for year-end accounting closure

negotiating trade-offs, by accommodating different requirements, or by defining alternative methods for applying the underlying capability.

New Product or LOB Planning

Top management may recognize an opportunity to introduce a new product or enter a new LOB in an emerging marketplace in a way that builds on key strengths of the current enterprise. Though some weaknesses may need to be addressed, rapid entry into a new market will be critical to long-term success.

A traditional enterprise might address this opportunity by forming a separate division or acquiring an existing company that avoids the burden and risks of adapting existing operations to the new business because existing processes and computer applications are designed to optimize each current LOB. However, at the same time, smart management understands that a new business silo will not effectively realize the strengths and potential economies of scale of the parent enterprise.

The agile enterprise is able to engage existing capabilities of the enterprise in the new LOB without penalizing the existing business. Top management is able to quickly configure a value stream in order to consider the impact on existing business, assess the value proposition of the new business, determine realistic operating costs and competitive pricing, assess the required investment, and develop a transformation plan to implement the new business.

The potential benefits of agility in introducing a new product line or business have been recognized in a number of industries, including financial services, telecommunications, pharmaceuticals, and transportation. The benefits include (1) increased visibility and control into the product line, (2) the ability to utilize a core architecture to improve data integration and consistency of implementations, (3) significant improvements in development schedules and time to market, and (4) higher customer satisfaction, in part due to reduced cost and improved quality of using established capabilities.

Outsourcing

Much of the cost of doing business goes into necessary operating activities that are not part the enterprise's core business and do not provide competitive value. Business operations such as finance and accounting, human resource management, and information technology require special skills and are increasingly complex, particularly for multinational enterprises. At the same time, these activities require considerable management attention and are challenged to achieve scalability and industry best practices for regulatory compliance, efficiency, and effectiveness.

Large enterprises have adopted outsourcing as a long-term strategy to mitigate these problems. IT outsourcing has been adopted in all industries. Outsourcing of accounting and human resource management services is gaining in popularity. The agility benefits for outsourcing include (1) scalability—the ability to quickly accommodate increased or reduced workload, (2) expertise—outsourcing providers can maintain skilled people to deal with change such as regulatory requirements, and (3) internationalization—a outsourcing provider should be prepared to support the client for expansion into new countries. It should be noted that small enterprises and startups in all industries can benefit immediately from agile outsourcing by reducing the start-up cost, duration, and risk and gaining scalability.

Outsourcing offers the opportunity to exploit the expertise and economies of scale of a service provider while reducing the management burden associated with these operations. However, the existing capabilities are often intertwined throughout the enterprise, and the divisions of responsibilities may be inconsistent across the enterprise. The disruptive effect of a transition to an outsource service provider could have a major impact on the rest of the business.

VDM can help clarify the scope of capabilities to be outsourced and the interfaces required by internal consumers of the outsourced services. It should also help define service level requirements for those interfaces. In addition, there may be capabilities or resources that are currently shared by the capabilities being outsourced and other internal value streams. This may require consideration of adverse effects on those retained capabilities such as loss of economies of scale and expertise.

The capabilities being outsourced are components of the current enterprise, just as an engine is a component of an automobile. A more powerful engine might require some changes in other automobile components, but the relationships to the controls and other components should be relatively easy to identify and evaluate.

Thus outsourcing is another source of substantial business value that can be realized in fairly early stages of enterprise transformation, as long as the integration is compatible with the strategic information-technology infrastructure. However, outsourcing can be better evaluated and implemented with less risk with VDM.

Governance

Governance involves ensuring that the enterprise is doing the right thing and doing it well. This can be difficult when boards of directors (or other stakeholders) must rely primarily on financial reports, market reports and occasional audit reports. The right thing and doing it well go beyond being profitable and gaining market share. They also go beyond regulatory compliance. A board of directors has a fiduciary responsibility to protect the interests of the stockholders going well beyond the next quarter.

The conventional enterprise reflects adaptations of enterprise designs that, in many cases, predate the use of computers. Responsibility for continued design has been delegated to large departments or LOB that focus on optimization within their local spheres of influence. Large departments or product lines tend to be physically isolated so that there is little interdepartmental collaboration or sharing of resources or expertise. In many cases, capabilities are developed rather than shared because it is easier to develop and adapt a capability if you own it yourself. Separate LOB may be the legacy of earlier, nonreconciled mergers and acquisitions.

The actions that must be controlled or measured for effective governance may be scattered across LOB and various activities embedded in their processes. A VDM conceptual model of the business at an appropriate level of abstraction provides an understanding of the context for governance. Based on this model, controls can be established, relevant events can be reported, and performance can be measured with clear accountability of responsible organizations. Some of these observations may be designed into the business operation, and some controls and performance measures must be independently evaluated to ensure objectivity.

Governance is discussed in more depth in Chapter 11.

Regulatory Compliance

Government regulation is an increasing concern. Managers are being held responsible for the integrity of their operations and protection of stockholder interests. Multinational enterprises must comply with business regulations of countries in which they operate as well as regulations for products or services in countries in which they sell. Not only are regulations constantly changing, but the regulations impose different requirements in different countries and changes to the business organization itself can create risks of violations. Regulatory compliance affects all industries.

Implementation of compliance is a challenge in conventional organizations because the affected processes may be undocumented and may be performed in multiple organizations in different ways.

The agile enterprise is able to quickly and reliably assess the implications of regulations to the business and plan appropriate changes and controls to ensure compliance. The consistent business architecture and robust business design model showing one or more applications of a relevant capability, clarifies responsibility, and accountability for compliance. Formally defined collaborations and business process automation support the implementation and enforcement of regulations. In order to address differences in different countries, capability methods must include business rules that consider the country of delivery and/or the country of origin of the product.

An important aspect of regulatory compliance is reliable recordkeeping. Formal definition and automation of business processes support the capture of appropriate records. Electronic identity and signatures ensure proper authorization and accountability for record content. Where regulated activities involve planning and decision-making by knowledge workers, adaptive case management technology can help apply rules and track compliance.

Outsourcing regulated activities such as accounting, purchasing, human resource management, and information technology development or operations reduces an enterprise's burden and provides greater assurance that appropriate expertise is applied to implementation of regulations and related changes. Of course, outsourcing still requires oversight and performance measurement at the interfaces.

Aspects of regulatory compliance are discussed in Chapters 5, 9, 10, and 11.

Technology Modernization

Technology modernization is required to remove the burden of maintaining obsolete technology and to replace it with solutions that exploit current technology and share the technical infrastructure needed for the agile enterprise.

Technology modernization may encompass broad replacement of legacy systems or any technology upgrade or improvement to a business capability. Many enterprises are captive to information systems developed long ago, many of which have locked the enterprise into ways of doing business that were optimal at the time but have since become outdated. The design of the systems as well as the technology used to implement them may be obsolete and difficult to support, change, or even understand.

Obsolete technology is a challenge in enterprises in every industry. The challenges are particularly pronounced in industries such as financial services and telecommunications, where there have been multiple mergers and acquisitions, with systems implemented in different technologies and tightly coupled to particular product lines or markets. The challenge becomes not only to upgrade technology but to reconcile the business logic and processes and to integrate consolidated capabilities from the legacy systems that support different LOB.

Duplication of functionality also occurs where the legacy systems cannot easily be adapted to support new LOB, so the legacy functions are duplicated in new systems. Replacement of legacy systems almost always requires major investments and entails substantial risk. But replacements of legacy systems without also providing enterprise-wide shared services only leads to more inefficiency and inflexibility—new legacy systems.

Analysis of legacy systems should start with application of VDM to discover the embedded capabilities and provide an abstraction of the structure of the systems and associated business activities. Value measurements can help define priorities and justify transformations.

VDM makes business processes visible and adaptable. Individual capability services should be relatively fine-grained with well-defined interfaces. The technology of implementation of a capability service should be hidden from consumers and other services it consumes behind a well-defined interface. Some capability interfaces may hide capabilities that remain implemented in legacy systems or purchased software products. Upgrades can be smaller in scope and selectively applied based on business value.

CSFs ON THE JOURNEY TO AGILITY

The transformation to agility is a journey. Appendix A outlines a Value Delivery Maturity Model that will provide some guidance in planning that journey. The specific roadmap for the journey differs for each enterprise because each enterprise faces different challenges. However, we have highlighted some CSFs, below, to help top management drive the transformation in the right direction. These do not define all the changes but identify those that are key indicators of progress. An enterprise-specific roadmap should contribute measures of progress on these CSFs.

Active Governance

Top management, with clear support of the governing board, must be committed to building an agile enterprise as a long-term undertaking. They must ensure that investments, improvements, and economies of scale are considered from a strategic enterprise perspective. In particular, information technology must be managed to control proliferation of diverse technologies, to provide a consistent information infrastructure, and to achieve economies of scale in technical resources. Departmental or line-of-business silos must give up control of duplicated capabilities to realize enterprise-level economies of scale and flexibility of shared services. Service units must be held accountable for compliance with service specifications, business rules, and security requirements. Finally, overall performance and progress must be focused on delivery of customer value and the long-term vision of the enterprise.

Value Delivery Business Models

To optimize enterprise operations and respond effectively to challenges and opportunities, top management must have models that provide information about the enterprise ecosystem, current operations, operating cost, quality and performance, and opportunities for improvements as well as new business. These models go well beyond the "executive dashboard," to enable analysis of disruptive events and trends, consideration of what-if scenarios, and exercise of operational controls. Value stream analysis must provide an understanding of the contributions to cost, quality, and performance for each current or planned product or service. Business activity monitoring should identify exceptions and trends in performance. Recognition of changing circumstances and tracking of changing circumstances should keep top management aware of the changing ecosystem.

Technical Infrastructure

A shared technical infrastructure must be established and maintained for economies of scale, integration, flexibility, reliability, security, and support for robust enterprise intelligence. This infrastructure requires initial investment that cannot be justified for individual application development projects; it is intended for use by most or all applications. The technical infrastructure includes services such as reliable messaging, authorization, sense and respond directory, regulations and policies directory, event notification, services registry, support for business collaboration, and more.

Service Management

Integration of services is fundamental to the agile enterprise paradigm shift. Managers must start to think in terms of providing services either directly to end customers or to other parts of the enterprise. This means formalizing capability offerings and the form of requests, responses, and related information exchanges. It means determining the costs of service units and the unit cost of using individual shared capabilities, including the costs incurred from other services used. It also means accountability for service level agreements, performance measures, security, compliance with policies and regulations, and responsibility for continuous improvement and adaptation to change. Much of the work of managing every service unit is very similar, and a common framework and supporting technology should be developed to minimize duplicated effort.

Moving Forward

The new way of thinking about, designing, and managing an agile enterprise requires synergy between business systems and supporting information technology. In subsequent chapters, we will discuss requirements of the agile enterprise and the key supporting technologies. The technologies are based on complementary, industry standards, and they represent the state of the art in information technology for business systems.

This book incorporates advances in technology and business methods that have emerged since the first edition. Technology will continue to change as will the business methods it supports. This edition describes the combination of technology and business that represent the current potential of an agile enterprise with consideration of anticipated advances. Chapter 11 outlines expectations for further advances that build on the vision presented in this book.

Business Modeling for Business Leaders

■ INTRODUCTION

Business leaders are confronted with increasing business complexity. This complexity is compounded when there are initiatives that cross traditional organizational boundaries and shared capabilities contribute to the value streams of multiple lines of business. In addition, optimization of capabilities requires an enterprise-level perspective and involves more than just cost, quality, and timeliness of operations—it depends on customer value delivery.

This complexity challenges the ability of managers to anticipate the consequences of proposed changes and to provide clear direction for the implementation of strategic initiatives. Management of this complexity requires computer-based modeling. Furthermore, such models are needed for accountability and control, for business analysis and design, for planning business changes, and for solution of operating problems. Models must allow each community of interest to focus on particular aspects of the business without other details getting in the way. At the same time, all communities must be assured that they are sharing a consistent representation of the business. In addition, modeling must support analysis of "what-if" scenarios with consideration of different business designs as well as different products and markets.

VDML (Value Delivery Modeling Language) was adopted by the Object Management Group (OMG) to address these needs of business leaders. It models a conceptual business design with different points of view. It provides sufficient detail for understanding of how the business works, or will work, without getting into the intricacies of exceptions and variations that are resolved in operational design and management of the business operations.

VDML fills a conceptual modeling gap between top-management strategic planning and the operational-level design and management of the business. It brings together multiple dimensions of the business design so that a VDML model can represent a consistent integration of multiple factors.

Building the Agile Enterprise. http://dx.doi.org/10.1016/B978-0-12-805160-3.00002-8

The level of detail supports the level of detail usually addressed by business leaders, but it also provides sufficient additional detail to validate a solution and to provide clear representation of the conceptual design of the business and consistent requirements for development of operational business processes and computer applications. Furthermore, the architecture of a VDML model supports the design of an efficient and effective business that exploits current computer and communications technologies. For example, capabilities are shared as services that can be engaged through secure, internet-based, service request technology supporting remote participants. Nevertheless, VDML can be used to model traditional system architectures and is particularly useful to identify embedded capabilities.

VDML does not specify the details of decisions and actions on individual units of production, but, instead, it statistically describes the flow of deliverables through activity networks per unit of production. At the same time, contributions of values are measured statistically for aggregation in value propositions. The aggregation of values can then be expressed in value propositions for different market segments or other stakeholders.

VDML also supports a broader perspective that includes customers, suppliers, and other business partners and the values they exchange in business networks. This provides for analysis of business models that rely on the participation of multiple business entities.

This chapter is about VDML. We will first examine the primary components of a VDML model, their relationships to each other, and their relationships to the business, followed by an overview of standard VDML graphical displays. Then we will consider VDML support for graphical displays that reflect Allee's Value Networks, Osterwalder's Business Model Canvas, and Lindgren's Business Model Cube.

VDML KEY CONCEPTS

The VDML language specification defines concepts and relationships used to represent the design of an enterprise. The fundamental purpose of an OMG modeling specification is to specify these concepts and relationships in such a way that when the language is implemented by different vendors, the models created with one implementation can be exchanged to function in a different VDML implementation.

This goal of interoperability extends to specification of the core VDML user interface so that it is the same when a model is moved from one VDML product to another. The developers of the VDML specification provided for a minimal set of user displays because it is expected that additional displays will be developed in response to needs of users that emerge as VDML implementations are used.

A VDML model may represent the design of a department within a company, a single company with customers and suppliers, or it may represent multiple companies, integrated to operate as an integrated, virtual enterprise with a joint purpose. VDML also supports modeling of conventional, silo-oriented business designs as well as an architecture based on integration of shared capabilities implemented as services.

Fig. 2.1 illustrates an overview of VDML concepts and relationships. Methods, Org Units, Communities, and Business Networks are special types of collaborations—participants interacting for a shared purpose. A collaboration has participants in roles that perform activities. Activities produce deliverables and contribute values that are the basis of value propositions to recipients of products or services. An Org Unit can have one or more method(s) that is a collaboration that provides a capability with roles performing activities and consuming resources.

VDML incorporates libraries of sharable concepts: a Capability Library, a Role Library, a Value Library, a Business Item Library, and a Practice Library. These libraries name and define key concepts in a VDML model. In addition, Measure Libraries define measures to be applied to VDML elements and to support computations, particularly measurements of value. VDML libraries are designed to be shared by different VDML models, different user communities, and different VDML implementations. These libraries of concept names and definitions may be developed for a specific enterprise, but it is expected that VDML tool vendors will provide initial

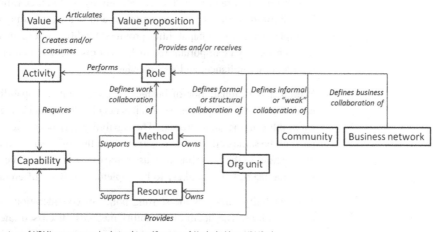

■ **FIG. 2.1** Overview of VDML concepts and relationships. *(Courtesy of Henk de Man, VDMBee)*

definitions to help new users get started, and that industry groups will develop and share definitions appropriate to each industry. The development of shared libraries is important to reduce the initial work of VDML modeling, but it is also important for promoting consistency for commonly occurring concepts that will improve compatibility of business industry standards, regulatory requirements, systems software, outsourcing, and other business integration initiatives. The application of these libraries will be described further in the sections for the associated concepts below.

In the sections that follow, we will explore these concepts and some more for a robust but abstract representation of how a business works from a business leader perspective.

Capabilities

In VDML, a capability represents the collection of personnel, facilities, intellectual property, supporting technology, and methods to perform a particular type of work. A VDML model can include a Capability Library with a taxonomy of capabilities. The taxonomy serves three purposes: (1) it helps a user recognize similar or equivalent capabilities that exist elsewhere in the enterprise, (2) equivalent capabilities are referenced with the same name since each concept is defined only once in the library taxonomy, and (3) it helps a user find a needed capability when exploring changes to the business. The taxonomy also provides the basis for a capability map display, discussed in Chapter 1, for consideration of needs for improvement. It is expected that industry groups may develop prototypical capability libraries.

Capabilities may reference Practice Definitions in a Practice Library. This is helpful for identification of best practices and in understanding differences in implementations of capabilities provided by different organizations. The differences may be important for such concerns as consolidations, security, regulatory compliance, and risk management.

Within a traditional, line-of-business organization, a capability may be embedded in a larger process so that it is not clearly distinguished from other capabilities in the same process. The capability may be applied in different parts of the same or different processes of the line-of-business. The different applications of the capability may use some of the same resources—possibly the same team, but it is likely to be implemented with different variables.

The capability library is the starting point for consideration of capability consolidations. The detail of capability methods, discussed later, provides additional insight on the potential for consolidation. A capability to be consolidated may include multiple, more granular capabilities in the library taxonomy. So, consolidation may involve multiple services associated with that capability to be managed by a single organization unit, described here as a *capability unit*.

A shared capability can achieve economies of scale with shared fixed costs, resources, methods, and expertise. When changes or policies must be applied to a consolidated capability, the changes need only be implemented by one organization. Only one organization is accountable for the value contributions of the capability. On the other hand, the LOB organizations that use the capability no longer have direct control over the capability implementation or operation, and there may be some trade-offs between the specific needs of a LOB and the needs of other LOB. These are factors to be considered when evaluating a consolidation. Consolidation may also be impractical when the needs for the capability exists in different countries so that there are barriers to communication or delays in transportation.

Collaborations

A collaboration is a group of people working together for a shared purpose. Usually, the participants have identified roles that describe the nature of their contribution to the collaboration, and a participant in a role is responsible for performing certain activities. Some collaborations may transfer some work to other collaborations. A supporting collaboration may receive inputs and provide outputs through delegation, or it may receive inputs and provide outputs through shared stores (discussed later).

In VDML, an enterprise is a network of collaborations that work together to achieve the purpose of the enterprise. VDML defines four specialized forms of collaboration: Community, Business Network, Org (organization) Unit, and Capability Method.

Community

A *Community* is a relatively unstructured collaboration where participants are described as *Members*. The members of a professional, religious, or political organization or a market segment are members of a community that share interests and goals. A market segment represents potential customers of a product or service. Shareholders are a community. Often a community will pursue a potential campaign or initiative, and selected members may become members of a specialized collaboration with a distinct purpose, where participants have more distinct roles and activities.

Business Network

A *Business Network* is a collaboration for interaction of business entities for exchange of money, products or services, or possibly other benefits. It is a cooperative exchange—there is no central coordinator. Each participant is described as a *Party*. These parties will have distinct roles and activities, and they will exchange certain deliverables and associated values. A Business Network may be displayed as an exchange of deliverables or as an exchange of Value Propositions (discussed later).

Org (organization) Unit

A typical management hierarchy is a composition of org units. An *Org Unit* is a group of people and possible suborganization units that work together at one level in the management hierarchy. The participant roles in an org unit are represented as *Positions*. An executive team of a company is an org unit; the leadership team of a division or department is an org unit; and a work group, team, committee, task force, or project team is an org unit. These are each part of a management chain where the managers are responsible for people, resources, and other assets. The typical org unit has a leader/supervisor/manager/director that is in charge of the org unit activities and allocation of resources. The person in charge is also a participant in the parent organization—the collaboration managed by his or her boss. This, along with the engagement of org units in roles of other org units, defines the management hierarchy.

As the owners of assets and resources, org units provide capabilities. These may be provided by simply staffing a formal collaboration that applies a capability or by staffing an ad hoc collaboration with appropriate resources. For staffing or providing resources or other business items for collaborations, an org unit has Stores and Pools (discussed later).

Capability Method

A *Capability Method* is a collaboration that specifies an activity network with activities, stores, roles, deliverable flows, and value contributions involved in the application of a capability. A capability method is an abstraction of a business process. The capability of an organization unit may be applied by different capability methods for different purposes. For example, an order entry capability may involve receipt of orders for standard products and receipt of orders for specialized products. So, the order entry organization might provide one capability method with activities for all products, or it may provide two different subcapability methods for the two more specific capabilities dealing with standard products vs specialized products. This will depend on the significance of the differences and the performance measurements of interest.

A capability method may be engaged as a service by delegation. A requesting activity sends a business item request and receives a business item result. A *Business Item* represents any form of deliverable that is conveyed in a VDML model. The requesting activity interacts through the defined interface and expects compliance with a level of service agreement. The exchange is "synchronous" because the requesting activity sends a request and waits for a response.

A capability method may also be engaged asynchronously by delivery of a business item to a shared store that is input to the capability method. This occurs less frequently, but typically occurs when there is a side effect of the primary operations or an exception that requires processing to proceed along an alternative path. In some cases, a deliverable of the alternative path may reenter the main stream at a later point through another shared store.

An organization that provides a capability is identified by a Capability Offer that is located by reference to the capability definition in the library. There may be multiple capability offers for a particular capability, each identifies a different organization that provides the specified capability. A delegating activity, discussed later, identifies a capability method by reference to the capability offer(s) for that capability.

As depicted in Fig. 2.2, a capability offer links a capability definition to an organization unit that provides the capability and a capability method (an abstract specification of a capability service) used by the organization unit to deliver the capability. In the diagram, there are two capabilities defined in the Library: Capability A and Capability B. Each refers to one capability

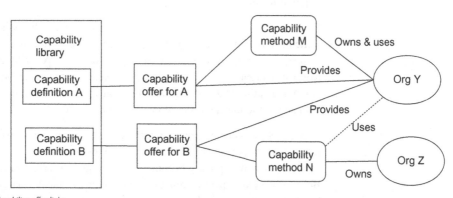

■ **FIG. 2.2** Capability offer links.

offer. Both capability offers refer to Org Unit Y, but the offer for Capability A refers to Capability Method M and the offer for Capability B refers to Capability Method N. However, Org Unit Y is both the owner and the user of Capability method M, but it is only the user of Capability N since Organization Unit Z is the owner of Capability Method N.

The provider of a capability method is usually the owner of the capability method. An owner organization is responsible for the design of the method (which usually includes automation), but the owner may be a separate organization from the provider(s). For example, the accounting organization may be the owner of a sale-processing capability method that is applied by multiple retail sales locations. The owner ensures consistency, policy compliance, and authorization. Each provider has the staff and other resources required to deliver the capability.

Roles

A *Role* represents a requirement for a participant in a collaboration. Each specific role is defined in the context of a collaboration, and each must have a name that is unique within the context of the collaboration.

Each role may be assigned to one or more activities in the collaboration. A participant in a role must be capable of performing all of the activities to which the role is assigned.

A participant in a role may be a person, a collaboration, or another role. In general, persons available for assignment to a role are persons in roles of other collaborations. For example, persons assigned to roles in a capability method are typically persons in position roles of the responsible organization unit. However, a person may be assigned to a role because they are assigned to another role that brings with it the capabilities and relationships required for that other role.

For example, a position (role) in an organization unit may be assigned (1) to a member role of a community, (2) to a performer role in a capability method, or (3) to a position role in another org unit. A manager position (role) in an organization unit X fills a position role in the parent organization unit Y indicating that the position in org unit Y *must be* filled by the person assigned to the manager role of organization unit X.

This is not the same as when the same person is assigned to two different roles. If a new person becomes a manager of organization unit X, then that new person will implicitly become the participant in organization unit Y. Because the participant is in both collaborations X and Y, that participant brings knowledge of collaboration X to collaboration Y, and vice versa.

When a role is filled by a collaboration, the assignment usually represents a delegation to an organization unit. That is, the basis of a conventional organization structure—a hierarchy of organization units. Assignment of an organization unit as a performer (in a capability method role) is to provide a capability available from that organization. That capability requirement is typically satisfied by a capability method and performers of that method that are typically managed by the organization unit (some may be from other organization units). The capability method is then engaged by delegation to apply the required capability. If the role filled by the organization unit occurs in multiple activities of a collaboration, then the organization unit must have the capability required by each of those activities.

VDML provides a *Role Library*. This supports consistent naming of roles. A role name must be unique within a collaboration, but the same name can be used in different collaborations. In order to avoid confusion, it is desirable that a Role name has a consistent meaning throughout the VDML model and the enterprise. We will see in Chapter 7 that this consistency of role names is also useful for management of access authorizations.

Activity Networks

Activity networks model the work of the enterprise. Activities are defined in the context of a collaboration. A collaboration *activity network* consists of activities and stores contributing to values and linked by deliverable flows that specify dependencies. Fig. 2.3 illustrates a simple activity network originating with entry of the collaboration and terminating with exit from the collaboration (triangles). *Deliverables flows* (arrows) are connected to activities with *ports (small squares on boundaries)*. Ports are cursor sensitive in a display for access to associated information.

An activity network begins and ends within the context of a collaboration. Activities are connected by deliverable flows, and collaboration activity networks are connected together through flows between collaborations. Any

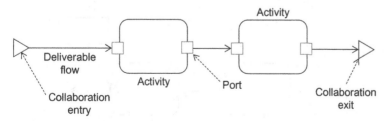

■ **FIG. 2.3** A simple activity network.

type of collaboration can have an activity network, but most activity networks will be modeled in capability methods.

This simplified view does not include all of the elements that can occur in an activity network. The following sections will start with further discussion of activities followed by discussions of deliverable flows, business items, stores, pools (specialized stores), and delegation.

Activity

An *Activity* specifies a unit of work to be performed by a participant. The participant is identified by the role associated with the activity. An activity is performed by one role. If there is a need for more participants, then the activity delegates to a collaboration among those participants. Delegation is discussed later.

Action by an activity depends on receipt of input deliverables. An activity may have multiple inputs, and the port specifications determine the inputs required to initiate actions such as all deliverables are required, any one deliverable is required, or multiple deliverables are required.

The performance of work and contributions of value of activities and the flows between activities are measured statistically. Within each collaboration, activity network measurements are based on one unit of collaboration production. The deliverable flows between activities define the portion of production routed out of and into each activity. The contributions of value are weighted according to the portion of production to which they apply. If there are multiple outputs, each output port will specify the percentage of outputs from that port. The output port also identifies the value contributions associated with that output.

Fig. 2.4 illustrates an activity with a value add element connected to its output port. The black output port indicates that there is value contributed since

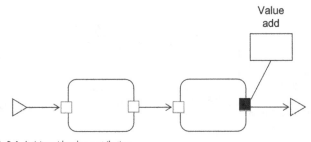

■ **FIG. 2.4** Activity with value contribution.

the value add element is not visible in a standard activity network view. Value adds are elements in a value aggregation network discussed later.

Deliverable Flow

A *Deliverable Flow* depicts the flow of a business item (deliverable) from a collaboration entry or the output port of one activity or store to the input port of an activity or store, or a collaboration exit.

By default, a deliverable flow is shown with a solid line. The deliverable flow may be distinguished as "tangible" or "intangible." A *tangible* deliverable flow is the default and is recognized in the business as formally defined in business process specifications. An *intangible* deliverable flow, indicated by a dashed line, is informal (eg, not identified in business process specifications) but is important to understand how the business actually works. This notation comes from Value Networks analysis (Allee, 2008) where the actual operation of the business is captured for analysis. Value Network analysis is supported by VDML.

Output ports determine the relationships between multiple outputs of an activity. Outputs may be mutually exclusive, concurrent, or based on a condition on the output port. The port specifies a *Planning Percentage* that is the portion of executions of that activity when that port produces an output and adds value.

Business Item

A *Business Item* element references anything that may be produced, consumed, conveyed, or stored in an activity network or exchanged by collaborations. This includes parts, products, and other physical things, as well as documents and oral or electronic communications that convey information necessary for subsequent action.

The name of the business item type is defined in the *Business Item Library*. The business item in the model represents the business item in the business and may include attributes that describe the business item. As such, the Business Item Library represents an abstract information model about things that are consumed, produced, and exchanged in the business. The same type of business item may occur elsewhere in a model, but it does not represent the same occurrence of the business item type unless the reference is to the same model element.

A business item may represent a person who is the subject of activities in the network. The same person may also be a participant in a role of the network. For example, a patient is admitted to a hospital and is the subject of various

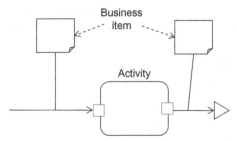

■ **FIG. 2.5** Business items on deliverable flows.

tests and treatment activities. Incoming patients may be held as business items in a store awaiting treatment. The same person has a role in treatment planning activities and as a customer for services.

Fig. 2.5 depicts business items associated with deliverable flows. A standard activity network view does not show the business items. The input and output of an activity may be the same business item element indicating that there is a change to the business item (some value may be added), but the business item is essentially the same thing, before and after the activity, with some modification.

Store

A *Store* receives and provides business items in an activity network. A store holds business items waiting for consumption by one or more activities. A store could represent, for example, a bin of parts, finished products in a warehouse, or orders waiting to be processed. Stores receive business items by deliverable flows and pass business items to activities by deliverable flows. Stores define inventory levels and delays due to business items waiting for processing. Since a store holds business items that have business value, a store has an org unit owner.

Fig. 2.6 illustrates a store providing input to an activity. The store may be the source of input to the collaboration, so there is no distinct collaboration entry element. Input to this store then occurs elsewhere in the model.

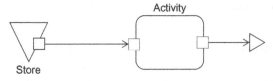

■ **FIG. 2.6** Activity input from a store.

Instead of entry by delegation, a collaboration may initiate activity in another collaboration by passing a deliverable through a shared store. The same store, identified by name, appears in both the sending activity network and the receiving activity network. A result may be returned later, through another store, or it may be passed on to another value stream. For example, a sheet metal stamping operation may produce a part for an automobile body, but the scrap sheet metal is passed on as input to another value stream where the scrap is used on the production of another product.

The flow of control through stores also represents the flow of many traditional business processes where deliverables, as well as responsibility, are passed from a process in one department directly to a process in another department. These inputs and outputs occur through Stores because they are "asynchronous;" the receiver may not immediately act on its input, and the sender does not wait for the receiver to accept. A store holds one or more business items it receives, waiting for a subsequent activity to accept each business item.

A specific shared store can appear in multiple activity networks. Each appearance of the shared store is then a receiver of business items or a supplier of business items. The multiple appearances of a shared store are views of a single store element that is identified in each view by the store name which must be unique within a VDML model.

In the trivial case, one activity network sends business items to the store and another activity network accepts business items from the store. Often business items will be sent by multiple activity networks to be processed by one activity network. Sometimes, one activity network produces business items that are consumed by multiple receiving activity networks. The store is essential to represent the business items that are held until a receiving activity network is ready to accept them.

In a capability-oriented architecture, we have described these flows through stores as "side-effect flows" because they often produce outputs that are ancillary to the primary operation of the activity network. For example, this may be used to represent a reporting flow or handling of exceptions. It may also represent a diversion of some of the production output such as scrapped units of production or material for a by-product. Generally, the scrap or by-product flow produces some value that offsets the cost of the mainstream product.

Stores are also used to represent asynchronous flows of deliverables between business entities. For example, a product shipment is generally sent when the sender has it ready and received to be held for processing. The sender does not wait for the receiver to be ready to process the shipment.

Pool

A *Pool* is a specialized store. A pool holds and tracks business items (resources) that are reusable. Conceptually, a business item accepted from a pool is marked as in use. When the reusable business item reaches a particular point in a series of activities, it is released and again becomes available for reuse. The pool computes delay in availability of resources based on the number of resources assigned to the pool and the duration of assignments of the resources. In a discrete event simulation or a system dynamics simulation, the pool would keep track of individual resources. Simulation is not included in the current version of the VDML specification.

Delegation

Delegation involves an activity of one collaboration engaging another collaboration to do the work of that activity. Essentially, the activity engages the other collaboration as a service. This is fundamental to the capability-oriented architecture where a capability is shared as one or more services.

Fig. 2.7 illustrates the implications of delegation. The group of boxes with black backgrounds, on the left side, represent the VDML model of capability methods linked through delegation. The scenario panels to the right represent different uses of the same capability method. The letters indicate different capability methods. Capability method G is engaged by both capability method C and capability method D. In each delegation, deliverable(s) are passed for each delegation to method G, so there are different deliverables and measurements associated with the different occurrences of method G.

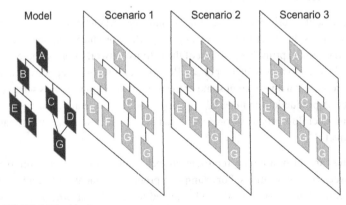

■ **FIG. 2.7** Activity delegation.

Scenarios

The Fig. 2.7 panels labeled Scenario 1 through 3 depict the model in different circumstances, that is, different scenarios. The gray boxes represent different contexts for the associated capability methods. In each scenario, each capability method has a different context, depicted by the gray boxes, that have the measurements associated with that capability method in that scenario. The delegation context also defines the inputs and outputs of the associated capability method in that context.

In this diagram, capability method G is engaged by capability methods C and D, so these define different contexts (gray boxes) in each of the three different scenarios. So, while there is only one specification for capability method G (black box), there are six different contexts.

A capability method can be engaged in multiple contexts in the same or different scenarios; in other words, the same capability method may be used in different lines of business, in other collaborations, or in different activities in the same collaboration. Each of these delegations may involve different subject matter and measurements. So, while the capability method model is the same, the measurements for each use of a capability method are independent.

The delegation context also identifies the exchange of value measurements that occurs in the delegation. The performance of a particular capability method may be evaluated in these different circumstances by looking at the measurements in the different contexts.

Note that Fig. 2.7 is not a standard display but is used here to illustrate relationships of elements involved in delegation.

A scenario incorporates a set of measurements that represent the performance of the business under certain circumstances such as for a particular production rate or product mix (as where a product has various options for each unit of production). This includes any measurements associated with activities, stores, roles, value adds, and value propositions.

A scenario element is the root context of a delegation tree. When a delegation is created, it is created in the context of an existing delegation (or scenario). The new delegation context is linked to the existing delegation context. This forms a tree of delegation contexts linked to delegation contexts depicted by each of the scenario planes of Fig. 2.7. When a user is working with a VDML model and assigns or looks at measurements, the user is working within a specified scenario, in other words, a specific delegation context tree. The circumstances associated with the scenario must be understood so that measurements are added and used consistent with those circumstances.

Value Contribution Network

The work of activities contributes values. The value measurements for a particular value stream are aggregated in value proposition(s) of that value stream that reflect the interests of customers or other stakeholders. In the following sections, we will discuss the network of value adds, the structure of a value proposition, the concept of the value stream, and the value library.

Value Adds

The values contributed by an activity are expressed as *value add* elements. The value add elements are associated with the output ports for which the contributions apply. For example, the cost of an activity is a value added. If the activity produces more than one output, some of the cost could be allocated to each output. On the other hand, the duration of an activity is also a value added. If there are multiple outputs, the same activity duration may be associated with each of the outputs. Note that outputs may be concurrent or may each be a fraction of the overall output.

The value contribution network is based on deliverable flows. An activity adds value associated with an output of a deliverable. The deliverable flows to another activity which contributes added value to its outputs and associated deliverables. Each value add element is linked to the value add elements of the same value type that are associated with deliverable inputs to the activity. At the same time, each value add is linked to the value adds of the same type that are associated with the outputs of the activity receiving the deliverable.

Value Aggregation

Fig. 2.8 illustrates the aggregation of value contributions adjusted for activity output percentages. This is not a standard diagram but is intended only to illustrate the value computations.

Activity A, the first rounded rectangle, processes each unit of production and has one output. The portion of production flow is represented by two numbers on the output deliverable flow. The first number, 100, represents the share of output of activity A, 100%. The second number represents the share corrected for the share of production directed to activity A; in this example, activity A receives 100% of production, so its output is 100% of production.

Activity B receives 100%, but it has two outputs, split between 80% for good product and 20% for defective products. Consequently, 80% of the total production goes to activity D, and 20% of total production goes to

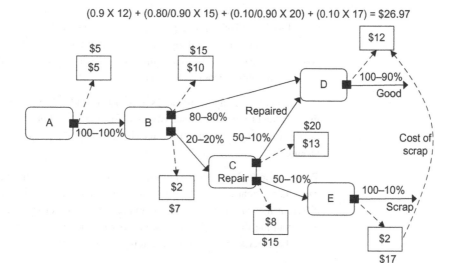

(0.9 X 12) + (0.80/0.90 X 15) + (0.10/0.90 X 20) + (0.10 X 17) = $26.97

■ **FIG. 2.8** Value aggregation example.

activity C. Activity C receives 20% of production for repairs and that is split, 50–50 between good and defective product on outputs. Since activity C has only 20% of production, the outputs are each only 10% of total production. The scrap output of activity C goes to activity E to handle the scrap, and 100% of that input is output as scrap representing 10% of total production.

The simple rectangles represent value add elements. They are associated with the activity outputs with dashed arrows. The number within each box represents the cost contributed by that activity that is associated with that output. For activity A, the total cost is $5 per unit of production and that is associated with all of the output. The number above the box represents the value allocated to that share of production which is also $5 for activity A.

For activity B, the added cost per unit of good production is $10, and the cost per unit of defective production is $2 (presumably the defects are caught before more is invested). The cumulative costs above/below the boxes are the sum of the input cost and the associated output cost: $15 for good units and $7 for bad units.

The defective units are directed to activity C. Activity C repairs half of the units at a cost of $13 and rejects the other half at a cost of $8 (presumably after attempting some repair). The two outputs now each represent 10% of total production. The repaired units are directed back into production at activity D.

Activity D now receives 80% of production as good units at a cumulative cost of $15, and 10% of total production as repaired defective units at a cost of $20 per unit. So the total input is only 90% of production. In addition, the cost of defective units is added into the cost per unit for the 10% of total production coming from activity D.

Consequently, the input costs and scrap cost are added as a weighted average that is added to the cost of activity D of $12 per unit of 90% of production. So the total cost per unit from activity D is $26.97 per unit for 90% of production.

These computations effectively represent measurement computations in a particular scenario. A different scenario will have the same structure, but different measurements. In our examples, unless otherwise specified, we will examine the model in one scenario with the understanding that there could be other scenarios with different measurements.

Value Proposition

A value proposition expresses the expected level of satisfaction of a market segment or other stakeholder based on the values associated with a product or service. A business relationship may be considered at a high level as an exchange of value propositions. The primary use of value propositions is for representation of the values offered to a customer.

In this section, we will consider a value proposition example, define the concept of a value stream, and discuss a business network exchange of value propositions.

An example value proposition is depicted in Fig. 2.9. The first column identifies the value type for each row. Three common value types are shown: Price, Duration (time for delivery), and Defects (number per unit). Other values will depend on the product or service and the interests of the recipient. We will focus on the Price row. The second column is the aggregated value for the value type of that row. In this example, we can assume that the Price is based on a profit margin added to cost. The cost is an aggregation of

Value type	Measurement	Satisfaction	Weight (%)	Impact
Price	$30	5	50	2.5
Duration (days)	5	4	20	0.8
Defects	0.02	3	30	0.9
			Net satisfaction	4.2

■ **FIG. 2.9** Example value proposition.

cost contributions from the activities that lead to production of the end product. So if the cost is $26.97 from the Fig. 2.8 example, then the profit is $3.03 per unit.

The third column is a measure of the satisfaction of the recipient market segment or other stakeholder. Here, satisfaction is a value from 1 to 5— nominally unacceptable, poor, fair, good, and excellent. The level of satisfaction for the value proposition should be derived from a formula applied to the value measurement of column 2 so that when the value measurement is updated, the satisfaction level will be adjusted accordingly. The translation of value measurement to satisfaction level will depend on the recipient. In this example, the market segment is quite pleased with the price, but not with the number of defects. The level of satisfaction of the market segment will tend to be related to the performance of competitors, so "excellent" could represent a significant competitive advantage.

The fourth column, Weights, defines weights assigned to the different value types. These factors are also based on recipient interests. Here the numbers are percentages indicating that the market segment considers the price most important, the defects are somewhat less important, and the duration is of relatively low importance.

The last column, Impact, is the weighted satisfaction level. This is computed for each value type by multiplying the satisfaction level by the weight and dividing by the total of the weights. The Net Satisfaction is the sum of the weighted measurements. In the example, the net satisfaction is 4.2 out of 5, closer to good than excellent, so, potentially, a modest competitive advantage.

A value proposition may also be applied to internal business operations. The aggregated value measurement of an internal capability method (a service) can be reported as a value proposition representing satisfaction of the internal consumers of that service.

A composite value proposition can be configured as an integration of multiple, contributing value propositions such as a value proposition that combines the value propositions of different market segments for the overall market value. A composite value proposition can be configured for top management or the board of directors representing the values delivered by a line of business for multiple products.

A value proposition can be developed for coupling the sale of a package of products. For example, a home theater may be offered as a package of multiple components, or a printer may be sold at a loss to generate sales of print cartridges.

Value propositions provide a useful perspective on a business network collaboration of business partners. For example, an Internet publishing business relies on submission of authors, contracts with advertisers, and subscriptions or purchases of consumers. Each of these contributes values and expects to receive values in return. If not all of the participants perceive that they receive greater value than they contribute, the business will fail.

Value Stream

In VDML, a value stream is the network of value adds and activities that contribute to the delivery of a product and associated value proposition(s). A value stream can be identified by tracing the deliverable flows and value add links backward from the value proposition and end product delivery. The same model can have many value streams that include many of the same capability methods. Conversely, a capability method may contribute to multiple value streams and may contribute to the same value stream in more than one context. Consequently, we may be interested in the impact of a change to a capability on the value proposition of a value stream or the value propositions of multiple value streams.

A value stream can be configured for consideration of a new product or line of business. Initially, the focus is on building a network of capabilities. To begin, there is no need to express the individual activities and deliverable flows, but rather to focus on delegations and direct flows (ie, through stores), of the value stream, incorporating existing capabilities and making placeholders for needed capabilities. The relationships between capabilities become a tree (or river with many tributaries) of capabilities. Subsequent development of the activity networks of the needed or modified capabilities will refine cost and other value estimates and may uncover the need for additional capabilities.

Conceptually, a value stream includes suppliers. However, the details of supplier's operations are usually not available. Instead, the performance of a supplier can be represented with a value proposition. The receiver can define the satisfaction formulae and weights. A supplier may have a contract involving multiple products and commitments that may be represented as a composite value proposition or exchange of value propositions. This is an appropriate level for evaluation of supplier performance.

For input to a value stream, it is the supplier's value measurements that are important. These may be incorporated into the aggregation of value measurements for the value stream. For example, the price (cost of purchase) and defect rate will be of interest. Duration may be important if the product is built to order and a supplier request occurs after receipt of an order.

Value Library

A Value Library provides the names, definitions, and measurement characteristics of value types. The library is a taxonomy to facilitate lookup. VDML vendors or an industry professional group may provide a value library with commonly occurring value types to promote consistency and make it easier for a business to get started using VDML.

Measures Library

VDML incorporates the SMM (Structured Metrics Metamodel) specification from OMG (Object Management Group). SMM defines the structure for definition of measures and for the representation and computation of measurements that occur in a VDML model. SMM also defines the mechanism by which different measurements are associated with each VDML scenario and delegation context.

In addition to the measurements in the VDML model, SMM defines a measures library that defines the characteristics of different measures. When a measurement is represented in VDML, an associated library element defines the characteristics of the measure. A value type element in the value library identifies a measure in the measures library that defines the characteristics of the measurements in value add elements and the value proposition entry for that value type.

As with the other libraries, VDML vendors or professional groups should provide value types and basic measures libraries. Once the libraries are established, a user should, for example, identify a value add for entry of a measurement, and the VDML system should offer a selection of value types.

Once a value type is selected, the measure characteristics are obtained from the measures library by a reference in the value type element.

VDML GRAPHICS

The VDML specification includes graphical elements for key concepts and a number of graphical displays of different aspects of a VDML model. Here we will provide highlights of displays to provide a general understanding of the graphical modeling capabilities. These will be complemented by tabular displays that are dependent on the particular implementation.

VDML Graphical Elements

Fig. 2.10 shows a sampling of VDML graphical elements. These elements are used in various ways in different types of diagrams. The following paragraphs provide brief descriptions of each of the elements in Fig. 2.10.

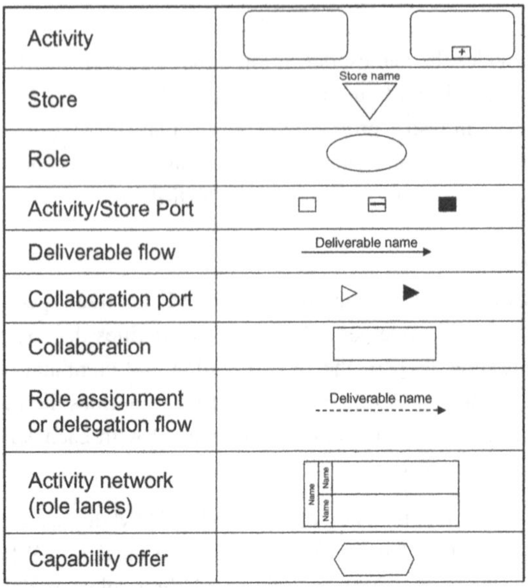

Activity	
Store	*Store name*
Role	
Activity/Store Port	□ ⊟ ■
Deliverable flow	Deliverable name →
Collaboration port	▷ ▶
Collaboration	
Role assignment or delegation flow	Deliverable name ┄┄┄┄┄►
Activity network (role lanes)	
Capability offer	

■ **FIG. 2.10** Sampling of VDML graphical elements.

Activity. A VDML activity is similar in appearance to a BPMN (2011) or CMMN (2014) activity; however, it represents a statistical occurrence of an activity, so an activity network does not have the detail of flow control. An activity with a plus sign in the little box is an activity that engages another collaboration through delegation.

Store. There is no element in BPMN or CMMN corresponding to a store. A store holds business items or resources pending their consumption by an activity. Stores provide for asynchronous communication (eg, store and forward buffer) where the receiver may be operating on a different schedule. For example, a store will occur in a collaboration receiving input from a customer or business partner over a business network collaboration.

Role. A role defines the need for a participant in a collaboration. Roles are visible in business networks representing the different parties engaged in the collaboration, and in collaboration structure diagrams (ie, an extended organizational structure).

Port. A port is attached to an activity or store or collaboration to connect an input or output. If the box has a black background, it indicates there is value contribution attached. If the output port has a horizontal line through it, there is an associated output constraint or a planning percentage such that only a portion of the output is directed to that deliverable flow.

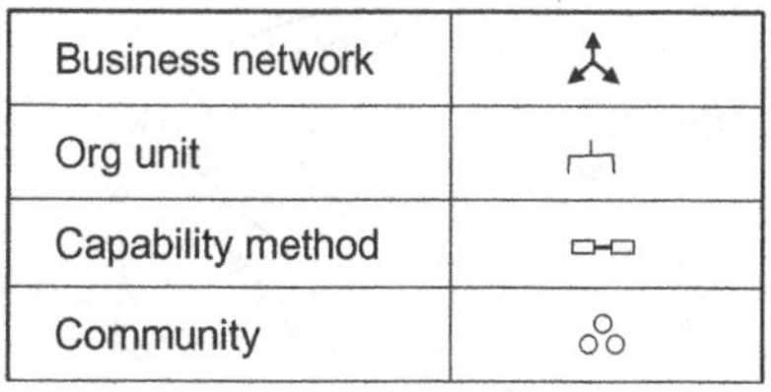

Business network	
Org unit	
Capability method	
Community	

■ **FIG. 2.11** Collaboration type icons.

Deliverable flow. A deliverable flow arrow indicates the flow of a business item from or to an activity or store, the input or output of a collaboration, exchanges between roles in a role collaboration diagram, or exchanges of value propositions in a business network. A dashed line may be used to depict an intangible (or informal) flow.

Collaboration port. A collaboration port, or entry/exit, occurs within a collaboration and indicates the point at which a delegation input enters the activity network, or where a delegation return leaves the activity network. A collaboration output port that has a black background has associated value contributions.

Collaboration. A collaboration is a simple rectangle that is used in several different diagram types. The type of collaboration is indicated by an icon in the upper left corner of the rectangle. The icons are shown in Fig. 2.11.

Role assignment or delegation flow. The dashed line is used to indicate assignment of roles to roles in a collaboration structure diagram, or to depict flows from/to collaboration ports within a collaboration, or to depict the link from capability offers to the capability methods they represent in a capability management diagram.

Activity network. An activity network can be displayed with roles shown as swim lanes containing the activities of the assigned roles with deliverable flows within and across swim lanes (see Fig. 2.13). An activity network can also be displayed without exposing roles, as just a network of activity rectangles (as specified, earlier) connected by deliverable flows.

Capability offer. A capability offer represents a capability available from an organization unit. The graphic is currently used only in capability management diagrams.

VDML Graphical Displays

The following sections briefly describe the various types of graphical diagrams defined in the VDML specification. Additional examples can be found in the VDML specification. The VDML-defined views are a basic set expected to be extended by implementers in response to market interest.

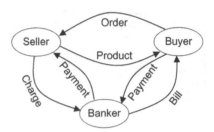

■ **FIG. 2.12** A role collaboration diagram.

Role Collaboration

A role collaboration diagram focuses on the exchange of deliverables between participants as depicted in Fig. 2.12. It is used primarily as a view on a business network but can be applied to view the relationships between participants in any collaboration.

Value Proposition Exchange

A value proposition exchange depicts the exchange of values between participants in a business network. This is somewhat similar to a role collaboration diagram except that one value proposition may correspond to the delivery of multiple deliverables, so the diagram is more abstract.

Activity Network

An activity network based on part of the role collaboration diagram of Fig. 2.12 is depicted in Fig. 2.13 with roles represented as swim lanes. This

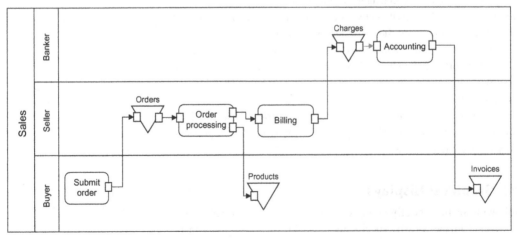

■ **FIG. 2.13** An activity network.

represents deliverable flows in the business network collaboration. A similar diagram may be used to represent deliverable flows in other collaborations. An activity network may also be represented without the role swim lanes, so the diagram requires less space.

Note the use of stores in this activity network. Since the participants are independent business entities, they will receive deliverables in stores because they may not be processed immediately. The store may contain a substantial number of inputs indicating a delay in processing.

Collaboration Structure

A collaboration structure is an extension of a conventional organizational hierarchy that includes additional roles and collaborations.

Fig. 2.14 illustrates a hypothetical collaboration structure. Field Operations has three regions, and a Campaign Committee that consists of Liaison representatives from each of the regions. Roles are ellipses. The Liaison roles have actors assigned (not shown). Each Liaison role is a role in a region but is also assigned to a Member role in the Campaign Committee as indicated by the dashed arrows. This illustrates roles of roles. The small ellipse above each collaboration indicates that it is filling a role in its parent org unit.

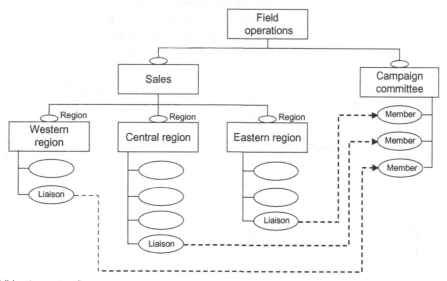

■ **FIG. 2.14** Collaboration structure diagram.

Capability Map

A capability map is a conventional graphical display. Capability rectangles are nested according to their positions in the taxonomy of the capability library. If certain capabilities are highlighted, then it is a "capability heat map." An example is illustrated in Chapter 1.

Capability Management

A capability management diagram, Fig. 2.15, shows one or more org units (large rectangle with the name on the top border) that may be linked by providing and consuming their capability methods. The boundary of an org unit contains capability offers (hexagons) that are each linked with a dashed line to the associated capability method (rectangle) used to fulfill the offer. The capability method may engage one or more supporting capability methods through the dotted lines to the capability offers of the associated organization units.

In Fig. 2.14, Capability Offer A of Org Unit X links to Capability Method A performed by Org Unit A. Capability method A engages Capability Method C through the Capability Offer C of Org Unit Y. Capability Offer B links to Capability Method B that is owned by Org Unit Y but is performed by Org Unit X which provides the Capability Offer.

Measurement Dependency

A measurement dependency network shows the measured characteristics that contribute to the computation of an end measurement. Each arc in the network indicates if the effect is positive or negative. Typically, the end measurement is a value measurement in a value proposition.

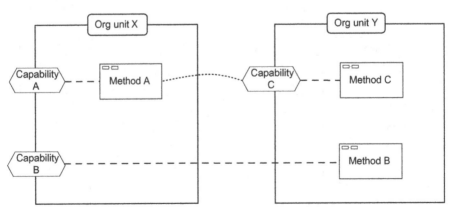

■ **FIG. 2.15** Capability management diagram.

RELATED BUSINESS ANALYSIS TECHNIQUES

The displays discussed above are included in the VDML specification to support understanding of the specification and to provide a minimal set for implementations. However, it is expected that implementers will develop additional displays based on user needs and market demand. Some displays may best be presented as tabular displays (spreadsheets).

Different business design and analysis techniques rely on additional graphical displays. Of particular interest are Value Networks displays based on the work of Verna Allee, and the multiple dimensions of the Lindgren, Business Model Cube (Lindgren et al., 2011) and the Osterwalder, Business Model Canvas (Osterwalder and Pigneur, 2010), discussed in the following sections. These techniques and associated displays can be supported with the content of a VDML model. Additional discussion of these techniques can be found in the Appendix of the VDML specification.

Allee Value Network

Support for the Allee, Value Network requires a display that is similar to the role collaboration display of Fig. 2.12, depicting the exchanges of deliverables between roles. A Value Network uses the distinction between *tangible* (formal) deliverables and *intangible* (informal) deliverables by using dashed lines for informal deliverables. These diagrams may also indicate a sequence of deliverable flows to improve understanding of the interactions.

A Value Network diagram may be derived from a collaboration activity network, but these are more useful when they depict a broader scope of exchange. The broader scope may depict observations of exchanges in an existing value stream to support analysis of existing business operations without regard for delegation to shared capabilities and the bounds of collaborations.

The broader scope may also be applied to a VDML value stream where the delegations are flattened to expose the participation of roles at multiple levels. A user might select a primary collaboration and then selectively expand the subcollaborations.

Lindgren Business Model Cube

Peter Lindgren has defined a *Business Model Cube* in which six dimensions of interest are defined and could be presented as VDML diagrams. The relationship of these to VDML concepts is discussed later.

> *Competencies.* A competency is a key capability (VDML) for which the enterprise possesses the necessary components to provide the capability.

For the Business Model Cube, this dimension will include the selected competencies that are essential to the particular business interest. These should appear as capabilities in the VDML capability library and could be flagged as competencies.

Network. The Business Model Cube network includes selected business partners that are essential to the success of the business being modeled. In VDML, these business partner networks will be represented in various business network collaborations.

Relations. The Business Model Cube expresses exchanges between internal processes and external business partners and customers that are critical to the success of the business. In VDML, these exchanges are represented as selected deliverable flows in business network collaborations.

User and customer. In the Business Model Cube, a typical customer is a direct recipient of the business product or service; a user is a typical participant in the activities or services of the customer. In VDML, the customer is typically a representative of a market segment (community collaboration) who is a party in a business network collaboration. Users may be represented as communities of individuals who interact through business network collaboration as part of the customer business relationship; in other words, the customer is the recipient of the value proposition and determines the more specific benefits provided to users.

Value chain. The Business Model Cube value chain is the sequence of high-level stages that define the operation of the business. In VDML, these stages are high-level abstractions of activities that engage much more detailed decomposition of the business operations.

Value formula (Profit formula). In a Business Model Cube, this describes the factors considered in the computation of profit. In VDML, profit may be computed from value measurements, such as cost, in one or more value propositions along with other factors such as profit margin.

Value proposition. In a Business Model Cube, the value proposition expresses the values offered to a customer or other stakeholder. In VDML, a value proposition expresses the same values, but these are supported by the network of value contributions along with satisfaction criteria and weights to represent the level of interest of the recipients.

Osterwalder Business Model Canvas

Alex Osterwalder has defined a *Business Model Canvas* in which nine dimensions of interest are defined and might be presented as VDML diagrams. The relationship of these to VDML concepts is discussed below.

Channel. A channel is a path for sales and distribution of product and services. In VDML, such paths are depicted with business network collaborations and a channel attribute.

Cost structure. In a Business Model Canvas, the cost structure describes all the costs to operate the business. In VDML, costs are a type of value contributed by activities and aggregated in value propositions for each particular product or service.

Customer relationships. In a Business Model Canvas, customer relationships are interactions with customers leading to delivery of products or services. In VDML, such relationships are represented as business network collaborations.

Customer Segment. In a Business Model Canvas, a customer segment is the segment of the customer market where customers have common interests or needs related to products or services. In VDML, the market segment is a community (collaboration) of customers.

Key activities. In a Business Model Canvas, key activities are typically VDML capabilities that are critical to the business and may be necessary for differentiation. In VDML, these key capabilities also may be identified with attributes to be highlighted in a capability heat map. Key capabilities can be identified as key competencies indicating that they must be retained within the enterprise (not outsourced) to preserve competitive advantage.

Key partnerships. In a Business Model Canvas, key partnerships are relationships with business partners that are critical to the success of the business. In VDML, business partners are identified in business network collaborations and critical (key) partners can be highlighted.

Key resources. In a Business Model Canvas, key resources are facilities, people, raw materials, etc., that are critical to the success of the business. In VDML, the key resources may be identified as key business items that may be scarce or not available to competitors. Most of these should be found as inputs to key capabilities (key activities, earlier).

Revenue stream. In a Business Model Canvas, the revenue stream is the income from sale of the product or service. In VDML, the revenue stream is represented by the exchange of value propositions in business network collaboration(s) between the business and market segments where the revenue is the sale price received from customers (represented in the value proposition received) minus the cost of the product delivered (represented in the value proposition delivered).

Value proposition. In a Business Model Canvas, a value proposition represents the values offered to the market. In VDML, there may be multiple value propositions reflecting the expected levels of satisfaction of relevant values to multiple market segments.

GOING FORWARD

In the next chapter, we will give further consideration to the analysis, development, configuration, and management of shared capabilities as the building blocks of the current enterprise and potential future business designs. Subsequent chapters will address implementation of an advanced agile enterprise and additional, supporting technologies. Chapter 11 will describe future work to further develop business modeling capabilities.

Business Building Blocks

A fundamental requirement for agility is the ability to configure existing components with minimal addition or adaptation to meet changing business needs. This requirement is addressed by VDM through the definition of sharable capability methods that can be individually modified or improved and integrated in multiple contexts to deliver related but diverse products or services. We define these business-oriented design concepts and relationships as a capability-based architecture (CBA).

The CBA is based on a service-oriented architecture (SOA)—the building blocks are integrated as services, but the CBA builds on the information technology of SOA to include the elements of business design that are addressed by VDML—collaborations, activities, deliverable flows, personnel, resources, values, and so on. From a business perspective, the services of CBA are collaborations—people and machines working together for a shared purpose. A business is a network of collaborations.

A capability method is a collaboration that specifies the activities and roles that provide a specific application of a capability as a service. A product is produced by a value stream which is a network of capability methods that delivers value to a customer or internal recipient. Capability methods are sharable services, and thus each capability method may participate in multiple value streams.

Capability methods are bundled into capability units. A capability unit is an organization unit that manages the capability methods along with the shared personnel and other resources that are applied by the capability methods. The capability unit may be responsible for a more general capability—such as machine maintenance, order management, warehouse management, field services, and product assembly—supported by the capability methods. A capability unit is implemented as a service unit at an operational level. A service unit implements the capability methods of the capability unit as business processes along with other administrative and supporting capabilities that maintain, adapt, and improve the capability unit implementation.

Management of resources by a capability unit results in sharing of resources for all of the value streams served by the capability methods of that capability unit. This sharing achieves economies of scale and other benefits from the elimination of duplication.

In this chapter, we will first expand on the characteristics of a CBA and its relationship to the more detailed operational business design. We will then focus on multiple aspects of value stream modeling. Next, we will consider issues related to management of capability units and expand on the requirements of operational business design. Finally, we will describe key components of the supporting information technology infrastructure.

CAPABILITY-BASED ARCHITECTURE

A CBA is the basis for design of all business aspects of the agile enterprise, including administrative services and business management. However, of primary concern is the design of the business to deliver products and services and the ability to quickly adapt to new market demands and opportunities. Consequently, our focus will be on the impact of CBA on lines of business and delivery of products and services to external customers.

In the following sections, we will discuss further the aspects of a CBA, particularly capability methods, capability units, value streams, and the operational implementation.

Capability Methods

A *capability method* is a collaboration that specifies the roles, activities, and deliverable flows to provide a particular service. This includes engaging other capability methods as supporting services. In general, a capability method receives deliverables from a requesting collaboration as input to its service and returns results. A capability method may also send and receive deliverables with other collaborations through stores.

Capability methods may have different degrees of structure, ranging from unstructured to fully structured with an activity network. The degree of structure depends on the level of detail in the model and the repeatability of the activities in the collaboration.

Many capability methods delegate to other capability methods. For example, a capability method can define the overall activities to produce a product. Such a capability method is then not generic but is specific to the product. The activities of that capability method, for the most part, will delegate to other capability methods where some may still be specific to the product while others may be generic, shared by other product lines. There may be multiple levels of capability methods delegating to other capability methods. At each level, a capability method should be limited in scope to confine its activities to a particular capability and delegate to other capability methods where a different capability is required, usually involving different personnel or key assets. The most elementary capabilities are the most sharable and stable.

Capability Units

A *capability unit* is an organization unit that is responsible for a bundle of capability methods and associated personnel, resources, facilities, and information that together provide various applications of a more general capability. A capability unit is depicted in Fig. 3.1 to include a bundle of capability methods and assets. Each of the capability methods provides a specific application of the capability.

A capability unit presents *capability offers* that identify the capability methods that the capability unit supports. There may be multiple capability units (organizations) that have some of the same capability offers. Consequently, when an activity requires a capability for delegation, one or more capability offers identify capability methods and associated capability units to provide the needed capability. The selected capability unit fills the activity role to provide the capability method along with the personnel and resources that are required.

Capability units are important because a capability usually involves some key assets that can support multiple capability methods. A capability unit implementation will also include additional services that support management and

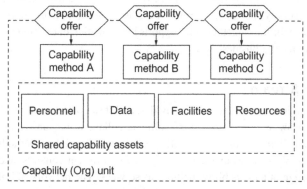

■ **FIG. 3.1** Capability unit and its capability methods.

control of the bundle of capability methods. A capability unit is implemented as a service unit at the operational level of design detail, discussed later.

For example, consider a shoe-repair shop as a capability unit. It has skilled shoe-repair persons, machines, materials, and ways to track the repairs of individual deliverables (shoes). There are several different capability methods for repair of stitching, replacement of heels, replacement of soles, and refinishing. Each of these services will utilize some or all of the shoe-repair shop assets. There will also be ancillary services such as cancellation of an order and change of an order. Additional support services based on other capabilities (that may be outsourced) will be used by the repair shop for accounting, purchasing, payroll, and marketing.

Note that a capability unit may manage all of the associated capability methods and all of the assets used by its capability methods, or it may manage some of the assets and delegate management of capability methods and some resources to suborganizations. In such a case, the parent and subunit relationships will align with the enterprise management hierarchy discussed in Chapter 10.

Capability Library

In a VDML capability library, capabilities are classified in a taxonomy. The nodes of the taxonomy are *capability categories* and *capability definitions*. The capability definitions for capability methods are leaves of the taxonomy tree. The capability library also contains capability definitions that identify capability units. A capability method definition can be associated with more than one capability unit, and a capability unit definition may identify multiple organization units that manage the general capability.

The capability taxonomy is not the same as the enterprise management hierarchy, and it is not the delegation tree of capability methods delegating to other capability methods. It provides a classification structure that brings similar capabilities together, and supports identification of existing methods that may meet a business need.

Value Stream

Collaborations can define roles, activities, and flows of deliverables. Deliverables flow between activities within a collaboration, and they flow between collaborations via delegation and stores. Capability methods provide sharable services that may be engaged in different contexts, and they may engage other capability methods as services. The network of collaborations (primarily capability methods) and their activity networks that deliver a particular product or service are called a *value stream*. A value stream is distinguished from a value chain by the level of detail that includes activities, deliverable flows, integration of shared capabilities, and value contributions.

The VDML model of a value stream includes the network of value contributions of activities to support value proposition(s) for the end product of the value stream. The value stream is thus the key structure for design and analysis of the work to deliver a product or service. An enterprise typically will have multiple value streams to deliver products or services to customers as well as multiple value streams to deliver products or services to internal recipients.

In a CBA, capability methods will be shared by multiple value streams. The capability library supports identification of the same or similar capabilities for potential consolidation. For development of a new or changing value stream, the capability library supports identification of capability methods to provide needed capabilities.

As a value stream is analyzed or a new value stream is developed, new capability methods may be added to the capability library. A capability method will be associated with a capability unit as the organization responsible for management of the capability method and associated assets. Alignment of capability methods with capability units and the capability unit position in the management hierarchy may be refined later to optimize sharing of assets and improvements.

MODELING VALUE STREAMS

VDML represents the configuration of multiple value streams using shared capabilities. The values delivered by each value stream can be traced to the capabilities that contribute to each value. The values contributed by each capability can be traced to its activities and any capabilities that it engages. From a VDM value proposition perspective, the enterprise is a network of value streams, each receiving values from its participating capabilities.

From an enterprise perspective, there are value streams delivering products or services to customers and others delivering products or services to internal consumers. The existence of a distinct value stream will depend on differences in the associated line of business, the character of the product or service, and the characterization of a unit of production.

The *value chain* of a line of business or product line will define major stages in the delivery of a product or service starting with product and market research and product development and potentially ending with customer field support services. The focus of a value chain is the general sequence of major operating stages that lead to delivery of value to an end customer. The stages are decomposed, potentially to several levels, to identify key capabilities affecting customer value. A value chain is used as the basis for definition of stages of a product lifecycle in Chapter 9.

A *value stream*, as used here, is more detailed and robust in the specification of a network of capabilities. It includes the flow of deliverables, the roles of participating people and organizations, the activities of participants, and the value contributions of activities. The entire value chain for a product or service could be modeled as a single value stream, but it is more appropriate and more manageable to define separate value streams for each of the primary value chain stages, particularly when the rate of production is significantly different. Value propositions should be developed for each of these value streams.

For example, product development has a long lifecycle as compared to a production process, and it contributes distinct values. The same value stream model for product development may be applied to the development of multiple products, so it is useful to consider this effectively as a supplier to the production process. At the same time, delivery of a new product specification is different from delivery of revisions to an existing product, so it may be appropriate for revisions to be modeled as different value streams although they may share many of the same capabilities. In addition, product development may have different value streams for different types of products. In any case, the value contributions of a product development value stream can feed a production value stream and ultimately impact the value proposition for an end customer.

A customer may receive a product that is a package of two or more relatively independent products like a set of furniture or appliances. In such cases, each of the products may have a value stream and value proposition with a composite value proposition defined for the package received by the consumer.

Implementation and management of a CBA requires modeling and transformation of existing processes and responsibilities. For an existing, silo-based enterprise, the production value streams for a line of business are likely intertwined in a large, complex process. The value stream will have embedded variations for the differences between the products or services of that line of business. In another LOB, there may be separate processes for each product or service with duplicated capabilities.

CBA requires identification of distinct capabilities, consolidation of equivalent capabilities for sharing, and the composition of value streams, using shared capabilities.

In this section, we will discuss approaches to development of a value stream model in VDML. We will focus on a single value stream as delivering a product or service to an end customer, but the approach is fundamentally the same for any value stream. Generally, analysis for an enterprise will start with a mainstream production operation that delivers end-customer value as a potential source of significant business value. As the enterprise agility matures, the scope of analysis will expand to include additional value streams, such as product development, and support services.

We will start by considering two complementary approaches to development of a value stream activity model: (1) top-down and (2) bottom-up. We will then consider identification and consolidation of sharable capabilities, followed by refinements to deliverable flows. Then, we describe development of the associated value contribution network. Finally, we will consider modeling the value stream in electronic commerce.

Top-Down Analysis

Top down analysis starts with the selection of a value stream and develops successive levels of detail. This may be based on an existing value chain model, or an industry framework, or both. We will consider each of these.

Value Chain Basis

Fig. 3.2A illustrates a conventional form of a hypothetical value chain used in strategic planning for an established, made-to-order product. This value chain depicts broad capabilities and an implied transition through those capabilities to deliver customer value. Each of the high-level capabilities is broken into supporting capabilities.

A value chain analysis focuses on the contributions of value for the end customer. This example business begins with sales and proceeds through product production, distribution, and support. The customer support capability functions somewhat independently, occurring when there is a reason for some action in the field. Consequently, it is appropriate to model this as a separate value stream. The value chain decomposition is sometimes described as a *process model*, but it is at most a high-level abstraction of the processes that actually deliver customer value. A value chain is not intended to be a process model but rather an abstraction of the flow of value contributions. Nevertheless, at times it is helpful to think in terms of a process breakdown to help identify the required capabilities.

It may be useful to use alternative forms for the value chain decomposition. The conventional value chain model is equivalent to a work breakdown

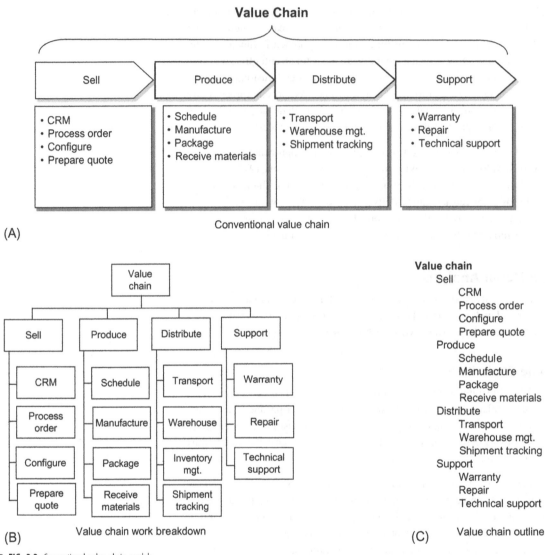

FIG. 3.2 Conventional value chain models.

structure, as depicted in Fig. 3.2B. Fig. 3.2C illustrates the same model in the form of an outline. The outline form is often a more convenient way to capture additional levels of detail, since it is easier to expand multiple levels. Regardless of the form, a conventional value chain model, if available, is a useful starting point for analysis.

The decomposition of the value chain identifies potential capabilities that may be implemented as sharable services. On further analysis, we may find that there are additional capabilities at each level that are less crucial but nevertheless necessary. The addition of deliverable flows will help identify the need for additional capabilities.

Starting from a value chain perspective helps focus on what the product line does rather than who does it. This helps ensure that the definition of capabilities is driven by the business of the enterprise and avoids repackaging the same old way of doing business. As capabilities are identified, they should be defined in the VDML capability library. As the number of capabilities increases, it is useful to start using the capability categories to group similar or related capabilities together and to start identifying capabilities that could be consolidated.

Industry Frameworks

Industry frameworks provide another approach to top-down analysis. Industry frameworks provide prototypical designs of enterprises in a particular industry, based on a consensus of industry representatives. The frameworks tend to define characteristic breakdowns of functionality and business processes that may align with capabilities. They may provide more detail and objectivity than a business-specific value chain. Of course, each enterprise may be different due to individual circumstances or manner of doing business, and these differences may be a basis for achieving competitive advantage in certain markets.

One advantage of an industry framework is that the capabilities will tend to align with implementations of capabilities in commercial enterprise applications and outsourcing services. Use of an industry framework does not mean that a well-defined conventional value chain should be abandoned; instead, together they define more insight for the definition of shared capabilities.

An industry framework may include an enterprise data model. The role of a consistent, enterprise logical data model is discussed in Chapter 6. Use of a framework data model should be strongly considered early in the development of a CBA for a particular enterprise, for two reasons. First, development of a good enterprise logical data model is a very large and time-consuming undertaking that will delay the CBA transformation and exceed the cost of acquiring a model. Second, the framework data model is more likely to be consistent with commercial software systems and outsourcing services as well as industry standards, so data exchanged between services have fewer data transformation problems.

The enhanced Telecom Operations Map (eTOM, http://www.tmforum.org/browse.aspx?catID=1648) from the Tele Management Forum (TMF), illustrated in Fig. 3.3, is one widely recognized industry framework. It is described as a business process framework but is similar to a capability map. It represents the processes of a typical telecommunications service provider. The TMF has defined a companion enterprise data model called shared information and data (SID, https://www.tmforum.org/information-framework-sid/) that supports the enterprise logical data model requirement discussed in Chapter 6.

Fig. 3.3 illustrates the eTOM framework at the enterprise level. There are three major process categories: (1) operations; (2) strategy, infrastructure, and product; and (3) enterprise management. These are described as level-zero processes.

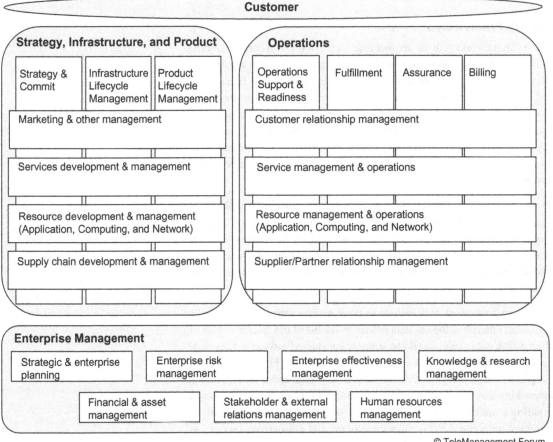

© TeleManagement Forum

■ **FIG. 3.3** eTOM telecommunications framework.

The operations category reflects the primary business operations. The strategy, infrastructure, and product segment defines processes for changes to the business; that aspect of agile enterprise architecture is addressed in Chapter 9. The processes in enterprise management are typically viewed as support services—those processes that are part of managing the enterprise, such as finance and human resources, but are not a direct part of delivering customer value.

The operations and the strategy, infrastructure, and product categories of Fig. 3.3 are each divided by vertical and horizontal partitions described as level 1 processes. The vertical partitions reflect functional capabilities. The horizontal partitions reflect primary enterprise objectives that cut across the functional capabilities. For example, customer relationship management (CRM) is an enterprise objective that requires participation and support from each of the functional capabilities. These objectives are optimized operationally in the operations segment and optimized from a business change perspective in the strategy, infrastructure, and product segment.

Fig. 3.4 shows more detail for the operations processes. These level 2 processes are shown at the intersections of the vertical and horizontal level 1 processes; each is in both a horizontal and a vertical level 1 process within the eTOM specification. Each of these level 2 processes is further detailed in subprocesses. Note that some level 2 processes span level 1 processes; these are effectively shared capabilities that may represent either shared work management service units or capabilities that can be further broken down to define shared operational capability units. A similar breakdown is defined for the strategy, infrastructure, and product level 1 processes. More detailed breakdowns also exist for the enterprise management processes. eTOM process models provide additional insights on capability requirements and the contexts in which they are used.

Value Stream Decomposition

As a first step in developing the detail of a value stream, a delegation tree should be developed based on the value chain and/or industry framework. Each node in the delegation tree is a potential capability method containing an activity network where certain activities delegate to the next lower level of capability methods.

Fig. 3.5 illustrates a delegation tree in which the solid-line arrows represent the request-response relationships from capability methods requesting services to those providing services. The dotted line represents the value stream—the sequence of execution of the capability methods as they contribute value toward the end product. This is a simplified portrayal, since

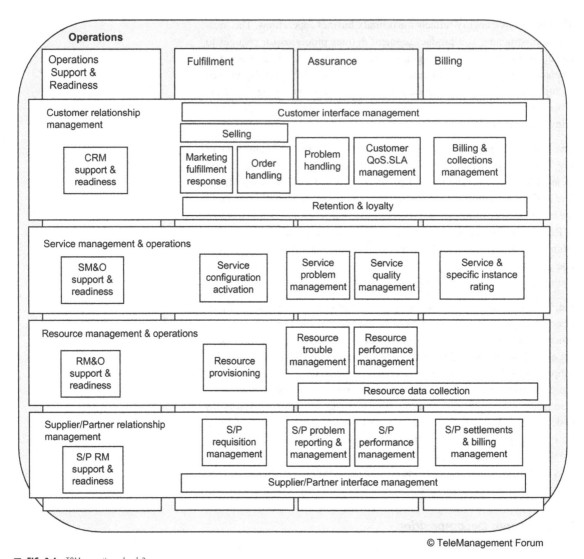

Operations

Operations Support & Readiness	Fulfillment	Assurance	Billing

Customer relationship management

Customer interface management

Selling

| CRM support & readiness | Marketing fulfillment response | Order handling | Problem handling | Customer QoS.SLA management | Billing & collections management |

Retention & loyalty

Service management & operations

| SM&O support & readiness | Service configuration activation | Service problem management | Service quality management | Service & specific instance rating |

Resource management & operations

| RM&O support & readiness | Resource provisioning | Resource trouble management | Resource performance management |

Resource data collection

Supplier/Partner relationship management

| S/P RM support & readiness | S/P requisition management | S/P problem reporting & management | S/P performance management | S/P settlements & billing management |

Supplier/Partner interface management

© TeleManagement Forum

■ **FIG. 3.4** eTOM operations, level 2 processes.

a value stream usually will have branches that are executed concurrently, like tributaries to a river.

Note that some of the capability methods are engaged more than once in the same value stream. The context in which they are engaged will likely affect the measurements of values contributed. If the value stream activities are sequential, then the time from the request to the delivery of customer value is the sum of the times it takes each capability method to contribute its value.

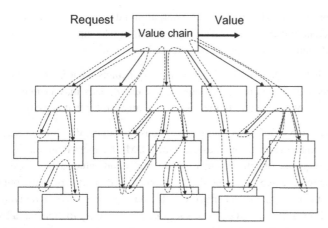

■ **FIG. 3.5** A delegation tree showing value stream.

The cost of the product or service will be the sum of the costs of executing each capability method.

It is useful to develop a delegation tree in an outline form as suggested by Fig. 3.2C. Text can be added below each of the capability name headings to describe the capability, along with the required input deliverable(s) and expected output deliverable(s).

The next step is to develop activity networks for the capability methods. This is detail that would be difficult to manage in the outline form of the delegation tree, so, at this point, we should start building the value stream model in VDML.

It is useful but not essential that the capability definitions in the value stream outline be transferred to the VDML capability library. An initial taxonomy should be developed using capability categories. This will help identify potentially shared capabilities which can then be identified by the same name in the different contexts in which they are used. The capabilities of capability methods must be leaves in the taxonomy tree. If convenient, related capability method definitions can be grouped under capability unit definitions. Note that the capability taxonomy is not the same as the delegation hierarchy.

Initial detail of the activity network for each capability method can then be developed based on the deliverables. Starting with the output deliverable of the value stream, work backward to identify the last activity of the top-level capability method that produces the end product. That activity must either be performed by a person or application/machine, or it must delegate to a supporting capability method. The output of a delegating activity becomes the output of the engaged capability method, and the input to the delegating activity must be the input to the engaged capability method.

Note that the name of a delegating activity depicts what is done from the perspective of the containing capability method. This may or may not be the name of the capability method that is engaged by that activity.

As deliverable flows are identified, the business items that flow as deliverables can be identified and posted in the VDML business item library. Note that a sequence of activities that incrementally add value to a business item can be represented as having the same business item as inputs and outputs rather than creating unique names for the business item in each deliverable flow. Sometimes it will be necessary to add an activity to create a deliverable that is needed as input to another activity.

An activity can only be performed by an individual performer or collaboration. If the activity requires multiple people, then the activity must engage a separate capability method with roles for the multiple participants.

Bottom-Up Analysis

Bottom-up analysis complements top-down analysis by examining the activities of actual business processes to discover activity networks and capability methods.

Traditional businesses usually have few shared capabilities as part of the delivery processes, and thus the capabilities are embedded and not identified in the processes. As a starting point, the work necessary to deliver a product or service is essentially the same whether the model is a traditional, product-line silo, or a value stream. The difference is the composition of a CBA value stream from sharable capability methods. Additional differences may emerge as the value stream is refined.

The top-down analysis should identify candidate value streams and existing processes that perform equivalent work. These processes are then the subjects of bottom-up analysis. The top-down and bottom-up analyses will eventually overlap and be reconciled to produce a more robust model.

This section uses a hypothetical example to illustrate how an analysis can use a spreadsheet to capture information about a current process segment with embedded capabilities and transform that process segment to a segment of a value stream that engages a sharable capability method.

Activity Data Capture

An analyst will start at the end of a process and trace the deliverable flows back through the string of activities and deliverable flows that produce the end product. The analyst should consider the purpose of the model and decide which inputs are of interest in a management-level model of the value stream. Then the analyst must determine if any alternative output deliverable flows are of interest and, if so, trace the output deliverable flows forward to develop the full activity network. Fig. 3.6 illustrates a resulting activity network segment arranged in approximate chronological sequence. Full chronological sequence is not useful where there are concurrent flows. It is most useful to keep together activities that occur in sequence.

Note that a value stream in the VDML model does not represent the flow of individual units of production but represents the paths of deliverables as fractions of production. As a result, gateways in an operational process will be represented as the flows of percentages of production in VDML. In VDML, variations in production rates are buffered by stores, and repeated execution (iteration) will be represented either as a capability method engaged for each iteration or activity value contributions that represent repeated performance of the activity (or group of activities). We will illustrate the analysis with a hypothetical process in which table legs are assembled to table tops and some defective tables are repaired.

In the spreadsheet of Fig. 3.6, the first group of columns identifies role names that are associated with activities. The role of each activity is indicated by an "X" in the intersection of the role column and the activity row. Note that role names need only be unique within a process/capability method. Some roles may be identified as appropriate in multiple methods and should be given the same names. It will likely be necessary to consider the general issue of role

#	Assembler	Packager	Repair scheduler	Repair technician	Method	Activity / Submethod	Table legs	Table tops	Table	Defective table	Defective table	Defective table	Table	Packaged table	Scrap table	Comments
3					Plant 1 assembly	Available legs (shared store)	O									Legs received from external source
4						Available table tops (shared store)		O								Table topse received from external source
5	X					Assemble legs to table	I	I	O	O						Assemble table with four legs
6						Pending repair (store)					I	O				Defective tables stored pending repair
7			X			Schedule repair					I	O		O		Schedule repairable tables based on
8				X		Repair						I	O			Make repairs
9	X					Package for shipment			I				I	O		Package good and repaired tables
10						Table for shipment (virtual store)								I		Tables awaiting shipment
11						Scrap (virtual store)									I	Scrap tables for disposal

■ **FIG. 3.6** An example for activity data capture.

names later in the VDML role definition library or an equivalent table may be developed in a spreadsheet, organized in a taxonomy.

The second major column is for method/process names. At this stage of analysis, there is only a segment of one process being considered. Some rows will be added in the next step of analysis.

The third major group of two columns has "Activity" overlapping with "Submethod." At this stage only the activity caption is relevant. Each of the detail rows contains an activity or store name.

The fourth major group of columns is labeled "Deliverable Flows." The name in each column is the name of a business item that flows from a source to a destination activity. There may be multiple deliverable flow columns with the same name indicating a flow of the same business item. The source activity is designated by an "O" for output, and the destination activity is designated by an "I" for input. So in one deliverable flow column, the source and destination activities are designated as output and input. The last column is for comments.

In the detail of the example, the first two activities are identified as *shared stores*. This means that the inputs to these stores come from other processes, presumably owned and operated by other organizations. Where inputs are directed to these stores, the stores appear as *virtual stores* because the actual stores are in the process we are analyzing. Stores are usually owned by the recipient as an input buffer.

Note that the activities in rows 6–8 deal with repairs, and row 11 deals with the tables that are scrapped. The good table output of row 5 is an assembled table that goes directly to "Package for shipment" in row 9. The defective tables (second output) go to the activity of row 6, which is a store, holding defective tables for repair. A store is appropriate since the production rate for good tables is much higher than the repair rate, and defective tables will occur at random times.

The final outputs of this process also go to stores: the tables for shipment and the tables for scrap disposition. Note that these are designated as virtual stores. This means that they represent stores that exist elsewhere, presumably owned by the organizations responsible for processing shipments and disposition of scrap.

Process Transformation

Fig. 3.7 illustrates the above example, transformed to create a repair service as a potentially sharable capability method. Rows 6–8 have been moved to the bottom of the spreadsheet, separated by a double line and given a method name of "Repair Service." In their place (between rows 5 and 9) is a sub-method call to "Repair Service." The call has input designated "D1" for

	Role Names						Method	Activity	Deliverable Flows									Comments
1																		
2	Assembler	Packager	Repair	Repair				Submethod	Table legs	Table tops	Table	Defective table	Defective table	Defective table	Table	Packaged table	Scrap table	
3							Plant 1 assembly	Available legs (shared store)	O									Legs received from external source
4								Available table tops (shared store)		O								Table topse received from external source
5	X							Assemble legs to table	I	I	O	O						Assemble table with four legs
								Repair service				D1			R1	R2		Call the repair service
9		X						Package for shipment			I				I	O		Package good and repaired tables
10								Table for shipment (virtual store)								I		Tables awaiting shipment
11								Scrap (virtual store)									I	Scrap tables for disposal
6							Repair service	Pending repair (store)					I	O				Defective tables stored pending repair
7		X						Schedule repair					I	O		O		Schedule repairable tables based on
8			X					Repair						I	O			Make repairs

■ **FIG. 3.7** Example with sharable service.

"delegation," and outputs designated "R1" and "R2" for the results for the repaired and scrapped tables.

In the Repair Service method, line 6 has an input of "I1" to correspond to the delegated input, "D1," and lines 7 and 8 have outputs O2 and O1, respectively, corresponding to the results of R2 and R1 of the above call.

The numbering of inputs and outputs is necessary so that the Repair method can be called by other processes without the deliverable flow columns of the call being aligned with the input and output columns of the Repair method. Each caller will refer to the input "D1" and the outputs "R1" and "R2." In this way sharable capabilities can be pulled out of larger processes and engaged in multiple contexts.

Each major process can be modeled with a spreadsheet. As subsequent processes are analyzed, opportunities may be recognized for using some of the already-defined sharable methods. Note that there can be additional levels of delegation, for example, if the Repair method was substantial, it might have sharable submethods pulled out as well.

This approach separates the activities and shared methods from the responsible organizations. This can be important for taking internal politics out of the restructuring analysis. Later, the organization structure for management of shared capabilities can be considered with a better understanding of the scope of sharing and the similarities of sharable capabilities.

Capability Reconciliation and Consolidation

Based on this spreadsheet-based analysis, capability methods can be defined in the VDML model. The capability methods from this bottom-up analysis of actual processes should overlap with the top-down analysis of capability methods. The capability names and deliverable flows of business items will help reconcile these two perspectives.

The capability library must be refined to provide appropriate classifications using capability categories. This will help identify capability methods that are similar. In some cases, a capability identified in the top-down analysis will be the same capability method identified differently in the bottom-up analysis. The details of the two must be reconciled to define one capability method with an appropriate name.

Capability methods that are classified as similar must be analyzed to determine if they should be consolidated as one shared capability method. Those that cannot be consolidated but share core elements should be evaluated as different services of the same capability unit. Note that it is possible that the same capability unit and associated capability methods could be provided by multiple organization units if required by considerations such as data residency (import/export regulations) and access constraints.

This consolidation achieves two important objectives: (1) it identifies multiple contexts in which a shared service unit can be applied and (2) it reduces the explosion of detail, since the detail of a consolidated service unit needs be expanded only once.

It may be necessary to modify the definition of some capability methods to consolidate them as shared services. In some cases, calling collaborations may need to be modified to provide a more appropriate scope or objective for a capability method so that a capability method can satisfy the needs of multiple, delegating activities.

Deliverable Flow Refinements

At this stage, we will focus on refinements to the deliverable flows starting with planning percentages, considering synchronous versus asynchronous interactions and modes of process optimization.

Production Planning Percentages

When a capability method has more than one output, a planning percentage must be assigned to each output. If they are alternative outputs, then the percentages should add to 100%. If they are concurrent outputs, then both percentages should be 100%. In rare cases, the outputs may be alternatives part of the time and concurrent part of the time, resulting in a total greater than 100%. These percentages may be different in different scenarios when they depend on product mix or random occurrences such as defects.

The statistical measurements associated with elements of a collaboration method are based on a single unit of production, and the cumulative value measurements can be affected by these percentages. In particular, planning percentages are a concern when deliverable flows branch or merge. For example, when flows have a concurrent branch, the cumulative cost of production should be allocated to the branches. When alternative flows are merged, the cumulative cost should be the weighted average share of the cumulative costs based on the planning percentages of the incoming flows.

At this stage, values can be assigned for testing purposes and to indicate the relationships between multiple outputs.

Synchronous Exchange

At this stage of analysis, most of the links between capability methods have defaulted to synchronous delegations.

A synchronous exchange is a simple request-response. The requester's action is suspended pending a response from the recipient. In VDML, this is represented as delegation by an activity to engage a capability method as a service. Only capability methods can be engaged in this mode.

Fig. 3.8A depicts a synchronous flow (for illustration only). The dashed boxes depict capability methods. Activity A engages capability method N. In capability method N, activities B and C are performed and a result is returned to activity A.

Delegation enables the capability method to be engaged in different contexts with different inputs where the activity network does not depend on the

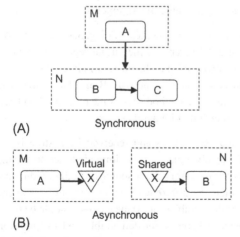

■ **FIG. 3.8** Synchronous and asynchronous flows.

source of the request. The measurements of the capability method will be dependent on the input and thus the context in which it is engaged. These measurements will be reflected in the value contributions associated with the response. The measurements of an engaged capability method are based on a unit of production of the engaged method. The measurements returned from the delegation are then adjusted by the calling activity to reflect the share of production of that context that is delegated to the engaged method.

Asynchronous Exchange

Not all interactions are synchronous. An asynchronous exchange occurs when a source activity sends a deliverable but does not wait for a response.

In VDML, a virtual store in the sending collaboration receives the deliverable flow, and the corresponding, shared (real) store in the receiving collaboration provides the deliverable to a receiving activity. The effects of this deliverable flow may be realized in a result received by the sender at a later time. This mode can be applied by any collaboration, not just a capability method.

The value measurements associated with a deliverable in a store must be factored into the measurements for the receiving collaboration. Essentially, each business item in the store can be viewed as a unit of production from the source collaboration, so the adjustment to measurements will be based on the number of business items from the store that represent a unit of production in the receiving collaboration. For example, tires may be delivered to a store to supply an automobile production line. Each tire is a source unit of production. However, since four tires are required for each automobile, four tires are a unit of production of the receiving collaboration. This will require adjustment of incoming value measurements.

An asynchronous exchange is depicted in Fig. 3.8B. Activity A in capability method M sends a deliverable to the virtual representation of store X. The deliverable is received by the shared (real) store X in capability method N where it can be accepted by activity B at a later time. The result may or may not be returned to method M or some other method later in the value stream via a similar link with another store.

A deliverable may be sent to and received by a store because (1) it is assumed that the receiver may not take immediate action and may be receiving similar deliverables from other sources, (2) the production rates of the source and recipient are different, (3) there are multiple sources or multiple consumers of the deliverables, or (4) the receiver should be free to determine and change how it will process the deliverable, and a shared store is a way of isolating the sender process(es) from the receiver process(es).

Generally, the shared store will be owned by the receiver. However, a shared store can receive deliverables from multiple sources and supply deliverables on demand to multiple recipients. The store should be owned by a common parent organization in the receiving management hierarchy.

A difference in production rate may also occur when the sender or receiver (or both) is operating in a batch mode. It may also occur when multiple units being received are used for each unit of the receiver's production, or only some of the units received are used by the receiver's production.

A service can be engaged asynchronously for a request-response exchange by agreement between the requester and provider. A deliverable can be sent to the provider's input store, and the provider later sends a response to the requestor's input store. However, at an operational level, this requires that the request carries the identity of the request and requester and the identity of the input store for the requester's response. In VDML, individual requests are not tracked, so it is sufficient for the production rate of the requests to equal the production rate of the responses.

A common application of an asynchronous deliverable flow (to a store) is to deliver exceptions for processing by another collaboration, for example, handling of scrap or rejection of a customer order. This has been regarded as a "side effect" flow since it initiates action not included in the response to a delegation.

Process Optimization

There are various techniques to achieve process optimization that may have implications to the value stream beyond the implementation of individual capability methods. The following are examples.

- Building to forecast vs building to order should reduce customer time to delivery
- Batch production, balancing setup costs against timeliness, and inventory costs
- Sequencing of requests as for an automobile production line, to avoid bursts of high work content at individual stations
- Sharing resources across capability methods
- Selection of operating location for utilization of special facilities or product distribution
- Sequencing work to manage priorities
- Managing rework

These factors should be considered as part of value stream design. Since they will likely impact the design of individual capability methods, they may indirectly impact other value streams or they may impact the ability to share certain capability methods. Since these factors can affect the success of multiple value streams, they should be considered from an enterprise perspective.

Value Contribution Development

Completion of the value stream requires the addition of one or more value propositions and value add elements for contributions of activities. A value proposition brings together measurements of the values that are important to customers in a market segment, and it computes a level of satisfaction for each along with an overall satisfaction level based on the relative importance of each of the value types. If there are subgroups of customers that expect different value measurements or give different weights to the values, then there should be different value propositions for these market segments. If there are market segments that buy products with different features, then it may be necessary to define different value streams that represent the flow and value contributions for the differences in features.

Each value proposition is supported by a value contribution network—the network of value adds elements that contribute to that value proposition. The following paragraphs describe development of the value contribution network. Note that a VDML modeling tool and predefined value and measurement library entries should make these operations much easier than they may appear here.

Identify Customer Values

Development of the value contribution network should start with a value proposition. For each value proposition, the value types of interest to the recipient/customer must be identified. This is the minimal set of values to be measured in the network.

Update Values Library

The value types of interest should be added to the values library if not already there. For each value type, the unit of measure must be defined. Value categories should be added to include new values in the taxonomy.

Attach Value Adds to Activities

Each activity in the value stream must be considered in order to attach value add elements for those value types of interest that are relevant to the work of that activity.

The value measurements of each capability method may be specified directly if more detail (an activity network) is not available, but in a more complete model, these measurements will be derived from the contributions of the activities within the capability method.

Insert Value Add Elements Into the Value Network

Each value add element must be linked into the value network for its value type. The value network generally parallels the activity network deliverable flows.

Assign Tentative Measures

It is useful to assign value measurements to each of the value add elements for testing purposes. These may be defined for a test scenario.

Define Value Aggregation Formulas

The formulas for aggregation of value measurements will depend on the nature of the value type and the associated share of production associated with the value add (the planning percentage of the associated output deliverable). Value measurements returned from delegation must be adjusted to reflect the share of production addressed by the requesting activity.

Refine Value Proposition

Each value proposition must be linked to the value aggregations for each value type of interest to the recipient. Note that there may be a different value proposition, with different values of interest for different market segments.

Define Satisfaction Computations

The aggregated value measurement for each value type must be translated to a customer satisfaction measurement in the value proposition. This formula will depend on the relationship between the value measurement and the satisfaction scale as well as the upper and lower bounds of satisfaction. Some value measurements may have a linear relationship to satisfaction while others may best be described by a curve. This formula is important so that changes to the model that affect value measurements will be properly expressed as customer satisfaction.

Define Weights

Weights must be assigned to each value type in a value proposition to reflect the level of interest the customer has for that value type. The default is to use the weights to compute a weighted average for overall customer satisfaction. These weights could also be computed with a formula for a nonlinear impact.

For example, an "unsatisfactory" satisfaction level for a value type could be very important while a "good" satisfaction level might be of less concern.

Participation in Electronic Commerce

An enterprise will engage in electronic commerce to exchange products and services with suppliers, customers, and other business partners.

Interactive Business Relationships

Asynchronous exchanges are the normal mode for a business network exchange because the exchanges with customers, suppliers, or other business partners are not tightly coupled. The parties in a business network (collaboration) send and receive deliverables asynchronously and a party may be involved in exchanges with many different business networks (other parties). In the business network, there are not shared stores, but it is expected that the receiving activity of each party will deliver input deliverables to a receiver's internal store for processing.

In general, electronic commerce between enterprises can be viewed as a loosely coupled integration of services in much the same way that services are used within the enterprise. Suppliers in a supply chain are providing the service of delivering products to the production process and the recipient later returns payment. Banks provide a service for accepting and cashing a check, and the check submitter receives credit for the payment. Transportation carriers provide services for pickup and later delivery of packages. The primary difference between internal services and electronic commerce involves concerns about security, trust, and autonomy.

In some cases, the information exchanged might not be private and the interaction may be trivial, such as in a request for a stock quote. The service provider may not be particularly concerned about the identity of the service user, but the service user is dependent on the identity and integrity of the provider for an accurate and timely stock quote. In other cases, such as the transfer of funds, identities of the service user and service provider are both critical and the information content is highly confidential. Security considerations are discussed in Chapter 7.

Trust requires a business relationship beyond technical compatibility. Each party must be assured that the other party will fulfill its obligations. Reputation may be a factor in determining the quality and reliability of the service. This assurance still requires human participation in the establishment of business relationships. In some cases, this will be established by consortia or other general affiliations that screen members and provide assurance of good faith relationships among them. A discussion of establishing trust is beyond the scope of CBA and the scope of this book, but electronic signatures that establish legal obligations are addressed in Chapter 7.

Business Networks

VDML models business network collaborations between the enterprise and its customers, its suppliers, and its other business partners. Two different views are defined for business network exchanges: (1) value proposition exchange and (2) deliverable exchange. Note that the other parties in a business network exchange are often typical participants such as a customer of a market segment represented as a member of a community.

In a value proposition exchange, each party is the sender and recipient of value propositions from other party(s). Each party must perceive a net gain from the exchanges in order for the collaboration to be viable. This is useful when considering a new business model, particularly where there are multiple parties involved. For example, a blog publisher, depicted in Fig. 3.9, must ensure that bloggers, advertisers, and readers each realize some benefit from participating.

In a deliverable exchange, the focus is on the flow of deliverables. One party may deliver a product and a recipient delivers payment. However, this exchange may be more complex if it includes related deliverables such as a proposal or quote and response, a shipping notice, an invoice, and a payment. The modeler must determine the level of detail that is needed to support the business design. Note that greater detail of exchanges may be deferred to the technical, operational design of service units.

It is important to link a deliverable exchange to its supporting value stream. The end product of a value stream may be delivered by an activity of the selling party to an activity of the customer party and another activity of the selling party receives payment which is delivered to a store for processing.

The operational exchange, the next level of design detail, is usually more complex, and different activities of a party may send and receive deliverables such as changes, cancellations, status reports, quotes, and other documents.

CAPABILITY UNIT MANAGEMENT

There are four primary aspects to management of a capability unit: (1) Capability method design, (2) management of resources, (3) management of operations, and (4) value optimization. These aspects may be all managed

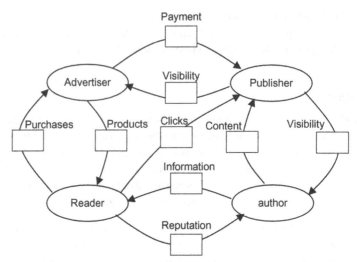

■ **FIG. 3.9** Example value proposition exchange.

directly by one organization unit, or some aspects may be delegated or acquired from other collaborations.

Capability Design

The operational design of an activity network is the responsibility of an organization unit that is the capability method owner. This will be separated from responsibility for performing the capability method when there is a need for multiple organizations to perform it. For example, a budgeting capability method may be defined by the accounting organization for use by all organization units. This can ensure policy compliance, security, or operating consistency. This may limit the ability of a provider organization unit (that performs the method) to innovate and improve its operations.

Resource Management

A parent organization unit, separate from a capability method provider, may have responsibility for resource management where there is an opportunity for economies of scale or workload balancing among similar capability methods. Typically, this will be a capability unit organization. The manager of resources owns stores. Consumable resources are used from a store and replenished by input deliverable flow. Personnel and other reusable resources are obtained from pools (a specialized store). These resources are assigned from their pool when needed and released when no longer needed. Not all personnel and resources for a capability are necessarily owned by the same organization unit, but their store must be accessible by the capability methods that need them.

Operational Management

Operational management focuses on the day-to-day operation of a capability method. The operational manager is in charge of the work being done, supervises the participants, and resolves problems. Generally, this will be the capability unit that offers the capability.

Value Optimization

Optimization of a capability is based on its impact on the value streams that use it, the values it contributes, and the importance of those values to the value stream consumers. Typically, there will be a trade-off between speed, quality, and cost. For some value streams, speed may be important where cost may be most important for other value streams. Since shared capability methods will impact multiple value streams, it is important that the impact of changes be evaluated from an enterprise perspective.

Consequently, capability service level agreements should include measurements of value contributions, and consumers of a capability service should monitor compliance, particularly for those value types that are important to their value stream customers.

If a capability method uses another capability method that makes a change affecting a value measurement, the value measurement change will show up in the value measurement of the calling capability method and any methods that call it, directly or indirectly. This propagation of effect works in the VDML model, but it may be more difficult to observe in business operations. This reinforces the importance of monitoring for compliance with a service level agreement.

Capability Outsourcing

An outsourcing relationship will take a somewhat different form. *Outsourcing* is the use of an external entity to provide a client with external services that would otherwise be provided by an internal capability method, capability unit, or complementary set of capability methods.

Analysis of capabilities should include capabilities that are outsourced even though the enterprise does not own the elements of those capabilities. The outsourced services must be integrated with the enterprise operations—they contribute values that must be considered in the resulting value propositions. An outsourced capability can achieve greater economies of scale and may be more scalable to respond to changes in seasonal demand or market share. Capability should be distinguished from competency where a competency of an enterprise requires that the enterprise own the elements of the capability, usually for competitive advantage. A capability should not be outsourced if it is important to differentiation in the marketplace or if there is no competition between outsourcing providers.

The enterprise will not have control over the implementation of an outsourced capability and must rely on marketplace competition to control the cost and performance of the services. The typical purpose of outsourcing is to realize economies of scale and scalability that cannot be achieved within the enterprise. As the enterprise organization is transformed to a CBA, it is important to consider outsourcing as an alternative to the transformation and consolidation of existing capabilities.

The exchange with an outsourcing provider will incorporate one or more capability methods (services) into one or more value streams. The outsourcing provider can be viewed as a capability unit with multiple, complementary capability methods. Depending on the nature of the outsourced capability, the delegations may be tightly coupled, the same as for an internal capability or they may be loosely coupled, asynchronous deliverable flows.

In general, the focus will be on the service interfaces and level of service agreements. The outsourcing provider implementation will be a black box, preserving the option of the provider to change its implementation to address new business challenges and opportunities.

There may be other exchanges through business networks for management of the outsourcing relationship and payment for services. Managers within the enterprise do not control the resources or the operations of the outsourced service units. The enterprise must manage the services on the basis of a service contract, costs, and performance metrics, along with assessment of the satisfaction of internal users with the outsourced service.

The service interfaces require close attention. The interfaces are more difficult to change because the same services are being used by other enterprises. In addition, all requirements must be reflected in the interface specification and service level agreement; otherwise, there is no basis for corrective action when the service does not meet expectations.

The service interfaces should be based on industry standards, if available. The enterprise should be able to switch to an alternative service provider if the current provider is not meeting expectations. Furthermore, the ability to switch to alternative services ensures competition between service providers to drive improvements in cost and performance.

Table 3.1 Risks and Benefits of Outsourcing	
Risks	**Benefits**
• Inability to take direct corrective action in service operations • Service provider failure could bring the enterprise to a standstill • No service employee loyalty to the user client enterprise • Burden of contract management—monitoring performance and enforcing service agreement • No competitive advantage • Risk of security delegation	• Economies of scale across multiple enterprises (cost savings and workload leveling, driven by competition) • Maintain regulatory compliance • Service can leverage and retain specialists to ensure quality • Service should be able to absorb changes in scale • May enable entry to new markets (eg, address regulations in another country) • Should implement best practices

Obviously, if the same services are available to competitors, they cannot be a source of competitive advantage. At best, outsourcing moves the enterprise to a best-practices level of performance. At the same time, the management of the enterprise does not have the burden of managing the implementation or ongoing operation of the service, although it is important for enterprise management to measure performance and enforce service agreements.

The risks and benefits of outsourcing are outlined in Table 3.1.

OPERATIONAL DESIGN

A VDML model is a conceptual representation of the business. In order to meet operational needs, additional design details must be added. Here, we will examine the necessary expansions of the CBA conceptual business design to develop the operational business design.

Operational Design Alignment

The building blocks of the CBA align with the operational design of the agile enterprise. The scope of business processes discussed in Chapter 4 must align with the scope of the activity networks of capability methods. The operational level models add details that include flow control for individual transactions; handling of exceptions; application of business rules; security mechanisms; accounting facilities; and ancillary services for monitoring, maintenance, and control of service delivery.

In an operational design, the service unit will correspond to the capability unit and include ancillary services as well as computer applications for management of the capability. Consequently, in a CBA enterprise, the VDML model used by management will align with the operational business design such that the model can properly be the basis for development of operational design details, and measurements of business operations will provide the value measurements of the VDML model for the same product offering and circumstances. This enables managers to refer to the VDML model to understand the context of measurements, the consequences of disruptions, the implications of proposed changes, and the viability of strategic plans.

Service Unit Design

A capability unit identifies an organization responsible for the management of a capability, its personnel, resources, facilities, data management, and the capability methods that provide associated services. A service unit expands on the capability unit specification to define operationally complete capabilities. Fig. 3.10 depicts aspects of a typical service unit.

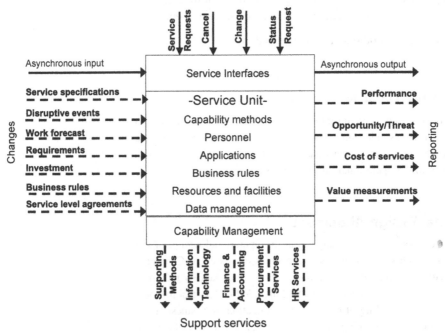

■ **FIG. 3.10** Service unit interfaces.

While this pattern implies considerable functionality beyond the VDML representation of the corresponding capability unit, VDML could be used to model these additional, detailed capabilities but that would obscure the business design abstraction. However, this could be modeled in VDML as a typical service unit pattern that engages a set of shared capabilities.

Note that not all capability methods will be implemented as information systems service units as described here. Some implementations may be completely embedded in conventional computer applications, and others may be implemented as human activities performed on physical deliverables with oral responses to questions and an individual or team that works according to a standard pattern of activities. In these cases, it may be necessary to implement specialized interfaces and protocols for integration with the enterprise information infrastructure.

Service Interfaces

The service interfaces on the top of the diagram are the interfaces for engaging the services defined by associated capability methods along with related services that are required for a full, operational capability. These are synchronous requests. Multiple services will require multiple processes that may all require consideration if the service implementation changes, although this will be easier to coordinate within one responsible service unit organization. It is also likely that specialized services will result in tighter coupling with users, in turn resulting in propagation of effects to users when the service unit makes internal changes. Each service unit should be designed to accommodate service parameters and specifications that enable a generic service to meet a range of user requirements.

There are also possible, asynchronous inputs and outputs—exchanges through stores. These must also be specified in the interface and performance specifications.

Note that though the focus is on service units that are electronically integrated and rely on automated business processes and applications, equivalent mechanisms must be considered where there are other manual exchanges based on paper or voice communications.

Supporting Applications

Most of the services managed by a service unit will involve some automated record-keeping or computations. These applications or tools are the responsibility of the service unit organization. The service unit must also take responsibility for the design of automated business processes.

Some services, such as a tax computation, for example, may be fully auto-mated and on the surface involve only a computer application. However, there is an organization responsible for the computer application and for ensuring its accuracy and reliability. Though people might not be directly involved in the operation, people maintain the tax rates and computations. This may involve other people or other services to identify changes to tax rates and regulations. There may be still other people involved in technical maintenance such as adapting the computation to new information technol-ogy. All these capabilities and associated responsibilities are part of deliv-ering a tax computation service. To the typical user, and from an executive management perspective, the tax computation service provides tax compu-tations in response to requests.

The implementation of the service obviously involves much more, including the use of other services. These implementation considerations are the responsibility of the service unit organization.

Changes

Fig. 3.10 shows a variety of inputs as changes. These are not part of the nor-mal operation of the services and are therefore not modeled in the capability methods. However, these inputs suggest that some action is required by the service unit organization to modify the services.

In the case of the service specifications and service level agreements, these will be the result of some collaboration involving representatives of the ser-vice unit, consumers of services, and enterprise leadership to ensure that they are appropriate from an enterprise perspective. A service unit is required to comply with its service interface specifications and its service level agreements. These specifications are effectively contracts with the rest of the enterprise. They may be changed as a result of new requirements or improvements in the service unit implementation, but they cannot be chan-ged unilaterally. Performance metrics are based on performance against these specifications, and users of the services, as well as potential future users, rely on conformance to the specifications.

Reporting

Fig. 3.10 also shows outputs for reporting on the right side of the diagram. Performance measurements and opportunity/threat identification are for con-sideration of higher management and may support investments or other action for adaptation or improvement of the service implementations. The cost of services supports billing for services as discussed later. These are related but not the same as the statistical costs in the VDML model. The value measurements are actual measurements that may be used to investigate problems or compute the averages that are needed to support analysis in the VDML model.

Support Services

The other services indicated with dashed arrows at the bottom of the diagram include supporting capability methods engaged through delegation, and administrative support services that are necessary for the service unit to maintain its capability, but they do not contribute directly to the value of each unit of production. These support services—accounting services, IT services, HR services, and procurement services—have their own value streams that deliver value for the management of the enterprise and the business operations they support.

Service Unit Management

Service unit management involves the work of administration, problem solving, and dealing with changes as well as other factors that affect the appropriate application of the general capability and the specific services that are offered.

In addition, the service unit is responsible for the internal operation of the service unit such as

- Management of resources within the service unit. This involves ensuring the availability of resources
- Workload balancing for optimal utilization of personnel and facilities across multiple capability methods and potentially with related service units under shared management
- Batch processing or other methods for optimization of cost (such as setup and maintenance) versus timeliness of operations
- Process improvement
- Personnel training and supervision
- Design and improvements of computer applications
- Implementation of business rules
- Maintenance of facilities
- Data management, including the security, integrity, and accessibility of associated master data (see Chapter 6) and data that support the service unit operation and reporting
- Risk analysis and mitigation
- Business continuity preparedness

Legacy System Service Unit

A legacy application may be "wrapped" in a service unit with interfaces appropriate to the capabilities it supports. It is important that the interfaces conform to the logical data model discussed in Chapter 6 and that they reflect industry standards if possible. The legacy application may then function somewhat like an outsourced capability where there is little control over the implementation.

Billing for Services

Billing for services is an accounting function supported by the observed cost of services. It is not explicit in the diagram, but it is an essential aspect of any service. Each service unit must recover its costs, and the cost of each service must include the costs of services it uses. This is essential for effective motivation and management decision-making.

The cost of services reported on the right of the diagram includes both the total periodic cost of the service unit and the cost that is billed for individual units of service. The cost that is billed is based on analysis that determines the direct costs plus an allocation of overhead costs for each unit produced.

Costs of support services will be incorporated as overhead in the activities or value streams they support. For example, machine repair is a support service that may be identified as a capability unit. It may have a routine and preventive maintenance value stream and an emergency repair value stream. Both of these will require acquisition of parts and personnel scheduling. The costs of these services will be billed to consumers of the services based on usage, or allocated by some other formula. The service unit will incorporate these costs as overhead for the cost of its units of production.

The cost of services internal to the enterprise is determined by financial cost analysts, whereas the cost of external services is determined by negotiation of service prices with external providers.

Accurate cost accounting is essential for four purposes: (1) pricing, (2) performance evaluation, (3) billing for services, and (4) enterprise design. Cost determines the profit margin on products and services. Without accurate costing, it is difficult to determine an appropriate price or even whether a product or option should be continued.

Cost is an indicator of the efficiency of a service unit. Costs provide a basis for accountability of service unit managers, planning for process improvements, investment in new methods, service unit redesign, organizational changes, consolidations, outsourcing, and technology upgrades. Billing can influence users with respect to the utilization of a service, and it may influence the behavior of the service unit personnel in attempts to reduce costs.

Determination of the cost of a unit of service is not trivial, since there are both costs directly attributable to the particular service and costs that are shared. For example, the service unit incurs the cost of an employee even if the total work of providing all services does not require the employee 100% of the time. Since much of the work of a service unit may be automated, considerable employee time may be allocated to problem resolution and process improvement. From time to time, these employees may engage in projects funded by outside initiatives so that the service unit cost may go down, but then local projects may be delayed.

Table 3.2 illustrates a hypothetical cost allocation for the Assembly Service applied to Product 123. This example illustrates the nature of cost accounting and some of the difficulty in defining reasonable cost for individual services. The example service provides three operations, A, B, and C. Operation A is the primary service. The rows represent variations in the request options where the first row, Base, represents the product without options. The Fixed Cost column is allocation of the total fixed cost of $8000 based on the variable costs in the column to the left. Different ways of allocating fixed costs may be more appropriate for different types of service units; for example, the option cost variances may be only associated with the cost of purchased material and not the costs incurred in performing the operations in this service unit. It may also be important to divide costs between labor and material so that sources of costs of a service and total product cost can be better understood.

Table 3.2 Assembly Service Unit Cost Model

Assembly Service	Operations						All Operations Total			
Product 123	A		B		C					
Request Attribute	Volume	Cost	Volume	Cost	Volume	Cost	Volume	Variable Cost	Fixed Cost	Net Cost
Base	400	4000	10	100	4	40	414	4140	$7419.35	$11,559.35
V	200	40	3	30	1	10	204	80	$143.37	$223.37
W	150	45	2	40	2	2	154	87	$155.91	$242.91
X	130	26	5	5	1	1	136	32	$57.35	$89.35
Y	10	50	0	0	0	0	10	50	$89.61	$139.61
Z	25	75	0	0	0	0	25	75	$134.41	$209.41
Total	915	4236	20	175	8	53	928	4464	8000	$12,464.00

This cost model represents costs for a time period—for example, a week—and the product mix that occurred during that week is indicated in the Volume column. For some analyses, it may be sufficient to consider the average cost contribution of this service based on a typical product mix. For other types of analysis, such as pricing, it is important to understand the costs of the various options as well as the typical volumes, since marketing strategy should reflect profitability of different products and product options. A robust cost analysis model would support consideration of costs and pricing under simulated variations of product mix.

Note that the total cost of a particular product configuration in a time period (ie, based on a specific mix) is computed here by adding the associated marginal costs of all the operations that contribute to that product. In the example, this would include the product base cost and the cost for any associated options. It must also include the cost of components produced by services that are not performed in direct response to a customer order, as where orders are filled from inventories. These may be included as cost of materials earlier in the value stream.

Consequently, billing rates for service units are approximations based on expected workload, product or service option mix, and use of support service units. If the workload goes down, the cost per unit goes up because there are fixed costs involved. Nevertheless, users of a service unit need to be able to plan for the costs they will incur as a basis for planning and decisions that may affect their operations as well as when and how this service unit is used.

Service Specifications

The following paragraphs describe key elements of a service unit specification:

- *Service unit name.* An identifier for the service unit that corresponds to the capability unit name in the VDML model.
- *Offering descriptions.* This is descriptions of each capability method being offered.
- *Versions and their life-cycle status.* There may be multiple versions of service implementation in different stages of their life cycles: There may be versions under development, multiple current versions during a rollout to multiple sites, or versions that are no longer active but could be restored if a serious problem is encountered with a current version. Distinguishing features should be described. Service unit versions include software, business process specifications, resources, skills, facilities, or other aspects of the service unit that change to achieve a new service unit implementation.

- *Interfaces and versions.* Every service offered by the service unit must have a well-defined service interface. An interface includes specifications of service requests and choreography if applicable. A single version of a service unit implementation may have multiple versions of an interface to accommodate the transition of users of the service unit from one version to another. Interface versions should also have effective dates, both when available and when deprecated.
- *Billing specifications.* This defines the basis for computation of service charges to be billed to service users.
- *Level of service specifications.* These are the performance targets for the service, primarily response times, scheduled availability, and quality of results that are measurable at the service interface.
- *Value contributions.* Identification of the value contributions associated with each service. Since measurements will likely vary depending on context, a VDML model or actual production should be the source of measurements.
- *Business continuity.* Specification of contingency plans for circumstances that could prevent continued operation of one or more services or affect recovery time.
- *Security.* The level of security requirements of the services goes beyond the interface and level of service specifications to address implementation considerations involving other forms of exposure or disruptions of service. This includes the security of stored data and potential functional intrusion. See Chapter 7 regarding security issues.
- *Used interfaces and versions.* These are references to the interfaces of other services used by the specified service. Different versions of a service may use different versions of interfaces to other services.
- *Scalability.* Capacity limits or nonlinear impact of changes in volume on cost, timeliness, or quality. Of particular interest is the extent to which the impact of change in volume of production reaches a hard limit or becomes nonlinear so that, for example, a higher volume increases or decreases the unit cost.
- *Access authorization policy.* This is a statement of who qualifies to use each of the services offered and the process by which authorization is granted if there is not a shared service for that purpose.

Master Data Management

A service unit requires data to support and record its activities. Data management services are implicit in capability units. While a service unit may share a database with broader scope, the service unit organization should be responsible for the timeliness, accuracy, integrity, and access control of its supporting data and operating records including data that support service unit reporting.

The primary source of records, *master data*, that represent the current state of the business, including records that represent legal obligations or commitments, must be the responsibility of specific service units. Typically master data will be the responsibility of the service unit where data about the associated entity are first created in the enterprise. Each type of master data (eg, customer orders and purchase orders) must be managed by a distinct service unit since updates may come from many sources and users from many organizations may need access. Replicas of master data may be held in other service units for performance or addition of data specific to the alternate service unit, but the master data must be updated for any persistent changes. Data management and master data are discussed more extensively in Chapter 6.

Store Specifications

There may be a number of stores involved in the services of a service unit. The operating measurements of stores should be monitored and appropriate actions taken to ensure that the stores properly complement the affected capability methods.

The following are general types of stores:

- *Queue*. A queue is a first-in-first-out sequence of individually identifiable business items waiting to be processed. The queue adds delay to the process. At the same time, if the business item arrival interval varies or the receiving process acceptance interval varies, then the queue can ensure that the receiving process always has input. The length of the queue may impact customer value.
- *Inventory*. An inventory store exists to provide resources on demand to support one or more processes. If the inventory goes to zero, the receiving process may be delayed. If the inventory accumulates, then the cost of inventory may be significant. In addition, if the need for the business item ends, then there may be a surplus for disposal.
- *Reusable resources*. Pools are specialized stores used for resources that are assigned and returned—typically personnel, facilities, or tools. The number of resources needed will depend on the production rates, the length of time in use, and the proportion of production units that require the resource. If there are insufficient resources, the shortage will cause delay.
- *Personnel*. When there are multiple people with required capabilities, they are assigned from a pool, essentially the same as other reusable resources. However, some people may have multiple skills but not all the same skills. This means that they may be in multiple pools and

assignments for one skill should consider that the person is no longer available for his or her other skill(s). The same may be true for some facilities that can meet the needs of multiple capabilities.

SUPPORTING INFORMATION TECHNOLOGY

Implementation of a CBA requires supporting technology. Much of that technology is based on SOA to support the operation and integration of service units. Advances in the last few years, particularly advances in business modeling, further affect the information technology infrastructure.

The potential organization of a tool and die shop illustrates how shared services and current technology can support agility. The shop uses job routings of work to engage a combination of services and to define the sequence of operations needed to deliver custom products. The shop has a number of specialized tools and machines, along with groups of specialized tool and die makers who operate particular machines and apply their skills. The various specialists provide different services.

As a job comes into the shop, a dispatcher prepares a job routing (ie, an ad hoc business process) that defines the sequence of services to be performed. The routing and operator instructions are delivered to tablets of operators as the work moves through the process steps. For some jobs a product or component may be fabricated from several parts by a team of specialists. The fabrication work is delegated to a fabrication capability method.

The operators record their actions and a porter picks up the work product and moves it to the next work station. Required tools are also routed to the next station through tablet instructions to the tool crib and the porter. Specialists may have multiple skills, so they may be assigned to different work stations and equipment based on workloads and job scheduling. The skills, tools, and machines used in each department remain unchanged, but a wide variety of products are produced. The shop is highly adaptive and efficient.

The adaptive routing of this example could be implemented with a product based on CMMN (http://www.omg.org/spec/CMMN/1.0). CMMN activities will engage various capability services as required to complete the requirements of each specific job. The routing can be adapted if there is additional or specialized work not initially anticipated or if there is rework required. Participants are notified when a job requires their action. CMMN is discussed in Chapter 4.

Of course, these automation capabilities may already be in place using specialized software. Application of a CMMN-based system will provide greater flexibility at lower cost including the cost of adapting to further advances of technology.

Technical Infrastructure

It is important that business and technical leaders have an understanding of the technology requirements and their business impact because the supporting technologies represent a significant investment that is essential to achieving the agile enterprise. Here we provide a general overview. We will start with discussion of key components of the technical infrastructure and then examine the implications of mobile computing and cloud computing. Subsequent chapters will discuss certain key technologies in greater depth.

An SOA is the underlying technology of the CBA. For the most part, electronic technology is expected to provide the medium of exchange of information. There are still other forms of media in use, particularly paper forms and voice communications. Nevertheless, today many paper and voice communications are being replaced by electronic communications on smart phones and tablets. Even documents that are attached to physical deliverables are likely identified by bar codes or RFID chips (radio frequency identification) and retrieved electronically.

Therefore, an electronic infrastructure—computing, communications, and associated software and supporting resources—is essential to SOA and CBA. The infrastructure must support standards and consistent implementation (1) to minimize cost and complexity, (2) to enable sharing and flexibility, (3) to ensure security, (4) to integrate applications in diverse technologies, and (5) to enhance speed, reliability, and economies of scale. With the Internet, the electronic infrastructure will support rapid communications with shared capabilities and human participants located around the world.

This infrastructure, along with adaptations for integration of existing systems, requires an upfront investment that increases the costs of early SOA projects but provides significant benefit and lower costs in the long term.

There are several fundamental components that must be part of the enterprise electronic infrastructure to support the integration and operation of service units. Fig. 3.11 depicts the key infrastructure components discussed in the following sections.

An integration component (including messaging, transformation, and access control) is associated with each of the services in Fig. 3.11 (the gray areas). Each service unit is capable of exchanging messages with any other service unit, and these exchanges could extend outside the enterprise. Additional technical details are developed in later chapters.

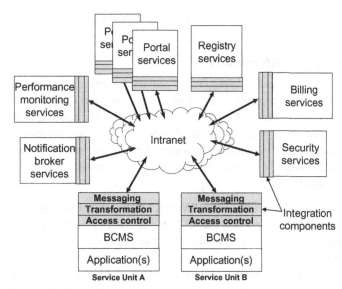

■ FIG. 3.11 SOA electronic infrastructure.

Reliable Messaging

Communications between service units are primarily through message exchange over the *intranet* (internal internet technology). Internet technology and middleware support the rapid, ad hoc exchange of messages between many sources and many recipients.

Messages must be communicated with *reliable messaging*. This means that the messaging system ensures that each message is delivered to a recipient once and only once. In a paper-based world, reliable messaging is accomplished with the use of original documents (so, there is only one) and transaction numbers such as an order number or invoice number.

In an SOA, requests for services and the interactions between requester and provider are communicated as messages. The communications are usually in a *store-and-forward* mode so that a message can be sent by one participant but held until the recipient is ready to receive and process it. A participant may send a message and continue to do other work rather than suspend activities until the recipient responds. This is described as *loose coupling* (more specifically, *temporal loose coupling*) because receivers need not be immediately available to receive messages.

Although these messages are communicated asynchronously from a technical perspective, from a business services perspective, the communications are very fast and support synchronous delegations and deliverable flows as well as asynchronous deliverable flows between collaborations as modeled in VDML.

Message Transformation

Message transformation is required to convert the sender's format of message content (if necessary) to a shared, exchanged form and then transformed to a recipient's form (if necessary). Fig. 3.11 depicts a message transformation capability at the interface to each of the service units. This anticipates that at various times, at a minimum, as new versions of services are implemented, there may be a need for transformation if only on a transitional basis.

Optimization of enterprise operation requires the ability to integrate and exchange data from multiple sources in the enterprise to support operations, analysis, planning, and decision-making. The diversity of sources and uses requires the ability to transform messages to correspond to the requirements of senders and receivers. The preferred approach is to exchange all messages in a consistent, neutral form, and transform a message specific to a sender or a receiver.

In the long term, transformations should be minimal, but transformations will continue to be required for interfaces to legacy systems and for transitions when business changes require changes to message content.

Differences in format, terms, and units of measure cause incompatibility that is relatively easy to correct. For example, dates may be expressed in different forms, such as *dd/mm/yyyy*, *mm/dd/yyyy*, *ddd/yyyy* (Julian), or other variations. Different terms might be used, for example, to describe employee status, such as *temporary*, *part-time*, *salaried*, and so forth, where they might be expressed in different languages but have the same meanings. Units of measure might be feet and pounds or meters and kilograms. Again, these are relatively straightforward but necessary conversions. Recipients of XML (http://www.w3.org/XML/) messages can allow for unexpected elements that are added for a new version, but more complex changes may require transformation.

For example, the same business entities may be represented, but with different identifiers for individual entities. Then there must be a cross-reference source to support a conversion.

Application adapters provided by integration middleware should provide for transformation between the application internal representation of data and an appropriate XML exchange representation.

Some messages may contain encrypted or signed content. This content must be retained by the creator or initial recipient of the document to preserve its validity. A working document, with encryption removed and signatures validated, may be shared for internal processing. However, the decryption and signature validation should be done by the master owner, not by the middleware transformation facility. This transformation might be performed by a shared security service unit that applies the appropriate keys for encryption and signatures or decryption and signature validation. Signed documents must be preserved in their original form for enforcement/accountability/nonrepudiation. Encryption and signatures are discussed in more detail in Chapter 7.

XML Data Exchange

The messages exchanges are in XML (eXtensible Markup Language) format. XML has been widely recognized as the preferred format standard for exchange of data between information systems that may involve different supporting technologies.

XML was recognized fairly early in the 1990s as a useful form of data interchange. It has several important characteristics:

- XML documents (ie, records) are somewhat self-documenting. Each element is tagged with a descriptive name.
- The fields are variable in length, with special characters designating the beginning and ending so that the format remains valid, even if the length of a field changes and text fields can take whatever space is required.
- A receiving program can select fields of interest based on the tags and ignore any other fields that may have been added by the sender, so the receiver can continue to use documents that have been expanded for other purposes.
- XML is used to specify the structure of XML documents (using XML Schema) so that shared specifications can be used for computational validation.
- XML is also used to express the transformation of XML documents by using Extensible Stylesheet Language Transformations (XSLT) so that there is a standard, computer-interpreted language for document transformation.
- XML is independent of the computing platform and computer languages used to send or receive it, so there is compatibility between diverse sending and receiving technologies.
- XML can be exchanged using HTTP and HTTPS, protocols of the World Wide Web, so that existing ports are compatible and the data can pass through existing firewalls.
- The widely accepted standard for electronic signatures is based on XML. Standards for encryption and signatures for XML documents are discussed in Chapter 7.

XML, along with XML Schema (http://www.w3.org/XML/Schema), XSLT, HTTP, and related standards, has been developed by the World Wide Web Consortium (W3C). Though other forms such as electronic data interchange (EDI) are still widely used, XML has emerged as the preferred form for exchanging electronic documents between systems and enterprises. The verbosity of XML that increases communication overhead is a trade-off for flexibility.

An example use of XML follows. This XML document is structured to contain a collection of customer orders—in the example, there is only one order with two line items:

```
<?xml version="1.0" encoding="utf-8" ?>
<Orders>
    <Order orderID="103">
        <Customer customerID="1234"/>
        <OrderItems>
            <Item>
                <Product productNo="223445"/>
                <Description>
                    100-watt speaker, Mahogany case
                </Description>
                <Quantity> 2 </Quantity>
                <UnitPrice> 235.95 </UnitPrice>
            </Item>
            <Item>
                <Product productNo="234523"/>
                <Description>
                    CD Player, Mahogany case
                </Description>
                <Quantity> 1 </Quantity>
                <UnitPrice> 167.95 </UnitPrice>
            </Item>
        </OrderItems>
    </Order>
</Orders>
```

The XML expressions are indented for readability. Each expression begins with *< name >* to identify the data element (where *name* is the name of the data element) and ends with *</name >* (a slash prefix) to specify the end of the data element. An element may contain a primitive value (ie, a data type that is not defined in terms of other data types), another element, or multiple elements. A primitive element may be expressed with both a name and value together, for example, the Product element in the example, by ending the value segment with /\>, and other attributes can be expressed with the name such as at the beginning of the Order element in the example. <*Orders*> could contain multiple orders, but in this case, only one order is shown, which starts with <*Order*> and ends with <*/Order*>. Within the Order are elements for Customer and Order Items. The Customer element only specifies the customer ID. There are then two order items, each containing several order-item attributes. XML structures are specified with a specialized XML language called XML Schema, so the format can be validated by a generalized computer program.

In many cases, these XML documents capture work products and decisions for which people or organizations should be held accountable, and some of these represent legal records or agreements that require encryption and electronic signatures.

Access Control and Security

The infrastructure must provide protection for the communications between service users and service providers using encryption as required. It must provide the means for determining the identity of participants (called *authentication*) and for determining whether participants are permitted to make certain requests or receive certain information (called *authorization*). These access control mechanisms must be complemented with logging and audit support, to ensure accountability and expose inappropriate accesses and attempts. Each service unit in Fig. 3.11 has an access control component that uses the security service. The security service unit includes identification, authentication, and authorization services.

In a CBA, many users are expected to directly or indirectly access many systems. This is partly because optimization of operations requires cross-enterprise access to data and because shared services may be used in a number of contexts. Users should be able to sign on once and then be able to access a number of systems for which they have authorization; this is called *single sign-on*. Security issues for SOA and the agile enterprise are discussed in more detail in Chapter 7.

Business Collaboration Management System(s)

Business Collaboration Management (BCM) is discussed further in Chapter 4 as next-generation Business Process Management (BPM) that comprehends, not just repeatable business processes and adaptive business processes but all forms of collaboration.

The technical infrastructure should include BCMS (Business Collaboration Management System) products. This includes a BPMN (business process modelling and notation, http://www.omg.org/spec/BPMN/2.0/) tool, a CMMN (case management model and notation) tool, and a DMN (decision model and notation, http://www.omg.org/spec/DMN) implementation to support automaton of business processes—prescriptive, adaptive, and ad hoc. BPMN, CMMN, and DMN are discussed in greater detail in Chapters 4 and 5. These tools should support modeling, execution, and analysis of performance for process improvement. Though an enterprise may have multiple BPMN or CMMN software products, preferred BPMN and CMMN products should be available for automation of business processes anywhere in the enterprise so that the same skills are required and the automation software is readily available as new processes are defined and deployed. Deproliferation of tools reduces licensing costs, eliminates incompatibilities, and enables everyone to use the same tools and representation in designing and improving business processes.

Note that there will still be collaborations identified in VDML that are not automated with BPMN or CMMN systems.

As more attention is given to the broad range of business collaborations, it should be expected that there will be more products to support collaborations and more industry standards. In Fig. 3.11, the BCMS is depicted as an infrastructure service, but it may include multiple services of multiple collaboration tools.

Notification Broker Services

A notification broker is a subscription service. All notices are directed to the notification broker. Systems and service units that act on events subscribe for notice by event type and may specify a filter to limit notices based on event notice attributes.

Events will become increasingly important as more automated support is provided for collaborations and people are engaged with mobile devices. Events and notification are discussed in detail in Chapter 8.

Registry Services

Registry services maintain current information about available services. At a minimum, a registry should provide links to available services so that users of a service can refer to a logical name of the service and be directed to the appropriate network address that may change over time.

In addition, the registry should identify different versions of service interfaces so that either a compatible version can be located or the interactions can be properly adapted or transformed. The registry should provide criteria for the selection of a service from among similar services. Within an enterprise, there may be only one appropriate service for a shared capability, but that is not always the case. For example, there could be services for different time zones or different countries, specialized for different product lines, or located in different physical facilities. The registry might also be extended for identification of approved external services such as supplier services, including, for example, suppliers that might be eligible to bid on a particular class of purchase request.

It may be useful to include additional information on each service for general reference, business management, system configuration, and change control purposes. The registry services should complement or extend the configuration management database (CMDB, https://en.wikipedia.org/wiki/Configuration_management_database) as defined by the Information Technology Infrastructure Library (ITIL). A CMDB supports management of computer applications and IT infrastructure.

It is also desirable for the registry to represent dependencies between services for data processing operations people to determine the implications of service failures and to plan for disaster recovery contingencies. However, a robust, current VDML model of the business should provide a better understanding of the dependencies from a business perspective.

Portal Support

Services are not only used by other service units but by humans as well. Even where a service is always invoked by an automated system, there likely is a need for human access to obtain information about the status of a request or associated data. The human users may come from across and outside the enterprise and include employees, investors, business partners, and customers. They need a way to find the appropriate services and to submit requests. This need for visibility of services to human users should be addressed by appropriate portals—a web site for each community of interest.

Generally, a portal is designed for use by a particular stakeholder community, and a community portal provides access to a variety of services of potential interest in that community. There may be multiple portals for participants in different collaborations where work is supported by specialized smart phone or tablet applications. Each portal should be owned by a service unit that manages the interactions with the associated community.

The design of a portal should address the particular needs of the stakeholder community, should have a consistent look and feel, at least for each community, and may include personalization features. Some portals will need to support internationalization. In addition, the service unit can address the need to translate the form of expression of requests and responses between the stakeholders' point of view and the internal services that respond to their requests. The infrastructure should support the necessary portal technology.

Performance Monitoring

Effective management of a CBA requires that performance data be captured and made available for monitoring and analysis. This should include evaluation of performance measurements against level of service agreements. It should be possible to obtain current performance data on any service. These measurements should be accessible in the context of a current VDM model of the business and viewed through a management dashboard as discussed in Chapter 6.

Billing for Services

Though costing is primarily a financial responsibility, the IT infrastructure must provide the mechanisms by which service uses are tracked and charges are computed and billed. A billing infrastructure may not be essential in the early stages of transformation to CBA, but it must be part of the strategic infrastructure design.

Billing requirements and cost allocation have been discussed earlier in this chapter as a service unit design requirement.

Mobile Computing

The proliferation of smart phones and tablets is changing the way people communicate and interact with computer systems. People can be always on line. They can obtain access to large records and documents and search for information to support their work.

This has a significant impact on collaboration and access to services. People can be actively participating in a collaboration with others who may be anywhere in the world. They may be notified of an important event, take immediate action, or engage others in resolution of the situation. They can request services and check the status of deliverables they need for further action, and track the status of initiatives from strategic business transformation to a crisis response. We will see the importance of this connectivity to adaptive processes in Chapter 4.

Cloud Computing

In the last few years, cloud computing has emerged as a viable approach to providing data processing services as a utility. Cloud computing adds an important dimension to enterprise agility. It can provide unrestricted scalability as well as seamless failover to move active applications to remote computing sites to ensure uninterrupted computing and communications services. It also means that an enterprise does not need to establish or maintain strong information technology capabilities to configure, maintain, operate, and secure computing and communications services.

At the same time, cloud computing will require integration of the conventional, enterprise computing infrastructure with the cloud infrastructure. This will require some new technical skills and may add complexity to customer support when the IT organization has neither direct control nor knowledge of the cloud operations.

The fundamental concept of cloud computing is that multiple computers are networked and integrated such that applications and data can be located anywhere in the network, resources can be allocated to accommodate changing workloads, and "failover" will relocate an application if it is executing in a node that fails.

There are a variety of alternative forms of cloud computing:

A *private cloud* is a computing network that is typically on the consumer's premises or in a provider premises but isolated from hardware running applications of other consumers. This form provides the greatest consumer control and also the greatest burden for management of the computing and communications environment.

In a *virtual private cloud* configuration, multiple consumers share a network of computing hardware, but each has a virtual machine environment (software) that executes and isolates conventional applications and data from those of other consumers. This gets the consumers out of the business of managing hardware and networking facilities, it provides more flexibility for scalability and failover, and it provides some savings from economy of scale.

In a *hybrid cloud* configuration, the consumer mixes the use of private and public cloud environments. For example, one approach is to keep the data and user interface facilities in the private cloud and run the applications in the public cloud. This minimizes the potential for exposure in the public cloud but is more complex and requires the consumer to remain involved in the full spectrum of data processing operations.

The *public cloud* approach supports multiple consumers (*multitenant*) with shared hardware and operating system. This configuration realizes the full potential of cloud computing for distributed computing, scalability, economy of scale, global failover options, dynamic load balancing, and more. Of course, it puts maximum trust in the cloud provider for reliability, security, performance, and regulatory compliance.

An extended cloud opportunity is for multiple consumers to share an application—a *multitenant application*). This achieves additional economy of scale and supports application billing based on use. But, note that this requires additional application functionality and places additional trust with the application provider to ensure security and maintain expected performance.

We expect the public cloud configuration will be the dominant configuration in the long term. Only very large enterprises will have the scale and expertise to realize benefit from a private cloud. The virtual private cloud may be useful for some applications since it should require the least adaptation of applications, but it achieves only limited virtualization, meaning that it cannot be as transparent in workload balancing, dynamic scalability, and failover. The hybrid configuration is a very cautious approach that requires the consumer to maintain considerable technical expertise and technical operating responsibility.

In the near term, enterprises should be cautious about deploying mission critical or high security systems in the cloud. The flexibility of deployment of applications and data raises additional concerns about data export regulations (data residency) since processing can potentially be transferred to a data center anywhere in the world when a server fails. The technology is still evolving. Eventually, it is likely that it will be very difficult to achieve better security or reliability than that provided by established cloud providers. At the same time, these will be very large providers and a software error might permeate the network and have devastating global, social, economic, and welfare consequences. They could become too big to fail.

■ SUMMARY AND FORWARD

In the first three chapters, we have introduced the emerging requirements for an agile enterprise, and we have introduced a new modeling language for designing, analyzing, and understanding how a business works from a business leader perspective. Then, we described a general approach to designing an agile enterprise based on value delivery management (VDM) and a CBA supported by an SOA infrastructure.

In the next five chapters, we will go deeper into the details of exploiting information technology for the agile enterprise. In Chapters 9–11, we will focus more on the enterprise transformation and the impact of the agile enterprise and supporting technology on the organization structure, governance, and leadership.

4

Next-Generation Business Process Management (BPM)

Business processes define how the repetitive work of the enterprise gets done at an operational level of business design. A business process defines the orderly interactions of process participants in roles performing activities, driven by events, messages, decisions, and exceptions to produce desired results. In this chapter, we broaden the scope of BPM to include all collaborations—people and machines working together to accomplish enterprise objectives. We will reference this broader discipline as business collaboration management (BCM).

Initially, business processes were defined for repetitive human activities. At a time when the operation of the enterprise was relatively stable and predictable, these processes described most of the work of the enterprise. business process management (BPM) emerged as a discipline for the development and continuous improvement of business processes. BPM has continued to focus on development and improvement of processes that are relatively predictable and repeatable.

Automation of business processes and business process modeling gave BPM more tools and controls for analysis, design, implementation, and evaluation of processes. Over the years, nearly all repeatable business processes in larger enterprises have become automated. At the same time, the workforce has shifted from people performing repeatable, rote processes to knowledge workers doing work that requires experience, and expertise to determine what needs to be done and when.

Now, advances in technology will provide similar automation support for the less predictable work of knowledge workers and managers. This will improve the coordination of work, provide guidance or pertinent information, capture information on activities performed, and improve the timeliness and quality of results. However, this requires new tools and a new way of thinking about the design of business processes. Some of the

Building the Agile Enterprise. http://dx.doi.org/10.1016/B978-0-12-805160-3.00004-1

knowledge work seems completely unpredictable, so there may be no apparent process except when the actions and interactions are viewed in retrospect.

Value Delivery Modeling Language (VDML) provides a conceptual framework for the definition and integration of this range of processes from repeatable to ad hoc. Business organizations bring together knowledge workers that solve particular classes of problems. These organizations typically form around repeatable processes that are based on related experience and expertise since those knowledge workers provide the on-going support, adaptation, and improvement of the repeatable processes in addition to performing more adaptive and ad hoc processes. Together, these repeatable processes and the less formal knowledge worker processes represent a *capability unit* at the conceptual design level.

We discussed in Chapter 3 how a capability unit aligns with a service unit in an operational business design. A capability unit manages capability methods to provide its capabilities as services. A service unit provides the operational implementation of the capability services along with ancillary, administrative, and support functions in support of its capabilities. Capability methods define the activity networks that are integrated into value streams and represent the conceptual requirements for operational business processes.

Consequently, to support the agile enterprise, a next generation of BPM should support operational design of the processes and other collaborations that implement the conceptual design of capability units and capability methods as well as other, operational level processes and collaborations. Most of these collaborations will be modeled with business process model and notation (BPMN) and case management model and notation (CMMN), but others will be more ad hoc, less predictable, or less amenable to automation support, so they may not be modeled. Nevertheless, they may be represented at an abstract level in VDML. Some capabilities will be provided by a small team of experts who will not benefit from automation, they may involve participants from other enterprises, or they may occur in environments not suitable to automation. Some collaborations will also be supported by knowledge management facilities discussed in Chapter 6.

In the following sections, we will first consider the business value of business process automation, we will describe characteristics of the operational, business process architecture for the agile enterprise, and we will highlight process design principles for the agile enterprise. Next we will describe business process modeling with BPMN (http://www.omg.org/spec/BPMN/2.0/) and CMMN (http://www.omg.org/spec/CMMN/1.0) to create operational business process specifications followed by decision model and notation (DMN, http://www.omg.org/spec/DMN/). DMN complements BPMN and CMMN with the expression of business rules and is discussed in more detail in Chapter 5. We will then briefly discuss the transformation of VDML capability methods to BPMN/CMMN models. Finally, we will explore further expansion of the next generation of BPM as BCM to address the full network of collaborations that are the way the enterprise actually works.

WHY BUSINESS PROCESS AUTOMATION?

Business process automation provides a number of business opportunities discussed in the following paragraphs. Even small businesses should be able to benefit from a process automation capability.

- *Reliability*. Process automation provides clear expression of who, what, when, and how participants must perform their assigned activities in order to achieve a process objective.
- *Capability composition*. Processes define how enterprise capabilities contribute and how they are networked to meet enterprise objectives.
- *Sharing*. Processes can engage shared capability services as subprocesses to deliver results. Sharing yields economies of scale from utilization of resources and implementation of improvements.
- *Control*. Processes can ensure control for efficiency, to meet requirements for compliance with policies and regulations, and to mitigate risks.
- *Resource management*. Processes that consume the same resources and manage the same business capabilities can be consolidated for economies of scale and workload management.
- *Visibility*. Information technology can greatly improve process visibility. Business process models expose the design of business processes. Runtime monitoring tools enable workloads and performance to be observed in real time. Operating statistics and audit trails support analysis of processes for process improvement and accountability.
- *Optimization*. Repeatable aspects of all business processes can be measured, and the impact of particular activities can be identified to determine where improvements are needed and to assess progress in implementation of changes.
- *Exploitation of advanced technology*. In recent years, mobile computing, such as smart phones and wireless tablets, has enabled participants to be engaged in a process as it happens from nearly anywhere, at any time, and relevant information can be accessed over the Internet.
- *Modeling*. Modeling supports consideration of process design improvement based on operational measurements along with many other factors such

as best practices, risks, accountability, authorization, share ability, and enterprise-level optimization.

- *Customer service*. Business processes can be driven by customer inquiries, orders, or order status requests over the internet for rapid response to a global marketplace.
- *Agility*. Business process modeling enables definition and adaptation of processes to be quickly developed, and process automation supports rapid deployment with minimal need for training of participants and oversight of the transition.

AGILE ENTERPRISE PROCESS ARCHITECTURE

The agile enterprise relies heavily on business process automation to achieve the above business benefits and to integrate and coordinate the many efforts of a successful enterprise. Traditional enterprises focus on the operation of independent lines of business. A typical process or series of processes take an order through all of the operations to deliver the product and receive payment. All of the required capabilities are embedded in this value stream process, tailored to the needs of the particular line of business. Similar processes feed the mainstream process with materials and supports. These processes could be very efficient (at least for the technology of the times), but very inflexible.

The agile enterprise requires a process architecture that enables rapid development and adaptation and exploits current technology. The following paragraphs describe the characteristics of that architecture.

- *Shared services*. A shared capability is implemented with a process that is engaged as a service. Shared services may engage other shared services. The scope of a process is limited to support of the capability it provides.
- *Closed-loop request-response*. In general, shared services should be engaged synchronously, so the requestor remains responsible for obtaining a result and the requested service is not required to deliver a result dependent on the source of the request. These are represented as delegations in VDML.
- *Asynchronous service*. Some capability services will be initiated by an asynchronous input message. This may initiate a different value stream, or it may enable concurrent processing with a later return delivered asynchronously. These are represented as flows through stores in VDML.
- *Choreography*. Interactions for coordination of independent processes (between business entities or independent organization units) are designed and implemented as choreographies.

- *Distinct business processes.* Business processes must be visible and separate from applications and provide the process context for the use of applications.
- *Service context.* The context of a service must include a process occurrence identity and related data for reference in ancillary services such as status reporting, changes, and performance monitoring.
- *Generic functionality.* A service process should not include activities that depend on the source of the service request.
- *Service unit.* A service unit is the operational equivalent of a capability unit where a designated organization unit manages a bundle of services and related resources, administrative functions, and technical support to maintain and adapt the services and optimize the utilization of resources.
- *Roles of roles.* It must be possible to specify a participant in a process role in terms of a role in another context. For example, a role in an order entry process filled by a person in a sales person role in a customer relationship management (CRM) process.
- *Input role assignment.* It must be possible for a service to pass a role assignment to a service it engages. For example, the surgeon for a patient is intended to be the same doctor as the one providing bedside care.
- *Reusable resource tracking.* A process must support tracking and availability of reusable resources, particularly people and equipment that are in limited supply.
- *Process integration.* Process interfaces must support seamless integration of BPMN, CMMN, and DMN (decision model and notation). DMN is discussed in Chapter 5.
- *Service registry.* Processes must be engaged through a registry so that introduction of new versions can be properly managed.
- *Runtime modification.* It is desirable to enable modification of a specific occurrence of a process at runtime to resolve a problem. In the alternative, it should be possible to trigger an exception that will cause an orderly termination or restart of the process.
- *Mobile device interface.* A mobile device application should provide each participant and/or manager with easy interaction with relevant processes including process and participant status. Status optionally includes completed and pending activities.
- *Participant alerts.* A participant and/or manager should receive text messages or other forms of personal alerts when action is required or delayed. A participant or manager should be able to post a condition to receive an alert when the process occurrence meets the condition.
- *Guidance.* A process should support presentation of participant guidance based on the current circumstances of the process occurrence. This includes guidance on decisions and planning in adaptive or ad hoc processes (discussed later).

- *Audit trail.* The execution of a process must generate an audit trail/ history of the process decisions and actions taken for future analysis and accountability.
- *Electronic signatures.* A process must support electronic signatures on records/documents created by, or approved by a participant, particularly if they involve management of assets.
- *Context tree.* A participant and/or manager should have access (with appropriate authorization) to the context tree of a process occurrence to examine the source and circumstances of the current request.

A number of these features are not necessarily supported by current business process systems, but all systems should support the basic structure of shared services and process design. The other features should be included as they become available.

PROCESS MODELING

The design and refinement of business processes is fundamental to management of an enterprise. We discuss process modeling here because it is important for business leaders at all levels to have a general understanding of the nature of process modeling and be prepared to discuss process models when investigating business problems or considering business changes.

VDML provides models suitable for the conceptual design and understanding of business operations. However, a VDML capability method is a statistical representation of the activities that apply capabilities, the flow of deliverables, and the creation of value, so it does not include operational detail required to process individual business transactions. VDML does represent the flow of deliverables (business items), whereas BPMN focuses on flow of control rather than statistical flow of deliverables (similar but different).

For example, a VDML process may represent an activity that receives inputs from two deliverable flows where the business items are matched and directed to one of two output deliverable flows. VDML may not address a possible exception where the input deliverables do not match, and it may define the percent of deliverables that flow to the alternative outputs, but it may not define the criteria used to determine which individual output flow is selected. We will discuss the possible complexity of VDML to BPMN transformation later in this chapter.

The operational equivalent of a VDML activity diagram may be determined by a transformation to BPMN or CMMN models, it may be embedded in the operational detail of a software product or legacy system, or it may be fully ad hoc, depending on individual expertise and represented in the abstract by a VDML capability method.

When an operational problem occurs, VDML may support analysis of the cause and possible source of the problem, but operational managers also must be able to understand and assess the processes of concern at an operational level of detail that is the focus of the operational workers and where the corrective actions must occur.

The architectural features discussed above apply to most operational business processes in the agile enterprise. This section will provide an introduction to modeling business processes with BPMN and CMMN. The discussion focuses on each of four types of business process models:

- *Prescriptive processes.* A prescriptive process can be specified in detail to define how each request is processed. That does not mean that each is processed in exactly the same way, but explicit decisions determine where different activities are required, where iterations occur, where exceptions are handled, and where the sequence of activities is affected by events. These are the repeatable processes modeled with BPMN, and such processes are automated with a system that manages the execution and tracking of each occurrence.
- *Adaptive processes.* The specific activities, events, and sequences of adaptive processes are not predictable, but they have patterns of activities and decisions that are typical of occurrences of a type of request. These have been called case management processes because the typical application involves a "case" and a "case file" that defines the current situation. These are modeled with CMMN and are implemented by a system that manages the case file, the emerging plan, the interactions of participants, and the tracking of status and events.
- *Cooperative processes.* A cooperative process is an interaction between two or more participants that are effectively independent business entities. The shared protocol is called a choreography. There is no shared system to manage the interactions, guide decisions, track the status, and make assignments. The participants are not concerned with the internal processes of other participants, only the observed behavior of participation. Each participant operates under a shared specification that defines the required actions of each participant and the interactions between them. The modeling specification for choreography is part of the BMPN modeling specification.
- *Ad hoc collaborations.* Conceptually, every ad hoc collaboration is different. These are collaborations that may only occur once, or they have significantly different issues and circumstances to address. Managers and executives are often participants in such collaborations. Although they are unpredictable, there are some common characteristics

of any collaboration that can be supported with automation, and automation can be provided by implementation of a small but useful CMMN model.

These four types are each discussed in greater detail in the following sections.

Prescriptive Process Modeling With BPMN

BPMN has been widely accepted as a business process modeling notation (ie, a form of expression) for prescriptive business processes—those that tell participants what to do and when. The following section provides and overview of BPMN that will enable managers to participate in process design and understand the specification of processes that drive the enterprise.

BPMN Example

Fig. 4.1 provides examples of the use of some BPMN elements. Participants in the overall process are designated by the separated boxes (pools) with the names of the participants at the top. The dashed arrows represent exchanges of messages. The focus of the diagram is on the process of the Seller. The Seller process (contained in the Seller pool) is started by a message from the Buyer. The Seller is partitioned into "lanes" representing different

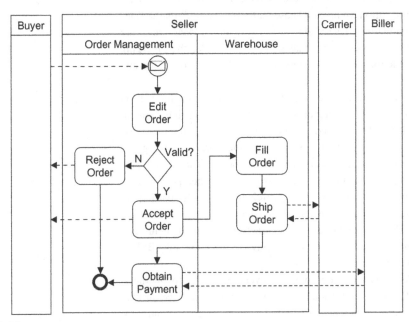

■ **FIG. 4.1** Example Seller process.

internal responsibilities. The Order Management organization (lane) edits the order, notifies the Buyer of acceptance or rejection, and obtains payment through the Biller after the order is shipped. The Warehouse (lane) fills and ships the order using the Carrier. Messages are exchanged between the Seller and the other participants. The Seller process ends if the order is rejected or after the Seller receives payment from the Biller.

Fig. 4.1 indicates exchanges between participants that can be expressed in a choreography, but here the sequence of exchange is defined by the internal process of the Seller. A choreography would define the interaction independent of the internal processes of all participants.

BPMN Notation

BPMN has 13 basic graphical shapes, as shown in Fig. 4.2. The figure also shows examples of frequently used variations on some of the basic shapes. Each of these shapes and some of their variations are discussed briefly in the

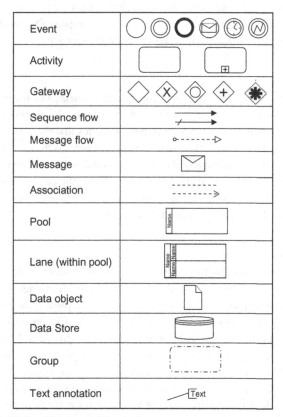

■ **FIG. 4.2** BPMN graphical elements (abbreviated).

following sections. For the most part, the general nature of an element is indicated by the external shape of the icon. More specific characteristics are depicted by the content of the icon.

Event

A *event* causes a process flow to start or stop. There are three basic types: a start event designated with a simple circle, an end event designated by a bold circle, and an intermediate event designated by a double circle. A default process start is an empty circle, and a default process end is an empty bold circle. Icons appearing within the circle define specialized types of events—for example, an envelope designates a message, a clock designates a timer, a lightning bolt designates an error. A message can start, delay, or end a process. A timer can start or delay a process. An error (or exception) can interrupt or end an activity or a process. There are other less commonly occurring events.

Events can define when a process is interrupted. When a process is interrupted, it may return an error or execute compensating activities to compensate for work already completed or messages sent.

Activity

An *activity* is where work is done. The default is a *task*, which denotes that there is no more detailed specification of the activity. A *subprocess*, designated with a plus sign (+) in a small box, indicates that the activity is performed by a more detailed process. The detailed process may be embedded and the activity can be expanded to show the detail, or the subprocess can be global (independent), meaning that it exists outside the current process and is shareable with other processes. Other activity specializations represent activities with repeated or concurrent executions.

Gateway

A *gateway* is a point in the process where flows converge or diverge. The default gateway (empty diamond) is an *exclusive or*. It provides for inputs from alternative paths to proceed on a single output path. If there are multiple output paths, only one can become active as specified by conditions on the outgoing paths. The *exclusive or* may also be designated with an X in the diamond. An *and* gateway is designated by a plus sign (+) in the diamond. It requires all inputs (from concurrent paths) to be active before it proceeds, and multiple outputs proceed concurrently, creating parallel paths. It may be called a *fork* for multiple outputs or a *join* for multiple inputs. There are other less frequently used gateway types designated with other icons.

The *complex* gateway is designated with an asterisk (*). It indicates that the action depends on a complex computation.

Sequence Flow

The solid arrow designates the control *sequence flow* of execution of activities, events, and gateways. The arrow enables the execution of a target activity, event, or gateway when the activity, event, or gateway at the start of the arrow is completed. Where there are alternative paths, as from an *exclusive-or* gateway, the default path may be designated by a hash mark across the arrow.

Message Flow

A *message flow* is designated by a dashed arrow. A message flow comes into or goes out of a business entity (ie, a pool, discussed in a moment). Messages may be exchanged between processes or between a process and another system. The agreed-upon specification of the sequence of message flows should be expressed in choreography.

Message

A *message* represents communication to or from an external business entity. It is communicated in a store and forward mode, so the recipient need not be immediately available.

Association

A document or other object may be associated with the process elements using a dashed line or arrow. The arrowhead is optional and may be used to indicate whether the object is an input or output to the associated process element.

Pool

A *pool* designates a business entity responsible for the process contained in the pool. Processes are bounded by the boundary of the pool. Actions that cross pool outside boundaries must be represented with message flows. In Fig. 4.1, Buyer, Seller, Carrier, and Biller are pools because they represent independent organizations. The Buyer, Carrier, and Biller pools are shown as empty because the focus of the diagram is on the Seller process, but the diagram implies that they have processes that send and receive messages, even though details of the processes are not known from the perspective of this diagram.

Lane

A *lane* is a segment of a pool that represents the role of an organization or person that is responsible for the process elements contained in the lane. In Fig. 4.1, Order Management and Warehouse are lanes within the Seller pool. They represent roles within the Seller organization. The Seller has overall responsibility for the process. The Warehouse has responsibility for the activities in its lane—Fill Order and Ship Order—and Order Management has responsibility for the activities in its lane.

Data Object

A *data object* is a unit of information that may be produced or used by a process element within a pool. The data are not retained beyond the scope of a process, but they are accessible by a subprocess.

Data Store

A *data store* holds data items beyond the scope of a process. This provides for asynchronous communication (store and forward) to other process(es) within the enterprise without the need for messages. BPMN assumes that exchanges within a pool are synchronous, and exchanges of messages between pools, representing independent business entities, are asynchronous. BPMN can also represent asynchronous communication within an enterprise when different processes place and retrieve data items in a data store.

Group

A *group* is a graphical representation of a shared characteristic of the process elements it contains. A group is not expected to have functional significance to the process flow but is used essentially for documentation.

Text Annotation

A *text annotation* is information added to a diagram to clarify the intent. It is documentation only. It is usually linked to a model element with an association line.

Attributes

BPMN also defines attributes associated with the graphical elements. *Attributes* are additional data that do not appear in the diagrams but would typically be accessed in a BPMN tool by selecting the graphical element to obtain a popup window with a list of attributes.

BPMN Choreography: Cooperative Process

A *cooperative process* does not have a shared control mechanism that directs the sequence of activities. Participants in a cooperative process are each responsible for determining when and what to contribute based upon a shared specification—a *choreography*. In VDML, a cooperative collaboration between business entities is specified as a *business network*.

In a cooperative process, the *tasks* are transfers of information or deliverables between the participants. Initiation of the next task depends on the internal processes of each party and their support for the shared choreography specification. Choreography assumes asynchronous communication with messages. The exchanges are asynchronous because the participants are independent entities that are not always prepared to immediately respond to a communication.

Without choreography, BPMN can still express the exchange of messages between pools of autonomous business entities. However, the possible sequence of message exchanges must be inferred from the internal actions of the participants. This gets complicated, quickly, particularly if there are more than two participants.

Choreography explicitly defines the "protocol of engagement," independent of the internal processes of the participants. It is a specification they can all agree with and rely upon for a successful engagement. In addition, it leaves the internal processes of each participant private, and they are free to change their processes as long as they continue to comply with the choreography.

Choreography Notation

Fig. 4.3 illustrates a trivial choreography. A rounded box is a *choreography task* and represents the delivery of a message. The bands at the top and bottom designate the sender and receiver. The sender band is white and the receiver band is gray. The solid arrows indicate the flow of control—the task to be executed next. Note that the sender of a task (white band) must be the previous task recipient (gray band) to represent a dependent action.

The *message flow*, indicated with a dashed arrow from a sender or to a receiver and an optional "envelope" icon, represents communication of information or a deliverable. The message (envelope) that initiates a task is white, and a subsequent message in the same task is gray. The envelope graphic is typically not needed since the white band indicates the source of a message directed to a gray band recipient.

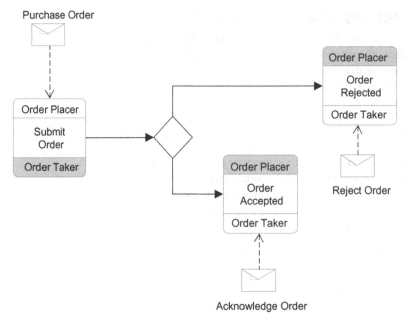

■ **FIG. 4.3** Simple choreography fragment.

The example diagram includes an exclusive-or gateway indicating that the previous task (Order Taker) must choose between the two output paths. The gateway does not operate directly since all decisions must actually be made by the participating parties—there is no shared entity directing activities. The sender must make the decision internally. Other BPMN gateway types can also be applied.

Order Placer and Order Taker are roles in the choreography representing participating entities. The choreography starts with a message containing an order from the Order Placer to the Order Taker. The Order Placer is the service user since it initiates the exchange and sets the context with the order content. The Order Taker receives the order and either accepts it or rejects it. The gateway (diamond-shaped) element indicates alternative paths.

Some services are accessed through a simple request-and-response exchange. The service user requests information and the information is returned, and there is no need to specify further interaction. This may be represented by a single choreography task with requester and provider messages; the return message is shown as a gray envelope.

A choreography specification defines only the interactions between the parties and not how the parties perform their responsibilities, internally.

Each party is free to define their internal processes as they like as long as they comply with the requirements established by the choreography. Of course, the content of the exchange or other agreements between the parties defines obligations of each as a result of the exchange, such as an obligation of the provider to deliver a product and the obligation of the requester to pay for it. This example choreography is quite trivial, but more complex choreographies may involve additional exchanges and participation of multiple parties that are coordinated to accomplish a shared result.

In addition to flow arrows, messages, and gateways, choreography also uses some other graphical elements defined for BPMN, above: events (circles), pools (named box but without content), and text annotation (dotted line to open box with text). A choreography task (with a heavy border) may call a choreography subprocess. A subprocess will have start and end events. Additional detail on these and other BPMN elements is a subject for a more advanced study.

Additional Cooperative Process Views

BPMN defines two additional types of process views that are based on the representation of related directed and coordinated processes: collaboration and conversation are discussed briefly here.

Collaboration is an unfortunate term since it is only used in reference to display involving message exchanges between pools, whereas a VDML collaboration is any interaction between persons, organizations, and/or machines for a shared purpose. A BPMN collaboration display may show (1) only messages exchanged between pools, (2) a choreography describing messages exchanged between pools, (3) messages exchanged between pools with processes receiving or sending messages from within one or more of the pools, (4) a pool, with or without an internal process shown, exchanging messages with a choreography, or (5) pools with processes sending and receiving messages through a chorography that defines the sequencing of the message exchanges.

Fig. 4.4 illustrates one form of collaboration view: messages communicated between a black-box pool (Order Placer) and the elements of another pool (Order Taker). This collaboration shows the Order Taker process that corresponds to the choreography of Fig. 4.3. This collaboration display could be extended to show message icons on the message flows with message names.

A BPMN *conversation* is an abstraction of a choreography. Fig. 4.4 shows a BPMN collaboration view of the choreography of Fig. 4.3 and the

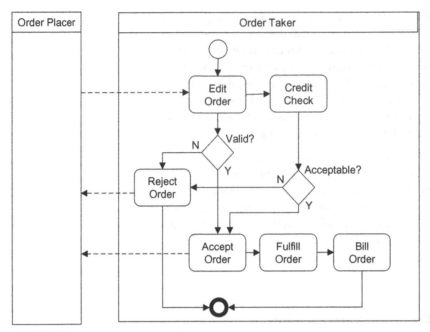

■ **FIG. 4.4** An example BPMN collaboration.

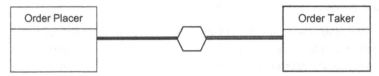

■ **FIG. 4.5** A simple BPMN conversation.

conversation of Fig. 4.5. A choreography of greater scope might show conversations between the Order Taker and a Transportation Carrier and the Order Placer and the Transportation Carrier. The conversation view is useful for an overview of a complex network of multiple participants.

Internal Choreographies

It is important to note that although the examples have involved business-to-business interactions, choreography can be applied to interactions within an enterprise as well. Two departments may have processes that involve interactions over a period of time as the work progresses.

As noted earlier, simple request-response interactions don't require explicit choreography, but conceptually they have a choreography as well. Essentially, every relationship between processes has a choreography, though it usually is implicit.

Often a process interacts with the same person several times, as defined by the role assignment. This sequence of interactions with the person can be described as a choreography, and this specification may be useful for understanding the responsibilities of the person assigned to the role. Often, what at first appears to be a simple request-response relationship evolves to a more complex interaction, particularly if the request is not immediately followed by a response.

Choreography essentially defines the restrictions participants must observe to achieve a mutually beneficial outcome from a relationship. In the next chapter, we will discuss business rules that are used to specify other forms of restriction on business operations.

Adaptive Process Modeling With CMMN

Over the years, with a focus on repeatable processes and automation, most of the rote, human activities of repeatable processes have been automated. The human activities that remain may be characterized as the work of knowledge workers—people who make decisions of how their work must be done and collaborate with others to plan and coordinate efforts. These are adaptive processes that vary depending on the particular situation as it evolves. Here we will describe these as *case management* processes where a case is "a situation requiring investigation or action" [Merriam-Webster]. CMMN has been recently adopted by Object Management Group (OMG) and is the only standard language for modeling adaptive processes.

Case management is a paradigm shift from design and optimization of repeatable processes that are the traditional focus of BPM. Adaptive processes are not repeatable but can be guided by best practices along with suggestions or alerts derived from changes in the state of a case. Many of the activities of adaptive processes occur frequently, but they may occur at different times in the overall process, they may involve different factors, and the actual occurrences and sequences of activities will vary. In addition, records that define the history and current state of the undertaking are central to the determination of actions to be taken. Nevertheless, repeatable processes and case management processes must work together to support the work of the enterprise.

With prescriptive (BPMN) processes, the balance between rote activities and knowledge worker activities has evolved to processes where work that requires a knowledge worker is assigned with general activity requirements and details are worked out by the knowledge worker. There are five problems with this approach:

(1) The process makes assumptions about the overall sequence of activities of the process that restricts best judgment,
(2) The interactions and coordination between participating knowledge workers are constrained,
(3) The specific actions of the knowledge worker are not captured to support analysis of better practices or resolution of problems,
(4) The process may not achieve timely response to changes in the situation,
(5) The knowledge worker may not have the benefit of relevant information including the insights of others, applicable regulations, or critical facts of the situation.

Adaptive processes address these issues.

(1) The sequence of activities can be adapted to the particular situation.
(2) Participants are expected to collaborate on planning and corrective action as the situation evolves.
(3) Plans, events, and activities are recorded as they happen, and knowledge workers can update their plans and accomplishments as they happen.
(4) A shared record of the situation (a case file) is updated by participants and external events so that critical events can be automatically recognized and appropriate participants notified.
(5) The system can define constraints and suggest actions based on the current situation to reduce omissions and expedite appropriate actions.

Modeling is key to successful automation support for adaptive processes. Knowledge workers cannot specify all of the detailed plans, monitor every change in the situation, and check for every circumstance that may affect decisions. The knowledge worker needs predefined plan building blocks—activities, process fragments, triggers, and guidance—that can be quickly assembled and adapted to the particular situation and revised as the situation evolves.

CMMN is an OMG specification for modeling adaptive processes. A particular CMMN case model focuses on a type of case where there are commonly occurring stages, plan elements, or plan fragments. A case model includes specifications for a case file (the record of the current situation and actions taken), triggers for important circumstances that may occur and reusable planning elements and patterns for the type of case. CMMN can engage directed, repeatable processes where applicable, and directed, repeatable processes can engage case management when knowledge work is required.

CMMN Notation

The CMMN specification includes a graphical notation for modeling adaptive processes. This section describes the primary graphic elements in Fig. 4.6 and "decorations" (icons) in Fig. 4.7, that qualify the primary graphics.

While these graphics are designed for modeling a type of case, it is expected that they will also be used by participants at runtime for planning and monitoring an active process and the process history. Therefore, modelers must keep in mind the level of process sophistication they can expect from the users of a model.

Primary Graphic Elements

The following paragraphs will discuss the primary graphic elements of CMMN in Fig. 4.6.

Case plan model. A *case plan* model contains the plan of a case. It is essentially a top-level stage, and it is the outer boundary of a case. The elements that can occur in the plan may be referenced in general as plan items.

Case file item. A *case file Item* is a unit of information that is stored in the case file. The information may be in any electronic form and may be a link to information in an external source. The content of structured items may be referenced by rules. There may be multiple versions of an item, but only the current version will be referenced by the case plan.

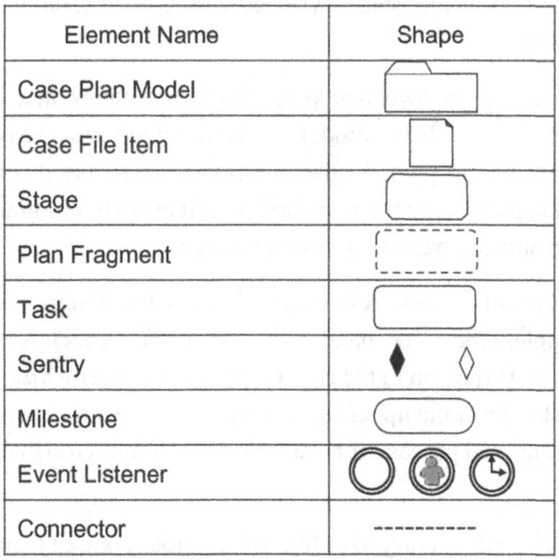

Element Name	Shape
Case Plan Model	
Case File Item	
Stage	
Plan Fragment	
Task	
Sentry	
Milestone	
Event Listener	
Connector	

■ **FIG. 4.6** Primary CMMN graphical elements.

Decorator Applicability	Planning Table	Entry Critrion	Exit Criterion	AutoComplete	Manual Activation	Required !	Repetition #
CasePlanModel	☑		☑	☑			
Stage	☑	☑	☑	☑	☑	☑	☑
Task	HumanTask only	☑	☑		☑	☑	☑
Milestone		☑				☑	☑

■ **FIG. 4.7** CMMN graphical decorations.

Stage. A *stage* (angled corners) is a group of plan items that occur together to achieve a particular purpose within a case. The plan items are only active if the Stage is active, and they will no longer be active when the Stage is completed. Stages can occur within a stage as for a hierarchy of activities in a project plan. Typically stages will occur in sequence, but they may also occur in parallel.

Plan fragment. A *plan fragment* is a set of plan items that often occur together in the case type being modeled. The fragment can be trivial or complex. Once placed in the plan, the plan items become part of the plan without any effect of the plan fragment boundary. The items in the fragment can then be changed to suit the particular circumstances.

Task. A *task* is a unit of work. A *human task* can be blocking—it waits for the human to complete the work (hand in the upper left corner). A nonblocking task has no outputs (person in the upper left corner). A *case task* will engage another case (folder in the upper left corner). A *process task* will be used to engage a conventional process, for example, BPMN (chevron in the upper left corner).

Sentry. A *sentry* enables entry to (white-fill diamond) or exit from (black-fill diamond) a plan item based on a rule. The rule has an *on-part* that identifies a triggering event, and an *if-part* that is evaluated when the on-part event occurs. The if-part must evaluate to true for the sentry to enable the plan-item entry or exit.

Milestone. A *milestone* is used to indicate progress and is achieved when specified conditions are met.

Event listener. An *event listener* (empty circle) is sensitive to changes that can happen in the case file or can happen to stages, tasks or milestones. Event listener is further refined as a timer event listener (circle with a clock) or user event listener (circle with a person). The start time of a timer event listener is dependent on a case file or plan item (stage, task, or milestone) condition. The duration of a timer event listener is dependent on a date and time, a duration specification, or a start-end interval specification. A user event listener is triggered by a user action. The user must be in one of the specified roles.

Connector. The dotted line of a *connector* indicates a plan item at the start of the arrow that must be completed for a subsequent plan item to become enabled. When connected to an entry sentry, the completion of the source plan item is the trigger for evaluation of the sentry.

Graphical Decorations

Graphical decorator icons are used to define specialized characteristics of graphical elements. Fig. 4.7 shows the decorator icons and graphical elements to which they can be applied. The first three (columns) appear on the border of planning items; the last four appear inside the lower border.

Planning table. The *planning table* icon appears on the top border of relevant planning items. When opened, a planning table defines the sub-set of plan items, essentially, a menu, that can be considered by a user when planning at runtime. The items that appear in the planning table are restricted by rules to those items that are appropriate to the current case context and the role of the person accessing the planning table. The plan items are described as discretionary since their use in the plan is subject to the discretion of the user. Discretionary items are shown with dotted-line boundaries. The context for planning based on a planning table is a stage or human task associated with the planning table. A planning table may contain links to other planning tables to form a menu hierarchy.

Entry criterion. An *entry sentry* appears on the border of a plan item and controls entry based on a rule. The rule is evaluated when the on-part becomes true (eg, the incoming connector becomes active) and the if-part evaluates to "true." Multiple connectors to one sentry requires an "and" event when all become enabled. Multiple connectors to different sentries requires an "or" entry event—any connector can trigger evaluation of its entry sentry.

Exit criterion. An *exit sentry* appears on the border of a plan item and determines when an exit can occur from the plan item. If the sentry if-part evaluates to "false," then exit from the plan item will be delayed until the sentry enables exit.

Auto complete. A stage (including a case plan) by default requires a person to enable exit from the stage allowing for additional plan items to be added prior to completion. If *auto complete* is set to "true," then the stage will go to completion whenever all of its plan items are completed.

Manual activation. If an associated plan item is enabled, a *manual activation* rule defines if an associated plan item requires activation by a human. The default is "true" (manual activation is required).

Required. If a *required* rule is "true," a plan item must complete before its containing stage is allowed to complete. The default is "false."

Repetition. A *repetition* rule indicates if an associated plan item is allowed to repeat. If the rule evaluates to "true," then the plan item will repeat (a new occurrence is created) each time its sentry enables entry. The default is "false."

The Case File

The case file contains, directly or indirectly, all of the information relevant to a case, including the case plan. The case file has a hierarchical structure composed of Case File Item Definition elements. These either contain the item of interest or may provide a link to the item of interest.

The case file is updated as the case evolves. Updates may occur from tasks in the case or from external sources. The case file is then the basis for occurrence of events of interest to the case—event listener and sentry rules refer to case file items. Of course, changes to case file items that are externally referenced cannot be referenced in event rules.

Case Modeling Challenges

CMMN is a new specification, and, at this writing, there is limited application experience. The CMMN specification defines modeling requirements and only implies the runtime functionality of a CMMN implementation. Consequently, there may be considerable differences between runtime implementations.

In addition, CMMN modeling is a new discipline. Certainly there are similarities to BPMN models, but the CMMN model developer must think differently about the possible evolution of a case and the roles of participants.

In the following paragraphs, we will consider potential features of runtime implementations and modeling practices.

Runtime Features Runtime features will depend on the innovation of implementers, but here are some to be considered.

Mobile technology. Access to mobile technology, such as smart phones and tablets, is fairly obvious, but case management should take full advantage of voice, video, text, email, and mobile applications. Mobile technology must not only connect participants to the case management system, but it must connect them to each other. They must be encouraged to collaborate.

Integrated forms. Forms must be designed for the requirements of the case type. Participants must understand that filling out a form updates progress on the case and communicates information to other participants. Forms must be designed to be quickly and easily completed. Known fields must be pre-populated. Traditional forms that capture everything must be broken apart to forms appropriate to particular aspects, so they can be completed and submitted without waiting to get more information.

Collaboration support. Participants need to know each other's status, not only their status on the case but also their availability for discussion. The result of collaboration between some of the participants should be communicated to the others. The conclusion to an email thread might be recorded as a result with a reference to the email thread. It should be possible to send a text message to multiple participants—more like a case team Twitter. Users must perceive the case management system as something that helps them do their job, not as a burden.

Web access. Tasks should be supported with relevant information. A user should be presented with key information from the case, along with a menu of links to information of potential interest from the case and from the Web. It should be possible to easily incorporate relevant links into the case file record.

Ad hoc listeners. Users must be able to define listeners (generates an event when a condition becomes true as personal reminders or alerts to others). This means that it must be easy to compose a listener condition. Potentially the user should be able to compose a condition by identifying a case file item type to trigger action on arrival or change and selecting from fields on that form or others for required values.

Inter-case coordination. Multiple cases can be related. This may be because one case engages another because a larger process engages multiple subcases, or there are other relationships with shared subject matter. Case listeners are driven by the case file, so a case listener cannot be driven by updates to a different case file. One approach is to have cases share a case file, but this may not be practical or possible for various reasons. Consequently, it should be possible to incorporate a case file item from another case. In order to make this information also available in the case record, the system should retrieve the target item when it becomes referenced by a listener and, subsequently, whenever it changes. This requires that the source case honor an event subscription request (discussed in Chapter 8).

Approval/concurrence. Certain actions in a case will require that a second participant concur or approve of an action. This should be an attribute of the task that requires approval and a subsequent approval task. The case file item requiring approval should not be updated until approved. The draft item might be held as a draft item pending approval. The participant that creates the item to be approved should retain control of the item until an approver has been identified and has given approval.

Case displays. Participants as well as others will need to view the current plan and history of a case. This requires displays at different levels of granularity and abstraction. For example, a display of stages without detail or detail of activities within a stage, or activities of a particular participant or activities affecting a particular case file item.

Dependencies. When a user adds planning items to a plan, each planning item may need to be connected with other planning items. The system should highlight where it may be appropriate to add connectors and assist the user in making the connections. For example, a task will often need a deliverable completed by an earlier task. A listener is not meaningful if not connected to a task to be initiated.

Rule-based guidance and constraints. It should be possible to associate a rule-based facility to selected tasks to provide guidance or validation for certain actions. The rules might be applied when the task is enabled or when it is committed. The rules may include not only case file facts but also questions to be answered by the participant. The action might also require approval by another participant who might also need the guidance. The guidance should become part of the case file record to define the circumstances when a decision was made.

Personal libraries. Participants, particularly case managers, should be able to maintain personal libraries of planning items by case type. These should not enable them to do things that they otherwise are not authorized to do, but this will not only enable users to improve usability and gain their support, but it may be a valuable source of improvements to the case model.

Modeling Practices The primary goal of the model developer must be to make it easy for users to do what they want to do that is not otherwise prohibited by their authorization, regulations, or adverse consequences. The CMMN modeling language is quite complex; the model developer must find ways to hide this complexity from the participants and, hopefully, make interactions with the case intuitively obvious.

Stages. A first step in case model design will be to identify stages that are meaningful to participants. This will define the basic framework for the case model, and it will also be used for others to check progress on the case. Stages may be associated with subteam activities that occur either sequentially or concurrently—this can help simplify the model for each of the subteams. Stages also should be the primary context for planning tables.

Definition of Roles. The developer must identify who (roles) may participate, how they may contribute, and the scope of their authority. This information will be important throughout the modeling effort and may evolve as the case possibilities become better understood.

Planning table design. Planning tables must consider not only the current case context, but the role of the participant that will be using the planning table. The purpose is not to restrict the participant, but to provide the right information and avoid presenting too much information. The planning table is a table of contents. It should start as an indented list, and then, a description of each selection should be added. This can be done in word processing. The description will help sort out both what the selection is for and what it should add to the plan.

Adaptable fragments. Plan fragments should not only be specific segments that may occur but most-common patterns that can be adapted to the particular circumstances. This makes larger fragments useful and reduces the work of planning the routine case. In some cases, a fragment may define the stages of an entire case to be supplemented or adapted by participants.

Ad hoc tasks. Participants will occasionally need to add tasks to the plan that were not anticipated by the model developer. There should be a set of relatively undefined tasks that the participant can select and adapt to the particular circumstances.

Adaptable listeners. Similar to ad hoc tasks, a participant may want to post a particular listener that is not typical of the case. The participant should be able to adapt a partially configured listener condition.

Case examples. Case examples are important food for thought. The current case workers should be asked for examples of unusual or difficult cases and how they were resolved. The model developer must then consider how each of these could be assisted with case management. Then the solutions should be reviewed with case workers.

Possible outcomes. Possible outcomes are a source of exceptional circumstances. Working backward from each outcome, the developer should explore the potential circumstances that could have precipitated the outcome. There may also be guidance, constraints, or listeners that could have avoided or mitigated adverse outcomes.

Case history. Case files should be examined for new patterns that could better be addressed by the addition or modification of plan fragments. Adaptations of fragments, use of ad hoc tasks, and adapted listeners require particular attention.

Agile development. Developers and their managers must expect that case model development is an iterative process. Developers must iteratively develop and refine the model with feedback from peers and users. New models or significant changes must be introduced with caution for fear of turning-off users, so they only use the system as little as possible. Feedback from users must be considered seriously and promptly.

Business manager role. It may be appropriate to include a special role in a case for the responsible business manager. This is not the same as the case manager. The business manager will want to know about the progress or delays in the case. That manager may have fragments with listeners for particular progress and timer listeners for delays in progress. When there are particular concerns about a case, that manager will want to post special listeners to keep track.

Guidance and constraints. A developer should look for actions or decisions that are either complex or time-consuming or have potentially adverse consequences. The tasks where such actions or decisions are to be made should engage a rule-based guidance component. This will require an appropriate extension to the standard CMMN modeling capability.

Ad Hoc Process Modeling With CMMN

CMMN should provide support for ad hoc processes—collaborations that each address different situations. Each collaboration may be different, but there are always some common elements.

The goal is to support personal tracking of individual activities and exchanges with other participants. Consider the support for managers. Managers are often involved in multiple collaborations with different teams at the same time. In some situations, a manager will initiate a more conventional case that can be modeled as a case, discussed above. In those cases, the top manager may have a role as the business manager, defined above. In other situations, the collaboration is less structured and predictable.

Model developers should interview managers to identify their typical stages, tasks, collaborators, documents, and outputs.

Roles. There may be a primary support person involved in a collaboration with other managers or subordinates. Possible roles may define differences in scope of authority and expertise. It should be easy for the top manager to define and add roles or delegate responsibility to a primary staff person. Possible roles might have individuals preassigned, so the focus is on selection of persons for the particular undertaking.

Tasks. Tasks may be very generic to be defined more specifically as they are added to the plan. Some tasks may be defined for typical contributions such as progress reporting and capture of minutes of meetings.

Team meetings. A plan fragment should provide for scheduling and initiating team or subteam meetings.

Schedules. Typical stages may be defined for types of collaborations, such as team formation, initial investigation and planning, problem solving, implementation planning, and approval.

Events (listeners). Managers may be concerned primarily about listening for availability of certain documents or delays in completion of tasks. Typical document types may be predefined with forms for tracking. A useful fragment may couple a generic task with a form and a listener for a due date within a simple fragment.

Objective(s). A form for multiple objectives and due dates can be used to create a case file item that can be updated as objectives are achieved so that listeners may be triggered for reporting or subsequent action.

Progress reports. A standard form can be defined for progress reports, possibly linked to objectives.

Shared documents. As work proceeds tasks may produce or update shared unstructured documents linked to the objectives.

VDML Relationship to Operational Processes

BPMN and CMMN provide operational models of business processes. They define the operations and flow of control for individual business transactions—one customer order, one purchase order, one customer service request, one expense report.

VDML, on the other hand, represents a conceptual model of the enterprise. While capabilities are, in general, applied by processes, some processes are embedded in legacy applications, some are too unpredictable to model, and some are simply conversations between knowledgeable participants, so they may be simply represented as collaborations with roles, but no specific activities. For interactions with common patterns and deliverables, the activities and flows represent statistical activity executions and deliverable flows. These are more abstract and thus less complex, but they are a better representation of the way people think about process flows.

VDML represents a mainstream capability as an application of a process consisting of roles performing activities contributing value, and linked by flows of deliverables. In addition, VDML generalizes processes as collaborations, focusing on how people and other collaborations interact to do the work of the enterprise. This generalization comprehends not only traditional business processes modeled with BPMN and the adaptive processes of CMMN, but it includes the informal collaborations between people of an organization unit, the telephone conversation between the customer and the customer support specialist, the strategic planning discussion of the executive team, and the ad hoc team that resolves the problem when a machine starts producing scrap.

While it will not be useful to always model these collaborations, VDML supports the representation and analysis of such collaborations and their capabilities and value contributions in the context of related organizations, value streams, and resources.

Thus VDML represents a more robust representation of how the business works rather than just how selected, individual processes work. It supports analysis of the impact of performance and value contributions by activities and their cumulative effect, through many activity networks (ie, processes) on the values delivered to customers.

Some VDML collaborations are just interactions between people. Some involve paper deliverables or the flow of physical products. Most of the repeatable processes and recurring types of collaborations will be modeled and supported by BPMN or CMMN for automation. Here we will focus on the transformation of those VDML activity networks that are appropriate for modeling and automation using BPMN or CMMN.

In some cases, it is possible to automatically translate a VDML activity diagram to a BPMN or CMMN process model, but in most cases, this will require some human intervention to add controls and optimize the flow considering the management of individual transactions. The reverse translation—abstraction of an existing process, is much simpler and there will be clear alignment of operational activities with VDML activities, although there will generally be more operational activities and process elements corresponding to a VDML activity.

In the following sections, we will discuss the relationship of VDML activity networks to the four types of process design discussed above.

PRESCRIPTIVE PROCESSES

Fig. 4.8 illustrates a fragment of a VDML activity network. A shipment and associated invoice are received into stores since they are coming from an independent business as an asynchronous exchange. One shipment may arrive before the invoice and another may arrive after the invoice. The Authorize Invoice Payment activity is to match invoice to shipment and either authorize payment or reject the invoice if it does not properly match a shipment. The input deliverable flows will each be one deliverable per unit of production. The output deliverable flows are alternative outputs, so the sum will be 100% of production.

Fig. 4.9 illustrates a possible transformation of the VDML fragment of Fig. 4.8 to a BPMN process fragment. This BPMN process fragment must address the possible payment for individual shipments. The invoice is received by the first activity. If the invoice arrives after the shipment, then the first gateway is satisfied (the shipment has been received). The second gateway is satisfied if the invoice has been received and the shipment is

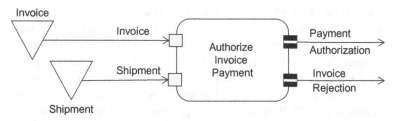

■ **FIG. 4.8** VDML activity network fragment.

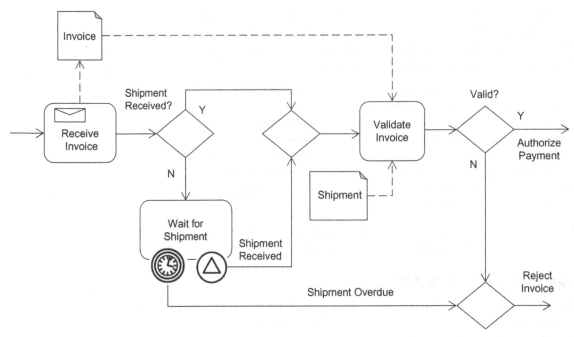

■ **FIG. 4.9** BPMN transformation of VDML fragment.

received within the time allowed, so control proceeds to the authorize pay-ment activity.

However, the invoice may arrive before the shipment, so the first gateway directs control to the Wait for Shipment activity. This activity completes if it receives an event for shipment received; otherwise, a timer expires for fail-ure of the shipment to arrive and the invoice is rejected. When the shipment arrives, it is matched to the invoice and the content is validated. If there is a proper match, payment is authorized, otherwise it is rejected.

The additional detail is a result of explicit handling of individual shipments whereas the VDML representation only addresses statistical measurements. The duration of the VDML Authorize Invoice Payment activity is different for the alternative outputs. For the Authorize payment output, it is the sta-tistical average of shipment received first and the amount of time waited for a shipment received later. For the Reject Invoice output, it is the average of the Authorize Payment duration for unmatched invoices and the expired time for shipments not received. The allocation of deliverables to the two outputs of the VDML activity are the percentages of production that are the "Authorize" versus "Reject" outputs of the process.

ADAPTIVE PROCESSES

A VDML representation of an adaptive process will include activities that, when they occur, will be somewhat predictable. Many activities may have relatively predictable measurements, but they will only affect the value stream measurements based on their frequency of occurrence. For example, measurements of activity durations will be more relevant to costs than to duration of the overall process since it is so unpredictable. Some activities will be dependent on deliverables from other activities, so there is some predictability of when they can occur.

Consider a collaboration for medical diagnosis in Fig. 4.10. The duration of each activity may be relatively predictable, but sometimes, some activities (here the three activities to obtain blood analysis) may not occur at all. An average duration for the examination can be computed based on the durations and percentage of flows out of the Examine activity, but the variance is substantial. An overall duration can be observed for the collaboration and associated with the value measurement for the collaboration rather than the individual activities.

In other cases, for example, a hospital stay, some activities, or groups of activities may be recurring, such as repeated blood tests or medication administration. These may be described in terms of duration and frequency of occurrence.

On the other hand, roles can be identified and assigned pending the need to perform the activities for those roles. The VDML model could be a collection of unordered activities and process fragments with associated roles along with a percent of occurrence (eg, percent of patients served by the activity). The repetition of an occurrence (if a patient is examined for vital signs every few hours) may be used to compute total occurrences based on the average patient length of stay.

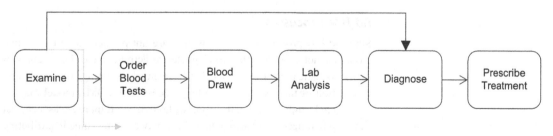

■ **FIG. 4.10** Medical diagnosis example.

This unordered collection can be refined in two ways: (1) dependencies should be shown when an activity requires a deliverable from another activity and (2) most cases pass through stages where only some of the activities are relevant to each stage. Stages may correspond to activities in a capability method where those activities each delegate to a collaboration of the activities within the corresponding stage.

Such a model is still of value from a top management perspective. The average cost of a type of case can be the basis for setting priorities for research into improved technology, methods, or case planning. The variance of measurements and occurrence of certain activities can be a basis for consideration of improvements. Measurements of other values of concern to customers will still be important and can be traced back to relevant activities.

The VDML model cannot provide more predictability than the CMMN case model, but the measurements and their variance can provide important insights not apparent from looking at a CMMN model. This also can provide a basis for managers to identify particular operating measurements for early identification of problem cases.

Cooperative Processes

VDML represents cooperative processes as business network collaborations. The exchanges can be represented as exchanges of value propositions, similar to BPMN conversations, or as exchanges of deliverables. The exchange of deliverables communicates the net effect of exchanges from a management perspective, avoiding the more detailed exchange of messages represented in a BPMN model. Consequently, the transformation between a VDML business network collaboration and a BPMN choreography is similar to the transformation of other VDML collaborations to BPMN processes as discussed above.

Ad Hoc Processes

Since ad hoc processes, by their nature, are not predictable, a conceptual model cannot provide detail to characterize activities and deliverables or define statistical measurements that have much meaning. Consequently, recognition of the need for an ad hoc process in a VDML model may be represented simply by a collaboration without detail. If there are aspects that can be generalized as recurring, then there may be some value in attributing value measurements to the collaboration.

BUSINESS COLLABORATION MANAGEMENT

BPM is a management discipline that focuses on the design of repeatable business processes and continuous improvement of the speed, cost, and quality of business processes. BPM emerged when much of the work of an enterprise was repetitive, human work—repeatable processes. BPM emphasizes the definition and documentation of repeatable business processes to optimize performance and as a basis for analysis and improvement. This includes both manual and automated business processes. BPMN has become the generally accepted standard language for specification of repeatable business processes.

The future of BPM is not clear. Advances in technology and business design are outside the scope of traditional BPM, and there is a need to redefine BPM to bring a broader perspective and new discipline to defining and modeling the way the business works.

As we discussed in Chapter 2, an enterprise can be characterized as a network of collaborations—people and machines working together for a shared purpose. In VDML, the detail of collaborations can include roles of participants, performing activities, exchanging deliverables, contributing value and exchanging deliverables with other collaborations. VDML represents an abstraction of collaborations appropriate for management-level analysis and decision-making. From this perspective, we propose BCM as the next generation of BPM.

BCM should link the conceptual business design supported by VDML to the operational design—the operational collaborations along with resource management and organizational alignment. In operational design, specific requirements must be defined for individual business transactions including activities, events, decisions, iterations, and exception-handling along with management of personnel, facilities, methods, and resources.

In this section we will assess the current challenges of BPM, propose a mission for BCM, describe the scope of BCM, assess the business value, and identify management challenges.

Current Challenges of BPM

There are four major challenges that should be addressed by BCM:

- Adaptive and ad hoc collaboration support
- Mobile computing, cloud computing and the Internet of Things
- How the business actually works
- Value delivery

We will discuss these in the paragraphs that follow.

Adaptive and Ad Hoc Collaboration Support

Case management opens the door to providing automated support for all kinds of collaborations, including ad hoc collaborations. The work of customer support requires adaptive processes. The work of claims investigation requires adaptive processes. The work of business transformation is an adaptive process. Much of the work of managers can benefit from adaptive process supports. This work no longer fits the traditional BPM discipline and persons with BPM skills and experience will need to develop new skills and methods to be successful in designing support for case management processes.

At first impression, a collaboration and a process are the same thing, but a collaboration exists when a purpose and at least two participants are identified. The process, as well as the roles for a collaboration may only emerge as the collaboration proceeds. At one extreme, a collaboration process may explicitly define possible patterns of execution for each occurrence of the associated collaboration, whereas, at the other extreme, a collaboration may have no predefined process but rather the process for an occurrence of the collaboration may only be known when the collaboration is completed—assuming the details of the execution are captured.

The following are some examples of collaborations that may benefit from additional computer and communications support: strategic planning, business transformation, project management, standards development, contract negotiation, CRM, process improvement, maintenance and repair, product planning, marketing campaigns.

Mobile Computing, Cloud Computing, and the Internet of Things

Recent advances in technology have further consequences for next-generation BPM. The internet and wireless access have enabled people to remain connected anywhere, anytime, with portable computing and communication devices: smart phones and tablets. The traditional mode of operation of repeatable business processes involves people sitting at work stations, interacting with computer terminals or desktop computers. Now people can participate from remote sites—while visiting a customer facility, while in transit, while visiting with different patients in a hospital, while investigating a crime scene, and so on. Furthermore, they can collaborate with others using voice and video, and they can be made immediately aware of new developments or a need for action. Members of a team can respond according to their roles and immediately collaborate for action planning. As a result of the connectivity and engagement, a much more detailed record of the actual activities, events, and outcomes can be captured. This can be the basis for process improvements and more timely action to mitigate adverse consequences.

The communication goes both ways. The Internet of Things (IoT) brings a focus on all of the sensors and devices that can be connected to the Internet. Remote observations and sensors can provide immediate input to the change of state of a process, case, project, machine, market, and so on. Remote devices can be controlled by service delivery, maintenance, security, and personalized responses, driven by automated processes.

These capabilities will be integrated with applications on the smart phones and tablets, as well as on-board computers in cars, trucks and railcars, household appliances, vending machines, utility network controllers, and on-line surveillance systems. In addition, the primary applications may be running in a public cloud, improving support for automation and information sharing for collaborations with customers, end users, and other business partners, around the world.

This integration provides access to performance and ecosystem data presented in the context of business models to support rapid response to changing circumstances, innovation, strategic planning, and governance. This rapid evolution of business and technology requires a comprehensive understanding of the network of collaborations that define how the business actually works along with models that make the complexity manageable.

How the Business Actually Works

While prescriptive, repetitive business processes direct much of the mainstream business operation of an enterprise, much of the actual business, and many critical activities, occur in collaborations that do not show up in any procedure manuals or organization charts. For example, the following collaborations must occur, but much of the activities, participants, and communications occur below the radar: innovation proposals, problem solving, risk mitigation, crisis response, value-proposition improvement. Consequently, the allocation of resources and coordination with other efforts may not be given appropriate guidance and support. There may be duplications of effort and omissions.

The consumption of resources may have the appearance of inefficiencies because there is not clear accounting for the occurrence and value of contributions. Instead there should be formal recognition for the contributions.

Furthermore, the initiation and participation in these collaborations relies on individual initiative and experience. When organization changes are implemented, or budget cuts require staff reductions, key participants may inadvertently be lost.

Value Delivery

VDML models will define value propositions and value streams from a top management perspective. VDML will support analysis of capabilities in need of improvement and setting of investment priorities. However, the actual delivery of value depends on the design and management of operational collaborations. This is more than business process design. It requires consideration of methods and tools along with resource availability and skilled personnel. Analysis of value delivery also requires capture of measurements from actual activities.

BCM Mission

The mission of BCM is to develop and improve the operational-level design and support of business collaborations to fulfill enterprise objectives, policies, and requirements of the conceptual business design.

Scope of BCM

The scope of BCM can be viewed from three perspectives: enterprise collaboration network, capability collaboration, and collaboration domains.

Enterprise Collaboration Network

Operational design focuses on how the enterprise actually works. This is more detailed than the management-level, conceptual model represented with VDML. The enterprise is a network of collaborations. Many of those are ad hoc and should be recognized for support and participation. Those that depend on the circumstances but can be characterized with roles, responsibilities, and exchanges of deliverables can be designed for case management. Of course, the best understood and recognized collaborations are the prescriptive, repetitive processes primarily involved in the actual delivery of products or services.

Capability Collaboration

Service unit design is focused on the aggregation of services for a particular capability and the affinity of services that may realize economies of scale from sharing personnel and other resources. Service units are based on capability units identified with a VDML model, but a service unit will have ancillary service interfaces and may bring together services for multiple, closely related capabilities. Service units should also be part of a larger shared services organization that brings similar services under shared management. Service unit design includes attention to automation, performance, and value creation.

Collaboration Domains

Collaborations can be classified as occurring in several different domains of business operation. Four different collaboration domains are described below.

Value Streams

As in VDML, we will define a value stream as the sequences of relevant activities of participating collaborations that contribute directly to the production of an end product or service. BCM should assess how collaborations contribute to value streams to develop and improve value stream service unit design from an enterprise perspective—applying management priorities to balancing the interests of different value streams and different market segments.

Ancillary and Supporting Services

Ancillary services are those collaborations that maintain or supply the facilities and resources needed by service units such as production scheduling, materials management, machine maintenance, and repair. Support services are collaborations that provide administrative or other services that support enterprise management such as accounting, purchasing, human resources, legal services, and data processing.

These collaborations are essential to the success of the business but do not directly contribute to production of the product or service. These services, in a sense, operate in the background. Their costs are typically recovered as overhead.

Meta Collaborations

Some collaborations work on the analysis and design of other collaborations—particularly the value stream, ancillary, or support services. These collaborations include process improvement, automation, problem resolution, and business transformation. Some meta collaborations also must operate on other meta collaborations.

Organization Structure

The organization structure should be extended and maintained to include the otherwise ad hoc and invisible collaborations that have identifiable business value. It is important to identify the existence, contributions, and organizational relationships to (1) recognize the contributions of participants and their allocation of time, (2) ensure that their purposes are aligned with enterprise objectives, and (3) reconcile potential duplications of effort or omissions through coordination and communication. The organization chart should be a living model of the management hierarchy and the roles of people in various collaborations. VDML supports this extended organization model, but the real, extended business organization structure must be a visible part of the day-to-day operation of the business.

Business Value

An enterprise should realize the following business values from a BCM practice.

Operating Efficiency and Reliability

Collaboration design and automation can improve efficiency and reliability throughout the enterprise.

Customer Value

Better design of shared collaborations can improve value contributions and optimization of values delivered to customers.

Employee Accountability and Recognition

Making collaborations visible and capture of activities and decisions improves accountability and provides a basis for recognition of accomplishments.

Alignment of Conceptual and Operational Business Design

If the conceptual and operational business designs are aligned, top management will have a better understanding of the actual operation of the business as well as more effective control of enterprise optimization, accountability, and transformation.

Agility

Agility is supported by well-defined, sharable collaborations as business operation building blocks.

Management Challenges

There are two important management challenges to the scope of BCM: resource management and performance management. These are not new challenges, but current challenges that become more visible with BCM.

Resource Management

Recognition and accountability for many otherwise informal and invisible collaborations brings with it a need for capacity planning and resource allocation. Without this visibility, individual managers provide informal accommodations for people contributing to these informal efforts when they believe the work is of benefit to the enterprise. However, they have a conflict of interest between contributing to this greater good, and fulfilling their primary responsibility for which they are accountable. When these additional collaborations are formal, they should be evaluated and budgeted based on their value to the enterprise. Unfortunately, this may create a bureaucratic barrier to getting things done.

It may be appropriate to allocate discretionary budget to managers to pursue the otherwise informal collaborations and, at the same time, implement mechanisms, possibly through collaboration automation facilities, to account for the effort and recognize the accomplishments.

However, in order to be effective, a participant must also have the necessary skills and experience for their role in a collaboration, and it is not appropriate for a manager to invest in collaborations that do not have some value to their primary area of responsibility. In order to provide proper support for each collaboration, it will be necessary to identify people with relevant skills and manage the allocation of their efforts to both their primary organization and other collaborations. This may best be managed as a pool of people allocated based on workloads, in part to value stream responsibilities and in another part, to ancillary collaborations to address enterprise priorities.

Performance Management

Evaluation of performance and accomplishments requires measurements of effort and contributions. If individuals are participating in multiple collaborations, potentially under different leaders, their performance across multiple assignments is difficult to assess. If performance is evaluated by an independent manager from an enterprise perspective, then the leaders of the collaborations in which an individual is a participant will sense a loss of control and commitment of the participant. Effectively, the individual must be managed as a shared capability that is engaged in multiple collaborations.

■ SUMMARY AND MOVING FORWARD

This chapter has focused on business process design, or more generally, design of business collaborations to include adaptive and ad hoc collaborations not previously addressed by BPM. This expanded scope along with advances in technology and the recognition of the enterprise as a network of collaborations, has highlighted the need for a next generation BPM to have a much stronger role in the operational design of the enterprise.

The next generation of BPM must complement the conceptual business design supported by VDML with operational, detailed design required for actual operation of the enterprise. We have discussed the design of collaborations of different types and in various contexts to provide a deeper understanding of the challenges and opportunities. Finally, we have proposed the development of a BCM practice to address this broader scope and fill the gap between the management-level, conceptual business design and the actual operation of the business.

In the next chapter, we will discuss business rules. At a detailed level, rules determine process flow of control and data integrity. However, rules must also be the mechanism for implementation of policies, the computation of guidance, problem analysis and business decisions, and, in some cases, the mechanism for generating a process. Rules make critical aspects of business processes more visible and manageable from a business perspective.

Chapter 5

Rules for Actions and Constraints

Rules are concise expressions of what must be true or when an action must occur. Rules express business requirements that reflect knowledge of the business and the business environment. Constraints specify what is possible, such as possible entries on a form. Rules with actions can drive business operations such as ordering parts when the inventory is low. Some rules enforce the integrity of business models and data. Some rules represent knowledge for decision-making, analysis, or planning. Some rules are used to express high-level business requirements for competitive advantage, governance, or regulatory compliance.

What makes rules important is that they enable a business person to express a restriction, inference, or circumstances for action but without the need to understand when the rule should be applied nor the technical details required to apply the rule. Essentially rules support a focus on what is required, not how it is to be implemented. If implemented appropriately, rules can also be a mechanism for quickly understanding and implementing business changes—agility. This makes rules a critical aspect for defining requirements for the design of the business and the information systems that support it.

Before computers, all business rules were applied by humans. Today, there are still some business rules that must be applied in human activities, including rules that are informally applied by experts to solve problems or provide advice.

Today, information systems are pervasive, so it is likely that many business rules are, or can be, implemented by information systems. In this book, we are particularly concerned with exploiting information technology for the application of rules because rules in automated systems are more efficient and reliable than those applied manually. Knowledge workers will continue to apply their experience and knowledge that may involve "rules," but those rules are applied with insights on when and how the rules are relevant to diverse circumstances.

Building the Agile Enterprise. http://dx.doi.org/10.1016/B978-0-12-805160-3.00005-3

Unfortunately, many business rules are currently embedded in application programs. When there are relevant changes to business operations, programmers must search program code to identify decisions that embody the current business rules. This can be expensive, time consuming, and subject to errors. There are application modernization tools available for mining business rules from legacy applications, but this still requires human analysis to distinguish business rules from less significant program logic. Even when these decisions are implemented in automated business processes, they may be overlooked when a change is required.

It is important for enterprise agility as well as good governance that business rules are implemented explicitly in information systems, so there is visibility and traceability from the business requirement to the realization of that requirement in the operation of the business. Computer-based tools for management of rules will (1) improve reliability of application, (2) improve the ability to change rules, and (3) improve governance—assurance the enterprise is doing the right things and doing them well.

In this chapter, we will first consider an overview of rules technology: the forms in which rules are expressed, rules in knowledge-based systems, and inferred rules in machine learning. We will then examine example business applications. Finally, we will consider how rules can be managed for effective enterprise governance and agility.

FORMS OF RULES

Rules are logical expressions that may occur in different forms. A rule expression may refer to specific things or their attributes or relationships, or the rule may be expressed with symbolic variables that are assigned specific references when the rule is evaluated. So we could have a logical expression that John is married to Judy, or we could parameterize the expression as ?X is married to ?Y. The latter expression could be applied to an appropriate database to identify all married couples. The following are typical forms of rules.

- *Constraint.* A constraint expresses a logical relationship that must be true. So a constraint might express that an employee birth date must be in the past, or that a new order cannot be accepted from a customer if the customer's outstanding balance due would exceed the customer's credit limit.
- *Logical inference.* A logical inference expresses a fact or conclusion that is true if a condition expression is true. So we might express that if a car has a dead battery, or it is out of gasoline, or it is flooded, then it won't start.

We can characterize this form as "then-if." We might instead express it as "if-then" as a car won't start if it has a dead battery, or it is out of gasoline, or it is flooded. This form is useful in diagnosis. Of course this example suggests our limited knowledge of reasons a car won't start. Logical inference rules are used in backward-chaining knowledge-based systems, discussed below.

- *Condition-action*. A condition-action rule is similar to the then-if logical inference. If the condition is true, then the rule specifies an action that should occur, for example, if car will not start and it is out of gasoline, then put gasoline in it. This rule is likely to be context dependent since you don't always want to put gasoline in a car that is out of gasoline. Condition-action or "production" rules are applied in forward-chaining knowledge-based systems discussed below.
- *Event-condition-action*. An event-condition-action (ECA) rule is a refinement of the condition action rule that expresses the context in which the rule is to be evaluated. So the event might be that the car has stalled then the condition is evaluated and the action is performed under appropriate circumstances.
- *Pattern recognition*. Pattern recognition is the computer application of complex conditions typically developed by machine learning techniques to recognize data patterns of interest. A computer system processes examples of situations that do or don't represent patterns of interest to develop the pattern recognition capability (effectively the rules). The representations of conditions are generally not meaningful to humans, and it is generally not possible to identify the specific reasons a pattern is recognized or rejected.

KNOWLEDGE-BASED SYSTEMS

Knowledge-based systems provide solutions based on the interactions of multiple rules. The rules represent knowledge learned from experts. Individual rules will be relatively understandable, but technical expertise is required to achieve the necessary structure and relationships of the rules for the knowledge-based system to function properly. While the decisions realized with knowledge-based systems are based on clearly defined rules, the results may not be so obvious.

There are two basic forms of knowledge-based systems; backward chaining, or *logic programming* systems and forward chaining or *production systems*. Both forms involve reasoning with rules, but they solve different types of problems and apply rules in quite different ways.

Backward Chaining, Logic Programming Rules

Backward chaining starts with an assertion that is true if an associated condition is true. Prolog is a well-known language for backward chaining or "logic programming." The condition may be evaluated by evaluating the truth of each element. The truth of each element, in turn, may be based on other conditions. Backward chaining is often used for diagnosis.

We might think of the basic form of a logic programming rule as then-if. For example, the "result" might be, "the car won't start." We then look for potential reasons—in other words, things that, if true, would cause the car to not start. So, in a rather informal form, the rules might look something like this:

```
Car-wont-start(?) <= Battery-dead(?) or Flooded(?) or Out-of-
gasoline(?)
Battery-dead(?) <= Lights-dont-go-on(?)
Flooded(?) <= Smell-gasoline(?)
Out-of-gasoline(?) <= Fuel-gauge-shows-empty(?)
```

Here the question mark (?) represents a reference to the particular vehicle under consideration. More complex rules might reference additional relevant entities or values.

If implemented as Prolog statements, the execution would start with the first rule, where we are interested in finding a potential reason that Car-wont-start could be true. In order for Car-wont-start to be true, one of the subsequent statements must be true, that is, Battery-dead or ...If we consider Battery-dead, we see that the next rule evaluates Battery-dead. If Lights-dont-go-on is true, then Battery-dead is true and the cause of Car-wont-start is found. If Lights-dont-go-on is false, then Battery-dead is false and we return to the first rule (we "backtrack") to examine the next possibility: Flooded. The nesting of rules can be very complex. The ordering and structure of the rules determines the order in which questions are asked. For example, if Lights-dont-go-on is true, we have completed the search and we need not ask about Smell-gasoline or Fuel-gauge-shows-empty.

Note that when one path of the search fails, the search returns up the search tree to explore an alternative path. This is commonly called backtracking and enables the exploration of alternative solutions. Some problems may have multiple possible solutions that can be identified and considered. Such alternatives might have different levels of risk or probabilities of success as in a medical diagnosis and treatment. The risks might be computed from multiple factors involved in a suggested action.

The example is quite trivial; it fails to demonstrate many capabilities of Prolog, it does not cover all possible causes of nonstarting car, and the result is fairly obvious. Much more complex problems can be addressed; among the most sophisticated is mathematical theorem proving.

Logic programming is important for implementing complex searches such as in diagnoses or identification of omissions and inconsistencies in models. The programmer can focus attention on defining the rules and does not need to deal with the mechanics of backward chaining and backtracking. Nevertheless, logic programming does require special skills and attention to the order in which statements are executed.

Forward Chaining, Production Rules

Forward chaining involves an alternative form of reasoning with rules, often called "*production rules*." A production rule is triggered when its condition is met in a model of the problem domain—the model is often called the "working storage." When a rule "fires" its action will update working storage causing other rules to fire. The actions of a sequence of rule executions produces (ie, production of) a working storage that is a solution to the problem.

Production rules are applied by a rules engine, as depicted in Fig. 5.1. A rules engine is a software product that applies rules to a problem. Generally, the rules reside in the runtime environment and, on request, the data representing a problem to be evaluated is loaded into the rules engine working storage. A Rete network (pronounced ree-tee) is created to link the rules to the working storage for efficient processing. The rules engine determines whether any of the rule conditions are met. If the conditions of more than one rule are met, the rules engine has logic to decide which rule to "fire" (ie, execute). When a rule fires, its action is performed. This action likely changes the data in working storage that defines a new, current situation; it may also cause some external effect. When the data change, the conditions

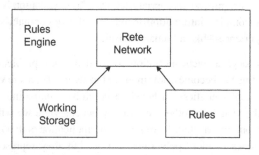

■ **FIG. 5.1** Production rules engine.

of a different subset of the rules may be met, and the rules engine again selects a rule to fire.

This general class of rules processing is called forward chaining because the action of each fired rule updates the working storage model and affects the selection of the next rule and subsequent chain of actions. The generally accepted mechanism for evaluating, selecting, and firing rules is the Rete algorithm.

Note that rules engines that implement production rules (forward chaining) also usually include backward-chaining capabilities where an evaluation of a condition requires examination of other conditions on which it depends.

The application of production rules does not include backtracking to explore alternative sequences of rule firings. Backtracking would require the engine to determine the point in the search where an alternative rule should be fired and the changes to working storage that would need to be withdrawn to pursue the alternative path. The Rete network links to working storage would further complicate the backtracking.

Production rules are used to produce a complex configuration or a plan such as a process or project or configuration.

MACHINE LEARNING

Cognitive computing is a recently popular phase for a collection of techniques for pattern recognition that mimics human cognition and learning. Recent advances emerged from work by IBM to develop a computer system that simulates human brain function. The laboratory implementation demonstrated a new computing paradigm. The vision is for a computer to provide the functionality of an intelligent robot—the ability to hear, see, and learn from receiving data in a variety of forms from multiple sources. Learned patterns and relationships are applied to analyze a new situation, reason about the situation and initiate or recommend appropriate actions. The expectation is to respond to complex, incomplete information, to draw conclusions or make suggestions based on experience—like a human advisor.

The vision is not yet a practical solution to current business problems, but cognitive computing has become a new industry buzzword. There are various definitions and characteristics attributed to cognitive computing. Some are focused on the vision and others are more practical. Here we will focus on systems that combine machine learning and the application of that knowledge. These techniques do not apply rules, per se, but they represent another approach to recognizing important circumstances and inferring results.

Neural networks are an early type of cognitive computing where the computer mimics the responses of neurons to various stimuli. Many examples of relevant circumstances are fed to the neural network, along with an expert's determination of the proper conclusion for each circumstance. The neural network learns to examine a situation and identify the proper conclusion.

Other cognitive computing techniques are being applied in analytic processes for identification of important patterns in natural language documents and "big data" collected from such sources as sensors, surveys, retail customer purchases, and web clicks.

Cognitive computing can provide valuable insights. However, cognitive computing systems must learn from substantial samples that are properly identified and cognitive computing results, generally, cannot be explained. At the same time, pattern recognition can be updated as circumstances change when it would take much longer for humans to define rules—assuming there is sufficient knowledge to identify the patterns of interest.

On the other hand, inferencing with rules may provide solutions for circumstances where there are few if any examples, and conclusions from forward and backward chaining can be explained by examination of the specific combination of rules that derived the result.

Developments in cognitive computing merit continuing attention.

APPLICATIONS OF RULES

While the previous section includes some examples of different types of rules, this section focuses on various aspects of business design where rules should be applied. The following sections describe the application of rules under the following topics:

- Data and model integrity
- Event filter
- Process flow control
- Process planning
- Selection
- Product design
- Governance

Data and Model Integrity Rules

Data integrity rules are first incorporated in data models and the design of databases. These rules may also be called business rules by developers of data models and designers of databases. They are constraints that exist in the real world. For example, a person cannot have a birth date in the future, and two people cannot have the same tax ID number. These rules do not change, and violation of these rules would indicate that the integrity of the associated database has been compromised.

Certain constraints are intrinsic to business concepts. For example, an organization unit cannot directly or indirectly report to itself, or a customer order must have at least one order item. These constraints ensure the validity of data when they are applied to data being entered by a person or received from another system.

Integrity rules may be considerably more complex. These rules may be defined in models and implemented in the computer applications. For example,

- In computer-assisted design models, a surface must have closed edges or the model is intrinsically invalid.
- In product specifications, for certain parts, there must not be more than one part number for the same application; for example, the conditions for use of different air conditioning compressors on a vehicle must be mutually exclusive.
- For process design, an iteration must have a termination condition.
- For an organization, a reporting relationship must not be circular.
- For a Value Delivery Modeling Language (VDML) model, the organization unit, management reporting relationships must not be circular (management hierarchy).

These constraints are defined to ensure the integrity of the model and are not dependent on the industry or the particular enterprise.

Some constraints are required to ensure data integrity from a business perspective. For example, a purchase order must be submitted or approved by a person with that level of financial authority. In this case, when a purchase order is entered, the rule will require an authorization that may direct a request, recursively, up the management chain until a person with sufficient authority is reached.

Data constraints are applied in databases to ensure that updates to not violate data integrity. In addition to constraints in databases, rules must be applied as data entry constraints and for validation of data received from other sources. Every field of every record created or received must be validated so that no actions are performed on invalid data. Processing of data should never reach the point where it is rejected in a database update.

This is not usually a concern in conventional systems, but when records are submitted to shared services, there is a greater risk that an invalid request could be submitted. Each service should apply the same rules to data received from other services as it would apply to data entered by a human. A service should be designed to be used in a variety of contexts and cannot assume that all sources are reliable. Similarly, a service may be used by new processes or processes that are independently upgraded or replaced in the future, resulting in potential incompatibility.

Event Rules

Event rules identify events of interest for monitoring or initiation of action. Event processing is discussed in detail in Chapter 8. Rules are important for recognition, filtering, and distribution of events.

External Events

External events may come as messages from other systems or machines, from human inputs and from sensors. Some events are communicated relatively infrequently and are individually evaluated to determine if they are of interest. Other events of interest may be in streams of data from sensors or other systems and may require consideration of inputs from multiple sources for recognition and validation. These inputs are filtered by analytics systems that can derive events from large, multiple streams of data, as the data are being received. Analytics systems are discussed further in Chapter 6.

As external events are received, event rules must be applied to determine the events of interest. In addition, external events, in particular, must be validated to ensure that the enterprise does not react to erroneous or fraudulent events. Validity may be evaluated by correlation of multiple sources, by data integrity rules, and by rules that validate against known, related data.

Database Events

Databases, particularly master-data databases, represent the current state of the business. A database management system can support rules called *"triggers"* to recognize changes in the state of the business that are of interest.

A trigger "fires" when its condition, referencing database elements, becomes true. Generally, it will not fire again unless its condition becomes false and then becomes true, again. A trigger initiates an action, typically an event notice, which is communicated to an application or process to perform a desired action. The ability to apply triggers is a database system feature.

Notification Broker

A notification broker provides a service of forwarding event notices to sub-scribers. Subscribers indicate the characteristics of events of interest and express conditions for qualification of individual events with rules. When the event broker receives an event it applies the subscriber rules to determine if and where the notice should be distributed.

Consequently, an event notice may go through several levels of constraints: the determination interest by the source or external event filter, determination of interest to the notification broker, and determination of interest to subscribers. It is likely that the subscriber will apply one or more additional rules to determine appropriate action depending on the purpose of the subscriber.

Process Events

Three types of events can affect a process: events from outside the process, event-condition-action events, and timer events. These events are discussed in the context of BPMN and/or CMMN processes.

Event notices from external sources will typically be received as asynchro-nous messages from an external source, another internal system, or a noti-fication broker. As noted above, the process may apply rules to further qualify and determine action depending on the process and the context in which it is received. In both BPMN and CMMN, the recognition of these events is represented by a circle—in BPMN it is an *event* and in CMMN it is an *event listener*.

CMMN assumes that events from internal activity (case file updates) as well as external sources will be applied to the case file where the effects will cause active event listener rules to fire, thus the case file functions as the clearing house for events to affect the active process. BPMN does not main-tain a "case file" representing the current state of the situation, therefore event elements are triggered by the receipt of messages or occurrence of time.

Machine Learning

Large volumes of incoming data may be analyzed to identify patterns of interest representing changes of circumstances in the data sources that may represent market activity, web queries, sales data, various sensors mon-itoring variables of interest. The occurrence of variances in a pattern can indicate a relevant event and trigger further inquiries and analysis.

"Cognitive computing" techniques are being applied in analytic processes for identification of important patterns in natural language documents and "big data" collected from a variety of sources.

Process Flow Control Rules

Some rules identify risks or expense to be avoided and divert process activity to mitigate or avoid the damage. Other rules recognize policy constraints that, under special circumstances or approvals, may be authorized. For example, all purchases of equipment must go through the purchase order process. However, if equipment is required to resolve a major disruption of operations, an individual can purchase the equipment and submit an expense report with appropriate justification. The constraint is violated, but there is a compensating process required.

Simple Flow Control

In a BPMN process, the simplest form of rule implementation is a gateway branch. The gateway condition is evaluated against one or more variables in the process context to choose between alternative paths. In CMMN, the entry/exit sentry controls what actions are initiated or completed. A CMMN sentry applies an ECA rule to enable the start or end of an activity. An ECA rule is evaluated only when the specified event occurs. The event will usually be an event within the process such as the completion of an activity. The ECA rule enables subsequent activity in the process. For the most part, the gateway and sentry decisions address variations in processing requirements. Alternative paths may be defined for differing circumstances or requirements, for compliance with a policy or regulation, or to direct control to an alternative path to resolve an exception.

For example, a policy rule might be, "if acceptance of an order will cause the customer's credit limit to be exceeded, then the order must be rejected." Instead of rejecting the order in our example, the rule might be changed to offer the customer an alternative payment option. Sometimes the same rule may be required at multiple points in different business processes. The credit limit rule might be applied in an order-change process as well, and a rule change must be reflected in both processes.

Decision Model and Notation

Sometimes circumstances are not so simple. There may be multiple alternatives described by multiple rules. The decision model and notation (DMN, http://www.omg.org/spec/DMN/) specification of the Object Management Group (OMG) defines a facility for representation of these complex rules in tables.

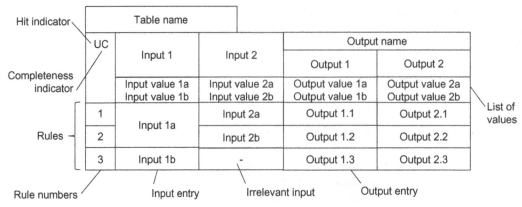

FIG. 5.2 Typical DMN table.

Fig. 5.2 illustrates the typical structure of a DMN table. The rules are the bottom three rows. There are two input variables and two output variables. The lists of possible values of each input and each output are indicated. The hit indicator, "U", indicates that each rule is unique (the conditions do not overlap). The completeness indicator, "C", indicates that there are no gaps between rules, full coverage.

Note that rules 1 and 2 have the same input 1 value, and rule 3 has an input 2 value that is irrelevant—the rule only depends on the input 1 value.

There are various possible hit indicators and completeness indicators that can prescribe the sequence in which rules are evaluated and how overlaps or gaps in rule coverage should be resolved. There is an expression language for specification of the conditions in a form to be interpreted by computer. Each input value or output value may be a computed value dependent on multiple variables. The table can also take various shapes and accommodate different numbers of inputs, outputs and rules. A tool that implements DMN and supports easy configuration of the table graphics and proper syntax of expressions.

It is most useful for business users to express the inputs and outputs as text to be converted to formal expressions by technical people. A table with textual descriptions can be relatively easy to understand and validate unless there are many rules or variables.

The decisions modeled with DMN are explicit and predictable.

Production Rules

In a typical process (such as defined by BPMN or CMMN), a rules engine and an applicable set of rules can be invoked by an activity at a particular point in a business process where there is a need for a complex computation to make a decision. This is typical of claims processing or product configuration. The rules engine is presented with all the relevant data, and the rules are applied. The rules engine returns a result, or it may return a failure to produce a desired result—the claim is invalid, the product cannot be configured, or the solution cannot be reached.

Forward chaining may be used to generate a sequence of activities for a project plan or an adaptive process, coordinating the work of different participants. This is equivalent to planning a trip. You make assumptions about intermediate outcomes, but if an outcome is not as expected, then you replan from that point forward. The end objective remains the same. Each plan identifies the best path to reach the objective from the current point under current circumstances and assumptions.

Alternatively, a process can be dynamically defined as each activity is completed. As an activity is completed or an event is triggered (or in anticipation), production rules can suggest the next activity(s) to be performed or considered for the particular situation based on the state of the process, the work product, and the objective. Rather than allow the rules engine to pick from the rules available to fire, the tentative action of each of the candidate rules could be presented to a knowledge worker. In such a process, there is no obvious, predefined flow, just a set of possible activities, events, and rules. This technique can fit quite well into an implementation of the CMMN specification.

Approval

In either BPMN or CMMN, a rule may call for prior approval for an action. For example, if a customer seeks a refund on a purchase, this may require that refunds greater than a specified amount must be approved by a manager with the appropriate spending authority. This decision may direct the flow of control to an approval service that will locate a person in the management chain with the necessary level of authority. Selection of an appropriate approver may be a backward-chaining rules process.

Complex Computation

A complex decision also may be performed by a rule-based system (forward- or backward-chaining inferencing) that is engaged as a BPMN subprocess or by a CMMN process task. For CMMN, the case file should provide the context information needed to support the inferencing process. In BPMN, the context is not as obvious but must be determined from process context variables associated with the input request record and inputs from the user.

In a typical BPMN or CMMN process, a rules engine and an applicable set of rules can be invoked by an activity at a particular point in a business process where there is a need for a complex computation to make a decision. This is typical of claims processing or product configuration. The rules engine is presented with all the relevant data, and the rules are applied. The rules engine returns a result, or it may return a failure to produce a desired result—the claim is invalid, the product cannot be configured, and the solution cannot be reached.

The complex decision could support a help desk operator with diagnosis of a customer problem or develop a bill of materials for a custom order.

Guidance

Rules may be used to provide guidance in an adaptive process (CMMN). The simplest form of guidance is a planning table where options in the planning table appear based on rules that include planning items based on the role of the participant and the current state of the case file. The choices might be influenced by collaboration with other participants.

However, the decision may require consideration of complex factors some of which the decision-maker might overlook. For example, the course of treatment of a patient with medications may depend on current vital signs, physical symptoms, allergies, other current medications, previous response to potential medications, and a balance of potential outcomes against potential side effects. A backward-chaining rules engine might be used to recommend possible actions or to identify risks of a proposed medication.

Forward-chaining rules might be used to propose a process or next step based on current circumstances in an adaptive process. Continued progress on the plan might depend on achieving expected progress guarded by sentries and event watchers to raise alerts or propose alterative actions.

On the other hand, backward-chaining rules might be used to identify multiple alternatives under the current circumstances and identify risk factors for each alternative. If some of relevant variables are not currently available, a backward-chaining process can be designed to consider options that do not depend on the unavailable variables or allow the participant to provide assumptions.

At the same time, rules can ensure that all relevant factors and possible alternatives are considered and provide measurements to provide guidance to the decision-maker. The rule-based system can also provide explanations of its conclusions and reasons for elimination of some options by consideration of the search paths that lead to each conclusion.

Optimization

Production optimization involves adjusting product mix or workload balancing to minimize cost, maintain quality, and adapt to changes in demand. Sharing of services and resources can improve economies of scale, but of course, sharing makes the problem more complex. The following paragraphs illustrate examples of production optimization problems that might be addressed with knowledge-based systems.

US Federal regulations for vehicle fuel economy require that a vehicle manufacturer not exceed certain average levels of fuel consumption in the vehicles it produces. This means that if the cumulative average is reaching the limit, then the product mix must be adjusted to decrease the production of vehicles with higher rates of fuel consumption. The fuel consumption of each vehicle depends on multiple factors including the weight and streamlining, in addition to the performance of various components. Rules can determine the expected fuel economy of each vehicle based on its features and components. This then provides the basis for computation of the cumulative average.

Average fuel economy is not a rigid limit since, if the limit is exceeded, subsequent production can compensate to bring the cumulative average back in line. This then allows production scheduling to optimize other factors when determining the sequence of vehicles on the production line.

Another form of optimization involves workload balancing. Returning to the vehicle production example, the work content of a vehicle can be determined by rules that consider the assembly operations required at each workstation. The work content will determine the distance a vehicle moves in each station while the work is being done (based on the line production rate). If two or more vehicles with high work content arrive sequentially at a workstation, the operator may end up out of his/her workstation, possibly beyond reach of tools or materials or interfering with the next workstation. The production line-up can be adjusted to space out these high-work-content vehicles.

Workload balancing may also occur with sharing of resources among multiple processes or services. Within a service unit, there may be multiple, different capability methods requiring the participation of people with similar skills. Sharing of services increases economy of scale but also will require more concurrent operations. Some people may have some skills that are more scarce, so bottlenecks can occur if the scarce resources are needed on multiple processes at the same time. Some requests may require more time or expertise than others. This is essentially a configuration problem, but the configuration is continuous as new requests are initiated and different skills are needed as work progresses.

Workload balancing is a common problem where participants can be assigned to a variety of roles in different processes, and the potential savings become greater when consolidation of capabilities provides the opportunity for economies of scale.

Selection

Backward chaining (or logic programming) is important for implementing complex searches. The programmer can focus attention on defining the rules and does not need to deal with the mechanics of backward chaining and backtracking. Nevertheless, logic programming does require special skills and attention to the order in which statements are executed.

For example, backward chaining can determine if the necessary elements to authorize a claim are present and return the allowable fee for the qualifying circumstances. This might include a determination that the claim has already been paid as part of another claim.

Diagnosis is another form of selection. Rules search for a diagnosis that exhibits the observed symptoms of a problem. Diagnosis is frequently a fundamental step in determining corrective action.

Rules provide the basis for selection of a performer to fill a role. Roles in any collaboration should be filled by people or service units that have the necessary skills, relationships, and authority to meet the needs of the collaboration while recognizing workload balancing objectives as discussed above.

Some collaborations are unstructured and require a mix of skills, relationships, and authority. For example, a task force may be assembled to address a particular business problem. The participants must have relevant skills, relationships to organizations that are affected by the problem and potential solution, and authority to gain access to the information needed to analyze and solve the problem. Not every person need have all the relevant skills, and it is likely that no one of them will have all of the organizational relationships or access authorization. Rules can be used to consider candidates for participation in the collaboration that, together, satisfy the requirements.

Different people with the same job classification may each have different, but overlapping skill sets and certifications. Assignments should reflect the level of demand for certain skills so that progress on some undertakings is not delayed because persons with critical skills are assigned to efforts that do not require those critical skills. This is again the workload balance problem discussed above.

A couple other factors may be considered. Even though activities within a collaboration can be done by different performers, assignment of one performer to a series of activities may result in higher productivity, quality, and job satisfaction. This continuity of participant must be curtailed where there is a requirement of separation of responsibility.

Product Design and Configuration Rules

Production rules are used to produce a configuration. Most often they are used for complex system configurations such as configuration of a complex product such as an automobile or a computer. For example, a rule may specify that "if a customer automobile order includes air conditioning, and if the order also includes an optional V-8 engine, then air conditioning compressor 1234 is added to the bill of materials." Another rule may specify that "if air conditioning compressor 1234 is included, and the order also includes power windows or power door locks, then the alternator must be replaced by a heavy-duty alternator."

Production rules might also be used for such computations as bill-of-materials generation, project planning, process planning, in-process inventory computation, design of experiments, or forecasting.

Since rules can be used to identify the parts required for a product configuration(s) this may be used to generate a bill of materials. An extension of the mechanism is to compute the addition of parts to correspond to a production-line sequence to determine assembled parts to determine inventory without emptying the production line.

Forward chaining may be used to generate a sequence of activities for a project plan or an adaptive process, coordinating the work of different participants. This is equivalent to planning a trip. You make assumptions about intermediate outcomes, but if an outcome is not as expected, then you replan from that point forward. The end objective remains the same. Each plan identifies the best path to reach the objective from the current point under current circumstances and assumptions.

Alternatively, a process can be dynamically defined as each activity is completed. As an activity is completed or an event is triggered (or in anticipation), production rules can determine the next activity(s) to be performed or considered for the particular situation based on the state of the process, the work product, and the objective. Rather than allow the rules engine to pick from the rules available to fire, the tentative action of each of the candidate rules could be presented to a knowledge worker. In such a process, there is no obvious, predefined flow, just a set of possible activities, events, and rules. This technique can fit quite well into an implementation of the CMMN specification.

A number of important features of a product can be computed (or estimated) using rules based on the configuration of the particular product (eg, car or truck).

- Weight can be computed as the sum of the components in the particular vehicle configuration.
- Cost of parts can be computed based on the particular configuration, but it is often more important to determine the cost based on product options (eg, air conditioning, power seats, sound system) which may involve different components for different vehicle configurations. Labor costs can also be computed based on product configuration. This can determine the cost of each unit, although idle operator time may be difficult to allocate. Overall production costs will be a function of the product mix.
- Fuel economy of an individual vehicle can be evaluated based on the components that affect fuel economy along with the impact of weight and aerodynamic characteristics of the vehicle model.
- Load capacity can be computed based on the suspension components and vehicle weight with some constraints based on the particular vehicle model.
- Failure mode analysis involves modeling components for analysis of potential failures and the consequences. This might be applied to the fuel system, the brake system, the drive train, and so on.

Design for Production

Rules can be used to apply design constraints for certain types of components and production operations, for example,

- Molded parts may require rounded edges and minimum thickness of sections.
- Stampings may limit minimum radii on creases and maximum draw on concave surfaces.
- Some parts may require minimum section thickness for heat transfer or strength.

Governance

Governance is the responsibility of the board of directors or other governing body to ensure that the enterprise is "doing the right thing and doing it well." Governance must be supported by the management of the enterprise, and governance will be a basis for evaluation of manager performance. Consequently, managers will also be concerned that organizations within their area of responsibility are doing the right thing and doing it well on a basis similar to the criteria of the governing body.

Governance involves (1) setting policies based on regulations, business objectives, good business practices, and monitoring compliance, (2) setting objectives, and monitoring performance, (3) ensuring accountability, and monitoring compliance with appropriate standards of conduct, and (4) identification of risks and assessment of risk mitigation or avoidance.

In this chapter, we are concerned with support of governance with rules applied in information systems. We will examine the mechanisms of governance in greater detail in Chapter 11. Much of governance involves the application of rules and measurement of compliance. This must be supported by a facility for management of the rules and traceability to their implementation as well as traceability from the effect of a rule back to the record of intent. Rules management is addressed later in this chapter.

Here we will consider the application of rules under the following topics:

- Regulations
- Policies
- Objectives
- Approval levels
- Monitoring

Regulations

Regulations are most often expressed in natural language text although there is interest in expressing them more precisely to remove ambiguity and support automated analysis for impact and compliance.

Regulations should not be applied directly to the enterprise but should be translated into policies appropriate to the particular enterprise. There should, nevertheless, be clear traceability between the regulations and the policies and rules that enforce them.

Most regulations are not published in a form that could be used directly by automated systems. There must be some transformation by humans to codify the required intent and identify where, if possible, the controls can be implemented in business processes or computations.

Some regulations are quite abstract, expressing an objective rather than a clear restriction on operations. The Sarbanes-Oxley Act (http://www. soxlaw.com/introduction.htm), for example, requires accountability and control. Executives must ensure accurate corporate reporting. This requires controls such as separation of duties, disclosure of conflicts of interest, restrictions on spending authority, and independent review of actions. In addition, there must be strict record-keeping for accountability. These measures are pervasive and must be addressed in the design of enterprise processes. Essentially, these are requirements for good governance.

Regulations must be interpreted in the context of a particular enterprise and in the context in which they will be applied. Furthermore, the approach to application of the regulation may reflect consideration of risks of violation such as the likelihood of accidents, oversights, or mistakes, as well as the potential consequences to the enterprise and individual employees.

For example, restrictions on shipment and storage of hazardous materials can be enforced by rules applied to shipping and receiving orders. Material control records should indicate which items are or contain hazardous materials. Hazardous shipments and material handling processes can include special handling based on the hazardous material identifier.

Some regulations can be very specific. Tariffs, for example, define the rates to be charged for specific types of service. Tax regulations are usually very specific as well. Similarly, hazardous materials regulations can be very specific about precautions and prohibitions regarding use, storage, and transportation. It may be relatively straightforward to implement such regulations.

In the future, regulations may be codified so that they can be interpreted and analyzed by computers. The semantics of business vocabulary and rules specification (SBVR, http://www.omg.org/technology/documents/br_pm_spec_catalog.htm#sbvr) from the OMG provides a formal way to capture and express rules in a natural language-like form. In fact this facility supports the specification of multiple vocabularies, so rules could be expressed in terms from different natural languages. The rules are represented in a computer model that can be used to analyze the rules for inconsistencies. The formal structure of the rules helps remove ambiguities. However, regulations will still require interpretation and development of controls based on the specific enterprise and the risks of violations.

Policies

A policy is a declarative expression of intent independent of specific business operations. For example, a policy might express that "any purchase of a personal computer or laptop computer must conform to an approved hardware and software configuration." The policy does not define an action to be taken nor who must take an action, but rather it defines a constraint on business operations.

A policy may require multiple rules with different points of application. At the same time, there may be degrees of enforcement or a level of discretion, where deviation might be authorized under special circumstances, as opposed to a level of absolute compliance with regulations where there could be civil or criminal liability. This computer purchase rule might have a level of enforcement which allows exceptions with prior approval—perhaps approval by the manager of the personal computer support activity.

Rules that express policies are a mechanism for governing the enterprise. Other management directives such as strategic initiatives, high-level business collaborations, organization structure, and allocation of resources are important aspects of enterprise management, but they have only indirect effect on how the enterprise actually operates. Policy rules define management controls that can have direct effect on daily operations as well as longer-term results.

Some policy rules may be incorporated in automated business processes or computer applications, and some rules must be applied to the behavior of humans. Where possible we should look for ways to manage and implement rules in automated processes and applications to ensure objective and consistent application and ensure agility in the ability to adapt policies to new circumstances.

Rules for implementation of policies, including those that reflect regulations, may affect many aspects of enterprise operations. Rules may be applied in business processes to enforce constraints defined by policies. Many forms are discussed under other topics in this section. Additional rules may be used to detect when policies are violated. These are discussed under "monitoring" below.

Objectives

Objectives are defined by management, in particular not only in strategic planning but also in response to concerns by the governing body. Objectives are to be measurable and time limited. This can be expressed as rules that determine if the enterprise has failed to meet an objective, and additional rules might raise attention to objectives where appropriate progress is not being achieved. Current measurements should be accessible from normal operating data. Rules can be evaluated at appropriate times and report if progress is not satisfactory or if the objective has been achieved or failed.

Approval Levels

For some persons, an action may not be authorized without approval by another person. There is typically one of several reasons for approval: (1) exception to a policy; (2) restriction of level of financial authority; (3) restricted access authorization; (4) requirement for separation of responsibility; (5) approval of a deliverable, particularly a project plan, acquisition, design or product; and (6) application of special expertise or responsibility.

Each of these requirements for approval can be expressed as rules to be inserted in business processes where authorization is required. A request for authorization may need to be escalated to reach a manager with appropriate authorization.

Security Authorization

A complementary authorization service is required for access control. A service should determine that requests are properly authorized which may include not only actions by requestors but also, when necessary, independent approval of a request. This requires a different process for application of authorization policies. Authorization is discussed in detail in Chapter 7.

Monitoring

Determination if an enterprise is "doing the right thing and doing it well" requires that the governing body monitor the actions, effects, and circumstances of the enterprise. Some of this is accomplished by reviewing financial reports, reports of exceptions as noted above, and other management reports. However, other mechanisms are needed to raise attention to other exceptions and external developments that indicate a need for special consideration. Here we consider the use of rules for monitoring under five topics: performance, level of service, threat recognition, time exceptions, and alerts.

Performance

Certain operational performance measures should be reported for normal business management. Reductions of customer satisfaction and profit will always be a concern. Significant variance in performance measurements, such as cost and defects, will be of concern. Triggers can evaluate measurements against acceptable levels of variance for all operations to report a need for attention. These detailed variances will be addressed by the responsible managers. Governance monitoring may focus on significant variance in end product value measurements as cause for attention. As necessary, with a value stream model (such as with VDML), these can be traced back to the responsible activities.

Level of Service Agreements

The agile enterprise will share capabilities as services. These may be out-sourced as well as internal services. All services must have level of service agreements so that the consumers of those services have a clear understanding of what they can expect and how it will affect their areas of responsibility.

Furthermore, actual performance of services should be tracked and reported for management oversight. Rules can be added to these reporting facilities or as triggers on an associated database to provide governance reporting of variances from the level of service agreements. In the alternative, periodic governance reports should highlight service level exceptions.

Time Exceptions

Time exceptions are situations when something is expected to happen and it is late or does not occur. Some time exceptions can be identified from records of activities and can be reported periodically or identified by database triggers. On the other hand, time events in BPMN or timer event listeners (CMMN) can be set to act when an expected action is over-due.

Time exceptions can be important for monitoring performance from a number of perspectives. For example, a time event could be set to report when delivery time for a product or service exceeds an acceptable duration. A time event can report when an objective is not achieved on time. A time event can report when supplier shipments are late. Some such delays may always be important, while others will be of interest when there is a particular area of concern to be monitored. Particularly serious delays should result in alerts that get immediate attention of top management with follow-up reporting to the governing body.

Ecosystem Alerts

Many factors of concern to the governing body are a result of changes in the enterprise ecosystem, such as economic factors, market demand, commodity and critical resource prices, international conflicts, disruptions in the power grid or Internet, and competitor announcements of pricing changes or new products.

Some of these factors, such as stock market indexes, can be monitored by reporting from specialized services that can provide regular updates. Rules or neural networks can be applied to identify significant trends and exceptions.

Other factors may require monitoring volumes of data such as publications, sales data or web clicks to discover announcements, trends, and world events that may affect challenges and opportunities for the enterprise. Recent advances in distributed computing, now called *analytics*, have made it possible to analyze large volumes of data in a short time. More recent advances have made it possible to analyze continuous streams of data from multiple sources. These data may be in different formats including unstructured data and images.

Many threats can only be recognized by human awareness of events in the world around us. However, rules can help recognize some forms of threat.

Market activity can be monitored from sales and other internet sources. Rules can be used to recognize significant changes in prices or demand. Analytics can be used to monitor trends from sales data for trends in market demand. Commodity prices can also be tracked to detect significant shifts, particularly commodities that have a direct impact on production of the enterprise.

Analytics techniques can be used to scan industry publications for research advances and competitor product announcements. Analytics is discussed further in Chapter 6.

ADMINISTRATION OF BUSINESS POLICIES AND RULES

Effective specification and management of business rules can ensure consistency in operating practices and compliance with policies, governance, and regulatory requirements. The ability to change and quickly deploy or modify business rules can have a significant impact on enterprise agility as well as the cost of implementation of changing regulations from political entities around the world.

We have talked about the many ways rules can be used to express decisions and constraints. Here we are concerned with rules that express business regulations or policies—*business rules* as opposed to *operational rules* that define operating efficiencies or practices and determine how a capability is applied. A control or decision that rises to an enterprise level of concern will be considered a business objective or policy.

A business objective of interest can be reported as achieved by a rule implemented as a database trigger for notification when a variable has reached a critical level. An objective may also be of concern when there is a failure to maintain a desired level or to achieve a desired result by a target date. It is appropriate that these objectives be observed in the dashboard of the concerned business leader(s). In general, such objectives are of temporary interest to particular stakeholders and, as opposed to policies, objectives do not, per se, control business operations.

Regulations come from outside the enterprise and policies come from top management and/or the governing board. Regulations must be interpreted as policies that are specific to the particular enterprise. To the extent their implementation may be automated, these should be expressed as computer-readable *business rules* that express the automated decision criteria. The regulations, policies, and rules should be centrally managed to ensure consistency and timeliness of rule implementation or change. Business rules will frequently affect different parts of the organization, possibly in different ways. Whenever a policy is changed, it is necessary to identify and adapt all the relevant rules.

A capability map, a taxonomy of capabilities (the capability library in VDML), provides a framework for identification of capabilities relevant to a policy. If there are many relevant capabilities, it may be appropriate to consider creation of a shared capability to implement the policy and engage that capability from the many affected capabilities. This is particularly true if implementation of the policy is complex, such as the implementation of rule-based reasoning.

Policies in VDML

To the extent a policy affects collaborations, activities, and deliverable flows, VDML can provide a context for the implementation of policies. Generally, such a policy will affect the flow of deliverables—a policy decision will produce an alternative flow. VDML can express the policy condition and define an alternative deliverable flow to resolve the policy violation or constraint.

However, additional deliverable flows may be avoided as too much detail in a VDML model where a policy violation flow should never occur, but the relevance of a policy can be included as an annotation on the affected activity. In addition, a policy may be characterized as a practice and can be represented in the VDML Practice Library for cross-referencing.

In general, a VDML model will assist in the identification of relevant value stream(s) and capability(s) that may be affected by a policy. Resources or deliverables that are referenced in the rules will also suggest relevant capabilities and activities (those that consume or deliver). This includes value streams in product development where product design and production engineering decisions may affect regulatory compliance, as well as value streams of support services such as purchasing, receipt and storage of materials, maintenance of equipment, and so on. Each relevant value stream should be examined to find the earliest point where a rule should be applied to avoid rework or the consequences of noncompliance. The value stream also supports consideration of the impact of the policy on customer values. The customer value impact may be a basis for reconsideration of the policy, reconsideration of the way the policy is translated to rules, or consideration of changes to the structure of the value stream or the product.

In addition, where the consequences of violation may be more severe, it would be appropriate to apply rules prior to potential occurrence of the undesirable consequence. For example, if there are regulations that apply to a product, it may be appropriate to inspect finished products for compliance prior to shipment. This may reveal a circumstance where an early stage restriction was overlooked. This is a particular concern where there has been a significant product or business change.

There may be multiple capability methods for implementation of a policy. For example, an employee termination policy should require termination of any authority for access to information or participation in operations. Similarly, a new assignment should result in reconsideration of existing authorizations. These controls may require not only a rule, but the initiation of a process to effect the required changes to role and authorization records. This requirement could be driven by a trigger on the employment record. While this might be considered a data integrity issue, the scope of effect is broad, and there may be some discretion required regarding the propagation of changes and the timing of their effect.

Mapping business policies and rules to capability methods and business processes will also provide the opportunity to recognize where policies may overlap or conflict. Note that not all policies will be implemented with rules. Some policies will affect the way processes are structured, the way activities are performed, or the way resources are allocated, including people, machines, and materials.

Ecosystem Conditions

A policy may require attention to certain market events or trends. The criteria for identification of changes of interest may be expressed as policies or rules. The translation of these requirements for analysis will be in internal responsibility of the analytics or enterprise intelligence service unit. These should be addressed by the Sense and Respond Directory discussed in

Chapter 9. If a relevant new or revised law or regulation is under consideration or has been adopted, this will be a situation to be reported in the Sense and Respond Directory. Such changes may affect not only activities and decisions but may require specific actions to achieve compliance of existing facilities, products, contracts, records, or other business items.

Consolidation of Control

It is desirable that implementation of policies and rules should have rapid effect. For example, consider an enterprise policy that "returns must be in original packaging, accompanied by the original receipt and received within 30 days of the sale." Suppose that a competitor starts a holiday season campaign drawing attention to their policy that "returns must be in original packaging suitable for resale, goods must be current stock items, and refunds without receipts are in the form of a gift card." It may be important to quickly implement a more accommodating policy to avoid potential lost business, particularly during the holiday season. This could take days if not weeks if there are different retail systems for different lines of business.

Consolidation of business control functions can provide a greater opportunity for rapid deployment of rules or codification of complex decisions. For example, computation of billing for specialized services might be a time-consuming manual process performed by individual, field service units, whereas consolidation of the billing function as a shared service might justify the development of a consolidated billing unit or an expert system solution. This is similar to the use of purchasing, accounting, and personnel services to control vendor selection, ensure control of financial records, and achieve consistency in personnel administration throughout the enterprise.

Regulations and Policies Directory

A Regulations and Policies Directory is needed to support an enterprise unit for administration of regulations and policies. Regulations must be interpreted to determine policies that are relevant to the particular enterprise, and policies must be expressed as rules that are precise expressions of intent and that can define relevant circumstances and be analyzed for overlaps and gaps. A policy may require multiple rules applicable in different contexts. The resulting rules must be deployed wherever they are appropriate, throughout the enterprise.

The Regulations and Policies unit must consider requirements for compliance with regulations and identify the appropriate organizations and processes where associated rules apply. From an enterprise perspective rules should be associated with capability offers. Capability offers identify not only the capability but the organization unit responsible for the capability and thus the organization unit responsible for application of the rule.

Relevant capabilities may be identified by analysis of value streams as discussed above, or by identification of other factors such as resources or deliverables affected by a policy. These are associated with capabilities where the policies may be applicable.

The directory must provide the linkage between regulations, policies, and rules. In the context of a VDM model, the implementation of policies and rules can be traced to capability offers and activities of capability methods, if appropriate. The VDM capability offers, methods, and activities are expected to align to operational models of service units, processes, and activities. Consequently, regulations can be traced to deployment in processes and activities, and the rules that implement policies (and regulations where applicable) can be linked back to the policy or rule that is the basis of the rule.

The Regulations and Policies Directory might also be the basis for analysis of the relationships between regulations and policies to consider overlaps, conflicts, and gaps. Rules reference business entities, attributes, and relationships in the rule condition expressions. The rule conditional expressions should reference these business entities, attributes, and relationships consistent with the enterprise logical data model as discussed in Chapter 6. Rules that reference the same business entities are related, so similar rules may be found by examining rules that reference some or all of the same business entities, and rule relationships can be further refined by identifying the references to attributes and relationships. There are various techniques for analysis of the relationships between conditional expressions (eg, using Venn diagrams).

MOVING FORWARD

Rules have a significant impact in chapters that follow. They define data integrity constraints, database triggers for events, and criteria for analytics in Chapter 6. They are fundamental to specification of access control in Chapter 7. They define events of interest and event notice routing in Chapter 8.

Chapter **6**

Enterprise Data Management

Data are the lifeblood of the enterprise. Without data there can bc no coordinated activity, no record of accomplishments, no ability to solve problems, and no plans for the future. Management of data is a critical responsibility and becomes increasingly critical as enterprises become international and require greater agility.

Data are the elemcntal form of enterprise information and knowledge. When presented in a useful form and context, data become information. When that useful form provides insights on experience, behavior, and solutions, it becomes knowledge. In this chapter, we are concerned with the management of data, involving capture, validation, transformation, storage, communication, and coordination of operations to provide information and knowledge in the pursuit of enterprise objectives. While data exist in many forms—on paper, in conversations, as measurements—here we are concerned with data in electronic form, communicated, stored, and computed electronically.

In this chapter, we will focus primarily on the data management architecture (DMA) for the agile enterprise. We will then discuss metadata—data about data—that is important to the structure, meaning, and credibility of data. Finally, we will consider a general approach to enterprise transformation to implement the DMA.

DATA MANAGEMENT ARCHITECTURE

The DMA defines the components and relationships that participate in the creation, storage, communication, and presentation of data in an agile enterprise. In the agile enterprise, data are stored in distributed databases that are contained and maintained by associated service units. All accesses to a database are performed by the service unit. A service unit is the master source of some of the data in its database, it may replicate some of its data from other service units, and it may manage some data for its internal operations. Data are shared, primarily, through the exchange of messages through the Intranet.

Building the Agile Enterprise. http://dx.doi.org/10.1016/B978-0-12-805160-3.00006-5

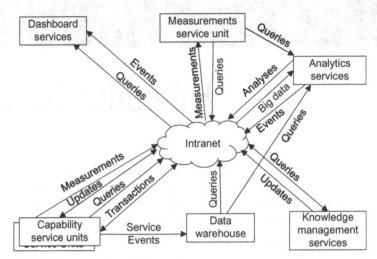

■ **FIG. 6.1** Data management architecture overview.

An overview of the architecture is depicted in Fig. 6.1. All of the rectangles represent service units. The underlying technical infrastructure is defined in Chapter 3, and details of notification requirements are discussed in Chapter 8. In the following sections, we will begin with a discussion of the general patterns and principles associated with this architecture, followed by discussions of each of the components depicted in Fig. 6.1.

General Patterns and Principles

There are several general patterns and principles that are key to the operation of the agile data architecture:

- Data ownership
- Service unit groups
- Data encapsulation
- Data sharing
- Access locking
- Legacy systems
- Outsourcing
- Legal records
- Data compatibility

These are discussed in the sections that follow.

Data Ownership

Each database is managed by a service unit that owns primary responsibility for the security, integrity, recoverability, and residency (geographical location) of the data. The database contains data for which the service unit is the master source along with data obtained from other service units and data created locally to support the service unit operation.

The agile enterprise will have many service units and thus many databases. The increased number of databases and frequency of shared data exchanges are enabled by internet technology, advances in middleware technology, and increased communications bandwidth.

The master data of a service unit may be data on a specific subject, or it may be a subset of data of a particular subject. For example, order management may be performed by different implementations of an order management service unit that serves different countries. Each service unit is then the master source for orders originated in its assigned geographical area.

Data Encapsulation

Every database or other form of data storage is accessed only by a service unit that is the data owner. This hides the particular data storage structure and technology from other users of the data, and it provides the opportunity to control access and the integrity of updates to the data. Every service *unit* has associated shared data and includes the services necessary for accessing the data and accepting updates.

Data elements for widely referenced business entities, such as customers, suppliers, employees, products, and the organization structure, each may be maintained in one or more independent service units.

Service Unit Groups

Service units may be clustered in a *service unit group* where they provide similar capabilities for economies of scale in the management of resources and technology. A group may share a database. When a database is shared by multiple service units, each of the supported service units has ownership responsibility and control for a portion of the database.

The service units of a service unit group must be managed by a common parent organization. This common manager has responsibility for the sharing of data between the service units. This group organization may improve performance by supporting sharing of data between the service units without replication that requires coordination of updates, but the cluster should, nevertheless, involve service units with similar capabilities that together represent a more general capability.

Data Sharing

A service unit will respond to the authorized queries against its master data, and it will honor requests for events to be generated when selected master data elements change. These change notices may be generated by actions of the service unit, but the notices can be managed more effectively if they are initiated by database triggers.

Master data may be requested from a service unit as needed, but for operating efficiency, a receiving service unit may store and maintain a replica of selected data obtained from the master source. Notices of change will keep the replicated data current (see notification service discussion in Chapter 8). The use of replication of data will depend on the frequency at which a receiving service unit must access the data, the frequency of updates to the data, and the volume of data that meet the recipient requirements.

Note that a service unit may associate local data with a business data entity without necessarily sharing all the data associated with the business entity. For example, the line items of an order might be replicated in the production service unit, while the status and operational detail associated with each line item remains local to the production service unit.

Access Locking

If synchronization is critical, requests to the master data service may require that data be retrieved from the master service unit with a lock (or "check-out" and later "check-in") that prevents changes to the locked data until the requester has completed the associated operation and releases the lock. A service unit may store data from another service unit without locking to reduce the need for frequent retrievals and locking of stable data elements. However, without locking, there is a risk that the retrieved copy will become out of synchronization with the master, while another operation relies on an updated version of that data. Notices of changes will provide the opportunity to update the copy, but then it is still possible that the recipient has already relied on obsolete data.

Locks should be avoided if at all possible due to the risk of performance consequences to other services that would be locked out and the risk that interactions of multiple lock requests could result in a deadlock.

For example, consider if A obtains a lock on X and B obtains a lock on Y, then B requests a lock on X which is suspended pending release by A, and

A requests a lock on Y that is suspended pending a release by B. Both A and B are then suspended pending further action by the other.

Legacy Systems

Some service units may be implemented as interfaces to legacy systems or purchased software that has not been designed for compatibility with the enterprise architecture. Data from these different sources must be accessible and combinable to provide a consistent view of enterprise operations. The service unit must provide an interface appropriate to its services and the data that are associated with it as a master data owner. The service unit(s) must ensure that the legacy system respects the ownership of master data of other service units. Compatibility is achieved through message transformation, discussed in Chapter 3.

Outsourcing

Services may be outsourced at a variety of levels of granularity. For example, a service could be as simple as a stock market query about a current stock price, or it may be outsourcing of a complex set of services that provide a major portion of the human resource management business function. Where the outsourcing represents a substantial business function, it includes management of enterprise master data, such as employee records in the case of human resource management outsourcing, and it may involve one or more external service units. Those service units, for the most part, will be capability service units, delivering business services, as discussed later.

The objectives for outsourced services should be the same as for corresponding internal service units. Services should have well-defined interfaces that are independent of whether the services are internal or outsourced. If the outsourcing is a substantial business function, it conceptually includes a number of service units characterized as service unit groups.

If the outsourcing provider implements best practices, the service interfaces should be consistent with service interfaces that its competitors either have or will have in the future. The outsourcing provider must provide access to its service units for sharing data that are needed or provided by other users within the client enterprise. For example, in the case of HR outsourcing, the client will need access to employee records along with a variety of services related to employment, benefits, compensation, and so forth, depending on the scope of the outsourcing.

Implementation of business capabilities as services should minimize the changes necessary for implementation of outsourcing. However, management of master data by the outsourced services must be reconciled with the internal service units that share that data. The internal organization responsible for management of the outsourcing relationship must have ownership responsibility for the outsourced master data.

The interfaces of the outsourced service unit(s) must continue to be supported for access to the outsourced capabilities and data. It may be necessary for the interface implementation to generate events and manage locks for changes to shared master data, and process updates for data from other sources.

Legal Records

The enterprise will receive and create electronic records that have legal effect, including internal records that involve authorization of transfers of assets or expenditures. These records should be represented in XML with electronic signatures. Some will also be encrypted for confidentiality. XML is discussed further regarding message exchange later. See the discussion of encryption and electronic signatures in Chapter 7.

These records must be preserved in their original form for the signatures and encryptions to remain valid. It is the responsibility of the service unit that creates the record or receives the record from an external source to preserve the original form along with a decrypted copy for internal sharing and processing. Some records will be cumulative, with cumulative signatures. Each extended record must be viewed as a new version of the record.

Data Compatibility

Throughout the enterprise, shared data must be compliant with a shared enterprise logical data model (ELDM), discussed further in the later section on metadata. The format of messages as exchanged must be consistent, but the format can be reconciled by the message exchange middleware discussed in Chapter 3. A service unit may use different internal formats for shared data and manage additional data elements and structures that are not shared.

However, shared data must not only have consistent elements and semantics (the meanings) but also represent a consistent point or period in time. Conventional enterprise applications control the relationships between the data they manage so that, within the scope of the enterprise application, data retrieved for a particular view are consistent. In contrast, service units are loosely coupled and must ensure that their database elements, particularly measurements, are consistent in time.

For example, some measurements may be accumulated weekly, while others are monthly. These measurements cannot be converted from one interval to the other.

Export Regulation

Enterprises often have operations in multiple countries. Many countries have laws or regulations that restrict the export of certain categories of data across their borders. This is particularly true for data related to personal privacy. The development of cloud computing has added the risk that such data could be deployed to a cloud computing node in a different country for workload balancing or to compensate for failure of another node.

Standards for control of data residency are currently under consideration in the OMG (Object Management Group). One approach could be to tag potentially sensitive data so that restrictions can be applied by the message exchange service based on the regulatory requirements affecting communication from the sender location to the receiver location. An attempt to send a message in violation of an export regulation should be detected at the sender. Of course this also requires that the message exchange facility knows the current geographic locations.

Capability Service Units

A capability service unit implements business capabilities and contributes to value streams.

Life-Cycle Ownership

Typically, a service receives a business request to produce a product or service for an external or internal customer. The request is pending until either it fails or the desired result is delivered. The service owns the request for the life-cycle of the request. This supports updates of the associated master data.

Consequently, a service retains responsibility for a request until all work is completed. Instead of transferring responsibility, the service unit delegates to service units that contribute to fulfillment of the request. The service unit that receives a request is the service unit that delivers the result.

In traditional, silo-based business systems, a request will be accepted by an organization and associated system, and when that organization's work is completed, it will transfer responsibility for continued work to the next organization. So each of these organizations has responsibility for a segment in the request life-cycle and thus responsibility for maintaining the associated master data.

Under certain circumstances, a request will be received as an asynchronous message that initiates another value stream, typically to deal with exceptions or support services. These have the form of a transfer of control. The service unit that accepts that transfer of control is then responsible for the life-cycle of that request for action. See the example in Bottom-Up Analysis in Chapter 3.

The service unit that receives a request is responsible for the master data records for that request. However, note that each of the service units engaged to contribute to the work receives its request and has life-cycle responsibility to resolve that request. As a result, a query for the status of a primary transaction is directed to the primary service unit that may, in turn, propagate the request through active delegations to provide more detail about the current status unless the delegation services send updates to the master data of the primary service. So the whole truth about a particular order, person, or product design may require propagation of a query to multiple service unit databases.

The identifier of the original request should be part of the request to each of the delegated services. This allows for data about a particular stage of processing to be requested directly from the service unit that performed that work.

Data Warehouse Support

Data on selected service events are sent to the data warehouse. These will be used for analysis of trends in performance and product or resource demand. The specific events and the scope of the event notices delivered to the data warehouse will depend on the value streams and business requirements for the data warehouse to support data analyses.

Measurement Reporting

Capability service units are the sources of value contributions. Measurements of value contributions may be taken at appropriate points in a service unit to correspond to collaborations and activities in the enterprise value delivery model. The level of granularity may vary depending on the level of concern and the ability of the process management services to capture appropriate measurements.

Potentially, detailed measurement reporting would be turned on when a particular value stream or capability is of particular interest and turned off when only high-level performance reporting is needed.

Measurements

The value measurements service unit captures individual value measurements and may report the latest measurement from a particular source, or it may develop statistical measurements for a period of time. If only a current measurement is reported, it may be appropriate to also report the variance for the last "n" reported measurements.

Note that in the long term, value measurements should be reported for value streams beyond the mainstream production operations so that various support services may also be monitored.

The measurements are in the context of the current value delivery model. This supports queries and reports on current and statistical measurements of performance of activities, capability methods, and value stream value propositions in the context of the current business design.

Note that this places a data capture requirement on the processes or activities being measured. A process that is engaged as a shared service must be measured in each of the contexts in which it is engaged. The measurements will differ depending on the requests. At the top-level process, some of the measurements for subprocesses can be taken from the results of activity that engages the subprocess assuming they can be and are measured at that level. If there are several levels of delegation with significant variance in performance from unit-to-unit of production, then performance may be difficult if not impossible to understand without the detail of the lower-level processes.

There should be a direct mapping between the VDM model capability methods and the operational business processes. The value types to be measured should be determined by stakeholder priorities.

Measurements should be captured for different scenarios, so there may be different measurements depending on product mix, production rate, and other relevant differences in circumstances. The modeling environment should enable business leaders to examine the differences between scenarios and monitor greater detail in areas of particular interest.

The value measurements service should also support tracking particular measurements for trends, variances, exceptional occurrences, and status related to objectives.

Separate value delivery models can represent to-be business configurations with measurement objectives for business transformation.

Data Warehouse

A data warehouse supports analysis of current and historical service events to identify trends, events, and correlations for insights on business operations and market patterns (based on customer orders). Current technology should support more timely and relevant data analyses.

Traditional Mode of Operation

Under established business intelligence services, a data warehouse receives inputs of events from business services as well as other sources and updates its database for an integrated view of the data. Inputs are typically taken as periodic batch extracts from production systems. The general assumption is that the cross-enterprise reporting is not time critical, so periodic updates provide data that are sufficiently current.

The process for feeding a data warehouse is often called *extract transform load* because the relevant data must be extracted from the production systems, transformed to a common format, and loaded in an appropriate manner to be reconciled with data from other sources. Transformation may include "cleansing" the data and merger of related data from different sources. The OMG Common Warehouse Metamodel (CWM, http://www.omg.org/technology/documents/modeling_spec_catalog.htm#CWM) specification provides a standard for modeling the transformation of data from different sources and different format technologies.

Agile Enterprise Data Warehouse

The agile enterprise supports more timely data warehouse analysis by accepting events as they occur. Unlike traditional data warehouse implementations, the agile enterprise data warehouse is limited to capture of internal events provided by capability service units and data from other sources are received by the analytics service unit. Possible events include initiation of a process, completion of a process, or completion of an activity within a process. Not all service events at all levels are of interest, so output of event notices should be turned on for events of interest.

The data warehouse provides these data for analysis by the analytics service unit. We include traditional *business intelligence services* under the heading of *analytics*. The measurements service unit provides another perspective for support of analytics.

BUSINESS METADATA

The integration of data from multiple sources involves data of differing quality and reliability. Within a single service unit, the quality and reliability of that service unit's data may be well understood, but as the users of data become more remote from the sources, the users may not understand the inaccuracies that can occur in the data they are using for analysis, planning, and decision making. Business metadata, such as the sources and credibility of data, should be captured with the data records being reported. Metadata is discussed further in a later section.

Analytics

Analytics refers to new mathematical and computational techniques for identification of important insights and opportunities from analysis of large volumes of data. Traditionally, data analysis has required substantial time investment in data collection and analysis, and it has been limited by availability of relevant data. More recently, large volumes of data have become available from many sources through the Internet and wireless communications. This includes data from tracking web activity, sensors, social media, and market activity. The Internet of Things will make large volumes of data available from a multitude of devices connected to the Internet.

Distributed computing technology has made it possible to rapidly analyze large volumes of data including unstructured text. Hadoop (http://hadoop.apache.org/) is an open source software product based on technology developed by Google for processing very large data sets in distributed computing clusters. The result is massively parallel computing that produces results in a fraction of the time required for conventional systems.

Various analytical techniques are built on top of Hadoop to analyze all forms of data: structured, semistructured (such as XML), and unstructured.

Analytics associated with "big data" has become an important aspect of strategic planning. However, it does require an investment, so the analyses should be focused on insights that available data can support and on issues that have value to the enterprise. The technology as well as the availability of useful big data are still evolving.

The agile DMA brings together three perspectives for analytics:

1. Big data provide access to specific, detailed events or actions both inside and outside the enterprise. The relevant events will depend on the industry and the particular enterprise.
2. The data warehouse service unit captures data from capability service events to support analyses of operational, customer, and supplier behavior.
3. The measurements service unit reflects operational performance that can be captured and analyzed at a range of levels of detail, for values including costs, timeliness, and quality measurements.

Business leaders should focus attention on aspects of the business that would have a significant impact on the business if business-as-usual assumptions were no longer valid. Assumptions may be related to customer demand, current technology, economic conditions, customer satisfaction, changing cost factors, changes in competition, and so on. Some analyses need only be performed periodically to discover and confirm patterns. Other concerns may call for continuous monitoring. Business leaders should work closely with analytics experts to identify meaningful analyses that may have a significant business impact.

In the final analysis, analytics is about mitigation of risk—risk of delayed response to a disruptive change, or risk of a missed opportunity that could have been revealed through a deeper understanding of an evolving business. Analytics does not provide business solutions, but it provides the basis for innovations and better decisions.

Dashboard Services

The agile enterprise architecture drives centralization of many planning and decision-making activities to ensure effective integration of services, optimize performance from an enterprise perspective, maintain or improve enterprise agility, and support governance. This strengthening of enterprise management and governance requires that enterprise leaders at multiple levels have access to a wealth of data from many sources and the ability to combine data from those different sources to gain appropriate insights and ensure accountability and control.

The dashboard concept arose from the vision of business leaders having real-time readings on what is happening in the business and the ecosystem so that the business can be driven with greater insight and agility in response to disruptions and emerging risks and opportunities. The dashboard service unit provides readings on business performance and opportunities that require management attention along with access to data for optimization and transformation of the business.

The dashboard must not just display raw data but must display data in context. The enterprise VDM model is a primary context for internal operating data. Additional models are needed for the context of market data, business transformation management, financial data, regulatory compliance indicators, and data on human resource management.

Dashboards must be tailored to the needs of individual business leaders. A dashboard should be initially configured by a technical support person, but it should provide controls that enable the user to refine the configuration as required to tap into and display events and measurements from selected services. The business leader should be able to identify certain measurements, trends, or events for continuous tracking; set alarms triggered by variance beyond expected or allowed limits; and look deeper into the models, ad hoc, to explore relevant factors. They should be able to selectively monitor certain business measurements or events and set thresholds for alerts.

Knowledge Management Services

Enterprise agility requires access to shared knowledge about how the enterprise works as well as knowledge that provides the basis for achieving optimization of operations and competitive advantage. Knowledge management involves the identification, retention, and retrieval of relevant insights and experiences. Much of this enterprise knowledge is in the heads of the enterprise's employees. Some of it has been or can be captured in textual documents. Still less has been codified in business rules and models. Knowledge management is critical to enterprise agility because it provides insights for determining what changes are needed and how to make them.

The primary challenge of knowledge management is to support knowledge capture and access and to engage the right people to contribute needed knowledge.

Traditionally, relevant documents and subject matter experts were managed within a departmental silo, often at a single office location. With a capability-based architecture, these functional capabilities are divided into more granular, shared services. The services may be geographically distributed, and some employees may work from home so there may be little informal, face-to-face contact. In addition, in support of adaptation initiatives, it is necessary to share knowledge more widely so that many factors can be considered to optimize from an enterprise perspective.

Knowledge management services, identified in Fig. 6.1 and discussed later, represent key aspects of the broader concept of knowledge sharing. Knowledge is an asset of the enterprise, but much of it is in the heads of its employees and will continue to be. Some of it can be captured for more effective sharing and to mitigate losses that result from employee turnover. Some knowledge can be encoded in computer applications as business rules (discussed in Chapter 5). Business models are also another form of structured knowledge. We have discussed business models in Chapters 2 and 4, and we focus on business models again in Chapters 9 and 11. Some individuals with expertise related to business capabilities can be identified by their current roles in VDM and BCM models and their contributions to knowledge management conversations and documents.

Here we focus on knowledge captured in electronic conversations and textual documents using existing practices and technologies. Both of these involve knowledge in text that is subject to web-search technology and analytics.

Knowledge Conversations

There are two popular forms of electronic conversations: email and group discussions. Both of these are based on communications among members of an interest group. An interest group has a web page that identifies the area of interest, the list of members, any access restrictions, and a form to apply for membership in the interest group. The web page should provide access to the email threads and discussions described below as well as the knowledge documents discussed later.

The interest group membership should be limited to enterprise employees. Members of an interest group should be self-selecting except that participation in some groups must be authorized if the interest group deals with restricted subject matter.

Email Threads

Email threads occur frequently between two or more participants with a common interest. Participants often share significant insights. This knowledge sharing should be captured and cataloged by the enterprise for future reference.

Each interest group, discussed above, should have a group email distribution list used to deliver relevant emails. An interest group member may have an insight to share and send a message to the interest group. More often, a member will have a question or an issue to resolve and will send an email for suggestions or opinions. In either case, the subject line should identify the topic to be discussed, and it becomes the identifier of the thread. The interest group web page should track all active threads by subject line. A member should be able to select an active thread to join.

Participants may come and go as the thread evolves. An email contributor may add a potentially interested, nonmember participant to a thread to join the discussion. Another participant may determine that the topic is not of interest to him or her, and opt out of the thread. All messages are captured and accessible from the interest group web page by all employees unless the interest group is restricted.

A participant in a thread may create a branch thread by changing the subject to a new topic. Members of the interest group should be notified of initiation of the new thread and opt in if they are interested. The original thread and the branch may both continue with the same participants, but each should be true to the topic in its subject line.

Group Discussions

Members of an interest group should also have the option of participating in a discussion where their comments on a particular topic are captured, in sequence on a web page. This service is patterned after LinkedIn and similar services.

A member can initiate discussion on a topic that will be announced to other members in the interest group. Any member that contributes a comment to the topic is optionally notified of subsequent comments by email. A discussion is closed if there are no new comments for a defined period such as a month (to allow for vacations or other distractions).

A branch discussion thread can be initiated to explore a new, related topic. The new topic is opened in a new web page and is announced to the interest group, so members can opt in. The contributors of the old topic continue to receive notices of comments to both the original and branch topics.

Knowledge Documents

Knowledge documents include two basic forms: authored documents and encyclopedia entries.

Authored Documents

An authored document is a natural language and/or a presentation file in a final form prepared by humans for human understanding. Authored documents address particular topics to support proposals, presentations, results of analyses, understanding of mechanisms, explanation of specifications, and capture of other knowledge of value for sharing and future reference. These data are just as important to the operation of the business as are structured data, but they are often given little attention from an IT perspective because they represent unstructured data.

Each document is given a unique identifier and a formatted header that includes the document type (from defined alternatives), tags for web search, an abstract, the author(s), the date created, a statement of the context (the associated project, initiative or other reason for development), links to previous and/or subsequent editions, and identification of relevant interest groups, the same as those discussed for conversations above. Each document is posted in a directory for the year in which it was created. Once an authored document is posted, it cannot be changed, but it may be linked to a newer edition.

Encyclopedia Entries

The encyclopedia is a wiki containing discussions of distinct topics. An employee may create a new topic with an associated discussion, a list of related, existing topics, and the identity of one or more of the relevant interest groups as defined for conversations above. The interest group members are notified of each new topic.

Persons interested in a topic may request notice of subsequent changes to the content. Anyone can add to or revise the topic content. The changes made by individual contributors are logged. Conflicting views should be included, identified, and subject to email discussion and potential resolution by an associated interest group.

METADATA

Metadata are data about data. Metadata are important for design of systems as well as for accountability and consideration of credibility. Metadata define the context of data and thus are essential to understanding the meaning of data. Consequently, metadata are an essential part of presenting data to users.

Metadata are a normal part of the technical design and operation of information systems. However, it is important to recognize that there are often additional business requirements for metadata. Metadata that specify the meaning and relationships of data elements are often called *technical metadata* because they are used for the design and implementation of systems. *Business metadata* refers to metadata that define the business context and quality of the data, such as the timeliness, source, and reliability. These metadata are important to business people because they can affect their reliance, interpretations, and resulting decisions.

For example, a customer order form provides metadata that describe the data fields. Data about the source, reliability, and timeliness of a record are metadata. Data about the structure of rules, neural networks, and business models are metadata. Computer programs are metadata although they are not usually described that way. So computers not only capture, store, and communicate data that represent things about the enterprise, but they also capture, store, and communicate data that specify what the data mean and what computers do with them.

In this section, we will discuss six forms of business metadata:

- Embedded metadata
- Data dictionaries

- Data directory
- Data virtualization
- Value delivery model
- Logical data model

Embedded Metadata

Individual records often contain some data that are about the data in the record. The most common is a time stamp, indicating when the record was created or changed. A record often contains the identifier for the person or device that created, changed, or approved the record. When a file, such as a document or a model, is created as a unit, then the file will have associated metadata. When a file or database contains records from different sources, it is often important to identify the source in the data for accountability, particularly if data from the different sources differ in quality.

Messages and other documents expressed in XML contain metadata. XML embeds identifiers of all data elements as well as data for encryption and signatures.

Data Dictionaries

Each database will have a data dictionary that defines the data elements, structures, and constraints of the database. In the DMA, there will be a separate database and associated data dictionaries for the database of each service unit or group of service units. Separate databases and data dictionaries are consistent with the hiding of service unit implementation and support the autonomy of a service unit, so changes can be made without reconciling the database design with other organizations.

Data Directory

Here, we define a *data directory* in the context of the DMA. The data directory contains the metadata needed to understand and manage the distributed databases and files of the DMA.

The data directory provides an overview of the data managed by each service unit including the master data managed by the service unit, and the data that is replicated from the master data of another service unit. It references the (ELDM, discussed below) to identify the business data entities. It identifies the business data entities of master data that is the responsibility of each service unit and it identifies the service units that also maintain replicas of the master data entities.

The data directory may include identification of the organization unit responsible for each service unit, and the geographical location of the service unit.

The data directory should include other business metadata that is not embedded in the actual data such as information about the quality and timeliness of the data. The data directory should also include data security requirements and information on data recoverability.

Data Virtualization

Data virtualization is software product capability that supports unified access to heterogeneous data sources in a form consistent with a unified data model such as the ELDM, discussed below. In the DMA, it will be desirable to perform queries that integrate data from multiple service units.

The data virtualization service requires that each service unit provide a mapping of its master data or any additional data that may be subject to queries to the associated elements of the enterprise master data model. This may include additional metadata that would be of interest to a requestor. The mapping specification may be based on the OMG CWM.

Note that the virtualization facility circumvents the rule that a database is hidden within its service unit and all accesses must go through the service unit. Updates through virtualization must be prohibited since that would undermine the control of the service unit to ensure data integrity. Queries must still be subject to access authorization, but access controls associated with the database may be sufficient. Queries might also be "depersonalized," so queries are unable to access data that could identify individual entities.

VDML Metadata

VDML represents two kinds of metadata: measure specifications and business items.

Measure Specifications

VDML captures value measurements. A Measure Library defines the measures, the Value Library defines the use of the measurements, and the VDML model defines the context in which these measurements occur. Various other VDML elements, such as participants, resources, and activities, may have associated measurements that describe their characteristics or behavior. For example, a store may record the number of business items waiting for an activity, or a deliverable flow may have a specified transit time.

The VDML model as context is important for reporting measurements of the Measurements Service Unit. Measurements received from business operations will be recorded on appropriate model elements. Users will look at the model to find relevant measurements.

Measurements may be captured in different contexts (eg, product mix or production rate) and associated with different VDML scenarios. The scenario defines the particular business context of the measurements.

These measurements may be reports of individual measures of occurrence (eg, one execution of an activity), or they may be statistical values with a mean and standard deviation representing the measurements during a period of time. Additional metadata may be associated with the VDML context element such as the source of the measurement. The association of measurements with activities, capabilities, and organization units provides identification of responsibility for performance measurements.

Business Items

Business item elements represent things that flow through activity networks and between collaborations. These may be records, orders, resources, products, parts, and so on. From a data modeling perspective, these are views based on a particular business entity. For example, a business item may be a customer order including order items, item detail, such as descriptions and prices, and a reference to the customer. The order is the key entity, identified by an order number, and the business item is represented as a nested data structure.

The VDML model does not include individual business items unless it has been extended to support simulation. The business item elements are described in the Business Item Library, and the data structure can be described to the extent it is relevant to the VDM analysis. The detail of the Business Item structure can be found in the ELDM. Additional metadata, such as data quality and range, may be included in the Business Item Definition and the data directory.

Enterprise Logical Data Model

The ELDM specifies the meaning, format, and relationships of all of the structured data of the enterprise that is exchanged between service units or is accessible through queries. It is an abstract metamodel, disassociated from the actual sources and storage of the data. *Physical* data models are used by technical people to define how the data are actually stored in databases as well as the data structures that may be exchanged by services and used within applications.

There must be an enterprise-wide understanding of the form and meaning of data exchanged, particularly since service user/provider relationships may be many to one or many to many and may change over time. The ELDM provides the common understanding for the exchange of data between service units and for management coordination, recordkeeping, planning, and decision-making activities.

Note that it is not essential that the business terms used to describe the data elements are the same throughout the enterprise, but the business concepts and the meaning of the data must be consistent. So data may be presented in a report or display in New York with English captions and annotations, and the same data may be presented in a report or display in Paris with French captions and annotations, and there need be no misunderstanding.

Development of an ELDM is a major undertaking, but some of the work has already been done. The enterprise would not function today if there were not some common understanding of the data in reports and records and the data communicated between systems. Sometimes the inconsistencies are not in the data per se but in what it is called in different departments. The current ability to exchange data requires that some degree of common understanding was developed in the past although that may not have been captured in a shared data model.

Industry Standards

From an industry perspective, understanding the data exchanged between enterprise applications was a major challenge of enterprise application integration. Suppliers of enterprise systems realized that the integration of their systems would be less costly and disruptive if they could exchange data consistent with a common data model, so they promoted the development of standards for exchange data. Many such standards were developed by the Open Applications Group, Inc. (OAGi).

Common data models are evident in industry standards such as those developed by the United Nations Centre for Trade Facilitation and Electronic Business, XML Business Reporting Language, and Human Relations XML. In the telecommunications industry, the TeleManagement Forum has developed a substantial ELDM called Shared Information/Data.

As the scope of electronic integration of the enterprise expands to include relationships with customers and suppliers, the scope of need for data consistency expands. When orders were exchanged, and coordination was accomplished by human-to-human communications, the people involved were able to compensate for inconsistencies, translating the terminology and the data formats as required. Computers are not so forgiving. Thus, there is a need for a shared specification for data exchange.

As a result of these forces, the world of information systems is converging toward a common LDM. Although new concepts emerge, we can expect this industry convergence to continue so that most differences will be only where innovative business solutions provide an enterprise with competitive advantage. For the most part, even significantly different business processes and product designs will use accepted interchange data models.

To the individual enterprise, industry convergence on a common data model reduces the cost of developing data models and database designs; reduces the cost of developing, maintaining, and executing data transformations; and improves the ability to measure and analyze operating performance and key indicators from an enterprise perspective. Consequently, it is the interest of every enterprise to align as much as possible to the emerging global logical data model.

Logical data models that should reflect the emerging common model are available as products for purchase or as a basis for consulting and integration services. Work on an ELDM should not start from scratch.

Data Modeling

In the meantime, each enterprise must establish and maintain an ELDM as the basis for exchange, storage, and retrieval of shared data. The primary form of enterprise data modeling is class models, generally associated with object-oriented programming and the Unified Modeling Language (UML, http://www.omg.org/spec/UML/2.4.1). These models provide a relatively robust way of representing business entities, their attributes, and their relationships. Implementations of computer applications usually employ relational databases, so for database technical design, entity-relationship modeling is more suitable, but we do not get into that level of detail here. We focus on class models that are the generally accepted form of logical data models.

A *class* defines the representation of similar persons, places, or things in the business domain. Class models rely on a concept called *inheritance*, whereby a class may inherit characteristics defined for a more general class. Fig. 6.2 illustrates a class diagram for a customer-order example. A class may represent a generalization of similar things, such as Customer, or it may be specialized to represent a more specific type of things, such as Retail

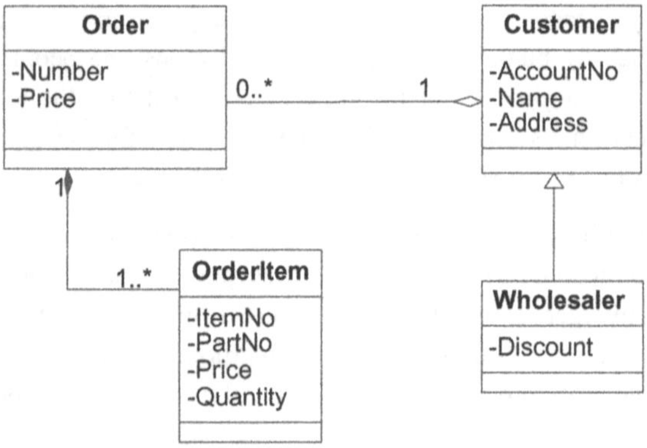

■ **FIG. 6.2** A class model.

Customer or Wholesaler. The more specialized class is said to *inherit* from the more general class, so characteristics of Customer are inherited by Wholesaler, as indicated by the open-headed arrow from Wholesaler to Customer in the diagram. This is a UML class diagram. UML is the generally accepted standard developed by OMG for modeling a number of aspects of an object-oriented application.

Inheritance provides a way to describe similarities between classes. Several different classes may inherit common characteristics from a shared parent class, or a specialized class may be defined as adding characteristics to a more general class. In the class diagram in Fig. 6.2, the Order, Customer, and Order Item classes show attributes of the classes within the boxes. The Wholesaler class is a specialization of Customer. Wholesaler inherits Account No, Name, and Address from Customer and has an additional attribute that is a discount specification that presumably is not meaningful for most customers. Wholesaler implicitly has all the other attributes and relationships of Customer, so a Wholesaler "is" a customer with an additional attribute. A Wholesaler can occur anywhere in a model or database that a Customer can occur. The numbers on the relationships indicate the *cardinality*, for example, an order must have one customer, but a customer can have zero or more orders (0..*).

The ELDM is represented with a class model, but the data may be expressed in different forms for storage and exchange. Generally, data exchanged between services are expressed in XML. Data stored in databases are most often in relational tables. Data warehouses have specialized data structures to support retrieval and analysis. Transformations between these and other representations can be modeled with tools based on the OMG CWM.

An ELDM must represent everything that may be shared through message exchanges, event notices, or queries. Service units may also include their local data since it will be related to the service unit master data and data it replicates from other service units. This may require thousands of classes, but not all these classes are implemented in a single database. A database stores the subset of the data that are of interest to the associated service unit or group of service units.

For example, in a manufacturing enterprise, incoming orders are captured by the order management service unit along with related sales and customer data. The order requirements are included in the delegation to the order fulfillment service unit, but without the sales and customer detail. The order fulfillment service unit will add data related to scheduling the order and may translate sales order specifications to production specifications before submitting the production request. During production, the production service unit may add data regarding the specific configuration, component serial numbers, or batches applicable to each order. So, as the order proceeds through fulfillment and closure of the sale, each of the service units will receive the data required to do their work and add data relevant to their work. Some data will ultimately be added to the completed master order in the sales organization and other data will be held as local, working data in the participating service units.

To get a comprehensive report on a customer order, it might be necessary to query several databases that hold data related to that order. When such reporting, analysis, or archiving occurs, the ELDM ensures that the data from different sources can be combined to produce a consistent representation and the meaning will be generally understood.

ENTERPRISE TRANSITION

The DMA suggests a major, technical restructuring associated with transformation of the enterprise. Here we take a brief look at key aspects of that transformation from a DMA perspective. The topics below are presented in approximate chronological order. See also the value delivery maturity model in Appendix A.

Messaging Infrastructure

The agile enterprise messaging infrastructure has been discussed in Chapter 3. It is fundamental to the integration of services. The infrastructure must include a notification broker to direct event notices to subscribers. Here we are concerned with communicating changes to data in databases.

These change notices may be needed to keep copies of data consistent with the master data, they may be needed to monitor status or measurements as they change, or they may be needed to initiate some action. More about the events and the notification broker is discussed in Chapter 8.

Requests for data transfers, the data transfers, and notices of updates should have a standard message format that is independent of the particular database technology.

Knowledge Management Service Unit

Work can start early to define interest groups, support conversations, capture documents, and support wiki authoring. There is minimal investment required in a supporting infrastructure, and the focus can be on providing incentives to contribute and web pages for collaboration.

ENTERPRISE LOGICAL DATA MODEL

The ELDM need not represent all of the data of the enterprise. The most important data are those exchanged in messages including event notices, data queries, and updates. The basic format of these messages must be defined. Data that are created and used within a service unit are less important, but individual service units must extend the ELDM to integrate the local data with the shared data. Within the shared-data subset, the initial focus should be on the application to shared services. Consideration also must be given to business metadata.

The starting point should be industry standards, where available. Purchase of an enterprise data model should be considered since it will provide a major step forward.

Preferred Database Management System

A database management system that supports triggers is an important component. Implementation hiding of service units includes the database and its management system, but support for triggers to support event generation will add significant value. In some cases, it will be worthwhile to consider conversion of the database of a legacy system to support triggers, particularly if that legacy system is to be "wrapped" in a capability service unit interface.

Opportunistic Service Unit Development

Service units should be developed based on opportunities for return on investment or competitive advantage. Some of these may be implemented by wrapping legacy systems with service unit interfaces; large applications may be configured as a virtual cluster of service units with a shared database. Each service unit will include supporting services for reporting status, responding to queries, requesting change notices, and so on. Consistent protocols should be defined for these supporting services for economies of development and integration of service units (see Chapter 9 regarding business transformation management). These supporting services may be implemented in phases depending upon the needs of services they support.

Data Warehouse Upgrade

If the enterprise has a data warehouse capability, it should be upgraded to accept service event notices as they occur rather than in batch. Priorities should be defined for tracking the events that provide the greatest potential business value. Existing systems as well as service units can be updated to generate event notices based on the priorities.

Analytics Service Unit

An initial analytics service unit organization should be established to provide analytics expertise, set priorities, and identify available sources of data. Initiatives should start small to implement some tools and develop working relationships, management appreciation of analytics, and insights on potential strategic opportunities. Development of an analytics capability is both a technical and a cultural challenge.

Data Directory

As service units are established, there will be an increasing need for information about the master data they each support and the services that replicate the master data. Additional metadata will also become increasingly important. A data directory service unit should be developed as the need emerges.

Value Delivery Model

Development of an enterprise VDM model requires a substantial investment. Value delivery modeling should start with a segment of a single line of business where there is a recognized need for improvement with measurable business value. The scope of the VDM model should evolve over time, driven by business value opportunities. The long-term goal is to develop and maintain a VDM model that represents the current state of the business and is the basis for modeling potential future states of the business.

Value Measurements

Output of value measurements should be part of the development of shared services. Priority measurements should be driven by customer value priorities. Measurement should focus on the results of business processes aligned with VDM model capability methods. Activity-level measurements may be developed later.

Although the current business structure may not be ideal, the VDM model collaborations should align with the current business process hierarchy so that VDM model measurements will reflect the actual performance of business operations. It is important for the VDM model to represent value streams that are being measured so that the measurements have the VDM model to define a context for the measurement data.

Model-Based Dashboards

Management dashboards should be developed to provide managers with access to up-to-date measurements and events. Measurements should be presented in the context of the VDM model and other models. The VDM model should provide support for viewing the broader business design context and related capabilities and measurements.

Investment in dashboard capabilities should proceed when there is a critical mass of measurements and events that are of interest to business leaders. Individual business leaders should not be introduced to dashboards if the dashboard does not provide more timely accurate and complete data of interest to the business leader by comparison to the information provided by their supporting staff.

MOVING FORWARD

Security is a fundamental concern for data management, and appropriate security mechanisms must be part of the data management infrastructure. Security is the focus of the next chapter.

7

Information Security

Fundamentally, information security is about managing risks associated with business records and information systems. With the advent of the public Internet and the World Wide Web, security risks have increased dramatically. Systems are exposed to public access and email messages can carry or link to corrupting software. Automation and electronic communications have added new dimensions to security concerns. Electronic integration extending beyond the walls of the enterprise has created additional security exposures. Security risks continue to evolve and expand as the scope of automation and integration expands.

CONVENTIONAL SECURITY

Many enterprises still have access control defined at an application level:

- *Identity management* uses local user identifiers.
- *Authentication* involves local user passwords.
- *Authorization* involves a local access control list for each user.
- *Access control* may be embedded in the application using the access control lists.
- *Accountability* may be implemented by an application tagging records with user identifiers and generating an audit trail.

Such approaches are only suited to small, closed communities of users. The design of security mechanisms has been delegated to technical people, and security administration has been delegated to technical and clerical people. But, even small, isolated systems are likely to be connected to the Internet and will be exposed to new risks. Managers often don't understand the nature of the risks and the necessary countermeasures until they experience failures.

INCREASED RISK FACTORS

Security cannot be sustained by adapting individual systems, particularly with development of an agile enterprise. Fragmented security systems increase complexity, diminish control, delay corrective action, and increase

Building the Agile Enterprise. http://dx.doi.org/10.1016/B978-0-12-805160-3.00007-7

209

security risks. Government regulations such as the Sarbanes-Oxley Act demand that managers take responsibility for ensuring accountability and control of enterprise assets and operations. Security is a fundamental aspect of accountability and control. Agility and efficiency require infrastructure consistency and thus consistency of security mechanisms. Capability-based architecture (CBA) supported by a service-oriented architecture (SOA) improves accountability and control through clarification of responsibilities, but sharing of services creates a number of new security concerns. Consistent architecture, technical infrastructure, and clarification of responsibility also bring with them opportunities for improving the quality, consistency, and timeliness of security measure implementations.

The fundamental security issues have not changed, and there are well-defined standards to address them. Nevertheless, the consistency, scale, and management participation necessary for an agile enterprise require significant technical investment and cultural transformation. Security is a major business risk factor for which top management as well as managers of each service unit must take responsibility and exercise control.

The following are sources of security risks of particular concern for the agile enterprise:

- *Expanded number of access points*. When organizations are divided into finer-grained service units, each of the services becomes a point of access from other systems and people. Each must have appropriate access controls.
- *Expanded communities of users*. Each of the more granular service units also has more users and more people interested in accessing data. These people may be in various organizations that would previously have been denied access. Each person must be identifiable, and authorization may involve a greater variety of specific restrictions.
- *Perimeter security*. It is no longer sufficient to protect against intrusions by creating barriers around the enterprise internal network. The internal network is typically accessible from many insecure sites, and there are an increasing number of internal points of access such as conference rooms and vacant offices.
- *Dynamic service relationships*. Service units can be replaced when responsibility is assigned to a new organization or new technology is installed. Service users should be redirected without disruption of service, but there must be assurance that redirection does not give access to an imposter.
- *Access across trust domains*. Some services require access from business partner or customer organizations that manage employee

identities, authorizations, and access control policies independently, so there must be a transformation from partner authorizations to appropriate internal authorization.

- *Electronic documents*. Paper is being replaced by electronic documents, which serve as the medium of exchange for assets and commitments between organizations both inside and outside the enterprise. Documents must be protected, and participants must be authenticated and accountable for their contributions and approvals.
- *Indirect access*. A user may request a service that in turn may access other services that the user might not otherwise be authorized to access.
- *Wireless and mobile devices*. Mobile devices carry data and are connecting to everything. They are connected through wireless communications that increase communication exposure.
- *Outsourcing*. Outsourcing can improve costs and response to new technology or business requirements, but at the same time, the enterprise must rely on the outsourcing provider to maintain an appropriate level of security.
- *Cloud computing*. Cloud computing potentially distributes applications and data around the world and shares computing and communications facilities with many people and organizations. In addition to exposure risks, international sharing raises new issues of regulatory compliance.
- *Business reconfiguration*. The agile enterprise can reconfigure the use of services to adapt to new challenges and opportunities, but change brings risk of new exposures, including new uses and adaptations of existing, shared services.

The purpose of this chapter is to provide an approach to management of security risks followed by an overview of security key technologies.

MANAGING SECURITY RISKS

Here, we begin with an overview of potential losses from security failures, followed by discussion of the sources of risk that can result in those losses, and, finally, measures for mitigation of the risks.

Potential Business Losses

Security does not contribute to the production of a product or service, rather security is about avoiding losses. Table 7.1 outlines six categories of potential business losses, and it identifies operational security risks that can result in these losses. We will briefly discuss the potential losses as a context for consideration of the operational risks.

Table 7.1 Potential Business Losses

Potential business losses	Operational Risks											
	Disclosure	Alteration	Unauthorized operations	Disruption	Destruction	Innovation exposure	Fraud	Repudiation	Denial of service	Data residency	Transition exposure	Residual content
Loss of assets	X	X	X				X	X			X	
Loss of productivity		X	X	X	X				X			
Time and cost of recovery		X	X	X	X						X	
Liability	X	X	X				X	X		X	X	X
Defamation		X					X					X
Competitive disadvantage	X	X		X	X	X			X			

Loss of Assets

This category focuses on financial losses that could be in the form of money or other things of financial value. Essentially, these losses are a result of an illegitimate transfer of ownership of assets.

Loss of Productivity

Various breaches of security may disrupt normal operation of the business causing delays and extra work to sustain operations. Essentially, costs are increased and results are delayed.

Time and Cost of Recovery

Recovery loss occurs when there is a failure or destruction of facilities or information where work products are lost and must be recreated, and the state of facilities and business operations must be restored. This includes the possibility the state of the enterprise cannot be fully restored.

Liability

Liability results from a breach of security that creates loss for another entity or entities such as customers, business partners, or others, including the possibility of identity theft. In addition, liabilities are created when the enterprise violates regulations where there may be enterprise or personal penalties.

Defamation

Defamation is any breach of security that causes damage to the enterprise reputation that may result in loss of business, lower credit rating, and disadvantage in business relationships due to loss of trust.

Competitive Disadvantage

Loss of competitive advantage may result from disclosure of proprietary information such as trade secret, strategic plans, business practices, or customer relationships that are elements of competitive advantage.

Operational Risks

Table 7.1 maps the above potential business losses to the types of operational risks that can result in these losses. The following paragraphs describe the possible risks. This is not an exhaustive list, but a reasonable starting point for analysis of risks.

- *Disclosure.* Disclosure of confidential data may occur through unauthorized access to a system or database or through obtaining access to a device (such as a laptop computer) or data storage medium (such as a compact disk or flash drive). Disclosure may result in liability to injured parties such as identity theft, or loss of business due to competitive disadvantage such as loss of good will or industrial espionage.

- *Alteration.* Data and programs may be altered by access to system storage, by alteration of data in communications, by entry of invalid data, or by a corrupted application. An application may be altered by installation of corrupt software, by downloading, or by intruder access through system vulnerabilities.
- *Unauthorized operations.* These involve the use of legitimate system functions without appropriate authority. Access might be by impersonation or by defective access control. In a shared services environment, unauthorized access might be accomplished by an authorized access that engages a supporting service that should not be accessible by the initial requester.
- *Disruption.* Disruption is when a system fails causing a direct or indirect halt of business operations. This could be a hardware failure, a power problem, a software failure, a software error, or a loss of communications.
- *Destruction.* Destruction is irreparable damage involving a loss of facilities and/or data. This may be the result of natural disaster, terrorism, or other physical event, but it could also be caused by a dysfunctional system that stores invalid data without a valid backup.
- *Intellectual property.* An enterprise can incur liability for unauthorized use of intellectual property such as proprietary software. Here, we are particularly concerned about patented computer-based solutions or copyrighted software. This may occur because an employee obtains protected software from the Internet or other source, or if protected software is inadvertently installed such as software included as a component of a supplier's software or an open-source product.
- *Fraud.* Fraud is an intentional misrepresentation or alteration of input to a system or modification of data within a system for a gain by the perpetrator. This may occur through tactics using authorized operations for unintended purposes or misrepresentation of otherwise valid transactions.
- *Repudiation.* The enterprise may rely on a representation or commitment by another business entity or person, and that business entity, or person denies making the representation or commitment. This is typically the result of business transition from signed, paper documents to electronic documents. A representation could be, for example, an assertion of quality or timeliness of a product, a sales agreement, or a false expense report.
- *Denial of service.* Denial of service occurs when an Internet server is flooded with generated requests that overload its capacity causing extended delay or failure. These requests may appear to come from many sources, so they are difficult to block or to hold the perpetrator accountable.

- *Data residency*. Data residency is a particular concern for cloud computing where data and applications potentially may be deployed and redeployed to computing resources anywhere in the world to achieve workload balancing and to compensate for failed components. Some countries have export restrictions on certain categories of data. Violation could result in significant penalties. Appropriate techniques for maintaining flexibility while ensuring compliance are currently being explored.
- *Transition exposure*. Any change brings a risk of exposure. New software errors may be introduced and mitigation measures may be overlooked. In an environment with shared services, a service may be engaged for new circumstances with new potential exposures and errors as well as new employees.
- *Residual content*. When devices and media are scrapped, they may have residual, confidential data. The owner of the device or media may have forgotten that it contains confidential data, or the device or media may have had a previous owner.

Setting Priorities

Security is about mitigation of risks. There are many security risks to consider. Security cannot be absolute, so it is important to give particular attention to the most serious risks. *What* are the values at risk, *who* might attempt to access or interfere with those values, and *why*.

- *What*: Consider what data or services are of the greatest concern and the nature of the potential risks. Some information is confidential and must be protected from disclosure. This may include personal data of employees and customers, business strategy, trade secrets, customer lists, product design, business records, and corporate financial data. Some application might be altered to transfer or destroy assets or capabilities.
- *Who*: For the various data categories or systems, who might present a risk: an employee; a thief; a competitor; a foreign government; a hacker; an investor; a partner enterprise; an equipment; or a software supplier, a programmer, an installer, or a maintainer? Also, consider natural disaster, political unrest, labor strikes, or other environmental factors.
- *Why*: If the "who" is an individual or organization, consider reasons they might be motivated to obtain data or corrupt data or services. This may include identity theft, competitive advantage, market strategy, disgruntled employee, dissatisfied customer, hacker taking on a challenge, or a terrorist.

Based on the answers to these questions, a priority list can be compiled to consider the current level of risk and potential measures for risk mitigation if not avoidance. Note that some mitigation measures reduce multiple risks.

Mitigation

The following list describes a number of common security mitigation techniques. Some of these may have broad applicability, and others may be more narrowly focused. It is impossible to ensure zero risk, so mitigation techniques should be applied to reduce risks to a tolerable level. These mitigation techniques should be evaluated for their cost and impact on the risks to information assets identified in the analysis of "what, who, and why" earlier. Some assets may require multiple risk mitigation techniques due to the complexity, severity of impact, or multiplicity of risk factors. Security experts suggest additional techniques. This list is intended to help business leaders understand the challenges, be able to ask intelligent questions regarding risks to the enterprise, and be prepared to plan for investment.

- *Encryption.* Encryption is a technique for translating data to an apparently meaningless form that later can be unencrypted (decoded) by an authorized recipient.
- *Hashing and signatures.* Hashing translates a block of data to a shorter "hash value" that is virtually unique for the hashed data. The hashed value is encrypted and signed by the sender of the data. A recipient of the data can apply the same hashing algorithm to create a hash value that will be the same as the first hash value if the data have not been changed.
- *Identification.* Identification is a mechanism for reliably determining the identity of a participant.
- *Authorization.* Authorization is a mechanism for determining if a participant has authority to perform selected operations or access selected data. Authorization may be dependent on the context or role in which the participant is performing.
- *Vulnerability scanning.* Tools are available to scan interfaces to systems and services to determine if known intrusion vulnerabilities have been resolved.
- *Penetration testing.* Tools are available to scan interfaces to systems and services and attempt to penetrate the interface based in techniques used by hackers.
- *Timely software updates.* Software updates frequently include changes to resolve vulnerabilities. When a vulnerability is identified, the risk that it will be exploited increases, so software updates should be timely but validated to ensure that new risks are not being introduced.

- *Redundancy*. Redundancy means that there are alternative facilities and duplicated data storage so that if a facility or data store is lost or corrupted, there is an available alternative. Data redundancy may range from a mirror image of data constantly updated, to a periodic snapshot copies with a log to bring the snapshot up to date. Redundant copies may be at remote sites. Facility redundancy may be extra equipment that can absorb additional workload, alternative data centers, backup power sources, alternative communications services, and so on.
- *Recovery*. Systems fail and must be recovered. In addition to resolving the cause of failure, this may involve shifting to alternative facilities, reprocessing to recover data, and resynchronization with other systems or business activities. Note that if the failure was a software fault, recovery on an identical system may result in a repeat of the same failure.
- *Virtual Private Network (VPN)*. VPN technology enables a user on the public Internet to establish a secure connection to an enterprise, internal network (or "Intranet"), and interact as though they were connected directly to the internal network.
- *Firewall*. A firewall is a communication facility that provides a barrier between the Internet and an Intranet thus restricting communications to selected ports and protocols. A firewall may also be a *proxy server* that translates network addresses so that internal devices are only known and accessible by aliases (proxies) in the public Internet.
- *Physical barriers*. A facility such as a data center or other exclusive area is protected from access by physical barriers with specific, controlled access points—a form of perimeter security.
- *Perimeter(s)*. Perimeters or perimeter security refers to the creation of exclusive domains that may be physical or logical. For example, the network of a campus may be isolated by firewalls that form a logical perimeter. Often, there will be multiple "nested" perimeters.
- *Layers of defense*. For high-security domains, access may be restricted in layers so that access must be successful through multiple barriers that apply different criteria, typically increasingly restrictive and more specific in functionality.
- *Compartmentalization*. Large enterprise network should use internal firewalls to partition domains each consisting of clusters of frequently interacting services and users. The purpose is to limit the scope of exposure if the enterprise perimeter is breached. This is similar to the use of bulkheads on a ship.
- *Monitoring*. Typically monitoring applies to observing patterns of communication and interaction on a network. The goal is to

recognize unusual patterns and levels of activity that may represent attempts to find and exploit vulnerabilities or achieve denial of service.

- *Alerts.* When a vulnerability is discovered, personnel responsible for the systems or devices at risk should be alerted for potential defensive measures. The recipients of the alert should be selected to minimize widespread awareness to people who do not need to know.
- *Virus detection.* A virus is a set of computer instructions that propagates itself to infect many computers and perform undesirable, often destructive behavior. Common means of transmission are by attachments to emails or inadvertent downloading from websites. However, viruses can also be communicated through other network intrusions. Viruses are typically detected based on computer code patterns which require that they be known or similar to be detected. They may also be detected in communications by special firewall appliances that recognize infection patterns.
- *Trustworthy personnel.* Many security breaches occur within an enterprise. At some level, some employees must be trusted to do their jobs including jobs to maintain security.
- *Least privilege.* Least privilege is a principle that people should only be authorized to access data and services they need to fulfill their responsibilities.
- *Separation of duties.* Access that carries high risk of fraud or abuse should require endorsement by two or more persons with distinct duties, so one person cannot violate security or corporate responsibility on their own. This is equivalent to requiring two signatures on a check.
- *Deterrent/incentives.* Risk is affected by the potential benefit derived by a perpetrator. If data have a substantial market value or if intrusion yields value to a competitor, then the risk is increased. For a hacker, the challenge of breaching security of a large corporation or government agency may be a significant incentive. On the other hand, the risk of getting caught and criminal penalties should be deterrents. Increasing deterrents or decreasing incentives are factors to be considered for mitigation.
- *Audit.* Audit of systems and security measures can identify unrecognized risks or needs for mitigation. An audit may also uncover risky behavior or practices that should be corrected.
- *Logging.* In addition to support for recovery, logging provides accountability. Logging may also support analysis of a security breach or attempted breach and help discover the cause of a security breach. Consequently, logging is important for corrective action, recovery and as a disincentive for misconduct.
- *Traceability.* Traceability is important in an environment with shared services to identify the origin of actions that may have been delegated

to multiple levels of supporting services. Traceability should be tied to logging to track paths of access.

- *Honeypot.* A honeypot is a false service or application that has vulnerabilities to be discovered by intruders and data that are fabricated to mislead or expose the thief. Tracking accesses may lead to identification and capture of an intruder.

In the following sections, we will explore some of the key security technologies and practices in order to establish an appreciation of the need for consistent mechanisms and for investment in security infrastructure. This is particularly important in this age of shared services, exposure to the public Internet, mobile devices, remote computing, and integration within and between enterprises in a global business environment.

SECURITY TECHNOLOGIES

The following sections describe key technologies that should be applied consistently, throughout the enterprise.

Encryption and Signatures

Encryption is a fundamental security technique. Data are encrypted to protect them from exposure in an unprotected environment or medium of exchange. Encryption may also be used to enable a recipient to determine whether data have been changed.

Simple encryption can be performed by a transformation using a secret algorithm. Since it is difficult to define new, secret algorithms for every situation, current practice is to perform encryption with a standard encryption algorithm and a unique key. The key makes the encrypted data infeasible to decrypt simply by knowing the algorithm. Note that there is no perfect form of encryption; the more secure forms simply make decryption exceptionally difficult.

Secret key encryption, however, requires that both the originator and the intended recipient of the encrypted data know the secret key as well as the algorithm. That requires, first, that the two parties establish agreement on a secret key and, second, that a different secret key agreement be established for every exchange relationship. Secret key encryption is, nevertheless, a commonly used technique.

Public Key Encryption

In another form of encryption, called *public key encryption*, an entity possesses two complementary keys: a public key and a private key. The public key can be known by anyone, but only the owner knows the private key. The application of public key encryption is illustrated in Fig. 7.1.

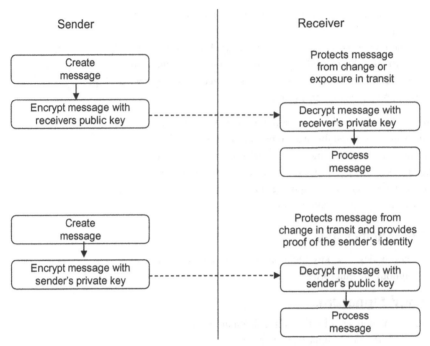

Sender   Receiver

FIG. 7.1 Public key encryption.

Data encrypted with one of the keys can only be decrypted by the companion key. This allows a sender to encrypt data with a recipient's public key, and only the recipient can decrypt the data using the private key. Conversely, a sender can encrypt data with its private key, and a recipient can decrypt the data with the sender's public key; this assures that only the sender could have originated the data, and the data have not been changed (but it does not keep the data secret). This system not only authenticates the sender but also establishes nonrepudiation of the content (in other words, the sender cannot deny sending it).

Public key encryption is the foundation of many industry security standards supporting Web services and shared internal services. A fundamental application is to create electronic signatures.

Electronic Signatures

The World Wide Web Consortium (W3C) has used public key encryption technology to define XML-Signature (http://www.w3.org/Signature/) as a standard for creation and expression of electronic signatures in XML documents. An electronic signature is formed by first processing the data to be signed with a standard *digest algorithm* that creates a "hash value" that is unique (as a practical matter) for the digested data. A change to the data would result in a different hash value. The hash value is then encrypted with the signer's private key. To validate the signature and the data, a recipient of the signed data applies the same digest algorithm to the data to recompute the hash value. This result is then compared to the hash value decrypted using the signer's public key. If the two hash values are the same, the signature is valid and the integrity of the data is assured.

Though public key encryption alone can ensure message integrity, the XML-Signature mechanism provides data integrity and nonrepudiation without incurring the cost of encrypting/decrypting entire documents.

The following is an example digital signature. Digest, key, and signature values are replaced with ellipses (...):

```
<Signature Id="SampleSignature"
xmlns="http://www.w3.org/2000/09/xmldsig#">
<SignedInfo>
<CanonicalizationMethod    Algorithm="http://www.w3.org/TR/
2001/REC-xml-c14n-20010315"/>
<SignatureMethod
Algorithm="http://www.w3.org/2000/09/xmldsig#dsa-sha1"/>
<Reference URI="#MySignedDocument">
<Transforms>
<Transform    Algorithm="http://www.w3.org/TR/2001/REC-xml-
c14n-20010315"/>
</Transforms>
<DigestMethod
Algorithm="http://www.w3.org/2000/09/xmldsig#sha1"/>
<DigestValue>...</DigestValue>
</Reference>
</SignedInfo>
<SignatureValue>...</SignatureValue>
<KeyInfo>
<KeyValue
<DSAKeyValue>...</DSAKeyValue>
</KeyValue>
</KeyInfo>
</Signature>
```

A brief description of these elements follows:

- *Signature*. The signature element (includes all of the following):
- *SignedInfo*. Specification of the information being signed (includes *CononicalizationMethod*, *SignatureMethod*, and one or more Reference elements)
- *CanonicalizationMethod*. The algorithm used to structure the *SignedInfo* in a standard way.
- *SignatureMethod*. The algorithm used to compute the signature.
- *Reference*. A link to an item being signed along with digest specifications (includes *Transforms*, *DigestMethod*, and *DigestValue*).
- *Transforms*. An optional set of transforms applied to the item being signed (includes one or more *Transforms* elements).
- *Transform*. A specific transform applied to the item being signed.
- *DigestMethod*. The digest algorithm applied to the item being signed.
- *DigestValue*. The value computed by the digest method.
- *SignatureValue*. The value computed by encryption of the *Signed-Info*, which includes the *SignedInfo* structure and the referenced content.
- *KeyInfo*. Optional information that may contain a key, certificate, name, or other key management information since the key may be available from other sources (includes *KeyValue* in the example).
- *KeyValue*. The public key of the signer (contains *DSAKeyValue* in the example).
- *DSAKeyValue*. The key value for DSA encryption as opposed to RSA encryption.

There may be multiple Reference elements for signing multiple objects. A reference may be to an element of the same document (which could be a complex structure) or documents referenced by URL.

Accountability and Nonrepudiation

Accountability is a deterrent to undesirable behavior and a basis for enforcement of commitments. For example, employees are less likely to embezzle funds if they know they will get caught. A customer is more likely to pay for a service if the customer agreement cannot be repudiated and acceptance of a product or service can be proved.

In the past, and still today to a great extent, accountability is established through written signatures on documents. A signature on a paper document can be written in the presence of a witness, and the identity of the signer is established not only by the writing but also by personal acquaintance of the parties and possibly credentials such as a passport or a driver's license.

There are three important issues concerning enforcement of electronic documents: (1) documents as evidence, (2) compound documents, and (3) preservation of authenticity.

Electronic Documents as Evidence

Today, agreements and commitments are increasingly established electronically; many are in the form of XML documents. Traditional computer applications were developed for recordkeeping within departments. Users of these traditional applications must establish their identity to access the system, and actions they take can be captured for accountability. Essentially, the computer record of their input is their signature. However, this "signature" is meaningful only within the context of the application, and it is reliable only to the extent that the records cannot be changed to misrepresent responsibility.

When an enterprise records information or commitments from an external person or organization, the existence of the record in a system that belongs to the enterprise is not sufficient to resolve a dispute over the content. Enterprises are increasingly outsourcing business functions that have traditionally been held within the corporation. Without proof of message authenticity, a corporation cannot hold employees of outsourcing providers or the providers themselves legally accountable for the actions documented in electronic records. Even within an enterprise, where substantial assets are at stake, individuals should have greater assurance that their responsibility cannot be forged through tampering with electronic records, and the enterprise should have assurance that people really can be held accountable. In addition, government regulations are requiring greater assurance of accountability for operating decisions and controls.

For example, when an engineer submits a purchase request with an attached specification, the engineer must be accountable for the content of the request and the associated specification. When his or her manager approves it, the manager also becomes accountable. It should be possible to prove what the originator submitted and what the manager approved.

The solution to this dilemma is electronic signatures. The mechanism for applying and validating an electronic signature was discussed earlier.

A signer is accountable and also protected from forgery because the signature could only have been created with his or her private key.

Electronic signatures should be used wherever written signatures would have been used in the past. This should include not only documents created with customers and business partners but also documents created internally to authorize expenditures and transfers of assets. Support for signing and exchanging electronic documents should be incorporated into or associated with business process management systems so that signed documents can be an integral part of business processes. Few if any business process management systems currently support signatures on associated documents. An infrastructure is needed that supports XML-Signature and PKI (Public Key Infrastructure, https://en.wikipedia.org/wiki/Public_key_infrastructure).

Compound Documents

The processing of business transactions frequently involves actions by multiple people or organizations; each of them contributes or approves aspects of the transaction, resulting in a compound document. The document defines the context and data associated with the particular business transaction. The document or portions of it move from one participant or service to the next to establish the context for activities and to capture results.

For example, extending our example, a purchase request and attached specification are originated by an engineer. That person's manager may be required to approve the expense and can add information regarding the approval. The request may then be directed to the purchasing organization to be reviewed and approved by a purchasing agent for compliance with corporate policies. The purchasing organization then proceeds to issue a purchase order (which may also be signed by the purchasing agent) that is incorporated by reference into the compound purchase request document.

Approvers cannot change what they received since it has been electronically signed by those who came before. Thus a compound electronic document may pass through different organizations for different purposes. The primary document may incorporate additional electronic documents by reference— for example, the specification attached to the purchase request might have been included by reference, and the electronic signatures would apply to the primary document and the referenced version of the specification.

Such situations are commonplace in paper-based systems. Current automated systems generally rely on records that are captured, processed, and retained in a single enterprise application with a defined set of authorized application users. With the automation of business processes and the movement of electronic documents among shared services, there must be consistent document integrity and participant accountability mechanisms that are effective across multiple business units as well as in exchanges with other enterprises.

XML-Signature allows each signature to apply to different portions of a compound document. Additional parts do not invalidate signatures on previous parts as long as the signed parts are not changed.

Preservation of Authenticity

Signatures ensure the integrity of the exchange of electronic documents; however, electronic business documents must remain valid for years. This fact places additional requirements on the handling of these documents.

First, a signed electronic document cannot be changed without the signature becoming invalid. In the signing and validation processes, a *canonicalization algorithm* is applied to ensure that the document is formatted in a standard way. This means that variations such as indentations and extra spaces produce the same signature value. But if the document is modified in any other way, the signature is no longer valid. This might occur, for example, if the document is converted to an internal computer form for processing and then regenerated for forwarding.

Thus a document cannot be transformed to comply with alternative data formats or element names required by a receiving application or service. If a transformation is necessary, the result must be considered a working document to be used by the recipient but distinct from the signed document. This creates some risk to the recipient that he or she (or the entity) may act on a misinterpretation or erroneous transformation of the original document as represented by the working document.

Signed documents should be archived in their original form. Note that documents included by reference must exist in their original form at the URL referenced in the composite document, since the reference is part of the signed data. This should be considered in the creation of the document so that the referenced documents continue to be available and the signature continues to be valid.

Over time, signatures may become questionable. A signer may claim that at the time he or she signed the document, his or her private key was compromised, so the document is a forgery. Records of a certificate authority (CA) (discussed later) can provide evidence to the contrary. If the signer gave no notice of revocation of the certificate within a reasonable time of signing the document, that would suggest that the signature was valid.

As a further measure, an "electronic notary" service might be employed. The electronic notary should be operated by a trusted third party. The notary can independently contact the signer to confirm his or her signature on the document. The notary signs the document as an independent third party. The notarized document and signatures can then be archived.

Identification and Authentication

Identification refers to associating a known identifier with a party. *Authentication* refers to determining if the party is legitimately using the identifier. There are three fundamental forms of identification and authentication: (1) what you know (such as an identifier and password), (2) what you have (such as a credit card, preferably a smart card with encrypted key), or (3) what you are (such as a fingerprint).

The traditional form of identification and authentication is through the use of an identifier and password. This approach has limited value. We refer to the entity to be identified as the *requesting party* and the entity requiring the identification as the *relying party*. The requesting party and relying party must first establish an initial trust relationship so that they agree on values of the identifier and password for the requesting party. For subsequent contacts, the requesting party's identifier is recognized by the relying party, and the password is a secret associated with the requesting party's identifier and known only to the requesting party and the relying party.

If the requesting party uses the same password for other relationships, there are multiple relying parties that know the requesting party's secret password, and there is an increased risk of exposure where all relationships would be at risk. In addition, various recipients may require different identifiers for the same requesting party. Consequently, the requesting party must keep track of multiple identifiers and passwords.

The use of multiple identifiers also makes it difficult to recognize where the same person should be authorized to access the same business transaction from different applications or when a person is violating a separation of duties requirement by performing two mutually exclusive roles.

Digital Certificates

Public key encryption and electronic signatures provide a more robust and convenient form of identification and authentication. To establish an initial relationship, the identity of a participant is established with a trusted third party. The trusted third party provides a *digital certificate* that the third party has signed containing the identifier and public key of the participant. The participant can then establish its identity by demonstrating that it holds the complementary private key.

A standard form for a digital certificate is specified by the Internet Engineering Task Force (IETF) X.509v3 (https://tools.ietf.org/html/rfc5280). A CA is a trusted third party, whereby entities can register their identities and public keys and obtain digital certificates signed by the CA. The CA also provides a certificate revocation list (CRL) of certificates for which the private keys have been compromised.

An X.509v3 digital certificate typically contains the following fields:

- *version.* v1, v2, or v3, designating the version of the certificate standard.
- *serialNumber.* A unique serial number that identifies the certificate.
- *signature.* Identifier for the algorithm used by the CA to sign the certificate.
- *issuer.* A unique identifier for the CA that issued this certificate.
- *validity.* The valid time interval, two times indicating the earliest time the certificate is valid and the latest.
- *subject.* A unique name that identifies the entity for which the certificate is issued.
- *subjectPublicKeyInfo.* Contains the public key for the identified entity along with an identifier for the encryption algorithm used with the key (next two items).
- *signatureAlgorithm.* Identifier for the algorithm used by the CA to sign the certificate.
- *signatureValue.* The value of the CA signature.
- *issuerUniqueID (optional).* A unique identifier for the CA that would resolve possible reuse of the issuer identifier used previously.
- *subjectUniqueID (optional).* A unique identifier for the subject entity that would resolve possible reuse of the subject identifier used previously.
- *extensions (optional).* Optional extensions that address special cases and restrictions, such as a certificate that identifies a CA and a certificate restricted to use for a specific purpose, such as for signatures only.

A PKI is a set of facilities to support the use of digital certificates for identification and authentication. Minimally, this involves a registration authority (RA) that validates the identity of entities seeking a certificate, a CA that issues and signs digital certificates and maintains a CRL, and directories where the certificates (containing the public keys) are available for access. An enterprise should implement a PKI for identification of its employees and service units.

Authentication of a party presenting a digital certificate is somewhat different from authentication with a password. The following steps describe an example exchange:

1. A requesting party submits its digital certificate.
2. The relying party validates the signature of the CA. This establishes that the certificate is valid.
3. The relying party checks the validity time interval to ensure that the certificate has not expired.
4. The relying party checks the CA revocation list to ensure that the certificate has not been revoked.
5. If the certificate is valid, it contains the identifier and public key of an identified party, but it is not yet established that this certificate belongs to the requesting party. The relying party may then encrypt a "nonce" (a unique bit string) with the certificate owner's public key and send it to the requesting party.
6. The requesting party returns a checksum computed with a standard algorithm and encrypted with its private key, using several established elements known to both parties, such as the requesting party's name, public key, the nonce value, and the requested service URL.
7. The relying party receives and decrypts the checksum and performs the checksum algorithm on the same elements to verify that the requesting party was able to correctly decrypt the nonce and encrypt the checksum (with the private key). The nonce with additional elements prevents an imposter from copying an encrypted checksum from a different exchange by the requesting party.

At the end of this exchange, a valid link has been established for subsequent exchanges. If the requesting party is a person, essentially the link is established with the person's personal computer and browser, with the assumption that the person is in control of the computer. In high-security circumstances, it may be necessary to establish that the person using the computer is actually the owner of the certificate through other forms of identity verification, such as queries about personal information or use of biometric devices such as fingerprint verification. This is described as *multitoken authentication*.

Two-Way Authentication

The described protocol shows how a requester can be properly authenticated, but there are circumstances in which the provider must also be authenticated. On the public Internet, people are often victims of identity theft or other fraudulent activities because they are directed to interactions with an imposter of a trusted provider such as their bank. Within an enterprise, service users should be able to have their requests redirected when a service provider is replaced or upgraded with a new address, but there is a risk of being redirected to a fraudulent service.

Where these risks are a concern, the service user should also authenticate the service provider. Service providers should provide a complementary protocol by which a requester can request and validate the provider's credentials.

Single Sign-On

A PKI provides the basis for single sign-on. An individual signs on to his or her personal computer to enable access to the private key; generally, users are not expected to remember their private key but have an easier-to-remember password to sign onto their personal computer. On the basis of their certificate and their private key, they can be automatically identified and authenticated for multiple systems. Legacy systems can be enabled with adapters to accept the certificates for identification. The approach reduces security administration and improves security by reducing risk of exposure of conventional passwords, since the user never reveals the secret key.

For the agile enterprise, service units and personnel must have identities that are recognized throughout the extended enterprise. It should be possible to establish ad hoc interactions with services to support enterprise level planning and decision making and to quickly adapt to changing business requirements. PKI and single sign-on are fundamental steps to achieve this flexibility.

Unified identification and authentication also enable one service to pass the identity of a requester through to other services needed to support the original request. This ensures that the requester does not do indirectly what he or she is not authorized to do directly. It also provides support for accountability back to the originator of a request.

The WS-Security (http://www.oasis-open.org/specs/index.php#wssv1.1) standard from OASIS defines a generally accepted approach to integration of standard elements to convey authentication information and ensure message integrity.

Runtime Authorization

It is not sufficient for a participant in an exchange to be authenticated and have a reliable identifier. The participant must also have appropriate authorization to participate in an exchange or access certain resources.

System access control is no longer a matter of defining which members of a department are authorized to perform particular operations or access certain data. Users of a shared service may come directly or indirectly from many different organizations, potentially outside as well as inside the corporation. Authorization and access control must be addressed at an enterprise level and, eventually, at an extended enterprise level, with an approach and administrative processes that work for all users and all services.

At runtime, a service unit should not need to deal with the details of the participant's roles or the details of the policies. Those data are maintained and applied by a security service, and the authorization determinations are made by the security service.

When a participant requests a particular service operation, a request is sent to the security service, specifying the participant, the type of request, and context data. The security service retrieves the participant's access authorization specifications, evaluates the relevant policies and the context of the intended action, determines whether permission should be granted, and returns that result to the requesting service.

When a party invokes a service and that service unit invokes another service, the actions of the second service unit must be based on appropriate authorization. This may occur in two ways: (1) the original party may authorize the intermediate service unit to act on its behalf, so the access to the second service is based on the party's credentials, or (2) the intermediate service unit acts on its own behalf on the basis that its actions are authorized to fulfill authorized requests it receives.

The first alternative creates the risk that the intermediate service unit could use the originating party's credentials to access resources it would otherwise not be authorized to access. This could be addressed by requiring both the originating party and the intermediate service to have appropriate authorizations. The second alternative relies on the intermediate service unit having an understanding of appropriate limitations on use of the second service and the results it returns.

Security Assertion Markup Language

An example authentication and authorization exchange is illustrated in Fig. 7.2. Central to this exchange is the use of Security Assertion Markup Language (SAML, http://www.oasis-open.org/specs/index.php#samlv2.0), a standard developed by OASIS that defines the form of expression of the authorization request and response in the exchange described at the end of this paragraph. Different security mechanisms may be used in conjunction with SAML, but a PKI is recommended. Note that in the diagram,

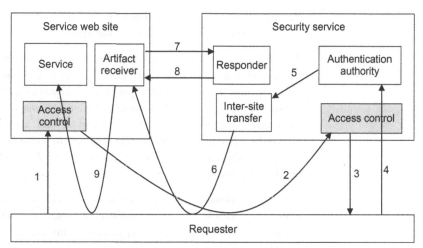

■ **FIG. 7.2** Access authorization.

arrows that loop back past the requester are redirections of the request through the requester, so responses always come back to the requester from the last-requested site:

1. The requester requests Service X.
2. Service X access control determines that the requester is not currently signed onto this service and redirects the request to the security service with an associated URL for the Service X artifact receiver that expects to receive a SAML assertion.
3. Security service access control determines that the requester is not currently signed on to the security service and issues a credential challenge to the requester. If the requester has already signed on to the security service, skip to step 5.
4. The requester responds to the credential challenge, and the response is processed by the authentication authority.
5. The original request to Service X along with authentication information is directed to the local intersite transfer service.
6. The request is then redirected to the original service site artifact receiver function, along with a SAML "assertion" that specifies the requester's attributes, the "responder" address (next step), and the URL for the original service request being forwarded from the security service.
7. The Service X artifact receiver submits a SAML authorization request, which includes the SAML artifact along with information about the request, to the security service's responder.
8. The responder applies appropriate policy rules to the SAML artifact and the request information and returns a decision.

9. An authorized request is redirected to the requested Service X; otherwise the request will be rejected as unauthorized.

This architecture separates the determination of authentication and authorization from the requested service. The attributes of the requesters and the services as well as the security policies are managed and evaluated by the security service. This allows these factors to be managed and controlled independent of changes to the requesters and services, and the overall permissions granted to individuals can be analyzed for consistency and appropriateness. Specialized hardware products, described as *XML appliances*, are designed for optimal performance of these access control functions.

Since this approach removes access control decisions from the resource being accessed, a legacy application may be protected by the same mechanism as current applications and services. This enables single sign-on within the scope of the enterprise and provides consolidated specification of access control for improved analysis, control, and accountability for authorization.

XACML Policies

The eXtensible Access Control Markup Language (XACML, http://www.oasis-open.org/committees/tc_home.php?wg_abbrev=xacml) is an OASIS standard for specification of policies and rules that define access authorization. Fig. 7.3 depicts an abstraction of an XACML authorization structure.

A *PolicySet* contains one or more policies and may contain *PolicySets*, making it potentially recursive. A Policy contains rules for determination of authorization.

A *PolicySet* contains a *Target* element, and a *Target* element may also appear in a *Policy* or a *Rule*. The *Target* element limits the number of policies and rules that must be considered for an authorization request based on the context.

A *Target* defines circumstances and things for which the associated *PolicySet*, *Policy*, or *Rule* applies. It contains *DisjunctiveMatch* (logical *or*) elements that in turn contain *ConjunctiveMatch* (logical *and*) elements that each contain *Match* elements. The result is a set of alternative sets of *Match* conditions that apply to one or more subjects (ie, participants) of the authorization request and the resources, actions, or environment to be accessed. Each *Match* contains an attribute value and a reference to an attribute in the context or subject attributes. When the target matches, the policy set, policy, or rule is further evaluated.

A *PolicySet* or a *Policy* may contain *Obligations*. These are specifications of required actions to be taken at the point of authorization enforcement.

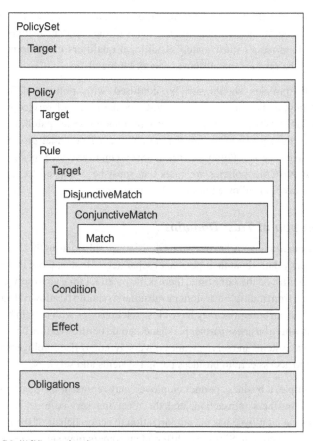

FIG. 7.3 XACML example policy set structure.

Within a policy, each *Rule* contains a *Condition* and an *Effect*. The *Condition* contains expressions that evaluate to true or false. These operate on attributes similar to those of the *Match* elements, but there are more complex functions that may be applied to determine the result. The *Effect* is the associated result if the condition is true and returns a value of *Permit* or *Deny*. Policy qualifiers can determine whether rule evaluation stops when the first *Permit* or *Deny* is encountered.

This discussion has been an oversimplified representation of XACML policy specifications. *PolicySet* and *Policy* have a number of other elements that qualify the interpretation and application of the policies. Rule conditions can also be very complex. The language is capable of expressing diverse authorization policies. The difficulty is that, as an XML form, it is quite verbose, and the intent of the policies is obscured by the XML details. A graphical tool is needed to provide appropriate abstractions.

The attributes referenced in an XACML policy must be present in the authorization request and the roles and attributes of the associated subjects, and the attribute names must match. Additional qualifiers can determine the action to be taken if the attributes cannot be found.

XACML policies should not be confused with policies defined by WS-Policy, a specification by the W3C for definition of service policies. The focus of WS-Policy is to express requirements and capabilities of services so that service users can determine whether potential providers are compatible. The WS-Policy assertions are essentially service specifications, whereas XACML policies are rules that must be evaluated to determine whether access is allowed or denied.

Federation of Trust Domains

A large enterprise may have separate divisions or subsidiaries that each manage security data about their personnel separately—that is, those in different trust domains. At the same time, there is the potential for shared services that personnel from multiple divisions or subsidiaries should be allowed to access. In addition, an enterprise may have close relationships with certain business partners where business partner personnel should be allowed to access certain enterprise systems and services, and conversely, enterprise employees should be able to access certain business partner systems and services.

For example, a business partner employee may represent the business partner in a business transaction, and the receiving service must determine whether the employee has the authorization to act on behalf of the business partner organization. Similarly, different customers may submit requests in the form of product or service orders. These requests may be submitted by authorized customer personnel. The receiving enterprise must determine that the customer representative is trustworthy and that the request is appropriately authorized by the customer organization or other trustworthy entity.

Essentially, these participants come from other trust domains. They are not known to the enterprise. Their trustworthiness must be established by another source that has been previously established as sufficiently trustworthy.

An extended enterprise may involve a number of suppliers and customers. Each of these has mechanisms for identity authentication and authorization of their employees and others who are expected to access their systems and services.

WS-Federation (http://xml.coverpages.org/ni2007-03-20-a.html), an OASIS standard, is a detailed language for specification of security federation.

Federation involves a cooperative relationship between trust domains so that participants known to one domain can obtain access privileges in another domain. The following steps are an example of the type of exchange required for service of one enterprise to allow access to an employee of a trusted business partner.

1. The relying domain security service locates the participant's home trust domain.
2. The home trust domain provides the participant credentials that specify attributes for relevant roles. These may be restricted to roles and attributes that are allowed to be shared with other trust domains.
3. The relying domain security service must accept the identity of the participant, probably as a temporary entity for the duration of the login, to support subsequent authorization requests.
4. The relying domain security service must transform and filter the participant's credentials to its local requirements (including limitations on acceptable roles), and the subject's credentials must be made available for subsequent access decisions.
5. The relying trust domain then proceeds with its normal response to the initial request using the subject's ad hoc identity and security assertions.

The requested service subsequently requests authorization(s) that apply the local policies and rules to the request context and the participant's credentials.

There may be different approaches to step 1. For example, the Liberty Alliance has defined an approach to work with Web browsers. This approach requires that a participant first log in at a home trust domain. The authentication service calls a common domain server to send a cookie to that participant and create a record that the user is logged in. The common domain server is accessible from all affiliated trust domains.

The relying security service acting in step 1 sends a request to the common domain service, which has access to the participant's cookie. (A cookie is only accessible to the domain that created it.) The common domain then returns the identity of the user's home security service to the relying security service. The relying security service must then obtain the participant's credentials as described in steps 2–5. The common domain service tracks the domains in which the participant is signed in so that it can propagate a logout or expiration of the session.

The Liberty Alliance protocol only works with Web browsers, involves more message exchanges to establish access authorization, and relies on a common domain server that represents a potential single point of failure for all participating trust domains.

In the absence of shared support for an industry standard, the most straight-forward approach is to establish partner employee identities within the enter-prise security system and grant restricted access similar to that granted to other personnel. This results in some increased administrative effort but avoids the need to develop and implement custom strategies and techniques that require continuing attention as business partners or their systems change.

Authorization Management

Specifications for authorization are quite technical and complex. Authoriza-tion is a management function, but managers must depend on technical experts to implement and maintain authorization specifications. Authoriza-tion management is increased in complexity in an agile enterprise to support the authorizations of participants in shared services.

Managers need a business-oriented way to give people the authorizations they need to do their jobs. The authorizations needed by a person will change as a person is given different assignments.

A person's authorization requirements are determined by the roles to which they are assigned. It should not be necessary to explicitly define access authorization for all the things an individual might need to do. If we define the access authorization requirements for each role to which people in an organization unit may be required to perform, then the actual grant of autho-rization should occur when the person is assigned to a role, and the grant can be in the context of the particular assignment (eg, regarding a particular order, a particular patient, a particular repair, and so on).

In the following sections, we will discuss the requirements for authorization based on role assignments.

Later in this chapter, we will discuss a spreadsheet-based authorization model and also Role-Based Access Control as a potential modeling standard in Chapter 11. In the absence of that standard, we will describe an interim solution, here, following a discussion of the requirements of authorization management.

Role Authorization Requirements

The access authorization needed by an individual depends on the role being performed by that person. If we consider that all activities performed by per-sons in an enterprise are in the context of a collaboration, then everything a person does is in the context of a role within a collaboration. Based on

VDML (Chapter 2), the collaboration may be characterized as an organizational unit, a community, a capability method, or a business network.

A collaboration will require that each role have access to certain information, the ability to perform certain operations, and responsibility for work involving certain assets or work products. The authorizations of participants are associated with the roles they are assigned, not specifically with the individual. Assignment of a participant to a role then determines the authorizations for the participant while in that role.

Every collaboration will have a responsible management chain of command that has primary responsibility for role assignments and authorizations of the participants. We will refer to the immediate manager in that chain as the collaboration manager.

- The collaboration may be an organization unit or a capability method provided by an organization unit, so the role authorizations are the responsibility of the management of that organization unit. The participants will be primarily from positions in the organization unit, and some may be engaged because they have relevant roles in other organizations.
- A community collaboration will involve members of a community, but their access to information or assets will be either managed by an administrative organization associated with the community or by the organizational managers of each of the participants (or both).
- In a business network collaboration, the management chain of each role participant will be responsible for the authorization of role accesses to the information systems and assets of that participating enterprise.
- When a role involves delegation to a service, the role must have authorization to access the required service. The engaged service unit will be responsible for authorizations of the roles and participants in its activities based on the context of the engaging activity.

Each role in a collaboration may be filled by a participant in another role. In most cases, participants will be in a position role of an organization unit. In many cases, a participant will be engaged because they are in a relevant role of a related collaboration. They will come with authorizations associated with the role that is the basis of their engagement. For example, a product planning committee may engage a person from marketing, a person from finance, a person from engineering, and so on.

Authorization of Individuals

Participants will obtain authorizations associated with the role in which they are performing. While the authorizations of the engaging collaboration may be redundant, they should be explicit for that role since the underlying authorizations are independently managed and may change. However, the assignment of individuals must be based not only on their roles but on their personal qualifications since it is the individual who actually does the work. A person need not come with authorizations to participate in a collaboration but must come with required qualifications. Collaboration managers are responsible for ensuring that candidates selected for a role are qualified to perform that role.

Participants should only have authorizations when they are needed. The authorizations of the individual will come and go as the individual's role assignments come and go. This is fairly straightforward except that when a role assignment X is based on another role assignment, Y, the assignment X is no longer valid if the individual is no longer assigned, directly or indirectly, to role Y. For example, if John is assigned to a role in a vehicle design committee because he is an engineer in the engine design department, he should no longer be in the committee role if he is assigned to a different department.

Access Control Administration

Up to this point, we have focused on what authorization management must accomplish. But, authorization administration requires business processes that define the actions to be performed by managers who have authority to grant authorizations. In an authorization administration process, an activity to grant authority will be context sensitive since the person granting or modifying authorizations must be restricted by their role in a responsible organization. A collaboration manager must be responsible for specification of role authorizations and the assignment of personnel to those roles. An asset (data or service) manager must be responsible for appropriate protection of the assets.

There must be accountability for changes to role performers and policy specifications. It should be possible to determine who granted authorization for a performer to take a specific action, and grantors should be able to periodically review their grants of authority (ie, role authorizations and performer candidates). In all cases, an audit trail should identify the grantor of authorization and when the grant of authorization was effective.

Here, we consider processes required at five stages of authorization administration: (1) specification of role authorization requirements, (2) identification of role candidates, (3) specification of access authorization policies, (4) approval of role authorizations and candidates, and (5) runtime role assignments.

Specification of Role Authorization Requirements

Specification of access authorization for a particular role is primarily the responsibility of the collaboration manager. The collaboration manager must initiate the grant of authority, but, in most cases, the information and assets are the responsibility of other managers. The collaboration manager, in fact, may not be personally authorized for some or all of the authorizations required for participants in the collaboration.

The collaboration manager must identify the roles of collaboration in the manager's area of responsibility. Then, the activities performed by each role must be examined to determine the access authorizations that will be required by that role. Authorization must define what asset can be accessed and what actions are allowable on that asset.

Access authorizations may allow general access to a service or access to all records of a particular type, but more often, access will be restricted based on the context of the collaboration. For example, patient records will be restricted to records of the patient under treatment. The collaboration context is a function of the information that is the basis of execution of the particular occurrence of a collaboration—a particular patient, order, customer, product, employee, etc. The context constraints must be included in the role authorization requirements.

Identification of Role Candidates

When a performer is assigned to a role, the performer will implicitly be granted the authorizations associated with that role. Thus role assignment is a grant of authorization. This would suggest that every time a performer is assigned to a role, the asset manager should approve the assignment. This could be a lot of work and require the asset manager to make some assessment of the qualifications of the potential performer for every assignment.

Instead, the collaboration manager should identify all of the candidates for each role and submit these candidates with the role authorization requirements for the approval of the asset manager. The effect is that all candidates are preapproved for the potential role assignments. The collaboration manager still remains in control of selection of the best candidate to fill a role for a particular occurrence of a collaboration.

Some performers may require a surrogate to perform certain actions in their absence. Essentially, a surrogate is identified as a person that is available for a temporary assignment that may be limited to certain roles of the primary performer. For purposes of authorizations, the surrogate performer may be included as a candidate for the selected roles. It will be up to runtime assignment management to determine when these assignments become active and inactive.

Specification of Access Authorization Policies

The asset manager receives role authorization requirements and candidates from the collaboration manager. Note that each role may require access to assets that are the responsibility of multiple asset managers. It is appropriate for the collaboration manager to provide some justification for the required authorizations. The policies must include context-based constraints. It is expected that the asset manager will work with a security specialist to formulate the technical policy specifications.

Approval of Role Candidates

Based on the role authorization policies, the asset manager should review and approve or reject the role assignment candidates provided by the collaboration manager. The level of scrutiny will depend on the level of risk associated with the assets to be accessed. The enterprise might provide some personnel attributes that would indicate the trustworthiness of the individual, potential conflicts of interest, need for separation of duties in a broader context, or other factors that might affect acceptability.

Runtime Role Assignments

Generic authorizations may specify that a role has access to customer orders or product inventories. However, many role authorizations are dependent on the collaboration context. A participant may not have access to all customer orders, but only the customer order that is the subject of the particular collaboration, and perhaps only authority to update a particular line item.

This becomes more complex in domains such as healthcare. A doctor is restricted to access of the patient records of the patient being served by a particular collaboration (ie, a particular case), but only if the patient has authorized access by the doctor or the treating organization. A role in the treatment collaboration will further restrict access appropriate to the specific responsibilities of each professional, and a patient may define further restrictions for authorization of certain roles or procedures. This may require authorization policies to have broader access to context data.

Context-based authorization may occur through delegation where individual participants are specified in the delegation. For example, a treatment collaboration involves certain treating professionals. When an activity engages another service (collaboration), some of those treating professionals may be assigned to roles in that engaged collaboration. These delegations may be explicit in the delegation, or they may be determined by reference to the context information (eg, the customer or patient records).

A performer may require ad hoc assignment of a proxy as a representative in a particular situation when the primary performer is not available. This is similar to a surrogate, but it is more likely to be unplanned, short term, and restricted to a particular role in a particular collaboration occurrence, such as one meeting of a standing committee. Again the proxy can be represented as a candidate for a particular role, but the candidate assignment is more likely to be ad hoc and thus may require ad hoc approval by the asset manager(s). The actual time and duration of the assignment must be controlled by runtime assignment management.

A Role-Based Authorization Model

Modeling tools are needed to appropriately manage grants of authorization. Managers must be able to easily express role assignments and policies and to periodically review all the specifications for which they are responsible as well as the performers who have been granted authority to access their assets. A potential standard for more robust role-based authorization modeling is discussed in Chapter 11.

Table 7.2, below, is an example for management of role authorizations using a spreadsheet for a hypothetical order management collaboration. The spreadsheet approach is not ideal but provides a manager with the ability to specify, understand, and manage authorizations and to specify requirements for implementation by a security specialist. It is also important for keeping track of authorizations as potential performers, applications, and processes change over time.

For each role, a role column identifies the service and data access authorization requirements, separation of duty requirements, and role performer candidates. The table is in four segments of rows: Request, Data, Separation of Duties, and Performer.

Request Rows

Within the Access column, the first segment of rows defines service requests. The access names that are not indented indicate a primary service request. The indented items indicate ancillary service requests.

The Context column identifies a business entity that is a focus of the service activity. The Scope column defines the scope of authorization at runtime

Table 7.2 Role-Based Authorization Table

				Role				
Scope	Context	Access	Request	Order Editor	Credit Check	Order Change	Discount Check	Liaison
				Service Access (X, Authorized Request)				
All	Product	Inventory						
	Product		Product status	X				X
One	Order		Reserve products	X		X		
One	Order		Restore products			X		
One	Order		Reject order	X		X	X	
One	Order		Order status request		X			X
One	Order		Confirm order		X			
Scope	Context	Data		*Data Access (A, Add; R, Read; C, Charge; D, Delete; L, Locked)*				
All	Customer	All content						R
All	Order	All content			R	R	R	R
One	Customer	All content		R		R	R	R
		Credit rating			C			
One	Order	All content		R	R	A, C, D	R	R
		Item price					C	
		Separation of Duties		*Role Restrictions (P, Primary Role; E, Excluded Role)*				
				E	P		E	
				E	E	E	P	
		Performer		*Role Candidates (X, Authorized for Role)*				
		John		X	X		X	X
		Mary		X		X		X
		Peter						X
		Sales Manager (Role)					X	

based on the Context entity. The scope may be unrestricted access to the type of entity (All) identified as the Context, or the Scope may restrict access to the "One" occurrence of the specified type that is the focus of the collaboration. If it is Scope of One, then context information will be required to determine authorization for the service.

An "X" in a Role column indicates that the request identified in that row is accessible to a performer assigned to that role.

Data Rows

The Data row segment defines access to databases. The Context column identifies the data entity type of concern for access. The Scope column specifies if "All" records of the data entity type are accessible, or if only "One" is accessible—the one that is the context of the collaboration activity.

The Access column identifies the level of detail to be accessed. "All content" indicates that all elements of the data entity record are accessible. If the Access column of a data entity row is blank, then only selected elements of the record are accessible. Selected elements are indented below the data entity row. A compound element (such as an order item) designated "All content" indicates that the subordinate elements of that compound element are accessible.

The Role columns indicate the type of access granted to each role. Here, the access authorization is further defined as Add (A), Read (R), Change (C), Delete (D), and Locked (L). For example, the Credit Check role has read (R) access to one customer record, and change (C) access to the credit rating data. The "Locked" designation indicates that the named element cannot be changed by that role.

Separation of Duties Rows

The third group of rows in the table specifies requirements for separation of duties within the context of one collaboration. The Exclusions (E) define those roles that are not allowed for a person in the Primary (P) role. In the example, note that a person in the Credit Check role is excluded from all other roles except the Liaison role; and a person in the Discount Check role is also excluded from all other roles except the Liaison role.

Performer Rows

The fourth group of roles, the Performer rows, identifies specific persons, and the "X" marks indicate the roles for which each person is authorized. John is allowed to fill any of these roles, but with the restrictions of Separation of Duty if he is assigned to either the Credit Check or Discount Check roles.

The Sales Manager role represents a role assignment in another organization that is the basis for assignment of a person to the Discount Check role. Note that the Sales Manager role will have access authorizations associated with that role such as sales data and marketing campaigns that are relevant when considering discounts. Since that performer assignment is managed by a different organization, the actual person may not be known, or, if known, may change independently. For such performers, each assignment to one of these roles must be approved by the asset manager. Performers identified by role might include persons representing customers, suppliers, or other external entities.

In some systems, an individual is allowed to designate a *surrogate* or grant a *proxy*. A surrogate is a person who performs for another primary performer in certain roles of the primary performer. This is typically a stable assignment, and authorization can be specified by simply defining authorized roles for the surrogate person that may be the same or fewer than the primary performer. The runtime collaboration support system must determine when the surrogate is to be engaged.

A proxy is a grant of authority as a representative of another primary performer in a particular context. The person designated as proxy should have the same authorizations for the roles of the primary performer that are required to exercise the proxy but restricted to a particular collaboration occurrence. In the example, the proxy might be for a particular order or a particular customer (multiple orders). This requires a restriction beyond the scope of the table that might be addressed by an additional "comments" column along with a corresponding role assignment mechanism in the runtime system.

With a role authorization model, the resulting authorizations are actually more considered and complete because the requirements are expressed in appropriate business terms and the performer authorizations are quite visible. When an employee gets a new assignment or is terminated, it is quite clear what authorizations must be addressed. A more complete role authorization modeling system could provide a more direct link between specifications like those in the table to express security policy specifications in the security service unit. This would be particularly valuable when systems change or new systems are implemented since it would not be necessary to change the authorization of every potential participant, only to redefine the authorization specifications for the new or affected roles.

Support for Administration

The role-based authorization table supports authorization administration. The service and data context and access columns define requirements for access authorization policies. The role candidates identify the potential performers, so they can be preauthorized for assignments to the associated roles. The separation of duty row defines constraints to be applied when actual role assignments are made. It would be desirable for process/collaboration management systems to enforce selection of role performers from the authorized candidates for the role.

Refinements

Some additional factors might be considered for addition to the spreadsheet model:

- The model does not explicitly support additional performer selection criteria for role assignments. For example, a doctor may be authorized to access a patient's records based on the role context, but a patient may require that only a particular doctor is acceptable for a particular role. There will be other circumstances where there are additional constraints to be applied when selecting a candidate for a particular role assignment.
- If roles in different collaborations require the same authorizations, it would be convenient to be able to represent each equivalent role in the same column of the table. It would also be convenient if they use the same name, but this may be misleading if the collaborations change and the roles require somewhat different authorizations. The table might be extended to provide multiple rows for the role names where each row represents the role names of equivalent roles in a different collaboration.
- The model does not reflect consideration of assignment to a role based on a performer identified in a delegation. For example, a patient has a doctor who will participate in bedside care, but the same doctor is to be assigned the role of surgeon in the operating room collaboration.

■ SUMMARY

Security is and will continue to be a major risk concern. While implementation of security measures can be very technical, it is important that business leaders understand that security management is about risk management. We started this chapter with an overview of risks and means of mitigation. In subsequent sections, we discussed the critical applications of encryption, access control protocols, and management of access authorizations. We also demonstrated the need for computer-based facilities for effective management control of access authorization.

A consistent, enterprise-wide security infrastructure is essential for management of the increased interactions and access points of shared services in an agile enterprise.

Mitigation of security risks has adverse effects. The implementation of a security infrastructure has a one-time cost. On-going maintenance, vigilance and threat, or intrusion response have on-going costs. Business and IT changes require careful review to prevent the introduction of new exposures. This caution and associated costs can be barriers to innovation and agility, and policies such as least privilege and compartmentalization can stand in the way of exploration of innovative ideas. Management must balance the risks against costs and the ability to respond to business challenges and opportunities.

Risk cannot be eliminated. If all the technical mechanisms are implemented, trust remains a key factor. People develop the applications, implement the security mechanisms, perform business activities, and make business decisions that can be sources of risk. This requires good selection and management of people, and awareness of the opportunities and temptations of their jobs.

Chapter 8

Event Driven Operations

VDM (value delivery management), CBA (capability-based architecture), and BCM (business collaboration management) can make an enterprise more flexible, accountable, and efficient, but they do not necessarily make it agile. The agile enterprise must sense what is happening and respond, and the responses must be timely and effective.

Business process automation helps streamline the movement of work through our business systems, but things happen that call for deviations from the normal process, and side effects of some processes require action by other processes. In an agile enterprise, these events must be communicated and initiate action.

For an agile enterprise, events and interactions are an important part of how an enterprise works. We do not just make information available to people who should take action, we send them a notice to pay attention. There are two fundamental levels of response to be considered. Some events occur that affect the normal course of business where we can identify who is responsible and can act more quickly or in a more coordinated way when it is time for them to act. Other events signal unfortunate or unexpected circumstances that disrupt the continued operation of the business.

In this chapter, we will first consider (1) how events drive the routine operation of the business and then (2) how events improve the response to operational failures that interrupt normal operation of the business. In Chapter 9, we will consider how changing circumstances drive changes to the enterprise.

ROUTINE EVENTS

Collaborations (including business processes and case management) respond to events, either events that occur within the collaboration or events from external sources. The most trivial event is the completion of an activity. Other events within a collaboration indicate a deviation from the normal

Building the Agile Enterprise. http://dx.doi.org/10.1016/B978-0-12-805160-3.00008-9
247

flow of activity. In addition, in many cases, an action occurs in one domain, but a response, a consequential action, is required by another person or in another domain. Events then are an important part of timely and effective collaboration, coordination, and awareness.

Some events have predefined recipients. Other events are communicated in response to an expressed interest. These may include notice of changes in status or measurements for monitoring or action when changes require special attention.

An event that is communicated in response to an expression of interest is delivered as an event notice message to a notification broker to be forwarded to interested recipients (see the discussion of notification broker later in this chapter). Event notices may be requested by many recipients from many sources of events. The linkage to event sources and recipients is an ongoing activity. Sources change and new sources will emerge as the ecosystem changes, and interest in certain events will come and go based on various circumstances.

We will consider routine events occur in the following contexts:

- Business process
- Case management
- Business network
- Coordination of collaborations
- Data updates
- Milestones
- Time expired
- Sensor events
- Performance management

Business Process

An event notice received by a business process may cause a business process to start or an active business process to alter its flow. A business process may issue an event to signal completion of an activity, to initiate action at a particular time, when an action or request is not completed in an allowed time, or to signal the occurrence of an exception (typically a problem that requires human intervention). Event notices received and issued are explicitly represented in BPMN (business process model and notation) (see Chapter 4). An event notice representing the occurrence of an exception may go outside the scope of the formal business process, for example, an operational failure event, discussed later.

Case Management

Case management in CMMN (case management model and notation) is driven entirely by events. Events drive responses to a changing situation, and they drive the flow of control as well as interactions between participants. Many case management events are equivalent to events in business processes. Events that drive a case are (1) an action that starts a case, (2) the completion of an activity or stage, (3) the occurrence of a point in time or expiration of a time delay, (4) a relevant change in the state of the data base representing the state of the case, or (5) an action by a participant. Any external event notice directed to the case is recognized as an update to the case database. Except for dependencies between activities, or time-based events, events of interest are recognized when there is a relevant database update from either an internal or an external source. The database represents the state of the world as the case sees it.

A case may generate an event notice to initiate action by a participant or another case or business process, or to report progress. From changes in the database, a case may generate other event notices that are of interest to others but are not necessarily of interest to the case.

Business Network

A business network interaction is similar to a business process except that the flow of control is through the exchange of messages. Message exchanges may be specified with choreography in BPMN. These interactions are fully defined, and any breakdown in the exchange will result in termination of the collaboration, possibly with event notices for problem resolution or performance reporting. The event notices, generally, are in the form of messages exchanged as specified by the choreography. A party expecting a response will use a time delay event to initiate an alternative action if there is no response. Recurring termination of a collaboration may be recognized as an operational failure (see later).

Coordination of Collaborations

Events may be exchanged between relatively independent internal collaborations, much like the exchanges between business networks. However, because the participating collaborations are within the enterprise, the interaction can be described and managed as a collaboration between the collaborations.

Data Updates

Data update events, or "triggers," are issued when notice of a particular change of state has been requested. They are explicitly anticipated and drive some action as determined by the requestor. The commonly occurring data update notice will be to inform another service unit that a state of interest has occurred or that there is a change to master data that the receiving service unit has copied and is keeping up-to-date.

Milestones

A milestone event notice is a declaration of the occurrence of significant progress in a long-running process, project or initiative. A milestone only exists if its occurrence is anticipated and is of interest for a person or a process. Most often it will be recognized in a database update.

Time Expired

An event notice indicating that a particular time has occurred or a period of time duration has expired as the result of initiation of a timer event. Consequently, the event notice is expected unless it is no longer a concern and is canceled. In some cases, it may trigger action as notice of an operational failure. Most timer events are specified within a BPMN or CMMN process.

Sensor Events

Sensors may detect many forms of event from tripping a limit switch, to recognition that a process variable is out of range, to the human selection of a button or mouse click in a kiosk, or to the image perceived by a television camera. The event notice is anticipated or there would be no sensor. That does not necessarily mean that there is currently an action pending for an event notice from every sensor. Some sensors may only be of interest under certain circumstances, so the messages must be filtered.

Performance Management

There are many measurements of performance that are captured by the measurements service unit (see Chapter 6). Monitoring will typically focus on variances that require corrective action. These are event notices for responsible managers, but sometimes they are part of a bigger picture that is of ad hoc concern to business leaders or analysts considering more extensive improvements. These may involve ad hoc subscriptions to event notices.

It is preferable that the events being measured align with the completion of activities in the current VDM model so that they can be interpreted in that context. Eventually, key events should be presented in a VDM model context to interested users in their personal dashboards.

OPERATIONAL FAILURE EVENTS

Operational failure events represent circumstances that prevent normal operation of the business. They may range from the failure of a communication link to a factory fire. The desired result is to prevent an interruption or quickly restore normal operation of the business. The event notices may identify an interruption of normal operations or indicate an increased risk of an interruption. Recognition of the need for such event notices is closely related to risk mitigation—early intervention before a potentially costly interruption.

The current business VDM modeling provides insights on the propagation of effect of these failures for a full understanding of the consequences and possibly the rate of increase in cost when it takes time to return to normal operation.

Case management is particularly appropriate to coordinate a response to a operational failure because each situation will be somewhat different and require different actions by different people. Case management can support the ad hoc planning and immediate and coordinated response as the case evolves.

The following sections characterize operational failure circumstances where notices are needed for prompt action. Each of these events would trigger initiation of a different crisis response case management collaboration. Related events are important for coordination of the response. Notices of these events and the actions being taken must also be directed to business leaders and others whose action or awareness is needed.

Community Infrastructure Failure

Transportation facilities, telephone, heat, light, water, and natural gas may be essential to operation of the business. Event notices should raise awareness of the outage to determine the potential duration and take appropriate action.

Personnel Absences

If the start of a production process, or the ability to maintain a level of service requires a certain level of staffing, it is important to know if the personnel are available. An event notice might be issued if people have not checked in at the designated starting time, and possibly a notice when the required staffing level is achieved.

Machine Failure

A machine failure or repair request may be critical to business operation depending on the availability of alternative machines. Critical machines might be polled to determine if they are available and active with an event notice issued if there is no response. For a less critical machine, an event notice might be issued, but no action may be required unless multiple machines become unavailable.

Product Defect Threshold

Some frequency of product defects may be expected, but at some level, it is appropriate to stop, find the problem, and fix it. An event notice is appropriate when that threshold is reached. In some cases, this may have a significant impact on the ability to continue business as usual. It is likely that event notices will be required for individual defects so that frequency can be assessed before more significant action becomes necessary.

Supply Failure

For operations that depend on consumable resources, an event notice is appropriate when the inventory approaches depletion (maybe X hours on-hand), and again if depletion occurs. For reusable resources, an event notice should be issued when there is a risk that the supply is insufficient, and another event if there is an unmet need.

Damaged Facility

An event notice should be issued if a facility is damaged such that continued business operation is at risk or is discontinued. Such events may require reporting by people on-site, but other operations sensors should also signal a work stoppage.

Natural Disaster

Natural disasters include storms, floods, droughts, earthquakes, fires, and volcanic eruptions. In most cases, there is information available about an increasing risk. Event notices should signal increased levels of risk to initiate assessment, tracking, and possible action to mitigate the damage. For some industries, such events may foretell an abrupt increase in demand for certain products or services.

Epidemic

The risk of spread of disease has been heightened by a shrinking world. Individuals can carry infectious diseases around the globe, overnight. Concerns about a bird flu pandemic have faded, but such risks remain. An epidemic could disable a critical number of employees. A pandemic could have a major impact not only on the ability of the enterprise to function but on the demand for products and services.

Civil Disturbance

Civil disturbance could include a strike, riot, act of terrorism, or robbery. In some cases, like natural disasters, there may be warning signs, indicating an increased risk for which there should be event notices. In other cases, there may be no warning, and an event notice is needed to trigger immediate action to mitigate the damages.

EVENT MANAGEMENT INFRASTRUCTURE

Event-driven operations require an infrastructure for communication of events to the persons or activities that need to be aware of events or take action as a result. The primary facility provides notification management. In the next chapter, we focus on sensing threats and opportunities. Here, most events are involved in internal coordination and collaboration or are reported by human observers.

Notification Management

The core of an event driven infrastructure is notification management, supporting publish and subscribe messaging. This facility filters and delivers notifications of events and other relevant circumstances.

Brokered Notification

Typically, as depicted in Fig. 8.1, a notification broker receives notices from *publishers* and forwards the notices to *subscribers* who have expressed interest in certain types of events. Notices are associated with *topics* and have attributes to describe the nature and context of the notices. Subscribers may specify constraints on the notices they want to receive. This may take the form of a topic designation and rules that filter notices based on notice attributes.

Note that a subscriber may subscribe to multiple topics, a publisher may publish notices of interest on multiple topics, and each notice may be forwarded to multiple subscribers.

The Organization for Advancement of Structured Information Systems (OASIS) has adopted the WS-Notification (http://docs.oasis-open.org/wsn/wsn-ws_base_notification-1.3-spec-os.htm, http://www.oasis-open.org/specs/index.php#wsnv1.3) family of standards. The interfaces and

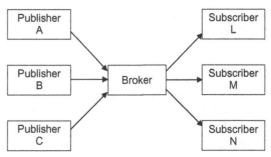

■ **FIG. 8.1** Brokered notification.

message formats for a notification service using a broker are defined by the OASIS WS-BrokeredNotification (http://www.oasis-open.org/specs/index. php#wsnv1.3) standard. Publishers register with the broker to identify the topics for which they publish notices. When the broker receives the first subscription for a topic, it will notify the registered publishers to begin submitting notices. If all subscriptions are withdrawn, the broker will notify the publishers so that they can stop issuing notices, thus avoiding unnecessary network traffic.

Nonbrokered Notification

As an alternative approach, under WS-BaseNotification (http://docs.oasis-open.org/wsn/wsn-ws_base_notification-1.3-spec-os.htm), a subscriber can request notices directly from a publisher. Fig. 8.2 depicts a nonbrokered notification topology. A notification directory identifies sources of events. Publishers need to register with the directory, and a subscriber then uses the directory to identify sources of events of interest and subscribes directly to those sources. A subscriber can define restrictions on the events of interest through specification of a constraint that operates on the attributes of the event notice.

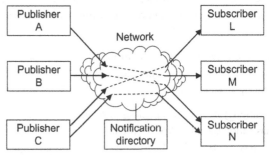

■ **FIG. 8.2** Networked notification.

This removes the event notification broker as a potential bottleneck. Before the general availability of Internet technology, a broker was necessary to eliminate a multitude of point-to-point connections; now with point-to-point connectivity and standard exchange protocols, a broker no longer simplifies the network. Note that Publisher C sends notices to Subscriber L and N, directly, whereas in the brokered notification, Publisher C would send a single notice and the broker would forward notices to Subscribers L and N. Subscription requests should be recoverable so that if the publisher fails or is shut down, notices will resume when the publisher returns to operation.

This mode is good if publishers stay the same. If there is a change in publisher, or if publishers come and go, subscribers would need to subscribe for each new publisher.

The absence of a notification broker makes management of event notification totally decentralized. It may be preferable to at least use a notification broker between internal subscribers and external providers to monitor the activity and contractual compliance for purchased services. A broker also provides a central point of control for directing notices to subscribers so that publishers can be replaced when necessary without searching out all subscribers. As an alternative, the event directory could function as a broker of offers and requests, while the publishers each send event notices directly to subscribers.

Access Control

An event notice can be a source of confidential information. Consequently, subscriptions for event notices must be authorized. The authorization must be granted by the source of the desired event notice. This is further complicated by the fact that authorization may be based on specific content of the event notice, such as data about a specific patient or a customer.

If the authorization is applied to the subscription request, then there must be a mechanism to remove the subscription when the authorization is terminated. Note that authorization may be quite dynamic as where different professionals may be authorized to receive notices for a particular hospital patient at different times, potentially at every shift change. There should not be a delay between authorization and the ability of the professional to participate in providing services nor termination of access when the professional is no longer authorized.

The nonbrokered approach enables authorization to be managed by the publisher since the publisher can validate the delivery of each notice to each subscriber.

Polling Service

Some sources of events, particularly external sources, are not designed to provide notification of changes but maintain web services with current information. A polling service can function as a notification publisher that obtains notices by periodically polling various sources for current information and comparing current state to prior states to identify changes.

This service, like other publishers, can have polling turned on or off depending on the presence of subscribers. This allows the polling services to maintain the possibility of providing notices on many topics, most of which are not currently of interest or may be of only occasional, brief interest.

MOVING FORWARD

Event processing has a significant impact on the timely and efficient operation of the business and the mitigation of failures and destructive circumstances. In the next chapter, we will consider the ability to respond to circumstances that require a change to the business in order to remain competitive and pursue threats or opportunities in a timely manner.

Chapter

9

Sense and Respond

Business and technology continue to change at an accelerating pace. Companies must innovate to improve their products and processes. Things are happening outside the enterprise that represent potential threats and opportunities. The market is changing, new products are being introduced, economic conditions are changing, international situations are affecting trade, competitors are pursuing new strategies, technology is changing, creating new markets and opportunities for improved efficiency, quality, or timeliness.

In today's world, an enterprise must be more sensitive to emerging challenges and opportunities and be prepared to adapt more quickly and significantly than in the past. Generally, we expect leaders to watch for changes that might affect them, or we expect executives to discover what is happing in the marketplace and the industry and deal with it in strategic planning. The agile enterprise must be better than that.

There are events, trends, and patterns of behavior in the marketplace or the enterprise ecosystem where the response should be to change the business. Sometimes the needed change can be addressed primarily by a particular organization unit and can be resolved quite quickly. Other responses should be broader in scope, particularly where the agile enterprise has shared capabilities that may impact multiple value streams. Still other threats or opportunities may require substantial or pervasive changes that must be defined and coordinated across the organization. Occasionally, there will be a potential opportunity to drive a radical industry change that could dramatically change the marketplace for significant competitive advantage (or disadvantage).

In this chapter, we will consider how the agile enterprise senses and responds to change. We will begin by considering the drivers of change and how we manage different levels of change. Then we will discuss transformation management using a value delivery management (VDM) model to define the future business design and phases of transformation. Next we consider the management of change through an example product life-cycle. Finally, we discuss enterprise-level business change support and sense and respond infrastructure requirements.

Building the Agile Enterprise. http://dx.doi.org/10.1016/B978-0-12-805160-3.00009-0

DRIVERS OF BUSINESS CHANGE

Occasionally the need for business change may be triggered by an event, but more often, the recognition of opportunity comes from realization of the impact of trends or relationships that create a synergy between emerging technology, declining costs, and market trends or emerging markets that may also be tapped by innovation. Some of these changes drive continuous improvement, and others drive significant changes in products or the industry.

This section will focus on the drivers of change to the business. We will describe these as relevant *circumstances*. These may also be associated with events, but circumstances more often involve a number of factors, trends, or expectations from which we may infer a business threat or opportunity.

So as we observe the development of new products in an industry, there are precipitating events, actions, investments, features, and market growth. Unfortunately, by the time there is a product and a market, the observing enterprise is already behind the competition. There is usually opportunity to become aware of a new technology, a market change, or a new business discipline as the basis of a competitive threat. For example, work on a new technical standard will typically begin years before implementations of the standard will come to market. The initiation of work on a standard is evidence of a demand that will eventually have consequential effects.

We should be aware of the evolving circumstances that drive the development of new products or services and decide when the potential customer demand (or other stakeholder) reaches a threshold that requires action to mitigate a threat or lead in the pursuit of the opportunity. This requires both broad industry knowledge and an understanding of the potential marketplace. In some cases, a radical change will represent a major opportunity (and risk) and will involve synergy with business partners, potentially including another industry.

A capability oriented architecture brings economy of scale that enables development of expertise in each capability and the circumstances affecting advances in that capability. This expertise should be encouraged and leveraged as a source of awareness and insights from outside the enterprise.

The enterprise must leverage the insights of the internal experts scattered across the organization. These are not only experts in their particular area of the business, but they live in the real world where, collectively, they have a diverse view of the enterprise stakeholders and potential markets, and, hopefully, some of them have an opportunity to attend conferences or standards meetings to have contact with industry experts.

The interest groups discussed for knowledge management in Chapter 6 are key to recognition of potential synergy of multiple trends and emerging technologies to form a new business opportunity. Participants in these groups should understand that such insights and innovations are part of their jobs. They are sources, and potential catalysts of new business visions.

This decentralized knowledge acquisition and innovation deserves some coordination and collaboration. A current enterprise VDM model will provide a context for this coordination and collaboration. Enterprise-level support is discussed in a later section.

Some changes will be incremental improvements that may support or improve market share. At the other extreme, some changes could dramatically change the market, the industry, and the competitive landscape.

In the following sections, we will consider sources of knowledge and insights about relevant circumstances, evaluation of the scope of impact of an observation or implication, and the role of executive staff organizations in providing business change support and leadership.

Sources of Knowledge

Underlying a new product may be an event such as the realization of an innovation or invention. While the invention is important, the development of a product and a market takes time and additional creativity. We may see the announcement of the new product as an event, but that is a milestone in a process. The success of the product will then depend on the readiness or development of the market—the development of demand and sales.

Significant circumstances seldom occur in a single event. Development of new technology and growth of a market may take years to develop. Below are a number sources of knowledge that can provide insight on things to come. Various employees should have access to these sources depending on their areas of expertise and roles in the business.

Public News Media

Employees at all levels should be aware of world events and changes in social, economic, and political circumstances. These affect the demand for products, the cost and availability of resources, the availability of funding for the enterprise and customers, and other factors.

Market Segment Industry Associations

Market segment industry associations are important sources of information on problems and concerns of customers that may suggest product improvements or problems to be addressed with new products or services. They may also suggest opportunities for synergy between industries.

Professional and Standards Organizations

Professional and standards organizations engage people who are aware of new ideas in their professions and they participate in the development of standards because those standards are relevant to their employers' capabilities or plans.

Industry Literature

Industry literature is a source of advertising by vendors that have something new to offer. The literature also includes articles on new approaches by members of the industry.

Industry Conferences

Conferences are forums for people to highlight their accomplishments and new ideas. In addition to listening to presentations, conferences provide the opportunity to have face-to-face contact where more detailed information may be revealed in personal conversations.

Competitors' Products

Competitors' products reveal new designs and features for potential competitive advantage, and they may also suggest new production techniques.

Government Regulations

Actions on development of new government regulations are good indicators of public concerns affecting business operations or products. These may have significant effects on current products or processes, or on the development of new products or services.

Analytics

Analytics applications examine large volumes of data of various forms to discover events, trends, or relationships. In this context, there may be opportunities to discover new markets developed by competitor products or pricing, but it should be possible to anticipate these developments before they occur. The circumstances in which new approaches are born usually exist months if not years before they appear in the marketplace. Nevertheless, analytics may help recognize potential markets or measure the size of existing or emerging markets, to establish when a market is ready for a new product or service, or which market segment may be the best target.

However, analytics requires focus. The computer cannot decide what is worthy of analysis, rather, leaders and analytics experts must consider the various sources of data that may be available and the particular entities, variables, and relationships that are important for identification of threats and opportunities. Buying habits of existing customers may also reveal opportunities. Note that a trend or change in a variable may be more important than its current value.

Collaboration

Collaboration of employees with other employees with related interests as well as with outside professionals is a key source of new ideas and refinement of possibilities. The formation of internal interest groups for collaboration is discussed in Chapter 6. Social networking such as LinkedIn provides the opportunities to collaborate (or observe collaborations) among professionals with similar interests. Members of an interest group can pool their knowledge and insights to innovate or predict potential products or services that could represent a threat or opportunity to the business. An interest group may also help determine how analytics can help determine relevant markets and the current or future viability of a product or service.

Employees throughout the enterprise should be encouraged to develop ideas for improvements of capabilities and products. Involvement with external sources of knowledge along with participation in internal interest group collaborations should cultivate many ideas. Interest group collaborations also should help select and refine ideas for further action.

With individual employees taking initiative and participating in interest group discussions, there will likely be some people looking at the same issues. There is a need for Sense and Respond Directory to capture and record the observations and ideas to encourage coordination and collaboration, and to drive input to persons or processes that should act on the information. This is discussed more, later.

Scope of Change

Fig. 9.1 depicts a business change framework. This aligns the scope of a change with organizational levels for evaluation and further development. The planning horizon indicates the general magnitude of the undertaking and the duration of the effort. The organizational scope describes the level and number of organizations involved and thus the level of collaboration and coordination required. We will briefly describe the planning horizons and then describe the levels of organization and their involvement in the implementations.

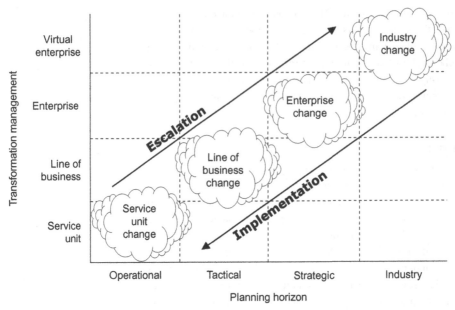

■ **FIG. 9.1** Business change management framework.

Planning Horizon

Here we are concerned with the significance of the undertaking and thus the cost, risk, and duration of the transformation. Potential changes may be recognized at the operational level but moved up to tactical or strategic level as the scope of impact expands.

Capability units and value streams clarify responsibility for many focused business changes. VDM clarifies the potential impact and requirements for collaboration and coordination as well as a shared business design of the future state. Tactical, strategic, and industry transformations require development of a future state VDM model.

In the following sections, we consider the four planning horizons: operational, tactical, strategic, and industry horizons in the above framework.

Operational Changes

An operational change is relatively narrow in scope as improvement to a capability unit or capability unit group, it is focused primarily on incremental improvement, and it has little if any impact on the consumers of its service(s) or the services that it uses. An operational horizon change would typically be implemented within a year but may be a bit longer if there is coordination required with other capability units.

Tactical Changes

Tactical changes have broader impact, generally focused on a value stream or line of business (LOB), and may require some adjustments to other value streams or lines of business as a result of changes to shared capability units. Development of a value stream for a new product as well as a significant change to an existing product for a new market would be tactical. Changes to multiple value streams within the same LOB may still be considered to be tactical except that it is likely there will be more impact on other lines of business through changes to shared services.

These changes rely on VDM models to ensure proper coordination and enterprise optimum impact on values of affected value streams. The tactical horizon is more likely 2–4 years since it will likely involve more analysis, design, and coordination of changes in multiple capabilities and multiple value streams, and, possibly, multiple lines of business.

Strategic Changes

Strategic changes are still broader in scope affecting multiple lines of business including some shared capability units. This would include merger, acquisition, divestiture, outsourcing, and changes to administrative support services. These changes require extensive use of VDM modeling for validation of strategy, assessment of impact, and specification of the to-be business design. Introduction of new information technology would also be managed at this level if it has an impact on multiple LOB operations, for example, new personal devices (smart phones or tablets), or use of cloud computing could require significant modifications to applications and personnel training. The strategic horizon could be 4 years or more, involve multiple lines of business, and potentially impact suppliers, business partners, and customers.

Industry Changes

Industry changes involve substantial departure from an established business model to effect an industry change of direction with new or significantly changed products and services for a new market.

This includes *disruptive innovation* as defined by Christensen (2016), where products capture a new, mass market that will respond to lower cost, less sophisticated products. The goal is to address a new, larger market that accepts neither the cost nor the need for complexity of competitor products. Cloud computing is a disruptive change that has drawn in a larger, less sophisticated market, and is now starting to erode the business of the traditional data processing center. The leader in industry change has the potential to capture a large share of the new market before competitors can respond and thus set the standards and build on the core business over time.

Levels of Response

Based on these planning horizons, we now consider how these relate to the levels of transformation management, the vertical scale of Fig. 9.1. Essentially, we start with the assumption that management of a change is the responsibility of the manager of the organizational unit affected. This may change as the nature of the change and the scope of its impact evolve.

VDM and the capability-based architecture (CBA) enable decentralized innovation by enabling employees and unit managers to see the big picture and understand how their ideas may impact the rest of the business. Employees at any level may become aware of opportunities or relevant changes in the business ecosystem. These may be topics of discussion in interest groups. The management chain of leading participants should ensure that proposals are brought to the attention of appropriate transformation leaders. Management controls, business processes that initiate change, and capability unit manager incentives must be appropriately applied to achieve a balance between local initiative and enterprise optimization.

A VDM model for the current business provides a context for consideration of the effects of a potential change. This helps determine the organizations and levels of management that may need to be involved in consideration of a change, it provides insight on the impact of the change on value contributions and their effects on value streams, and it provides the basis for determining the enterprise-level optimum effect that may involve trade-offs.

In addition to the organizational scope of a change, there may be funding thresholds that require that a change be proposed to a higher level of management for approval of funding.

As the total transformation becomes clear, requirements on lines of business and the individual capability units will become clear, and responsibility for implementation of specific components may be delegated back to the LOB and capability unit organizations consistent with the VDM model and a phased implementation.

Capability Unit Management

The lowest level of transformation management is the capability unit. Some changes have an effect specifically on the operating activities of a particular capability unit. Resolution of these circumstances can be implemented immediately by the capability unit manager unless they require substantial investment or will adversely affect service cost, quality, or timeliness. In a CBA, the approach to implementation of service operations is internal to the capability unit, as long as it does not adversely affect service users or services used.

If a capability unit manager implements changes that improve the cost, quality, or timeliness of its operations, it must remain compliant with its interface specifications and level of service agreements of the capability unit. Some changes to interfaces and performance may be acceptable if the related capability units concur, particularly if there is off-setting value, otherwise pursuit of the changes may need to be escalated to a level appropriate to the scope of impact of the change. Shared services will have multiple recipients of their services to reconcile. Collaboration is required with related capability units to ensure continued compatibility and compliance with service level agreements. Services that are unique to a value stream—typically those that define the high-level activities—will only be concerned with the needs of the particular value stream.

For example, plans for transformation of a capability implementation may start at the capability unit level, but if the change has a functional effect on consumers of the service or services it engages, then there are broader implications to consider. This may still be resolved at the capability unit level by collaboration with the affected recipients and providers. However, if there are many other organizations, or if the change suggests a change to the corporate VDM model, then there may be cause to raise transformation to a higher level of management. The same applies to expanding scope of changes at the LOB level and the enterprise-level. Furthermore, if the planning horizon is longer, management at a higher level may be appropriate since other initiatives and considerations may come into play.

Incremental Change Generally, changes managed by a capability unit will be incremental. This may include improvements of cost or quality or one of the following.

Regulatory compliance. Compliance with regulations may only require changes to the capability unit. They may have some effect on users of a service, but that will not remove the need to comply. Collaboration may reveal ways to comply without undesirable side effects.

Information technology. Information technology could be applied for automation, improved access to information, technology modernization, or better communication and coordination.

Production technology. Production might be improved with new or better tools or machines and potentially by changes in materials or production scheduling; however, consideration must be given to adverse effects on value contributions.

Business process. Process improvements might save labor, material or reduce scrap or defects.

Product. Product changes might improve manufacturability or maintainability or improve product appeal with new features or appearance. However, for a shared service, potential effects on other products must be considered.

Propagation of Change If changes to internal operations adversely affect the cost, quality, or timeliness of the service for some users, the capability unit manager will need to negotiate with service users to justify the change or demonstrate to enterprise leaders that there is a net gain to the enterprise. Changes that do not affect the interfaces and do not increase cost or degrade the level of service should not be a concern to service users or providers.

In some cases, there may be a need to change the capability unit interface, and this will require other units to make complementary changes. Fig. 9.2 depicts relationships between service users and service providers. Capability unit X is both a user of capability unit Y and a provider to capability units A, B, and C. A change to the service interface of capability unit X may require changes to all the users of capability unit X, here represented by capability units A, B, and C. If a change impacts the value contributions of capability unit X, it affects the competitive position of the value streams served by capability units A, B, and C, because A, B, and C must bear the cost and depend on the results of capability unit X in the delivery of their services.

Consequently, the solution should be the result of collaboration between the capability unit manager of capability unit X and the managers of the user

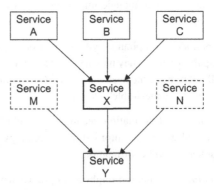

■ **FIG. 9.2** Change propagation.

capability units A, B, and C unless the changes also impact the users of capability units A, B, and C.

Note that enterprise governance should require that changes to capability unit interfaces be approved at an enterprise-level to ensure that the solution is optimal for the enterprise, particularly for future needs that might not be represented by current service users.

A capability unit may require changes to a service it uses. In the diagram, capability unit X may need changes to capability unit Y. If so, the capability unit X manager should work with the manager of capability unit Y to develop the changes. However, capability unit Y may have other users, such as capability units M and N that are not apparent to capability unit X. Thus capability unit X may need to engage both capability unit Y and all the users of capability unit Y to accomplish the change. The change should occur easily if all users see a net benefit; otherwise, they either agree that it has value to the enterprise or the decision must be made at a higher level in the organization. This includes consideration of the cost of change as well as any increase in operating cost as compared to the business value of the change.

If a change to a service provider increases the cost or degrades the performance of a user, that user is in turn accountable to its users. In the diagram, suppose capability unit Y makes a change to improve the quality of its product, but this causes a cost increase. This cost increase is incurred by capability unit X along with the other services that use capability unit Y. This affects the obligation of capability unit X to its users, A, B, and C. This effect propagates up the chain of users until it becomes evident in one or more value streams or otherwise affects enterprise performance. At that level, the impact on the enterprise and the ultimate customer can be evaluated.

Changes that have a propagation of effect to one or more value streams must be evaluated in the context of relevant VDM scenarios. This will highlight the impact on value propositions and provide a basis for objective consideration of enterprise-level trade-offs.

One-Time Costs Even if a capability unit manager makes a change that reduces cost over time, there may be an investment, and thus an increase in costs, incurred in the short term. It would not be desirable for all improvements to be impeded by opposition to cost increases by users. This should be addressed with an appropriate funding mechanism. The cost of change might be recovered over time, so improvements that would be recovered within a certain number of years would be authorized and amortized for cost recovery. The capability unit management chain has primary responsibility for making such changes. Changes that would increase the unit cost of services to users should be approved by the service user managers and/or the affected LOB managers. The enterprise must establish appropriate procedures to ensure an appropriate level of budgeting, approval, and concurrence by affected managers.

For example, a machine repair capability unit may determine that an investment in a diagnostic tool would reduce the cost of repairs. If the return on investment is acceptable, the cost of the tool can be prorated, reflecting the return on investment so that there is no net cost increase to service users. This would not affect the capability unit interface. On the other hand, shifting from a failure-response mode of machine repair to a preventive maintenance mode requires a different relationship with service users and thus a change to the service interface—which may put an additional burden on service users while reducing the impact of failures on the operations of the service users. This also requires a change in the cost model. This can be resolved through collaboration with service users but should still require enterprise-level approval of the interface change.

Changes Out of Scope For a particular business change, there may be no solution that can be implemented within a single capability unit or through a collaboration among the service manager and service users. This may be because the change has long-term consequences or significantly impacts the enterprise product or service. The resolution of these exception events must be escalated to the LOB manager or managers. In some cases, the need for change may come to the attention of a capability unit manager but not have a direct bearing on his or her operation. Notices of these events should be posted for distribution to more appropriate recipients. If appropriate recipients have not been predefined, the event notice must be escalated up the management chain.

LOB Management

The LOB manager has a broader perspective on needs for change. The LOB manager is concerned about competitive position of value streams for the products or services that he or she manages and thus can assess the implications of changes in a market context. All LOB managers should be able to view the delivery of customer value in the context of a product life-cycle for their LOB (see the product life-cycle discussion later in this chapter).

A LOB manager will also have capability units that are unique to specific value streams or to the LOB. Some changes to these will be internal to the capability unit, but optimization of the particular LOB will always be the primary objective.

As with the capability unit manager discussed previously, the LOB manager may be able to work with one or more shared capability units to resolve changes of limited impact. These are essentially operational adjustments.

Observations that indicate a change in market demand or an opportunity for competitive advantage should be primarily directed to LOB managers and market analysts. They must translate a change in market demand to a change in sales forecasts, and then, using the value stream, they must determine the implications to the services used to deliver products or services. This may have a significant impact on the workload of service providers, but it might not require any change in functionality.

Some enhancements call for significant changes to the product or service or need to be coordinated across a number of services that are only indirectly related. For example, a new product technology may require changes in product engineering activities, production activities, field service activities, and supply chain relationships. The design and implementation of these changes requires cross-organizational coordination and control. VDM support for substantial transformation management is discussed later in this chapter.

These changes are more likely to involve improvements of value streams and value propositions of other lines of business. Planning and implementation must involve VDM modeling analysis along with collaboration among representatives of all the affected lines of business, the business architecture organization, and other shared services and business support services. These changes will likely involve changes to shared capabilities, and these must be reconciled with other lines of business that share those capabilities.

The Cost of Change   The cost of such changes must nevertheless be determined and considered in the decision to change. Change implementation may be owned by the LOB manager but managed and performed by transformation capability units. The affected provider capability unit managers have the primary responsibility for change implementation. If the change adversely affects their other users, the impact on those users is part of the cost of change and could be an increased burden on other LOBs. Unless the affected product lines agree, the issue should be escalated to the executive staff level in the organization.

Value stream relationships in a service-oriented architecture supported by VDM modeling make it possible to determine the full cost of change as well as the full cost of a product, including the indirect impact on related products and services. Each product is the result of contributions of value and cost from the services used to develop and deliver the product. Each service must report its true cost, including the cost incurred in using other services and the recovery of costs for improvements.

In some cases, a needed change has effects that reach beyond the responsibility of the LOB manager. This includes an opportunity for a new LOB, a need for substantial realignment of business operations, consideration of a merger or acquisition, or a technology change that exceeds a threshold for investment in new capabilities. These exceptional circumstances should be escalated to the executive staff.

Later in this chapter, discussion of a product life-cycle process reflects the requirements for collaboration with other organizations in the development and implementation of a new product or substantial LOB changes.

Enterprise Management Transformation that has broad impact and requires coordination across major organizations must be managed from an enterprise perspective. These changes arise from new business opportunities and threats that are not specific to a LOB. This includes (1) consolidations of capabilities or significant changes to shared capabilities; (2) creation of a new LOB; (3) a merger, acquisition, divestiture, or outsourcing; (4) changes to customer or supplier relationships; and (5) introduction or upgrade of pervasive technology (typically information technology).

The executive staff should be aware of any circumstances, internal or external, that can cause significant and sustained change in market demand, operating costs, personnel, investment, and supply chain relationships for consideration of countermeasures or changes of strategy. Enterprise management must bring an overall perspective through strategic planning. Strategic planning and implications to the agile enterprise are discussed in the next major section. A transformation management process is discussed later in this chapter.

Virtual Enterprise Management

A virtual enterprise is an enterprise composed of multiple companies that work together for a shared purpose—a collaboration of companies. The companies involved in a virtual enterprise each expect to realize benefit from the collaboration, otherwise the virtual enterprise will not survive. This is represented in a VDM model as a business network exchange of value propositions.

The decision to participate in a virtual enterprise will be the result of enterprise management strategic planning. Strategic planning will continue to focus on the virtual enterprise relationships and the role of the parent enterprise in this business arrangement and the marketplace. See the discussion of strategic planning in the next section.

Industry Change Generally, the purpose of the virtual enterprise is to create a stronger business than the participants can achieve on their own. Formation of a virtual enterprise suggests a change to a business model that is not consistent with current industry relationships. It will have a significant industry impact and will involve a greater investment, duration, and risk than a transformation that is contained and managed within the single enterprise.

While the industry change may involve multiple companies, one company will be the focus of the transformation as the company that will realize the major competitive advantage among its competitors, and likewise the one that will take the greatest risks, making the industry transformation a primary focus of that company's efforts for several years.

The participants will work together for seamless integration of their products and services and potentially participate in joint sales or integrated customer solutions. This will involve adoption or development of shared standards for seamless integration of complementary products and services as an aspect of the expected competitive advantage.

An industry change usually brings a new business model or at least a substantial change in the nature of a product or service. A radical change has the potential to take advantage of the cultural inertia of competitors because they are heavily invested and comfortable with business as usual.

Convergence of Factors Generally, the change becomes viable because of the convergence of multiple factors—potentially multiple industries. Consider the introduction of iTunes by Apple. It was not just a new music download service, and it changed the recording industry—a new business model. There was already a transition to digital music, and cheap memory enabled collections of music to be stored on a small, portable device. Recording studios and artists were already losing to the distribution of pirated music. Apple gained the advantage of being first to provide the service to serve the market and develop relationships with members of the recording industry. A mass market was driven by low prices and easy access to a very large library of recordings that was more convenient (and legal) than access to pirated recordings.

The market factors did not suddenly change, they converged over time: digital music, very small player devices with lots of memory to hold many recordings, internet access to a library, recording companies and artists losing money to pirates, and an existing market of people enjoying their personal collections on portable devices. The strategy could have been developed much earlier. If it was introduced too soon, it might have failed. A key was to make the commitment and develop the details and relationships at the right time.

For Apple, the disruptive event occurred when there was a commitment to the strategy. For the industry, it occurred when iTunes was announced.

Of course, there was a lot more to the success of iTunes than commitment to a strategy. There was implementation of the service, synergy with mobile devices, the development of a profit formula, development of marketing strategy, the acquisition of content, and the delivery of value to the affected artists and enterprises.

So what could a competitor do? Could they have beaten Apple to market with an alternative service? Probably not. But they might have anticipated such a move and built a complementary strategy. Apple changed, not only the portable recording device industry, but the music industry as well.

So to create an industry change requires (1) an understanding of the marketplace, including the behavior of the end customers, (2) understanding of the potential of the core technology, (3) relationships with key participants, and (4) having the capability and courage to deliver.

STRATEGIC PLANNING FRAMEWORK

Strategic planning defines what the enterprise is now and what it is expected to be in the future. It is primarily the work of the executive team and supporting staff, but it must reflect the values and interests of the governing board and investors.

In the agile enterprise, strategic planning must be an on-going activity. In this section, we will first consider a conventional framework of strategic planning and then discuss how this might be modified to address the concerns and capabilities of the agile enterprise.

Conventional Strategic Planning

Fig. 9.3 depicts a high-level view of the BMM (business motivation model) strategic planning framework, an OMG specification. This structure has received widespread acceptance as a useful framework, and it is a good foundation for strategic planning for an agile enterprise. The concepts are typical of common strategic planning practices.

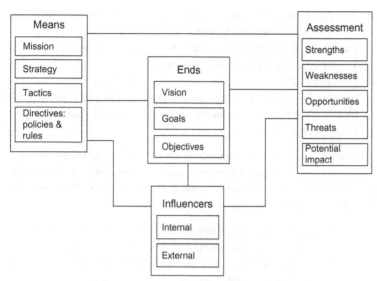

■ **FIG. 9.3** The business motivation model (BMM).

Strategic planning is primarily the responsibility of the CEO with the participation of his or her direct reports. At the same time, there is a need for a support staff to gather information, support the analysis, develop the work products of the strategic planning effort, and coordinate with related activities. The leader of the strategic planning capability unit typically reports to the CEO. The following points briefly describe each of the elements in Fig. 9.3:

Ends. Ends describe the ideal future state of the enterprise; they include vision, goals, and objectives.

- *Vision*. A vision is a future, possibly unattainable state of the enterprise. It may be a characterization of the way the enterprise should be viewed by others, for example, as leader in a particular industry, preferred employer, innovator, etc.
- *Goals*. Goals are more specific aspirations for the enterprise, but they tend to be on-going rather than having a point of completion. Goals support the vision.
- *Objectives*. Objectives are achievable, measurable results that support goals with a defined time of completion.

Means. Means are the mechanisms by which ends are pursued. The components of means are mission, strategy, tactics, and directives.

- *Mission*. The mission is a general statement of the on-going purpose of the enterprise—a generalization of the value to be produced.

- *Strategy*. Strategy is a plan or approach to supporting the mission and achieving ends, particularly with a focus on goals.
- *Tactics*. Tactics are specific, near-term actions in support of a strategy. Tactics typically focus on achieving objectives.
- *Directives*. Directives define restrictions or requirements on how business is conducted. They include policies and rules. Policies are high-level statements of intent. Rules are specific constraints on business operations.

Influencers. Influencers are sources of effects that must be considered in assessment and planning. Influencers can affect the conduct of business, positive or negative, but do not have direct action or control. There are internal and external influencers.

- *Internal influencers*. Internal influencers are things within the enterprise, such as culture, attitudes, thought leaders, infrastructure, beliefs, and capabilities, that influence how business is approached or conducted and how new ideas are developed.
- *External influencers*. External influencers come in a wide variety, such as competitors, customers, the economy, governments, and technology. Changes in these influencers may have a significant impact on business opportunities or the viability of the enterprise or its undertakings. These are sources of change outside the enterprise. See the section on drivers of change, earlier in this chapter.

Assessment. Assessment deals with the evaluation of the impact of specific current and changing factors that should be considered in planning future pursuits or direction. Strengths, Weaknesses, Opportunities, and Threats (often referred to as SWOT) are not a normative part of the BMM specification but are widely used. Strengths and Weaknesses are internal; Opportunities and Threats typically come from the environment. Influencers, along with strategies, tactics, and transformation plans, are inputs to assessments. An assessment effort will determine potential impact.

- *Strengths*. Strengths are those factors that make the enterprise competitive or give it competitive advantage. Strengths are important in considering new undertakings.
- *Weaknesses*. Weaknesses are those factors that could put the enterprise at a disadvantage with respect to competitors or the capability to undertake a new pursuit.
- *Opportunities*. Opportunities represent potential growth or improvement of value and include such things as new endeavors, new markets, and advanced technology that may create a new market or provide competitive advantage.

- *Threats.* Threats are circumstances that could put the enterprise at risk. These may include actions by competitors, economic, political or social events, natural disasters, supplier failure, shortage of resources, or lawsuits. They may include missed opportunities that could impact market share.
- *Potential impact.* Potential impact captures the results of assessments— potential gain or loss. Typically, the affects of these impacts are relative to current or future business endeavors.

Adaptations for the Agile Enterprise

Fig. 9.4 depicts the BMM framework modified to support strategic planning for an agile enterprise. The modifications are highlighted with double boundaries.

We have made five changes: (1) expanded on the content of vision, (2) added business architecture, (3) changed influencers to enterprise intelligence, (4) replaced potential impact with risks within assessment, and (5) added transformation and standards and technology to means.

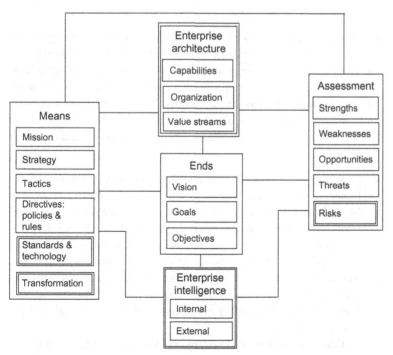

■ **FIG. 9.4** Strategic planning for the agile enterprise.

These five changes not only connect strategic planning to the operation of the enterprise; they provide the means for insight and participation in governance by the Governing Board. Along with Strategic Planning, these changes align with the executive staff capability units described in the organization structure in Chapter 10. We discuss their roles in strategic planning activities in the following list, and their broader capability unit capabilities and responsibilities in the organization structure discussion.

Vision. The content of Vision is expanded here based on Collins and Porras (1996). These added elements provide a stronger corporate identity.

- *Core ideology.* The core ideology consists of two elements that could persist for as long as the enterprise exists:
  - ○ *Core values.* A few guiding principles for the operation of the enterprise.
  - ○ *Core purpose.* The most fundamental reason for the existence of the enterprise.
- *Envisioned future.* A significant ambition for the future.
  - ○ *Audacious goals.* These are inspirational goals that may not be possible.
  - ○ *Vivid description.* An inspirational vision of what the enterprise should be in the future.

Business architecture. Adding this component makes the design of the business a key part of strategic planning. It provides insight on both the current enterprise design and implications of potential designs of the future. Within the Strategic Planning activities, Business Architecture is a component supported by the Business Architecture capability unit, discussed later. There are three key components that support the strategic planning process: Capability Units, Organization, and the Value Streams.

- *Capability units.* The capability units component is a model of the formal, integrated capabilities of the enterprise, which support the Means and are the basis of the Assessment. Capability units and resources for the capability units are managed and leveraged by the organization. Capability units are an addition to the standard model because they are the building blocks for implementation of Strategies and Tactics, and they are the focal point for assessing Strengths and Weaknesses as well as Risks. Specification, configuration, and implementation of capability units become means to realization of the strategic plan.

  Capability units are also the targets of strategies and tactics. Strategies and tactics are developed for capability units when we address threats and opportunities, possibly requiring some adaptation of existing capability units and occasionally requiring the development of a new capability unit. The investment required to implement strategies is lower and more predictable with capability unit building blocks. For the most part, shared capability units remain stable as the products or services of the enterprise change. This means that they continue to operate effectively and potentially continue to improve.

- *Organization.* The organization structure defines responsibility for management of operations, resources, and facilities to fulfill capability unit requirements. The business architecture must align organizational goals and incentives as well as other factors that achieve synergy, to promote optimal performance of capability units. The organization structure is not the capability unit integration network but instead represents the relationships between people that manage and participate in capability units, perform the work, and adapt the enterprise to changing business needs. Organization design is discussed in Chapter 10. The organization structure also determines the responsibilities of managers for compliance with rules and regulations and mitigation of risks.
- *Value streams.* The value stream concept is fundamental to VDM model. A value stream defines the network of capability units that contribute to the deliverables and values delivered to a customer. The enterprise consists of a number of value streams. The primary value streams produce end customer value and generate revenue for profit-making enterprises. Other value streams produce value for internal customers and stakeholders.

  In many cases, the focus for strategic planning is on value streams and the participating capability units to deliver value, manage cost, and ensure compliance with rules and regulations. Analysis of a production value stream reveals the contributions of cost, quality, and timeliness of individual capability units in the delivery of results to customers. This provides perspective on where to invest in improvements.

  In evaluating new products and assessing a LOB, the full life-cycle of products and service offerings should be considered as discussed later in this chapter. VDM analysis of a potential value stream can reveal both the ability or inability to deliver value and the direct impact on other operations and lines of business of the enterprise, including the utilization of strengths and the need to resolve weaknesses.

  In the past, there has not been a direct linkage between the strategic objectives and the design of business operations to achieve those objectives. Generally, strategic planning has relied on the mental models of executive leadership to identify required changes and define initiatives for change. Initiatives can suffer from the lack of a detailed and balanced understanding of the effort required and the consequences to the rest of the enterprise.

In the agile enterprise, value streams make it all real. They are the connection between change at a strategic, enterprise-level and the operation of the business, both in terms of current operations and future plans.

Enterprise intelligence. As a component of strategic planning, enterprise intelligence provides visibility of the current state of the enterprise and provides insights on forces for change—those influences, both from inside and outside the enterprise, that affect the operation and future of the enterprise. Enterprise intelligence includes knowledge management, analytics and data warehouse, and it is the primary manager of information regarding observations on changes to the enterprise ecosystem. Note the section on drivers of change earlier in this chapter. Enterprise intelligence also provides input to the formulation of ends and the assessment of means. It gives an enterprise perspective on both the data collected and the presentation of information for planning and decision making.

Assessments. Risks are added to assessments.

- *Risks.* Risks are the potential effects of opportunities and threats on the success of the enterprise. Risks include latent risks in the design and management of the enterprise as well as risks associated with the pursuit of enterprise initiatives and noncompliance with regulations. This is the assessment aspect of risk management. An audit and risk assessment capability unit, discussed later, provides the capabilities needed to assess compliance and risks along with mitigation.

Means. Transformation and standards and technology are added to means.

- *Transformation.* Strategic initiatives require more than statements of strategy, tactics, and directives. They require planning, coordination, and accountability. The transformation component addresses the broader scope of concerns associated with changing the enterprise to achieve strategic objectives. A transformation management unit provides the capability to address this strategic planning component and provide visibility into transformation plans and progress. The transformation management process is discussed in more detail later in this chapter.
- *Standards and technology.* This makes specification of standards and the selection of technology a key component of strategic initiatives.

Standards and technology are important to both products of the enterprise and the internal operation of the enterprise. For organizational agility, standards are essential to interoperability of capability units; the ability to combine and compare data from multiple sources; and the efficiency, reliability, and flexibility of information systems. A standards and technology capability unit, discussed later, provides the capabilities needed to address this strategic planning component.

TRANSFORMATION PLANNING

Strategic planning should work closely with business architecture to define a "to-be" business design at sufficient detail to validate the intended changes to the business from an executive perspective. Business architecture must then further refine the design with additional levels of detail to establish the consequential changes at the level of specific capability units to provide a clear definition of requirements for the transformation planning and management.

Currently, VDML can be used to provide one or more business scenarios representing stable states of the business. The to-be model will represent a desired future stable state and an as-is model will represent the current state. In general, it will be desirable to create models for intermediate stable states representing phases of transformation.

In order to manage the transformation, it is necessary to determine the specific changes that are required to transform from one phase to the next and identify dependencies between these changes. Fig. 9.5 depicts that process.

These changes are effectively activities in a transformation plan, and the dependencies between changes are dependencies between the transformation activities. Selected changes are then the basis for definition of strategic objectives for progress reporting to management. Of course, the transformation plan becomes the basis for more detailed monitoring of progress.

The VDM business design model enables the implementation of many changes to be delegated to the LOB managers or the individual service managers, as long as the requirements and scope are defined by the VDM model and the solutions are not suboptimal from an enterprise perspective. The VDM model will identify the relationships between a capability unit and other capability units and multiple value streams for consideration of propagation of effects.

Substantial transformations take years, and new circumstances will emerge that require response before the current transformation is completed. In

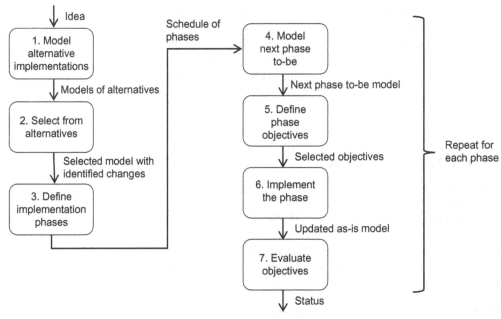

■ **FIG. 9.5** Transformation management process with VDML.

addition, phases support periodic evaluation of progress and possible course correction.

The following sections describe a process for planning and management of phased business transformation supported by VDML (Fig. 9.5).

Model Alternative Implementations

VDML provides the ability to represent an implementation with enough detail to identify the capabilities affected and new capabilities required, if any. This provides a reasonable basis for estimating the cost and duration of transformation. The value stream analysis will provide an assessment of the value contributions and potential customer value proposition(s). The details of these estimates should be supported by the organizations that are or will be responsible for the contributing capabilities.

Select From Alternatives

Management consideration of cost, duration, and customer satisfaction provides the basis for validation of the proposed business change as well the basis for selection of the best alternative. It is likely that it will be necessary to consider trade-offs between cost, timeliness, and customer satisfaction.

The result of this step is a clear, consensus definition of the final, to-be business configuration. This provides the basis for continued alignment as operational details are developed by participating organizations.

Note that over the course of the transformation, new factors and potentially new strategies will arise, and it will be necessary to revise the to-be business configuration to provide new, refined guidance to the transformation participants and the details of the transformation plan.

Define Implementation Phases

Phases of implementation should be based on the expected, overall duration of the transformation, the significance of the changes, and the necessity for coordination of changes among different organizations and their capabilities. Each phase should be an incremental step in the right direction, ending with a business configuration that is acceptable and stable until completion of the next phase.

This may require a fairly detailed analysis of the dependencies between capabilities and their effects on customer satisfaction for the target value stream as well as other value streams that might be affected.

Model Next Phase To-Be

While the overall plan should define the expected phases, the next phase, for each iteration, will require the most detail and must reflect the actual results of the preceding phase. Progress on each phase will not be perfect, some assumptions will be revised and some phase objectives will not be met, so the next phase will require some adjustments. Each new phase is based on this step.

Define Phase Objectives

Each plan for the next phase should identify critical success factors (objectives) for that phase so that progress can be monitored by management and timely adjustments can be considered for the plan and availability of resources. The achievement of these objectives, or not, provides a basis for detailed planning of the next phase.

Implement the Phase

This is where most of the work gets done. The capability methods and resource requirements of the VDM model are transformed to development of changes in service interfaces and service level agreements, business processes and applications, acquisition of facilities, and staff training and recruiting.

Evaluate Objectives

The completion of each phase must be evaluated against objectives. Success should be further evaluated by consideration of the value measurements once the completed phase has become operationally stable. Some capabilities may require further refinements to realize expected value contributions. Unless this is completion of the final, to-be phase, the transformation proceeds with the *model next to-be phase* step, mentioned earlier.

The final phase should achieve the design and expectations of the originally anticipated, final, to-be business design. However, by that time, there will likely be new, strategic objectives and a new, final, to-be business design. Strategic planning and transformation should become a continuous process.

EXAMPLE PRODUCT LIFE-CYCLE

Implementation of a new product or LOB is an example of a different form of transformation. This process is effectively orthogonal to the above transformation process. For the most part, the production engineering stage is where the new value stream is implemented.

It is possible that the new product value stream is only a reuse of existing capabilities. However, if there is a requirement for new or modified capabilities, these should be incorporated in transformation planning as discussed in the previous section. It is most likely that such changes will affect the production operation value stream rather than the other stages discussed below.

The goal of the new product life-cycle is to develop and implement the delivery and support of a new product. This will involve one or more product development value streams that together spans the product life-cycle from concept to field support.

We use a value *chain* perspective, illustrated in Fig. 9.6, to define stages in the life-cycle. A value chain typically depicts general stages in the development and delivery of a product or service to a customer—it does not depict a flow of deliverables like a value stream. Different industries and companies will have different value chains but with a similar purpose. In this example, we use a value chain of a hypothetical manufacturing company.

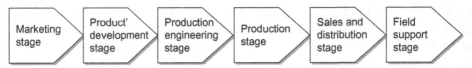

■ **FIG. 9.6** Example product life-cycle value chain.

The capabilities of each stage of a value chain tend to be distinguishable in the personnel and other resources involved, as well as their unit of production for delivery of a new product. Therefore each stage will have a relatively distinct set of capabilities, and we have used those distinctions as the basis for bringing together shared services that support that stage, both for product development and for on-going support for business operations in an example organization model in Chapter 10.

The work of a stage does not end when the next stage begins, but it shifts to a different mode of support.

Consideration of the life-cycle of a hypothetical product will illustrate how different shared services organizations interact and contribute value to the end product. We use a value chain based on a manufacturing enterprise with stages marketing, product development, production engineering, production, sales and distribution, and field services. We will step through these stages focused on contributions to the development and refinement of the product and its value stream.

The LOB responsible for the product is responsible for managing the overall collaboration that drives the product life-cycle capabilities including an on-going change management collaboration. The LOB-driven collaboration will engage shared services in each stage as well as interorganizational collaborations. Development of the product vision and commitment to development occurs in strategic planning prior to initiation of the marketing stage. Value contribution measurements will be captured and reported throughout the life-cycle. The start of each next stage is a major milestone based on readiness and continued commitment.

We assume the enterprise is an established manufacturer with an established LOB, and we are implementing a new product. Note that this is not intended to be a recommended or complete model, but only an illustration of the interorganizational collaborations and capabilities involved in each stage.

The LOB product management team develops the details of the product life-cycle services as the life-cycle develops, and the overall coordination and tracking of progress is performed by the enterprise transformation management unit.

Marketing Stage

The marketing stage is enabled by a strategic plan defining a product vision, a management commitment to initiate the marketing stage, and creation of a product management team in an appropriate LOB.

The marketing stage solidifies plans for development of the product to support an enterprise commitment to the next stage. Marketing has participated in strategic planning in support of the product vision and the decision to proceed with the marketing stage for this product.

Marketing

- Marketing will perform further and on-going market analysis based on analytics and studies in order to clarify the market segment(s), the expected product volume and lifetime, and the competitive position.
- Market segments and initial value propositions will be developed based on assessment of customer values and priorities, particularly pricing.
- Marketing will collaborate with enterprise architecture, product development, and production engineering regarding product design, features, and cost.

Business Architecture

- Enterprise architecture has participated in strategic planning for this initiative and has developed an initial production value stream model to assess capability requirements, key competencies, cost of implementation, and production costs.
- A business model cube (see Lindgren under Related Business Analysis Techniques in Chapter 2) has been developed with strategic planning and will be refined along with development of more detail in the value stream model.
- One-time and recurring cost estimates will be developed in collaboration with product development and production engineering.

Strategic Planning

- Strategic planning will continue to collaborate with marketing, enterprise architecture, and the responsible LOB organization regarding the product vision, the business model cube, market assessments and the implementation cost, status, and objectives.

Regulatory Compliance

- Regulatory compliance will collaborate with enterprise architecture, product Development, and production engineering to review the product features and the production value stream to identify regulations that may apply to product features, materials, or production operations.

Product Development

- Product development will develop a conceptual product design in collaboration with marketing, the responsible LOB organization, and enterprise architecture. This conceptual design will be the basis for further feasibility analysis, refinements to the value stream model and cost estimates.

Production Engineering

- Production engineering will assess production capabilities based on the production value stream model, and will identify key suppliers (outside capabilities), costs of equipment and facilities, and production staff skill requirements.
- Production engineering will collaborate with production regarding the impact on staffing, facilities, and equipment.

Human Resource Management

- Human resource management will assess staffing requirements in collaboration with production engineering and production.
- Human resource management may need to support temporary or contract staffing for the preproduction stages.

Finance and Accounting

- Finance and accounting will develop financial plans and budgets in collaboration with the involved organizations.
- Accounting will establish accounts for cost accounting and track one-time and recurring costs throughout the life-cycle.

Risk Management

- Risk management will collaborate with the LOB organization, marketing, product development, and production engineering to assess market risks, operational risks, and product liability risks associated with the new product.
- Risk management will also participate in the change management collaboration.
- Risk management will collaborate with other organizations, as required, to mitigate risks.

Product Development Stage

The product development stage will begin with a decision by top management that the product will be viable and profitable, and that the costs and risks are acceptable.

Product Development

- Product development will develop a complete product design. The design will be refined based on collaboration with marketing and production engineering considering customer appeal, value propositions, and manufacturability.
- Product development will include development of prototypes and product testing.
- Product development will develop product maintenance, diagnostic, and repair materials for field support as well as user manuals.

Business Architecture

- Enterprise architecture will continue to refine the production value stream model based on collaboration with the LOB organization, product development, and production engineering.

Production Engineering

- Production engineering will collaborate with product development regarding manufacturability and production capability requirements.
- Production engineering will identify requirements for suppliers and their capabilities.
- Production engineering will periodically refine estimates for facilities, equipment, and staffing based on further development of the product design and the value stream model.

Marketing and Sales

- Marketing, in collaboration with sales and the LOB organization, will develop a marketing plan including advertising, incentives, product configurations and features, sales projections, and threat analysis.
- Proposed pricing will be developed in collaboration with finance and accounting, the LOB organization, production engineering, and production.

Risk Management and Regulation and Policy Compliance

- Risk management along with regulation and policy compliance will continue to participate in collaborations to identify risks and relevant policies and to mitigate risks and ensure compliance.

Production Engineering Stage

The production engineering stage begins when the product design is determined to be sufficiently complete. Additional product design refinements will be required as further testing and development of production capabilities identify design problems, or marketing identifies changes in customer interests or competition.

Production Engineering

- Production engineering will continue to collaborate with product development regarding production capabilities.
- Production engineering will acquire facilities, install equipment, develop tooling, and develop manufacturing processes.

Procurement

- Procurement will collaborate with production engineering to acquire facilities, equipment and tooling, and to negotiate contracts with suppliers.

Human Resource Management

- Human resource management will collaborate with production engineering and production for recruiting and training of production personnel.

Information Technology

- Information technology will collaborate with production engineering, production, distribution, sales, and field services to implement necessary changes to systems to support the new product.
- Information technology will work with enterprise architecture, production engineering, and production to implement new or changed capability unit business processes.

Production

- Production engineering will collaborate with production regarding testing of new equipment, tooling, and manufacturing processes as well as staffing and staff training.
- Production will collaborate with information technology regarding information system requirements and implementation.
- When new capabilities and processes are in place, production engineering, and production will collaborate in pilot production operations.

- Product engineering will collaborate with product development and marketing in testing and evaluation of the products from pilot production.
- Supplier schedules and initial parts inventories must be established in anticipation of production.

Marketing and Sales

- Marketing in collaboration with sales will develop advertising along with sales projections.
- Marketing and sales will make arrangements with channels, develop sales materials, and provide staff training materials.

Sales and Information Technology

- Sales and information technology will collaborate to implement changes to sales forecasting and order processing and tracking.

Field Services

- Field services will collaborate with product development to refine maintenance and repair materials and train staff.

Risk Management and Regulation and Policy Compliance

- Risk management and regulation and policy compliance will continue to participate in collaborations to identify risks and relevant regulations and to mitigate risks and ensure compliance.

Production Stage

The production stage starts when the product design and production engineering are completed and facilities, equipment, materials, capabilities, staff, and business partner relationships are in place to sell, produce, and support the product.

Effectively, the distribution and sales stage and the field support stage are enabled at the same time as the production stage, but from a customer and product flow perspective, sales and distribution come after production (except for a build-to-order product), and field support comes after sales and distribution.

Production Operations

- Production will collaborate with marketing, product development, and production engineering to improve production operations.

- Production will collaborate with production engineering for changes to production capabilities.
- Any changes to shared, production capability units must involve collaboration with other recipients of the same services to resolve any impact on their value measurements or changes in the service interface.
- Individuals in the production organization will come up with innovative ideas to improve operations or the product. They will collaborate informally within production before collaborating with marketing, product development, and/or production engineering regarding potential implementation.
- Production operations will fill the pipeline to support the production process.

Finance and Accounting

- Finance and accounting will participate in collaborations regarding the budget impact of product or production changes and changes in production volumes.
- Accounting will establish cost accounting and unit cost measurements for the new product production value stream.

Marketing

- Marketing will continue to monitor market trends and disruptions and collaborate on their impact on production schedules, product design, pricing, advertising, and promotional campaigns.

Product Development

- Product development will develop product improvements and collaborate with production engineering and production as required to implement the revisions.

Sales and Distribution Stage

The sales and distribution stage is enabled at the same time as the production stage, but from a customer and product flow perspective, sales comes after production (except for a build-to-order product).

Marketing

- Marketing and sales collaborate on advertising, promotional campaigns, impact of market trends, and responses to competition.
- Marketing, sales, and product development collaborate on product design options and improvements.

Sales and Distribution

- Sales and distribution collaborate with product development and production engineering regarding customer complaints and defects.
- Sales will deploy sales training and advertising.

Procurement

- Procurement must evaluate and reconcile carrier and supplier contract compliance.
- Procurement collaborates with sales and distribution regarding complaints about carriers.

Field Services Stage

The field services stage is enabled at the same time as the production stage, but from a customer and product flow perspective, field services comes after production and sales and distribution.

Field Services

- Field services collaborates with product development and production engineering regarding product failures and problems with maintenance and repair.
- Customer services collaborates with marketing and product development regarding customer feedback.
- Field service personnel will be trained in product maintenance and support.

BUSINESS CHANGE SUPPORT

People throughout the enterprise represent a valuable resource for identification of emerging threats and opportunities as well as insights and creativity in the development of solutions. However, these contributions need to be orchestrated for a harmonious result.

A VDM model provides a shared understanding of the dependencies and propagation of effects of changes so that these different perspectives and initiatives are aligned. In this section, we discuss the roles of executive staff units in unifying these efforts.

Strategic Planning Unit

A strategic planning framework has been discussed in the previous section. Strategic planning is the responsibility of top management, but it must be supported by a team that facilitates the discussion and pulls together the detail of an enterprise strategic plan. The strategic plan is no longer a document prepared every 3 years with a consensus of abstract ideas, but rather a constantly changing framework for guidance of efforts to evolve and adapt the enterprise to address threats and opportunities in a changing world.

The strategic planning team must consider how various initiatives, from capability unit incremental improvements to radical, industry initiatives fit into the strategic plan framework (or don't). The executives must also use VDM to validate initiatives and defined transformation phases, and they must consider the risks of strategic plans and initiatives. This may affect approval and funding for some initiatives, consolidation of some initiatives, alignment of timetables for related initiatives, or guidance regarding enterprise priorities. This requires close communication between the strategic planning, enterprise architecture, and response oversight.

Transformation Management Unit

The transformation management team is responsible for coordination, collaboration, and tracking of threats and opportunities and resulting transformation initiatives at two levels: the sense and respond directory and program and project management.

Sense and Respond Directory Unit

Transformation begins with a recognition of a threat or opportunity that requires some response. The sense and respond directory accepts notices of observations that require attention and it links that notice to appropriate persons or processes for awareness and a response. This result may range from resolution with no further action to exploration of emerging trends and technologies, to initiation of major transformation initiatives. The purpose of this service is to keep track of all the business change related activities and facilitate communication where there is potential synergy or overlap and to ensure that observations get appropriate attention and follow-up.

With a multitude of employees and internal interest groups exploring potential threats and opportunities, there could be a lot of duplicated and inconsistent effort. This directory might include taxonomies for products, technologies, and capabilities for assignment of individuals as contact persons to receive distributions of notices and for ensuring that all areas of interest are monitored at some level.

Based on the taxonomies, topics can be directed to persons with particular interest, or a person higher in the hierarchy should accept a notice to determine who should follow-up. The follow-up person can then be added to the hierarchy for that topic.

Tracking of the response will continue until some action has been taken or initiated. When action is initiated or action has been taken, the disposition of a threat or opportunity will be reported and conveyed to the originator and other interested parties.

If a transformation effort is initiated, large or small, a link to that effort will be captured with milestones identified. As milestones are achieved, these are to be reported and communicated to interested parties.

Status and progress notices may be distributed through the general notification service once an implementation effort is identified.

Program and Project Management Unit

Program and project management (PPM) applies to transformation efforts that involve active participation by multiple organizations. The overall initiative should be managed by the PPM team, but subprojects should be assigned to organization units that have responsibility for transformations within their area of responsibility.

Tracking of the projects, status and milestones are then included in the sense and respond directory and the PPM team will be responsible for collaboration and coordination among the various, related efforts. The PPM team must also identify potential synergy or conflicts between independent efforts and facilitate coordination and collaboration to reconcile differences and optimize results.

This is somewhat similar to a conventional Program/Project Management Office, except that the role is to support planning, coordination, and collaboration and to provide status tracking, not to directly manage the transformation projects.

As the enterprise adopts case management technology, much of this activity can be coordinated with a case management (CMMN) system, and much of the tracking, supporting, and reporting can be automated.

Business Architecture Unit

Business Architecture is responsible, among other things, for analysis, development, and maintenance of VDM models of business design. The current enterprise VDM model is the basis for understanding the context in which changes are considered and proposed. Some models represent proposed future states for validation and evaluation of changes. To-be models represent intended future states.

Business architecture is also responsible for obtaining measurements for activity cost and value contributions, and for review of capability unit interfaces for consistency and for approval of interface changes.

The current VDM model should have different scenarios for value measurements to provide the context and estimates for analysis of changes. New value streams can be configured primarily from shared capabilities so that there is good basis for estimation of measurements for a proposed value stream. These measurements are also available for analysis of improvement opportunities and for determination of an enterprise optimum for changes affecting multiple value streams.

Operational changes represent incremental modifications to the current business model. These are considered for compatibility and for the impact on other capability units and on value streams.

Tactical changes are more significant, so there is a focus on the desired design of one or more value streams and the capabilities that may be modified or developed to support the future value stream(s).

Strategic changes and transformations involve substantial changes that require more extensive modeling and analysis of future value streams and supporting capabilities. Generally, these will involve some reconfiguration of existing capability units and possibly addition or modification for some new capability requirements.

Industry changes go beyond strategic changes to consider the business models and value exchanges with business partners along with development of new value streams, again leveraging existing, shared capability units.

In all of these analyses, the goal is to avoid creating redundant capability units and to optimize the values delivered by multiple value streams where there may be some trade-offs of values between different value streams.

Regulations and Policies Unit

The business transformation may be affected by existing regulations and policies and it may make the enterprise subject to additional regulations. The relevant regulations must be identified and interpreted in the context of the business in order to be implemented as policies. The VDM model provides the context for implementation of policies. In this context, most policies should already be implemented, so there is a pattern for implementation in new activities. New policies will require analysis to determine appropriate implementations.

Risk Management Unit

Risks are a very important aspect of change. A change may increase or decrease operational risk or other risks such as failure rates or liability. A change has a cost that is expected to be recovered as a result of the change, but there is risk that it will cost more and the return will be less, or the effort will fail. It may be useful to consider the cost of insurance as a representation of the cost risk.

Risks must be considered in the context of the current and future VDM models both from the perspective of the propagation of effects and the costs involved due to potential loss of business and the cost of recovery. The risk perspective will also help identify those aspects of the transformation that require close attention, and the limitation of the scope of transformation phases to mitigate the consequences of delays or rework on implementation dependencies.

As the planning horizon gets longer, the risks become more substantial.

The risks of incremental changes to capability units are relatively small, so the losses from overruns, delays and even failures may be painful, but they seldom threaten the viability of the enterprise. Initiatives at the LOB level can be more serious leading to losses both in investment and in revenue. Again, these are serious, but probably do not threaten the viability of an enterprise with multiple LOBs.

Risks of undertakings at the enterprise-level, however, could be very serious due to the magnitude and duration of the effort and the amount of business that is at stake. Consequently, we must assume that top management will be cautious about taking on such initiatives and will monitor progress closely.

Industry change is high risk with the expectation of high reward. However, there is also risk if the opportunity is not pursued. There is risk that a competitor will pursue the change and will take over the market. If top management decides not to pursue an industry change, then they should consider ways they can mitigate the risks if their competition does pursue it.

There is also a risk of undertaking an industry change before the opportunity is mature. If the product is good, the relationships are solid and the marketing effort is good, but the customers are not ready or economic conditions are poor, the business may fail.

Consequently, in considering industry changes, top management has a number of choices:

- Abandon the idea as too risky or too expensive but consider possible mitigation if a competitor pursues it.

- Postpone the pursuit and wait for circumstances to become more favorable. Again there is a risk that a competitor will pursue it.
- Wait for a competitor to take the risk and create the market, but be prepared to catch up by developing key capabilities, value streams, and business partner relationships in advance.
- Wait for a competitor (potentially a start-up) to pursue it and after success is shown, acquire the competitor. This is a common strategy among large corporations, although they do not necessarily recog-nize the opportunity and decide to wait.
- Commit to the change. This of course has the risk of failure, but there is also a risk that it will cost more or take longer than anticipated. In the meantime, the effort may cause other opportunities to be missed.

The important point here is that doing nothing may have a greater risk than the risk of failure.

Risk management should make a risk assessment of alternative courses of action. The assessments must involve collaboration with other parts of the organization with expertise in different aspects of the undertaking.

Marketing

Marketing has a key role in refining the product design, determining the market size, and estimating pricing potential and promotional costs in the initial assessment, and in sales promotion when the product goes to market. For an industry change, this may involve collaborating and supporting the marketing organizations of the business partners. VDM modeling will help estimate production costs and product features as a basis for pricing and estimates of market demand.

Other Supports

Contributions will also be needed from other organizations such as

- Staffing costs from Human Resource Management, possibly involving requirements for special skills based on new and expanded capability capacity.
- Supplier selection from procurement considering new product requirements and business relationships considering supplier value propositions.
- Financial planning for funding and return on investment from finance for governance and risk assessment.
- Potential requirements from regulatory and policy compliance must be considered related to product design, customer usage, and regulated

production operations as well as regulations such as energy conservation, safety, and environmental impact.

- Potential legal liabilities from corporate counsel related to injuries to employees, customers, or others as well as violations of government regulations and intellectual property.

SENSE AND RESPOND INFRASTRUCTURE

A sense and respond infrastructure provides automated support for recognition, filtering, publication, notification, coordination, and tracking activities. The information technology organization is responsible for the technical infrastructure to support these activities. Key facilities are a sense and respond directory, analytics for monitoring of external circumstances, and complex event processing (CEP). The notification service discussed in Chapter 8 also supports sense and respond capabilities.

Sense and Respond Directory

Response oversight is supported by a shared sense and respond directory service to define key persons to receive notices of events or relevant circumstances as well as to track activities and progress related to collaboration, analysis, and transformation.

The focus here is on observations that may require ad hoc action or business change initiatives. This information should support coordination and reconciliation of overlapping efforts and status reporting to management. Observations should directly send messages to individuals or initiate business processes or case management efforts.

The current VDM model should help identify the capability units and value streams that may be affected by changes in technology, products, markets, business models, and other factors so that these threats and opportunities are brought to the attention of appropriate persons.

Analytics

Analytics is a discipline for analysis of "big data" to analyze events and trends and discover insights in various domains. Recently developed technology supports processing massive amounts of data with distributed computing to accomplish analysis in a reasonable amount of time at a fraction of the cost of traditional methods. For most companies, this means processing using a cloud computing service.

The decision to use analytics should be based on careful consideration of the available data and the value of the potential insights. This should be accomplished with the support of an analytics expert who can provide insight on what can reasonably be expected and the cost.

Internally, there are sources of critical data such as actual sales, or sensors on equipment or transport vehicles. Capture and analysis of these data is important to understand circumstances related to the particular enterprise.

For external events, it may be very difficult to get event notices directly from the source. For example, competitors are not going to provide event notices that enable the enterprise to monitor their activities, or if they did, the events might not be a true representation of what is happening. So, we need to look for *consequential or precursor events*—events that precede or occur as a result of the root cause event. For competitor events, we might look at product announcements or patent applications, which are much less likely to be misrepresented and more likely to be accessible. Analytics may help discover some of these events or trends that are not immediately obvious from looking at the data.

Some observations will be duplicated, coming from different observers. Some represent different events resulting from the same root cause. Some event notices are simply ignored if the frequency becomes overwhelming. Consequently, we need to analyze what events are really needed and which event notices should be shared for different purposes. For example, an increase in the price of crude oil results in increases in costs of materials and transportation and may result in a reduction in demand for certain consumer products or services. These consequences may be relevant to a number of different enterprise activities. Some of these relationships may be addressed by CEP, discussed below.

Depending on the industry, there may be existing sources of important events and circumstances. For example, Neilsen (http://www.nielsen.com/us/en/about-us.html) captures massive amounts of data on current retail sales and television viewing (among other things) from countries around the world and can also provide various analyses of these data. Such sources of external data and analyses should be considered in lieu of development of analytics for a particular enterprise.

Complex Event Processing

CEP is a technology resolving some of the uncertainty of event notices and for inferring events from other events and the surrounding circumstances. A CEP service is both a subscriber and publisher of events. For example, the National Association of Securities Dealers (NASD) monitors news feeds to analyze the relationship of company news events to stock trades, to identify potential insider trading and fraud.

Recipients of notices should deal with various ambiguities, redundancies, and credibility of the event notices they receive, particularly from external sources. Generally speaking, the recipient of an event notice should perform some form of correlation and filtering of events to avoid unjustified or duplicated resolution activities.

It may be appropriate, given a certain magnitude of consequences and business risk, to initiate a response immediately, even with an event notice of questionable credibility. However, such a process should be designed to take into consideration later event notices or the absence of supporting event notices at certain points in the subsequent activities. These considerations cannot be programmed into a CEP system but must be part of the business logic of the resolution process.

Inference of an event relies on timely and accurate information on related events and circumstances. If the conclusion is to be based on the occurrence of two independent sources of event notices, there must be allowance for different delays in the delivery of the event notices. If the inference depends on related circumstances, there must be accurate and up-to-date information about those circumstances. The inferencing mechanism and event specifications must take these timeliness and accuracy factors into consideration. It is likely that the result of the inference can only be a probability that a particular event has occurred. It may be appropriate to publish an event notice only when the probability exceeds a particular threshold.

An approach is to capture and retain a sequence of events for a period of time or a number of events for each event source or stream. Thus the sequences of events can be viewed as relational tables. An SQL-like query can join entries from multiple tables to find combinations of events that would suggest the occurrence of an underlying event of interest. This allows corresponding event notices to be considered together, even though they may have been received at different times. These queries can potentially include information about related circumstances. With special tools, queries can be implemented such that they are applied continuously as event notices are received.

At this point, it would appear that CEP is primarily applicable to specific areas of concern such as fraud detection or security threats where there is a fairly focused domain of expertise and relevant events and the value derived from the inferred events is high. It essentially performs as a real-time expert system. At the same time, some of the analysis capabilities anticipated for CEP may be accomplished faster and at lower cost by analytics.

Internal sources of events are more controlled, and it may be effective to infer underlying events more directly, possibly adjusting for differences in timing. For example, warranty claims might be correlated with production events if the event notices are aligned based on the production date of the product. In this case, the receipt of warranty claims might trigger efforts to prevent or mitigate the consequences of similar production events. This, of course, requires a long history of production events.

Events may be captured and stored in a data warehouse; many enterprises already have such data warehouses for certain categories of events. Data mining is applied to data warehouse records to discover patterns and relationships that occur over time.

Events in Context

A broader spectrum of events can be captured and retained for future reference. When an event of concern occurs or is inferred, engaging in *look-back* at preceding events helps put the event of concern into context, to both understand the full nature of the event and discover potential causation.

By analogy, suppose a person is discovered murdered, but there is no source of information about events preceding the murder—no information about how the victim got where he is, no telephone calls, no witnesses, no information on where his acquaintances were at the time of the killing. In this situation, it is very difficult to identify the perpetrator. These events are key to discovering the context of the murder and, so, the murderer.

Beyond the potential to look-back, the precursor event patterns can be studied to infer the potential occurrence of another unfortunate incident to be anticipated and prevented. The focus of attention can then shift to analysis of risk patterns to react earlier and to either prevent or respond more quickly to mitigate the effects of the undesirable event.

Verification and Consolidation of Event Notices

Besides inferring underlying events, there is a need to correlate events from multiple sources to either confirm the occurrence of an event or avoid repeated responses to the same event.

Event notices from some sources may be unreliable. For example, event notices derived from news feeds may be the result of misinterpretation. There is often a need to confirm the event from another source. The speed of reporting may vary significantly, from minutes to days or longer. It may be appropriate to separately report such event notices, with an indication of the tentative nature of the notice (ie, having business metadata that reflect the quality of the event notice). The recipients of these notices would need to act accordingly.

Some events have many observers. These people may observe the event in different ways, characterize it differently, and publish event notices through different channels. It would not be desirable or appropriate to initiate an independent event resolution process for every redundant event notice. It may be necessary to leave the resolution of these redundancies to the subscribers. In some cases, the subscription criteria may limit reporting to certain event notices, reducing the number of redundant notices received. However, there is a risk that some events are not reported through all the possible channels, and when we ignore some notices, some events may be overlooked. Another approach is to notify event observers when resolution is identified (ie, a resolution event) so that they need not give further attention to the event notices they have received.

CEP systems may provide mechanisms for resolving these issues; however, the resolution may differ depending on the action to be initiated. The subscribers to such events should provide appropriate criteria for analysis and filtering of events.

MOVING FORWARD

Requirements of sense and respond have a significant effect on the organization, governance, and culture of the agile enterprise. The effects on the organization structure will be reflected in the next chapter, and we will consider the implications to governance in Chapter 11.

The Agile Organization Structure

An enterprise organization structure defines the relationships among people, along with their respective responsibilities and authority, as the basis of their collective efforts to achieve enterprise objectives. It also defines the chains of command through which enterprise management exerts leadership, accountability, and control of resources.

Current-day organization hierarchies often reflect groupings of people engaged in functionally related activities. However, in some cases, the clustering is based on business relationships required decades ago, the remnants of mergers and acquisitions, or the independent evolution of various product lines.

An agile enterprise changes these relationships by breaking down departmental silos into value streams and shared services driven by value delivery. The participation and relationships of people continue to be important in the agile enterprise, but the workforce has shifted from performing rote production tasks to knowledge work: maintaining capabilities, managing exceptions, and resolving needs to address business challenges and opportunities.

In the agile enterprise, we combine the workforce shift to knowledge work with shared capabilities and a network of services, contributing to value streams that deliver enterprise values. Service units provide enterprise capabilities that can be engaged in a variety of enterprise pursuits. This is a sort of "hyper-matrix" structure because collaborations are connected by deliverable flows; value streams; responsible organization units; delegations from service to service; delivery of events; and teams for planning, coordination, innovation, problem solving, and other purposes that involve interorganizational participation.

The management hierarchy in an agile enterprise is a hierarchy of organization units responsible for budgets, personnel, and other resources, from the collaboration of top management to service units with people who do the actual work of the enterprise. The grouping of organization units under a parent organization unit brings together organization units that have

Building the Agile Enterprise. http://dx.doi.org/10.1016/B978-0-12-805160-3.00010-7

similar capabilities and operating characteristics that enable them to work together for economies of scale and comparable leadership and incentives. The organization hierarchy is not about products, but about capabilities.

At the lowest level, capabilities are implemented by service units that perform the management and operational details to perform capabilities and contribute to value streams. Similar service units are grouped together in a parent organization unit. The parent organization unit operates at a more abstract level to manage the service unit and report to the next level in the hierarchy. At increasing levels, the collaborations become more abstract and the composite capability becomes more general.

The management hierarchy, for the most part, brings together service units that have similar capabilities and objectives. The primary objective of the management hierarchy is to optimize the operation of its service units and to adapt the service units to changing business requirements.

In the following sections, we begin by considering the impact of the VDM perspective. We then will outline agile organizational design principles. Next, we will discuss an example, high-level organization structure. Finally, we consider a general approach to transitioning an organization to achieve the agile enterprise based on the Value Delivery Maturity Model in Appendix A.

VDM PERSPECTIVE

Value delivery modeling (VDM) brings three important perspectives to the design of an enterprise organization: (1) the collaboration network, (2) shared capabilities, and (3) value streams.

The Collaboration Network

The basic structure of the organization is changed by collaborations as a basic unit of composition. A collaboration engages people and other collaborations to accomplish its purpose. Collaborations include loose associations at one end of a spectrum, and formal organization units at the other end. Collaborations of various forms define all working relationships in and between enterprises.

VDML (Chapter 2) defines four specialized types of collaboration: business networks, organization units, communities, and capability methods. Business networks define relationships between the enterprise and other business entities. A community is a loose association of members with a common interest that may form more structured collaborations for initiatives of community interest. A market segment is considered a community collaboration among customers with shared product interests. An organization unit is part of the formal enterprise structure and is responsible for the management of people and other resources and facilities including funding. A capability method defines an application of a capability through a recurring collaboration pattern as a service.

A hierarchy of organization units forms the traditional management hierarchy that is extended to additional collaborations that manage resources such as project teams and business transformation initiatives. A capability method is performed by an organization unit that is responsible for the assignments of people, availability of resources, and management of capability method performance. Interorganization collaborations define interactions between members of different organization units to do work for enterprise purposes ranging from transformation planning to ad hoc problem resolution meetings. The network of collaborations involves all of the people engaged in the work of the enterprise, many people in multiple collaborations. Most of these collaborations are not represented in typical organization structure diagrams.

Fig. 10.1 illustrates a segment of an extended organization structure model using the VDML graphical notation. This diagram depicts representation of collaborations beyond the traditional management hierarchy. The rectangles each represent a collaboration. Those with a fork icon represent organizational

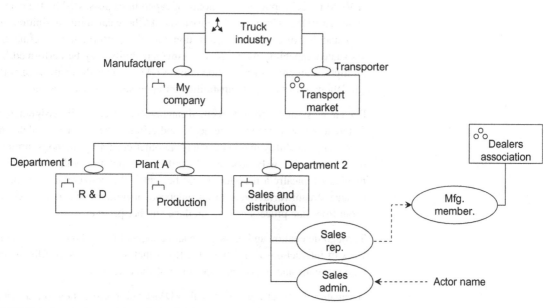

■ **FIG. 10.1** An example, extended organization diagram.

units. Those with a three arrow icon represent business network collaborations. Those with a three circles icon represent communities. An ellipsis represents a role. Each collaboration with a small ellipse on top has in a role in the connected collaboration. A large ellipsis represents the role of a person in the associated collaboration. The dashed lines indicate that the role at the source of the arrow is assigned to the role at the head of the arrow. So the Sales Representative fills the role of a Manufacturing Representative Member in the Dealers Association.

Obviously, a more complete organization diagram could become very complex. However, such an organization structure should be accessed on-line since it will include collaborations and role assignments that are constantly changing, and the on-line service should provide for interactive viewing that allows the user to browse selected segments and abstractions of the overall organization structure.

Capability Units

A capability unit is an organization unit that manages the resources and performance of a capability. That capability unit can offer one or more capability methods for application of the capability. A capability method is a collaboration that specifies the activities, roles, and flows of deliverables that apply the capability as a service.

A VDM model captures a taxonomy of capabilities possessed by the enterprise in a VDML Capability Library and links those capability definitions to the capability offers of the organization units that perform and/or define the associated capability methods. The same capability may be performed by multiple, alternative organization units. VDM includes the analysis of consolidation and sharing of capabilities for economies of scale and control.

Each request for a capability method can involve different role assignments, different performance measurements, and different occurrences of deliverables. The capability method can engage other capability methods through delegation, or it may send a deliverable as input to another capability method—typically a message would be sent if the deliverable is input to a value stream for delivery of an independent product or service such as scrap from one process used to produce another product.

Through delegation and message sending, capability methods define a network of interactions and deliverable flows that represent the fulfillment of value streams and the overall operation of the enterprise.

A capability unit at the conceptual, VDM-level, corresponds to a service unit at an operational level. A service unit specification includes additional technical details and ancillary services that are not included in a VDM model. Ancillary services operate on active service requests for such action as requesting status or cancelation. Additional services of a service unit provide data management functions and engage administrative services. See more on service unit details and operational design in Chapter 3.

Capability methods (collaborations) are the building blocks of value streams. The enterprise can respond to new business opportunities by configuring a new value stream from existing capabilities. This implicitly defines the organizations that will participate in a new business.

Value Streams

A value stream is a network of flows of deliverables that converges at the delivery of a product or service to a recipient. Generally, there is a main stream that sets the pace, based on the receipt of customer requests or a production schedule. Alternatively, a value stream may be viewed as a tree structure with the root at delivery of the result and branches up the streams of deliverables. Multiple value streams can share branches at different levels where services are shared. Thus each capability method may be engaged in multiple value streams and may be involved more than once in the same value stream. Note that recipients of the result of a value stream may be internal consumers of the product or service.

A capability method returns a deliverable in response to a service request, and it delivers value measurements based on the specific use of the capability method. The value measurements can be defined in greater detail as contributions of value by each of the activities in the capability method. These measurements are based on a unit of production, and they are aggregated to support measurements for each type of value in one or more value propositions for the output of the value stream. Value propositions may differ for different customers based on different levels of customer satisfaction and priorities.

Value contributions of a capability method are the responsibility of the organization unit that performs the capability method and provides the resources. Value contributions affect every value stream in which the capability method is engaged, but the measurements will vary depending on the context in which the capability method is engaged. Thus the organization unit must be accountable for performance to its management chain and to each of the recipients of its services as well as the value streams in which the recipients participate. Some capability methods may contribute to all value streams. An organization unit also must hold accountable each of the services that are engaged by its capability methods.

The operational structure of an agile enterprise is based on value streams composed of capability methods. A value stream will typically have unique capability methods that define the high-level operations required to deliver its product or service. These capability methods will engage other capability methods to develop more detail of the value stream. At some level, a capability method that is unique to the value stream will engage a shared capability method, and because the called capability is shared, any capability engaged by that shared capability method is also implicitly shared (even if it is only engaged by the one method).

SERVICE UNIT DESIGN PRINCIPLES

This section will focus on patterns and principles that influence the design of a service unit as a building block of the agile enterprise organization structure. There are a number of factors that affect organizational design. We will explore these in the sections that follow.

Note that we focus on a typical, automated service unit with a full complement of ancillary and supporting capabilities. Some capabilities may, in fact, be implemented as interfaces to legacy applications or engage an individual or team that operates without automation due to the circumstances and nature of their work.

While we have some capabilities (capability methods or capabilities of individuals) that are dedicated to a single value stream, there will also be many capabilities that are shared (or intended to be sharable) and thus are independent of any particular value stream.

There may be some capabilities that are similar in some ways, but are, nevertheless, clearly different capabilities. These may be candidates for limited consolidation in a single organization unit as a service unit group. In other cases, it is inappropriate to consolidate, but there may be value in applying the same capability method specification to be performed in different service units—replication.

In this section, we will consider the factors that go into applying these design alternatives. We will begin by discussion of the appropriate scale of a service unit as an elementary organizational unit. We will then focus on the grouping of service units, both those unique to a value stream, and those that are sharable, and then the factors that define a single service unit. Finally, we will consider the replication and outsourcing of service units.

Service Unit Scale

How big is a service unit? A service unit is not limited by span of control since a service unit may have specialized teams. We include in Fig. 10.2 the diagram of service unit interfaces from Chapter 3 to highlight the implied scope of a service unit implementation.

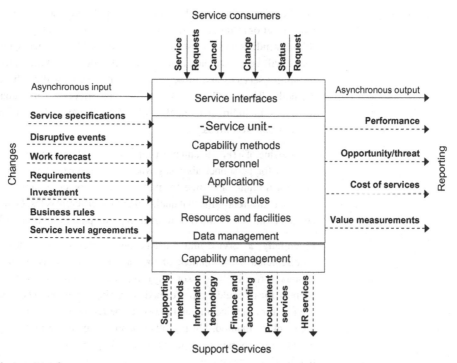

■ **FIG. 10.2** Service unit interfaces.

A shared service unit provides a capability that is applied as a service by one or multiple related capability methods. In addition, the service unit has ancillary collaborations for maintenance; problem resolution; and management of personnel, facilities, and resources. Some of these ancillary collaborations may engage other shared services such as expense reporting, purchase requests, and personnel promotions.

It is acceptable that a service unit could include a capability method that is used by its other capability methods, but it should only be engaged by methods of the same service unit. A service unit might also perform methods that have a shared method specification—the specification is shared, but each service unit provides the staffing and resources to apply it. We discuss this further as replication, below.

There will be roles for individuals in a capability method that apply the associated capability. There will be roles for individuals in some of the ancillary services although many of those may be fully automated. There will be opportunities for persons in a service unit to participate in capability methods of other service units such as for submission of an expense report to Accounting, and submission of a purchase request to Procurement. There may be roles for individuals that maintain and adapt the service unit as problems occur or as required by business or technology changes. There may be roles for individuals to ensure security and resolve data management issues. There will be individuals involved in collaborations with recipients of the capability services and those services that are engaged by the service unit methods. There will also be individuals involved in management of resources, including personnel assignments, and availability of consumable and reusable resources.

The staffing of a service unit must consider all of these requirements as well as reserves for personnel absences, vacations, turnover, changing workloads, time for training, and time for participation in other collaborations. People will have different skills that qualify them for different roles. Generally, some personnel must be skilled or trained to participate in multiple roles.

Essentially, a service unit must be big enough to efficiently meet these requirements. Development of the capability hierarchy in the Capability Library (effectively a taxonomy) may define detailed capabilities where each of these could be performed by a single person. These are too fine grained for a service unit and may each be represented by an activity within a capability method. On the other hand, a capability method of one role might be performed by a person from a large team for capability methods that merit a service unit.

Those fine-grained capability methods that do not merit the scale of a service unit should be brought together as alternative methods of a more general capability. If they are quite different, then they should be part of a service unit group where they share the service unit group management and supports.

A Service Unit Group

We will first consider a service unit group before we consider a service unit because the criteria are less restrictive. We will then consider the additional criteria that would qualify a service unit. A service unit group is the placing of multiple service units under the same management primarily for coordination or economies of scale, and for sharing of ancillary activities. These service units are not sufficiently the same to be fully consolidated into a single service unit, discussed later. The following are factors to be considered for formation of a service unit group.

Minimum scale. It may be necessary to form a service unit group to achieve minimum service unit scale as discussed earlier. While there are still separate service units, they can achieve the scale requirements through group economies of scale, discussed below.

Economies of scale. Economies of scale can come from better utilization of resources, technology, database management, and sharing of ancillary and management activities. A service unit group need not achieve all of these economies of scale.

Resources. The obvious economy of scale comes from pooling resources assuming the service units have similar resource requirements. Resource sharing may include personnel, equipment, facilities, and consumable or reusable resources. The personnel can be pooled, and workloads can be balanced to reduce the total staffing requirements. Scheduling of pooled equipment and facilities can improve utilization thus reducing the total requirements. A minimum inventory of resources can be less than the sum of the minimums that would be required by the individual service units.

Technology. Similar capabilities will involve similar technologies. Expertise in the technologies can be shared, so higher levels of expertise can be developed and maintained. This expertise can foster innovation in the implementations of the participating service units.

Databases. Licensing and support for a shared database should cost less when compared to separate databases for each service unit.

Ancillary activities. The service unit group can provide or consolidate ancillary services and administrative functions for economies of scale including implementation of design changes and policy compliance.

Complementary service units. Certain service units may participate concurrently or in sequence in a value stream. There may be opportunities for improved coordination in the scheduling of operations or the continuity of personnel as a unit of production flows from one service unit to the next.

Complementary work products. The capabilities of certain service units may be complementary such that they both participate in the same value stream to produce deliverables that will later be combined. There may be efficiencies or qualities to be realized through collaboration on corresponding units of work.

Degree of data sharing. As members of the same service group, service units may share a database so that they can share data directly rather that exchange messages to access shared data or coordinate updates.

Level of support. Where a service unit requires a critical level of support for reliable operation, it is possible that the supporting service unit might be brought together with the supported service unit for closer coordination. However, the supporting service unit should only be engaged within the service unit group, so it does not have a conflict of interest between serving the group and serving an outside recipient.

Service Unit Consolidation

A particular goal of the agile enterprise architecture is to share capabilities as services, whereas traditional organizations tend to duplicate capabilities in LOB silos. In the agile enterprise, all capability implementations will be incorporated in service units. Service unit consolidation brings together the otherwise redundant service units.

The following sections describe factors that suggest the consolidation of otherwise separate capability implementations.

One capability. The consolidated service unit should represent the implementation of one capability. This may require that the service unit be described as providing a more general capability than some or all of the consolidated service units. Not all of the consolidated service units need to bring all of the shared capability methods.

The capability implementations being consolidated may each represent a particular application of the capability due to the context in which they are being used, and it may be appropriate to include some or all of those applications as capability services within the service unit. However, as much as practical, these applications should be generalized so that they can provide the same services in multiple value streams.

Additional economies of scale. The consolidation of service units will be expected to improve economies of scale in the categories discussed for service unit groups, earlier. If greater economies of scale are not achievable, then the implementations may not represent a single capability.

Consistency of implementation. It should be possible to reconcile different method implementations that have corresponding inputs and outputs. Consistency leads to greater agility by enabling changes in business and technology as well as improvements to be resolved once and monitored for compliance. It reduces the cost of implementation, maintenance, and adaptation.

Note that a shared service does not necessarily operate in an identical fashion for every user of that service. The value measurements of activities may be different, some activities may be performed more or less frequently, and the activities may be performed according to different product specifications. Consequently, a shared capability must produce a deliverable appropriate to each value stream it supports.

Consolidation of control. A shared service can be in important mechanism to ensure the consistent and reliable implementation of policies and controls. A service unit may be important for separation of control from the collaboration being controlled, and it consolidates the control if it is required in multiple value streams.

Separation Factors

It is not always appropriate to consolidate capability implementations (or service units) into a single service unit or a service unit group. The following sections describe factors that suggest that consolidation is not appropriate, and the separation requirement may suggest that service units should be in separate branches of the organization hierarchy.

Separation from service recipients. The level at which a shared service unit and a recipient of its services has the same management must be the same level of reporting or higher for all of the recipients of the shared service. This is to ensure that the shared service unit is encouraged to treat all of the recipients of its service equally, or at least as appropriate to enterprise optimization.

Close affiliation of the service unit with some recipients can be a problem, particularly if the shared service is created from a segment of an existing organization and remains under the same management. Other service units that are expected to use the shared service are likely to believe that they are receiving lesser quality of service due to management priorities and personal relationships, even if the joint manager does not exercise such influence. There may also be a tendency to tap some of the personnel for work of the previous organization.

Different value chain stages. Value chain stages are each focused on creation of value for the end customer, but in different ways that tend to begin at different times in the end-product life-cycle. Value chain stages are significantly independent in purpose, technology, and skills. As a result, each value chain stage will have distinct value streams and will have different capabilities. See the discussion of a product life-cycle in Chapter 9.

While different stages come into play at different points in the end-product life-cycle, they each continue to impact the end-product throughout its life-cycle. As the product develops through its life-cycle, each stage, in turn, will become dominant, and the previous stages will continue to support adjustments to the product life-cycle for new insights and developments.

Service priority. Services that support production operations or provide customer support generally have a high response-time priority and require immediate attention. These should not be consolidated with services that have longer-term efforts.

Demands for immediate action will often interrupt and disrupt the long-term efforts, and performance metrics will be significantly different.

For example, product development services should not be on call for customer support services even though they may have the required skills and knowledge.

Service delivery locations. Some service units and the collaborations they engage will involve direct contact with customers, physical resources, communities of users, or business partners in different geographical areas, so it is not effective to consolidate these capabilities. It may be important to perform the same services in different countries in a way that is more culturally sensitive or that observes data export regulations. Some services may be distributed to different time zones to utilize daytime work hours while providing around the clock services as for customer service. At the same time, with the Internet and collaboration services, colocation of personnel may be unnecessary.

These geographic circumstances can be addressed in three alternative ways: (1) a distinct service unit is located in each area, possibly replicating the capability method(s), (2) individual service personnel work remotely from a central service unit operation, or (3) a single service unit has operations that are in multiple locations. In all cases, there should be consistent service interfaces.

Where there are distinct service units in different locations, the implementations might not be the same in all locations. This might be a function of differences in infrastructure, culture, regulations, or resource availability. These differences might be addressed with a shared capability method that engages specialized, shared methods depending on the geographical domain.

If there are strong differences among the various locations, it is likely that a decentralized organization of separate service units is necessary. These services still may be brought together in groups based on their geographical proximity. At the same time, these services may utilize centralized, shared services that achieve economies of scale and consistency in certain aspects of their operations. This model is typical of some retail operations.

Where the activities are primarily individual employee activities, there could be a single service operation that manages and coordinates the field activities, but the field personnel work remotely, interacting with the service applications for support, assignments, and data entry. This is typical of sales operations, where people spend most of their time visiting customers.

Some service units may simply operate with employees who participate remotely from home or client sites, thus avoiding the need to relocate new employees and making assignments to employees based on their proximity to clients.

Finally, a single service unit may have distributed operations so that the service users make requests of a single service and the service determines where the activities are performed. This could be a model for an engineering service where different specialists are located in different operating sites. For a service that delivers a complex product, various aspects of product development or production might be located in different countries, to optimize the use of expertise and variations in levels of compensation.

Separation of duties. Separation of duties is generally required to offset personal conflicts of interest and prevent inappropriate transfer of assets or disbursement of funds including fraud or embezzlement. Typical applications are expense claims, vendor selection, payment of invoices, hiring, and promotions.

It is appropriate to separate service units that implement critical controls from the service units to be controlled. This avoids privilege for certain people or organizations and ensures that management policies and controls can be quickly, reliably, and uniformly enforced. This separation is evident in the separation of accounting, human resources, and procurement services from the organizations that they support.

For example, funding is controlled by the accounting organization, and business units must establish budgets and obtain disbursements through accounting services. Generally, accepted accounting practices define requirements for separation of duties for financial controls.

Similar services might be implemented for such activities as customer quote preparation, application of government regulations, or allocation of expensive resources.

Separation of duties may also be needed where there are competing objectives. For example, it is appropriate to separate inspection operations from the manufacturing production organization or testing services from a product development organization. This also applies where critical records must be maintained or valuable assets could be at risk.

Incompatible culture. Business culture is a rather subjective quality. It is a product of shared values and working relationships and methods. Consolidated service units may provide the same capabilities, but they may bring different approaches, priorities, roles, and expectations. It may not be possible to clearly identify the culture of a service unit, but there are factors to consider.

For example, the methods and the roles of participants as well as the stature associated with certain roles are relevant. If these are significantly different in the service units under consideration, it is very possible that there will be a lack of harmony in the consolidated service unit. The consequences may be disputes over responsibilities, poor quality work, significantly low productivity of some workers, and increased turnover. There may be similar problems up the management chain, but the most severe discord will occur among people doing the actual work.

Different value priorities. The services brought together in an organization hierarchy should have compatible measures of performance. Two different service units are not expected to have the same service objectives, but the metrics relating to quality, duration, methods, resource management, and responsiveness to users should be compatible, particularly at lower levels in the hierarchy.

Replicated Service Units

Where the same capability is provided in multiple locations, it is important to use the same method specifications to enable advances, new business opportunities, and compliance with policies and regulations to be implemented quickly, and without redundant transformation efforts. This will require collaboration among the multiple sites to reconcile any relevant differences.

The following factors should be considered.

Increased costs. The replicated service units will not realize the economies of scale that could be achieved by a single service unit. This may be reflected not only in costs but also in an inability to respond to changes in demand or employee absences and turnover.

Essentially, the benefits of replication must offset these costs.

Multiple transitions. Changes in technology or business requirements must be rolled out to multiple sites, so there will be time periods when not all of the sites are operating with the same methods. This may cause some confusion and coordination problems.

Redundancy. Multiple implementations of a capability will eliminate a single point of failure assuming that the implementations really are independent implementations, and when one fails, the consumers of that implementation can switch to the other.

Barrier to innovation. The requirement for all sites to have the same processes is a barrier to innovation because an innovator must get all of the sites to agree to the innovation.

Outsourcing of Service Units

Outsourcing can provide greater economies of scale and relieve management of dealing with specialized services, particularly when there are complex or international regulations involved.

Interfaces. Interfaces for outsourcing may occur at various levels for service units as branches of an organization hierarchy or value stream. In either case, the impact on shared services must be considered. The capabilities to be outsourced may be shared with other organizations or value streams, and the outsourced organization or value stream(s) may depend on service units that are provided by other organizations or value streams. These dependencies should be minimized since they will require adaptation of the outsource provider and will require continued attention. VDM modeling will be a valuable source of information on these relationships.

Core competencies. Outsourcing should not occur with services that are core to the operation of the business or represent competencies that are a basis for current or future competitive advantage.

Relationship management. The relationship with an outsourcing provider must be "owned" by a manager within the client enterprise so that there is a single point of contact for negotiations and contract enforcement. The management of the contractual relationship should be in the procurement organization, but management of the operational relationships should be assigned to a manager positioned where the associated service unit(s) would be if they were internal. The primary responsibility is to ensure that the needs of the internal users are met with appropriate cost, quality, and timeliness.

Service level agreements. As with any service unit, outsourced services must have clear service agreements covering level of service, clearly specified service interfaces, management of master data, and sharing of data managed by other service units. The outsourced services must deliver appropriate value measurements along with deliverables.

Here the owning manager is directly responsible for compliance with the service agreements and service interfaces. The procurement organization is responsible for the contractual relationship.

Adaptors. There will be a need for adaptation and thus some negotiation of service interfaces provided and used by the outsourcing provider. Additional issues may arise in the future as the provider introduces operational improvements or changes for regulatory compliance. Changes that impact an interface should be addressed by collaboration at an enterprise-level, as with other transformation initiatives, including representatives of service consumers, the outsourcing owner, and contract manager.

MANAGEMENT HIERARCHY

In an agile enterprise, organization units in the management hierarchy are responsible for managing resources for the delivery of services. The leaves of the hierarchy are where the work of capabilities is actually done. The hierarchy brings together service units that have similar capabilities and objectives. This aggregation of organization units with similar capabilities facilitates the development of expertise, economies of scale, alignment of incentives, and adaptation to changing business requirements.

From an organizational perspective, we focus on service units where each service unit is a cluster of services for the same capability. A service unit group is an organizational grouping of related service units, at the next level up the management hierarchy, for economies of scale such as sharing of a workforce, equipment, and special skills. The management hierarchy should reflect degrees of affinity of capabilities from the consolidation of capabilities in service units with successively lesser degrees of affinity going up the management chain. Note that the delegation hierarchy of services engaging other services is not the same as the management hierarchy.

The top-level management hierarchy brings a focus on the overall enterprise for management of the business, optimization of operations, and response to business threats and opportunities as well as advances in technology.

The management hierarchy is enhanced for an agile enterprise (1) to support agility and (2) to support governance, management, and optimization of a dynamic enterprise.

In this section, we will examine the executive-level management structure under the topics of governing body support, executive staff, administrative support organizations, and business operations. The overall structure is depicted in Fig. 10.3.

Governing Body Support

The board of directors or other governing body should be able to see the same information that is available to top management, but generally, access will be selective, based on current concerns. We will examine the responsibilities of the governing body in greater detail in Chapter 11. Two responsibilities should report directly to the governing body since they could have a conflict of interest with the CEO: (1) Audit and Risk Assessment and (2) Legal Counsel.

Audit and Risk Assessment

These activities require an assessment of how the business works with consideration of the integrity of operations and record-keeping and the level of risk undertaken by management decisions and business operations.

Risk is a topic of considerable concern given the increased risks associated with government regulations, potential liabilities associated with product

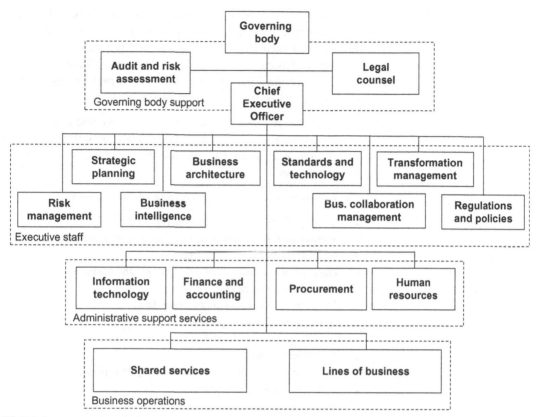

■ **FIG. 10.3** Top management organization structure.

defects, and breaches of security. Shared services have the potential to increase risks through broader exposure of systems and the creation of consolidated service units that could be single points of failure. Risk assessment goes beyond consideration of deviations from expressed operating requirements and considers business circumstances, practices, events, trends, and enterprise design that create notable risks to the enterprise. Understanding and eliminating, mitigating, or deciding to tolerate risks is an important concern for executive management as well as the governing body.

Audit is combined with risk assessment because both are concerned with identifying risks. Audits generally focus on compliance with record-keeping and compliance with policies, regulations, and standard practices. This group may not perform all levels of audit, such as security and recoverability of systems, but it should ensure that such audits are objectively performed.

Audits and risk assessments are not intended to resolve risks or fix problems of accountability and control, but they should assess the risk mitigation, and the effective level of risk, and they should identify audit problems and evaluate the resolutions. This separation of duties to evaluate from duties to resolve is important so that those assessing the risks or identification of problems do not become invested in the solutions.

There are always risks. The purpose of this service unit is to ensure that executive management and the governing body, as well as other stakeholders, are aware of the risks and that they are at least mitigated to an acceptable level.

The following are examples for the scope of risk assessment:

- Social, political, and economic disruptions
- Overlooked threats, opportunities, and loss of market share
- Investments and money management
- Single points of failure that could cripple the business
- Loss of enterprise assets
- Exposure of systems or confidential data
- Failure of programs or projects
- Regulations and legal liability
- Risk to reputation
- Failure to meet or improve upon industry best practices
- Employee working conditions
- Supplier performance

Information security risks are discussed in Chapter 7, and risks of business change are discussed in Chapter 9.

The business design using VDM modeling provides a valuable context for consideration of risks and audits. Value streams and service units identify where work is done, resources are consumed, policies should be enforced, and decisions are made along with the organizations responsible. The flow of control and deliverables identify the consequences of failures and thus the scope of risk and effects of efforts toward mitigation.

Each risk situation should be documented along with the level of risk. Resulting corrective action or mitigation efforts should be documented and followed by reassessment to ensure that an acceptable level of risk is achieved.

Operational risk management is part of the business architecture unit since it is closely related to business design. Mitigation of other risks is the primary responsibility of the organization units in which the risks arise.

Legal Counsel

Legal counsel must deal with a variety of issues that we will not elaborate here. However, some companies fail to recognize the importance of intellectual property to their competitive position. Employees should be encouraged to develop and propose patentable ideas. Some internal techniques may be subject to trade secret protection. Product names require trademark protection, and copyright or possible copyright infringement may be important for some publications. These are likely to be of increased importance in an environment where innovation and adaptation are becoming increasingly important. Legal counsel must also identify various sources of liability and suggest means of mitigation.

Executive Staff

Executive staff services provide support to top management and the governing body by providing information, development of detailed analyses and plans, facilitating collaboration and coordination, developing and applying policies, and providing oversight of performance and transformation. Each of these may be viewed as a service unit, and some of the services may involve participants from other organizations, or they may engage shared services of other organizations. These organizations provide services to top management or on behalf of top management, and often collaborate with participants of other organizations to solve problems or develop plans.

Executive staff services must report to the CEO or a person reporting directly to the CEO to ensure that they function with an enterprise-wide perspective. The executive staff services provide the mechanisms for governance and transformation of the enterprise. The services are under the CEO but should provide support to the governing body as well.

Strategic Planning Unit

Strategic planning is the responsibility of top management, but it must be supported by a team that facilitates the discussion and pulls together the detail of an enterprise strategic plan. See Chapter 9 for details on a strategic planning framework and coordination of transformation activities.

Strategic planning has new insights and supports from the other executive staffs as well as employee initiatives to identify challenges and opportunities, using VDM models for business conceptual design and context for assessment, design, and implementation of initiatives.

Business Intelligence Unit

Business intelligence has responsibility for analytics, data warehouse, measurements, and knowledge management. See Chapter 6 for more on these data management services.

Business intelligence also has responsibility for support of the interest groups with such facilities as email distribution lists, webinars, and group web pages.

The goal is to provide information for analysis, planning, process improvement, and risk analysis for top management as well as others involved in solving problems; optimizing performance; and assessing threats, opportunities, and transformation proposals.

Business Architecture Unit

Business architecture is responsible for defining the architectural characteristics of the enterprise and for development of the detailed, conceptual business design based on top management requirements.

Business architecture will develop and maintain in-depth VDM models of the current business design with associated value measurements for performance and change evaluation. It will develop to-be models to validate innovations and strategic initiatives and will develop transitional phase conceptual models that represent a top management consensus to drive and harmonize transformation efforts.

Business architecture provides the VDM models as the business context of measurements presented in executive dashboards.

Risk Management Unit

Risk management is a major business concern. Risk assessment, discussed earlier, has a primary responsibility for identification of risk factors and determination of the severity of the risk. Risk management is responsible for supporting the enterprise management to identify and manage risks with efforts to avoid or mitigate risks. This requires close work with business architecture to design the business to minimize risk and to introduce measures to mitigate risk such as rapid response to resolve a disruption of operations.

While VDM modeling provides a context for consideration of risks, not all risks occur in that context. Some external risks may be mitigated by business design and rapid response. Risk is a major business concern and requires close coordination of business architecture with risk management.

Regulations and Policies Unit

Note the discussion of regulations and policies in Chapter 5. Regulations must be interpreted in the context of the particular business and expressed as policies. Additional policies must be defined to address concerns of the governing body, to mitigate risks, and to define operating requirements.

VDM provides an understanding of the business design to identify where compliance is a concern, determine the mechanisms for reliable application of the policies to ensure compliance, and avoid redundant enforcement efforts.

Regulations must be traceable to policies and policies must be traceable to the activities where they are to be applied as discussed in Chapter 9.

Standards and Technology Unit

The role of the standards and technology unit is to lead efforts to develop and adopt relevant industry standards and emerging technologies for product design and business operations, particularly information technology. Furthermore, this unit must coordinate efforts to identify and evaluate the business impact of new standards and technologies.

Standards participation. The standards and technology unit should develop recommendations and manage budget for representation of the enterprise in industry standards organizations and particular standards development efforts. This is a source of insights on interests of competitors and potential areas of competition as well as technology trends. Standards and technologies are particularly important for information systems where there is continuous industry change.

Adoption of standards. The standards and technology unit should lead internal collaborations to evaluate the business impact of adopting specific standards and technologies and to develop proposals for implementation.

Information technology product selection. Standards and technology should be the leader in the development of the enterprise logical data model, and the owner of on-going maintenance and compliance enforcement, and it should lead collaborations on the selection of information technology products. The objective is to (1) ensure compatibility for exchange of information between service units; (2) ensure compatibility of data for cross-enterprise access and integration of information; and (3) promote economies of scale in information technology of service units, information system development, and systems maintenance by avoiding unnecessary technology diversity.

Standards compliance. Standards and technology should review product designs, system designs, and other business practices to assess compliance with adopted standards and technologies.

The IT services organization has primary responsibility for recommending standards and preferred products. The standards and technology unit is responsible for determining which standards and product preferences are appropriate from an enterprise perspective. Representatives from the various departments of the enterprise must collaborate in these decisions as well as decisions regarding deviations from the standards and preferred products.

Product acquisition and application development processes must include review by the standards and technology service unit, and deviations from standards should be authorized only if there is a clear business case for the deviation. This consideration must reflect the likelihood that the loss of economies of scale experienced by the IT service units will persist many years into the future, whereas the benefits of using a noncompliant solution may be only temporary.

Transformation Management Unit

The transformation management unit is responsible for coordination of transformation initiatives starting with the sense and respond directory to communicate notices of threats and opportunities for further action as well as program and project management to coordinate the multiple transformation initiatives, reconcile overlaps, and facilitate collaboration. See transformation management in Chapter 9 for more details.

Program and project management. Program and project management (PPM) supports the coordination of enterprise changes and the planning and tracking of transformation efforts. The PPM team should provide support for project planning and progress reporting independent of the individual project teams. Project responsibilities should be assigned to organization units that have responsibility for transformations within their areas of responsibility.

Identification, planning, and reporting of status and milestones are supported by the sense and respond directory that is managed by the PPM team. PPM will ensure that an observation that may represent a threat or opportunity will be brought to the attention of an appropriate person or process, and that the issues will be resolved by either a decision of no action or the initiation of a process for appropriate response. PPM will be responsible for collaboration and coordination among the various related efforts. The PPM team must also identify potential synergy or conflicts between independent efforts and facilitate coordination and collaboration to reconcile differences and optimize results.

For example, suppose there is an insurance enterprise initiative to consolidate four claims processing activities into one shared service unit to achieve economies of scale. A new service unit will be formed and positioned in the management hierarchy to be relatively independent of the organizations currently managing claims processing. The requirements for the new service unit, organizational implications, the impact on the related service units and lines of business, and the expected investment and return on investment are developed by business architecture in collaboration with affected organizations. Each of the four organizations that have processed claims in the past is expected to use the shared service unit. The IT organization is required to adapt, acquire, or develop the automated business processes and application software for the consolidated service unit.

A steering committee (collaboration) chaired by PPM might be formed with representatives of the affected organizations, including IT, business architecture, and BCM. PPM is responsible for a program plan that coordinates project plans, including an application development project and an organization transformation project. PPM, along with the steering committee, is responsible for requirements change control. PPM must coordinate, directly or indirectly, issues of training, cultural change, alignment of goals and incentives, BCM, and standards compliance. A community of affected personnel might be formed to provide a forum for discussion and resolution of personnel issues and concerns.

As the enterprise adopts case management technology, much of this activity can be coordinated with a case management (CMMN) system and much of the tracking, supporting, and reporting can be automated.

Business Collaboration Management

The purpose of the BCM unit is to provide a center of expertise and collaborate in the formation, recognition, automation, integration, and participation in appropriate collaborations. BCM must assist in the definition and automation of business processes, case management (collaboration) specifications, and decision management notation (DMN) for expression of rules. The BCM unit will provide support for both transformation implementation and incremental improvement. Note that while business architecture is focused on collaborations at a conceptual level, BCM is focused on the increased detail of collaborations at an operational level.

Administrative Support Organizations

The traditional administrative support services are finance and accounting, procurement, human resource management, and information technology. These already separate management of their shared services from the product value streams that they support.

Administrative support services essentially provide separation of control, economies of scale, and specialized capabilities that are more effective if managed independently.

These support services also provide shared services to each other, so the management of these shared services is also separated from the recipients of the services.

Difficulty occurs when a support services organization needs to use their own shared service units. While this violates the separate management principle, this is mitigated by the fact that the support service performance is measured by its level of service to other organizations, so there is a greater risk that it is the internal recipients of these shared service units that will suffer from neglect rather than that the shared service units will be affected by undue influence.

These services may be engaged through participation in collaborations with supported organizations, through receipt of requests for services, or in response to events that require their attention.

In the following paragraphs, we will focus on services from each of these organizations that require particular attention for the agile enterprise.

Human Resource Management

Employee orientation. To support an agile, value-driven enterprise, HRM should focus particular attention on the impact of service unit autonomy, the challenges of continuous change, and the need for appropriate incentives. This may involve the services of industrial psychologists.

Temporary and contract personnel. The agile enterprise will have changing service unit workloads adapting to new business challenges and opportunities. HRM will need to support arrangements for temporary and contract employees with short notice. Procurement may need to provide flexible contracts with personnel contractors.

Finance and Accounting

Value measurements. Value measurements are a critical part of assessing performance of the enterprise, particularly for accountability and governance. It is appropriate that the capture and accuracy of these measurements be the responsibility of accounting.

Internal billing. Every service should bill the recipients of its services for the cost of its services, including overhead and the costs of services it uses.

Accounting must manage the internal billing system, including the allocation of the overhead cost for unit of production, for value delivery analysis.

Adaptive budgets. Each service unit should have a budget. Particularly at this level of granularity, it is not appropriate to lock in a budget for a year. There is a need to make budgeting more adaptive to changing variable costs and to provide more timely authorizations and effective notations on variances.

Procurement

Outsourcing. Once outsourcing is determined appropriate, procurement is responsible for outsourcing contracts, including negotiations and contract enforcement. The contract manager must work closely with the outsourcing service manager/owner that has oversight and problem resolution responsibility for the outsourced services and their interfaces with other internal services based on VDM.

Value contributions. The impact of the cost, quality, and timeliness of purchasing service units has an impact on both product development and production operations. Delays in purchases can affect the timely introduction of new products and their success in the marketplace.

The cost, quality, and timeliness and other value contributions of supplier products and services have a direct impact on production value streams. Procurement is responsible for the values delivered by suppliers and for enforcing their compliance with level of service agreements.

Virtual enterprise. Procurement should be prepared to analyze and negotiate relationships with potential partnerships if a virtual enterprise strategy is adopted.

Information Technology

Information technology contributes to a number of agile enterprise capabilities, outlined below. For more detail, see each chapter with a description of supporting information technology.

Analytics. Information technology must support the analytics tools, databases, and data capture facilities.

Knowledge management. IT must provide the systems for knowledge management as discussed in Chapter 6.

Dashboards. Dashboards represent a management tool to be supported by IT services. Dashboards must be linked to events and measurements in the operation of the business.

Infrastructure management. IT is responsible for management and operation of the technical infrastructure, including computers, communications, and data storage as well as email, notification service, security facilities, business process systems, and case management systems.

Optimal use of information technology. The IT organization, like other service groups, is responsible for optimization of its operations. In addition, it is responsible for bringing new technology into the enterprise for applications where there is appropriate business value.

Service unit automation. IT service units support automation of business service units and other collaborations. This includes development of automated business processes, development of supporting computer applications, implementation of commercial software, transformation of legacy systems, systems integration, problem resolution, and technical support.

Strategic planning. The CIO should be a member of the strategic planning team, the same as other enterprise executives. The CIO brings a perspective on advances in technology and the application of technology to optimize the operation of the enterprise.

Business architecture. Business architecture requires technical support for a number of its responsibilities. In particular, it requires support for VDM and other modeling tools, capture of value measurements for VDM, and transformation planning. IT personnel are needed, along with BCM, to translate the VDM conceptual models to operational system models to implement the details of the systems and processes.

Enterprise intelligence. IT supports development of the enterprise logical data model, knowledge management facilities, analytics tools, and so on. See the data management services in Chapter 6.

Enterprise transformation. IT must provide the technical capability to develop and deploy detailed business processes and applications; integrate service units, applications, and business rules; transform legacy applications; and implement appropriate security facilities.

Standards and technology. IT provides the primary input for defining and implementing information systems standards and technology selections driven by a need to minimize diversity and achieve economies of scale in IT service units.

Business Operations

The business operations organizational units manage the service units that deliver the enterprise products and services. There are two basic categories: lines of business and shared services.

Lines of Business

An enterprise will have one or more LOBs. An LOB delivers products or services to customers.

Product life-cycle management. A line of business is responsible for management of the life-cycle for each product. See the example life-cycle in Chapter 9. The LOB will manage the top-level collaboration(s) that drive the life-cycle stages and directly or indirectly engage shared services to do the detailed work. As the product evolves through improvements and adaptations, capabilities of the life-cycle stages will be involved in varying degrees in the transformations.

LOB value stream management. Each LOB manages value streams for its products or services. At the top-level, a value stream will have service units that are unique to the LOB. These service units will engage other service units that directly or indirectly engage shared services to perform the detailed work.

Shared Services

In the agile enterprise, much, if not most of the actual work of the LOBs should be delegated to shared services.

Each shared service unit, directly or indirectly, must report to an organization unit that is organizationally higher than all organization units that are recipients of its services. This is to ensure that one value stream does not have undue influence over the operation or optimization of the shared service. This basic principle is a key factor in the design of the management hierarchy for an agile enterprise. Consequently, there is a fundamental separation of LOB organizations from shared service organizations.

We have already identified shared services for the business administration services: finance and accounting, human resource management, procurement, and information technology. This leaves the remaining shared services that include more direct support of LOB operations.

We have partitioned these remaining support services using value chain stages to identify lifecycle stages. Most of the value chains in an industry will be very similar, and thus it should be possible to define a value chain that reasonably supports all of the product life-cycles of the enterprise. Each of the value chain stages involve different capabilities and different value streams and thus are a basis for grouping the shared services.

A shared services organization will support multiple value streams that are relevant to its participation at various product life-cycle stages. For example, the product development stage will at least support a value stream for product development and another for product revisions. The primary capabilities of these value streams will be LOB capabilities, so there will be different value streams associated with different LOBs and there may be different value streams for product lines within a LOB. A shared services organization, like the traditional support services, will have service units that support some of its multiple value streams but also like the traditional support services, the performance of the stage is based on contributions to the success of that stage for all products. The value measurements of these value streams contribute to the overall success of each product and the enterprise.

Interorganizational Collaborations

Beyond the stable business organization structure, there are some collaborations that are continuous and others that will occur from time to time to coordinate the efforts of multiple organizations. These collaborations should be visible in the extended organization chart. Some examples follow.

Requestor collaboration. A person requesting a service or initiation of some action may do so by initiating an ad hoc collaboration with one or more persons of the service provider organization. The purpose is to develop a consensus on the proper action.

Peer to peer. A group of peers may come together to solve a problem, develop a proposal, or coordinate efforts among their respective organizations. Such collaborations may grow out of exchanges among members of an interest group (see the discussion of knowledge management in Chapter 6). The group may choose a chair person from among the participants.

Coordination of initiative. A collaboration may be initiated by one organization to engage participation in an interaction by other organizations. This could include coordination of changes in a transformation initiative. In this case, the initiating organization may provide supporting resources and might provide compensation for the time of the participants and other costs incurred by the participating organizations.

Enterprise-level optimization. Optimization of shared services requires enterprise-level leadership in a collaboration to resolve different interests of service providers and service users. The goal is to develop a feasible and optimal solution using VDM to configure and evaluate alternatives based on costs and duration of change and the impact on affected value propositions.

Innovation. Some innovations can be pursued within the scope of a single service unit; however, an innovation with broader impact will require collaboration for refinement with peers representing technical and organizational perspectives. Such collaborations should be encouraged to enable the innovator to develop the idea sufficiently for higher management consideration.

Contract negotiations. Representatives of procurement, affected service units, and supplier representatives may collaborate to arrive at a contract agreement.

Customer relationship management. Sales representatives and various other product experts may collaborate with customer representatives to develop a sales agreement or maintain a customer relationship.

ENTERPRISE TRANSITION

This section provides insight for enterprise transition to the agile enterprise by providing the basis for planning the future organization structure. Changing the organization structure drives changes to the business and helps align the objectives of people with the objectives of the enterprise.

Development of an agile enterprise seldom starts with a blank slate but must deal with the realities of an existing organization. This is a multidimensional transformation. The approach must evolve. The following sections focus on organizational aspects of the Value Delivery Maturity Model discussed in greater detail in Appendix A.

Level 1, Explored and Level 2, Applied

Organizations at level 1, explored, and 2, applied, should focus on consolidations of capabilities to realize business benefit with reasonable return on investment.

For example, multiple claim payments systems of an insurance company or multiple order management systems of a manufacturing company or multiple billing systems of a telecommunications company might be consolidated with redesign to create appropriate capability service units. At least some of these service units should be in anticipation of sharing with future value streams.

These value streams must be built on the agile enterprise information technology infrastructure to support message exchange, notification, and message transformation and should incorporate service unit databases based on the data management architecture of Chapter 6. Message and event exchanges must be based on an enterprise logical data model of at least sufficient scope to specify the messages exchanged for the new value stream(s).

In addition, information technology should implement tools for analytics and knowledge management. A small analytics activity should be established, and support for knowledge management should be implemented as described in Chapter 6. These facilities should be used as soon as possible to gain acceptance and start to show business value.

In most cases, this should result in service units that achieve significant economies of scale through consolidation. Alignment of these service units with the organizational hierarchy should give consideration to the design principles and management hierarchy design factors discussed in this chapter.

Once there are initial stage support service organizations established, these organizations should aspire to increase their shared service units by consolidation of capabilities from LOBs. These should be justified by realization of economies of scale and, in some cases, improved control.

Level 3, Modeled

To achieve level 3, modeled, all production value streams should be modeled, and work should be under way to consolidate capabilities into shared services. Shared services must be organizationally separated from the LOB capabilities they support. This will provide the basis of a plan for further consolidation of capabilities and the transformation of production value streams.

Transformation of value streams should be one at a time, at least initially, to develop the disciplines and skills for transformation. After the first value stream transformation, the second should help drive the consolidation of more capabilities for further economies of scale by sharing service units established for consolidation(s) of level 2 and the first production value stream.

At the same time, establishing a new product through the product life-cycle could be a significant driver for further development of the stage support service organizations and could increase understanding and acceptance of the strategic direction of the enterprise.

As value streams are implemented, they should be measured and the measurements captured in a measurements database. Initially this may be limited to time and cost averages of capability methods, but work should be under way to capture actual measurements at activity levels where the operational activities correspond to deliverable flows of the VDM-level, conceptual activities, so the measurements have meaning in a VDM model context. This will require measured activities to issue events to communicate measurements.

Planning for transformation of administrative support services may be deferred except that compatible service interfaces should be implemented for integration with the transformed value streams. In addition, consideration should be given to outsourcing with appropriate service unit interfaces to be provided by the outsource provider.

Level 4, Measured

At level 4, measured, much of the organization should be transformed, particularly those elements involved in production value streams. The executive support services should be established and should be developing their enterprise leadership roles. Service specifications should be formally defined, and the capture and reporting of performance metrics should be supported by the infrastructure, enabling greater empowerment of service unit managers and their people to pursue improvements. The organization structure should be near to an agile enterprise design.

Measurements should be captured and managed consistent with VDM scenarios to provide a context for the measurements. Information technology must support a dashboard capability and provide user support for key executives with plans to expand to all mid-level managers.

Strategic planning should be supported by enterprise intelligence, business architecture, standards and technology, regulations and policies, and transformation management. Business architecture should maintain current and proposed VDM scenarios and measurements for analysis and planning, including value propositions, for alternative futures. At least one transformation initiative should be supported by specification of transformation phases with VDM. Strategic planning as well as sales forecasts and product planning should be supported by analytics insights on market trends and opportunities. Mechanisms should be in place to encourage innovation and support collaborations for refinement, formal recognition of innovation, and investment.

Level 5, Optimized

At level 5, optimized, the organization structure should be transformed based on the organization design principles and hierarchy factors discussed earlier in this chapter. The agile enterprise organization structure should be in place to support continuous change, optimization, and effective governance. Strategic planning and transformation are continuously active and adapting to threats, opportunities, and changes to the enterprise ecosystem.

MOVING ON

In the next chapter, we will consider changes in leadership roles.

Chapter

11

Agile Enterprise Leadership

In this chapter, we focus on the impact of the agile enterprise on business leaders. We start by highlighting the leadership supports of the agile enterprise. We then define four levels of leadership that have fundamentally different roles. Next we discuss the impact of the agile enterprise on each of these leadership roles. Finally, we discuss ways an enterprise can be an industry leader and a list of next generation standards for further improvements to the agile enterprise.

AGILE ENTERPRISE LEADERSHIP SUPPORTS

In this section, we review aspects of the agile enterprise that support improved enterprise leadership. We discuss these under the following topics:

- Business collaboration management (BCM)
- Capability based architecture (CBA)
- Value delivery management (VDM)
- Business models
- Transformation management
- Transparency
- Sense and respond
- Innovation
- Master data management
- Information security
- Accountability
- Policies and regulations
- Risk management

Business Collaboration Management (BCM)

Traditional management hierarchy fails to recognize the responsibilities and interactions by which an enterprise actually functions. The enterprise is a network of collaborations. BCM focuses on the purpose, responsibilities, relationships, activities, and exchanges of deliverables of collaborations of various forms. The BCM model of the organization should assist in defining and supporting these collaborations with resources and automation.

Collaborations take many forms including business processes, organization units, committees, task forces, projects, interactions with customers and suppliers, and the application of capabilities (eg, capability methods). Understanding the purpose, roles, and contributions of collaborations is essential for understanding how the enterprise actually works, and for recognition of the values contributed by individual employees.

BCM not only clarifies the importance of the collaborations, but it clarifies the need to devote personnel resources to the efforts, beyond their traditional roles as members of an organization unit. In addition, the development of case management technology based on case management model and notation (CMMN, 2014) can substantially improve the efficiency and effectiveness of collaborations.

CMMN (2014) automation can provide guidance and advice to support planning and decision-making, it can improve communication and coordination, and it can provide a shared understanding of the current state of the endeavor.

Improved efficiency applies at all levels of the organization where people work together without predefined activities and interactions. These essential interactions can all be more effective if they are formally recognized, supported with automation, and engage appropriate participants.

Capability Based Architecture (CBA)

Capabilities are critical building blocks of the enterprise. Sustained capabilities can be consolidated as sharable capability units for economies of scale as well as consistency and control. These are offered as services through well-defined interfaces with defined levels of service for performance measurement and accountability.

This accountability for performance applies to the oversight of immediate management and extends to the consideration of the governing board, depending on the significance of the capability contributions and performance expectations.

Capabilities are delivered by individuals or collaborations in specific organization units, so the integration of capabilities is based on the integration of collaborations, and the activities and exchanges of deliverables in a capability method are specified as a collaboration. Thus capabilities are aligned with business processes and linked to responsible organizations.

A well-defined capability unit encapsulates the implementation of the capability to enable specialized technologies and continuous improvement without the burden of coordinating changes with related capabilities.

Value Delivery Management (VDM)

VDM involves modeling and analysis using Value Delivery Modeling Language (VDML, 2015). A model incorporates the collaborations of BCM and the capabilities of CBM. They define the contributions of values to value streams and value propositions for delivery of products and services to customers as well as internal recipients.

VDML provides the context for analysis and evaluation of capabilities because the impact of value contributions and changes to a capability can be evaluated in multiple value streams for the impact on customer satisfaction in multiple market segments. A new business opportunity can be evaluated and implemented by composing a value stream from existing capabilities with possible refinements and development of new capabilities where necessary. This is a critical capability for assessment and deployment of strategic plans.

The participation of capabilities in multiple value streams achieves economies of scale and supports analysis of the value contribution impact of changes to a capability implementation on value propositions of multiple value streams to achieve an enterprise optimum.

VDML supports scenarios for analysis of the impact on value propositions of different business contexts such as product mix or changes in other operating variables and for phases of business transformation.

Business Models

Business models based on Lindgren's Business Model Cube or Osterwalder's Business Model Canvas can be developed to describe a business under consideration and then developed in more detail using VDML to support detailed analysis and implementation. Alternatively, business models can be derived from a VDML model to provide a very abstract representation of key aspects of a product line or line of business for discussion with investors or other stakeholders.

Transformation Management

VDML significantly reduces the gap between strategic planning and the development and management of strategic initiatives. A detailed business design can be developed using existing capabilities with likely changes to support planning of capability changes and development of new capabilities as required. This can be compared to a current VDML model of the business to clarify details of the transformation. As a result, there will be a detailed, consensus business design to ensure more consistent transformation efforts in the organizations responsible for the new or revised capabilities. Objectives can then be defined based on the projected value contributions and the cost of more specific transformation projects.

Depending on the degree of transformation, VDML models may be developed for interim stages of transformation so that progress can be evaluated more frequently with viable, measurable advances. In addition, it is likely that there will be other initiatives introduced during a transformation effort that can then be introduced into the to-be model and reflected in remaining and possibly additional stages of transformation.

Transparency

The VDML abstraction hides complexity of operational details to make the design more consistent with a management perspective and more manageable for consideration of alternative business designs.

The VDML abstraction of collaborations and activities aligns to organizations and operational business processes so that VDML measurements are an accurate abstraction of operational performance. Measurements of operational value contributions provide objective measures of performance that are associated with the responsible organization unit. In addition, a VDML model can be used as the context for measurements from actual business operations so that leaders can examine the detailed capabilities and activities that contribute to value levels in value propositions and can trace the impact of changes in value contributions on multiple value streams.

The alignment of VDML activity networks with operational business processes provides an overview of operational business processes for compliance with capability unit service level specifications as well as the ability to identify the specific capabilities and activities that could be targeted for value stream performance improvement. Management dashboards should support monitoring of selected performance measurements and progress toward selected objectives in the context of a VDML model.

Sense and Respond

The sense and respond directory provides a classification of events and circumstances that require follow-up. This provides a mechanism for employees throughout the enterprise to report circumstances that may be

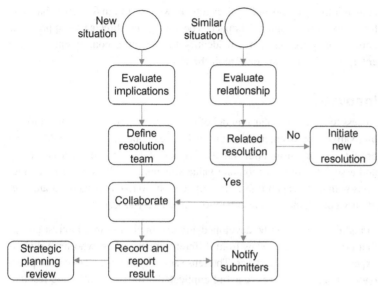

■ **FIG. 11.1** Sense and respond process.

relevant to the enterprise so that information will be communicated to an appropriate person or process, and the status and resolution of the circumstances can be monitored.

Fig. 11.1 illustrates the general concept of the sense and respond process. A new situation is posted and raised to the attention of a person or process. If there is merit, a resolution team is identified and collaborates to define an appropriate resolution. The result is recorded including those that are abandoned. In any case, feedback is provided to the original submitter(s). If appropriate, the resolution is forwarded for action in strategic planning. Additional individuals may subscribe for notice of events and resolutions that may affect their area of responsibility.

The process identifies the possibility of another, similar situation being posted. It is considered for consolidation with the active resolution if it is effectively the same or suggests refinement, otherwise it is addressed in an independent resolution initiative.

This facility allows individuals to determine if a circumstance has already been reported and if some action has been initiated. It can also help identify where different individuals or groups are working on the same or a similar problem so their efforts can be coordinated or consolidated.

Circumstances of concern must include potential risks to current operations or future success of the enterprise such as economic, social, epidemiological, and political events as well as internal events that may have cross-organizational impact. These must be directed to appropriate persons or processes that can identify the potential consequences to the enterprise and mitigate or exploit the effects.

Innovation

Access to a current, robust model of the business is important for exploring innovative improvements in current business operations. A VDM model provides clear information on the impact of innovation on a capability and associated organization and value streams as well as specific interactions with other capabilities. The implications to risk management and regulatory compliance can also be more effectively assessed.

In addition, ideas can be developed and explored in shared interest groups that bring together persons from different organizations who have diverse experiences and perspectives. The sense and respond directory can help reconcile related initiatives to avoid duplicated efforts or conflicting results.

Knowledge management provides access to relevant documents, email distribution lists, and shared web discussion pages to solicit input on problems or suggestions on solutions. This supports ad hoc collaboration on topics of shared interest.

Master Data Management

Master data is the authoritative source of enterprise data on a particular area of interest. Alignment of master data management with associated service units aligns a segment of enterprise data with the organization that has primary responsibility and expertise for creation, update, and integrity of that data.

The data directory identifies the sources of master data and replications. A master data service receives and validates updates from other capabilities, and supports requests for notices of specific changes to the master data to initiate relevant actions and support updates to replicas.

Organization units responsible for master data must be accountable for data security, accuracy, availability, and metadata (data about the source, quality, and timeliness of updates).

Information Security

In this age of the Internet and integrated, interactive systems, information security is a major issue. A number of major corporations have had security failures exposing large numbers of people to potential identity theft. The agile enterprise must include a consistent information security system and it must provide manager-friendly role-based access control.

A consistent architecture reduces complexity and consequently potential oversights in protection. It provides ease of authorized, cross-organizational access, and it supports efficient and effective maintenance and monitoring to detect intrusions and attempted violations and response to new threats.

A consistent architecture should also include processes for authorization of special circumstances by raising the request for a controlled action to an appropriate level of authority, for example, a customer order or expense request that exceeds an authorized limit, or an action that is restricted by a policy to independent review or approval by a person with special knowledge or responsibility.

Role-based access control enables managers to quickly and easily provide appropriate authorization for an individual, or terminate authorization that is no longer appropriate (see Chapter 7). The authorization should clearly identify the grantor of access authorization.

Role-based authorization support processes can improve management control and awareness of the access authorization granted to individuals, and can more reliably terminate authorizations when employees change assignments or leave the company. VDM will help identify the authorization requirements associated with different roles.

Accountability

Accountability is important for performance evaluation, but it is even more important for actions that could have consequences to the assets, integrity, or liability of the enterprise. Accountability applies to external entities such as customers and suppliers as well as employees.

A key element of accountability is reliable signatures. Public key infrastructure provides the management of identities and keys for signatures on electronic documents. An electronic signature can establish that a document represents the authority of the person(s) whose signature(s) have been applied, and it establishes that they were in agreement with the content of the document.

Electronic signatures should be applied wherever an action is taken or approved that involves the transfer of assets or an action that could have adverse effects on the operation or integrity of the enterprise. This should include acceptance of responsibility to perform an action or exercise a control in compliance with an assignment, policy, or regulation.

Policies and Regulations

Regulations and policies must be appropriately applied to control business operations. The source of regulations must be identified and each regulation must be transformed to a policy or policies that express how the regulation applies to the particular enterprise. The regulations and policies should be captured in a directory that supports analysis of interactions including categories, such as their purpose and the data entities and attributes affected.

Policies must be linked to the specific organizations and activities where they are to be applied supported by a VDM model. Where appropriate, processes must be defined for deviation from strict application of a policy. Deviations from policies must be recorded for accountability.

Risk Management

Risk management is defined by Douglas W. Hubbard in his book, The Failure of Risk Management, John Wiley and Sons, Hoboken, New Jersey, 2009:

> *The identification, assessment, and prioritization of risks followed by coordinated and economical application of resources to minimize, monitor and control the probability and/or impact of unfortunate events.*

Risk is a critical consideration in planning, decision-making, investments, and business design. It is impossible to eliminate risk, and there are not well-defined disciplines or tools for assessing risk. The governing board assesses risks and reviews the risk catalog for completeness and adequacy of mitigations.

Levels of risk must be balanced against the cost of mitigation to arrive at acceptable levels. We discussed security as techniques for mitigation of information risks in Chapter 7. We discuss development of standards for risk assessment near the end of this chapter.

A VDM model provides a context for identification and evaluation of risk. Potential unfortunate, internal events can be identified, evaluated, and mitigated for each capability and for the consequences to the affected value streams. Single points of failure can be considered for backup or redundant operations. Unfortunate events can be considered for interruption of operations, cost and duration of recovery, and potential impact on customer values.

Where capabilities can mitigate risk, the associated organization unit should be accountable. In addition, unfortunate external events and their consequences to the enterprise should be identified for resource availability, market demand, or technology advances and for economic, social, political, or environmental events. These unfortunate events can then be assessed for their impact on capabilities and associated value streams and customer values.

An assessment of the financial impact of an unfortunate event might be based on an estimate of the cost of insurance that would compensate for the loss.

VDM can also help clarify when one unfortunate event impacts multiple aspects of the business, so one possible event does not become interpreted as independent events on each capability or value stream giving the impression of a much higher level of risk.

At the same time, the risk of an unfortunate event may change over time based on related circumstances or the occurrence of another unfortunate event. Consequently, it may be necessary for mitigation methods to be reconsidered. For example, a homeowner may enjoy the pleasant environment and recreational activities of a home on a river or lake. However, when there are heavy storms or a large snow-melt upstream, the homeowner would be well advised to prepare for a flood. These changes in risks may be identified and resolved through posting of events to the sense and respond directory where responsibility is identified for initiation of appropriate action.

We will see the potential for further advances in risk management in the last section of this chapter. In the absence of a comprehensive discipline and supporting tools, an agile enterprise should develop and maintain a directory containing sources of risk, the probability and severity of the risk, potential means to eliminate or mitigate the risk, and identification of circumstances when certain risks are exacerbated.

LEADERSHIP LEVELS

In the following sections, we define four levels of leadership depicted in Fig. 11.2: the governing board, top management, capability management, and knowledge workers. In the next section, we discuss how these roles should change in an agile enterprise. In the final analysis, all of these levels of leadership have a responsibility, within their sphere of influence, for ensuring that *the enterprise is doing the right thing and doing it well.*

Governing Board

The governing board along with top management is responsible for "governance." The following is a formal definition of governance:

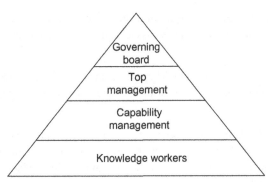

■ **FIG. 11.2** Levels of leadership.

[Governance is] The set of responsibilities and practices exercised
by the board and executive management with the goal of providing
strategic direction, ensuring that objectives are achieved,
ascertaining that risks are managed appropriately and verifying that
the organization's resources are used responsibly.

(Board Briefing on IT Governance, second edition, ©2003 ITGI;
all rights reserved.)

This definition has also been adopted by the International Federation of
Accountants (IFA) as expressed in *Enterprise Governance—Getting the*
Balance Right, 2004.

In brief, governance is ensuring that the enterprise is doing the right thing
and doing it well. The board has an oversight role. It represents the interests
of the investors, or for a government organization, the interests of the public
for whom tax dollars are invested. Investors are concerned about the sustain-
able success of the enterprise that may be reflected in a profit, but is also a
function of relationships with the recipients of products and services as well
as suppliers, business partners, and the community at large. Doing the right
thing involves meeting or exceeding investor expectations, and doing it well
means efficiency, quality, and integrity. This expectation ultimately extends
to the expectations of the other three levels of leadership.

In the traditional enterprise, success is measured, to a great extent, by return
on investment and growth. These are objective, but crude measurements. In
the following sections we will see how the agile enterprise can better ensure
that the enterprise is meeting or exceeding expectations, and doing it well.

Top Management

Top management is responsible for managing the resources of the
enterprise to achieve the strategic, tactical, and operational purposes of
the enterprise, and for supporting the governing board in fulfillment of

their responsibilities. This involves strategic planning, organizing, adapting, and investing in resources to fulfill the enterprise purpose. This includes monitoring and control to ensure that appropriate objectives are met, that the enterprise is successful in meeting the needs and demands of its customers, and that it is enabling the success of its suppliers and business partners.

Capability Management

Below top management, there may be multiple levels of capability managers. These are the managers of the management hierarchy. These leaders are responsible for managing their assigned resources and ensuring the sustained and reliable operation of their segment of enterprise operations. Generally, they have specific authority to spend money and hire and fire people. They are responsible for directing the solution of problems within the scope of their authority, collaborating with others and for informing their management chain of challenges and opportunities that have implications beyond their scope of authority.

Knowledge Workers

In any organization where there is actual work being performed, there are knowledge workers who understand operating details and are essentially responsible for continuous improvements and keeping the operation running. They may do mainstream work but they are also leaders in a particular aspect of the business.

These are the people who typically are the actual problem solvers, but they do not have formal authority for directing the activities or responsibilities of others. At the same time, they may have explicit authority and responsibilities in interorganizational collaborations by virtue of their insights, experience, or credentials. Most importantly, they have authority by virtue of their skills and experience.

LEADERSHIP IMPACT

In the following sections we discuss the implications of an agile enterprise to leaders at the four levels outlined, earlier.

Governing Board

The governing board has traditionally focused on the financial condition of the enterprise. For a profit-making enterprise the focus is on profit and growth. For government and nonprofits, the focus is on outcomes, but the board tends to leave the operation of the enterprise to the CEO.

The board of an agile enterprise should be expected to do more because they can, and investors should expect it. The agile enterprise enables oversight by the board that goes deeper into "doing the right thing and doing it well" because technology enables greater transparency and accountability. Investors are more concerned and aware of how the enterprise is being managed as a result of some high-profile cases of mismanagement and the recent global, financial crisis.

Most investors are not constantly watching the financial markets and moving their investments, but expect their investment to be good in the long run. To properly represent the interests of these investors, the board must ensure that top management is looking well beyond the next quarter financial reports. Investors are more concerned about the vision of the enterprise, expanded to include core ideology, core values, and core purpose as discussed in Chapter 9.

Oversight must ensure that the agile enterprise is actually prepared to adapt to threats and opportunities, that it fully utilizes the knowledge and experience of leaders at all levels, and that it delivers the values that are important to its consumers. The technologies of the agile enterprise make it possible to more effectively evaluate the challenges and the results.

Agility

Agility is more than an adaptive business design. It requires awareness of external changes affecting the enterprise, it requires innovation to maintain or improve competitive position, and it requires continuous strategic planning and transformation. The world is changing too rapidly for strategic planning to occur annually.

The sense and respond directory discussed in Chapter 9 provides a record of identified threats and opportunities and the responses. This information can provide important insight of the governing board into the enterprise agility.

Risk Management

Risk is a major concern of investors. While there is always some risk, risks undertaken by the enterprise should not be only discussed behind closed doors or undertaken by the CEO, alone.

The board should have access to a risk management catalog identifying the sources of risk, the potential severity of the risk, mitigation measures that have been implemented, and the residual risk. The level of risk may change as a result of changes in business circumstances. The sense and respond directory should drive reconsideration of affected risks.

The risks of business as usual should be assessed as a baseline. Threats and opportunities represent new risks and potential needs for change. Change brings transformation risks, both in the transition, and in the future state of the business. The board must understand the risks of a change as well as the risks of continuing business as usual. The benefits of change must be worth the net risk of change. The board must understand the threats and opportunities and be assured that the planned changes are properly developed and evaluated, and the transformations are well-managed.

Value Delivery Management (VDM)

The fundamental impact of VDM is management with models. VDM models provide a clear understanding of how the business operates currently and potentially in the future. They provide a context for understanding the impact of change.

The governing board should expect the enterprise to maintain current and future VDM models and make them available so that board members can understand business problems and plans in context including measurements and value propositions. VDM models should also support business model abstractions such as those of Lindgren and Osterwalder for consideration by board members and investors. The as-is model must be consistent with the actual business design and performance measurements.

The board should be informed of plans and progress to achieve a full, agile enterprise based on the value delivery maturity model (see Appendix A).

Accountability

The agile enterprise must be more transparent in order to be accountable for performance, implementation of improvements, and resolution of problems. Performance of all capabilities must be reported against service level agreements.

Management dashboards should be available to the governing board to provide measurements in the context of VDM models, to report progress toward objectives, and to consider contributions of values that affect customer satisfaction.

The sense and respond directory enables the board to monitor relevant events and circumstances along with timeliness and appropriateness of responses.

The board can also review the regulations and policies directory that provides a record of all policies and all regulations that are transformed to policies along with links to the capabilities that must apply the policies. Periodic audits should validate the completeness and compliance with requirements.

The board should have supporting staff to perform analysis and oversight activities and report to the board. This is reflected in the suggested organization structure of Chapter 10, with audit, risk assessment, and legal counsel reporting to the board. The board should also have access to results of analytics and competitive analysis for consideration of the enterprise standing in the marketplace.

Consistent Architecture

The information systems architecture of the agile enterprise represents a significant investment. It is essential to the effective implementation of the agile enterprise and is an important aspect of the value delivery maturity model.

Consistent architecture is fundamental to efficiency, effectiveness and flexibility of integration, security, data management, event processing, support of processes and collaboration, and management of shared services. The governing board should require and monitor the timely implementation of a consistent architecture to align with progress on the maturity model.

Industry Leadership

The full value of the agile enterprise is not realized by incremental improvement, it is not realized by being able to quickly adapt to advances of competitors, it is not even realized by delivering the best value to customers because that will change. It is achieved by taking the lead in the industry; by getting ahead of competitors, defining the industry direction and exceeding the expectations of customers and investors.

The sense and respond directory will provide a record of awareness of advances and new applications of technology along with responses to this awareness. The governing board should review the list of alerts and responses to assess the leadership position of the enterprise.

The board should expect the enterprise to be active in the development of standards, methods, and regulations that help to improve the cost and quality of industry products and services, to ensure that members of the industry maintain business integrity, and to provide appropriate visibility of risks to investors and other stakeholders. As a leader, the enterprise is then positioned to be an early adopter and realize competitive advantage.

Top Management

The leadership model of top management defines the context for leadership of the next two levels. Top management must develop a new way of thinking about and providing enterprise leadership that involves employee empowerment and inspiration.

Traditional top-down management is no longer appropriate. While top management has awareness of the breadth of issues facing the enterprise as a whole, people within the enterprise have the depth of understanding that is necessary for effective planning and decision-making as well as innovation and improvements. The VDM modeling capabilities, along with the knowledge management facilities of Chapter 6, identify sources of detailed knowledge.

Top management must inspire pursuit of a vision and a general commitment to success of the enterprise. Employees must realize personal value in collaborating with others and contributing to make the enterprise great. This must be reinforced by formal recognition of individual contributions and support of cross-organization collaborations.

Value Delivery Management (VDM)

VDM modeling must become a fundamental approach to top management planning, decision-making, performance evaluation, and problem solving.

VDM models are key to enterprise level optimization of capabilities in a business with multiple value streams of shared capabilities.

VDM models should be used to validate innovations, define new value streams, and assess the costs and benefits of such initiatives.

Measurements of actual performance, i.e., activity value contributions, should be captured in the context of a current VDM model of the business.

Business leaders should have personalized dashboards for monitoring performance and progress on objectives. A VDM model of the current enterprise should define the context for dashboard measurements.

Continuous Strategic Planning and Transformation

Strategic planning can no longer be an off-site exercise conducted once every year or more. The world is changing too fast and an enterprise that does occasional strategic planning will get left in the dust. Furthermore, transformation to address a threat or opportunity cannot wait for the current transformation to be completed, but new initiatives must be incorporated in transformation plans.

Strategic planning today does not adequately drive the enterprise. Most strategic initiatives fail to meet expectations and take far too long. Not only must there be a seamless connection of strategic planning to business transformation, but strategic planning should be a continuous process that unifies continuous change. This also requires that there be continuous measurement in the context of a VDM model to assess problems and progress.

Transformation planning must include the necessary changes to business methods, organization structure, incentives, and delegation to engage all employees in contributing to the advancement of the enterprise.

VDM modeling can support incremental transformation by defining the altered state of the enterprise at operational stages representing less ambitious transformations, leading to the currently defined future state. As new initiatives are defined, they may be incorporated in the current and future stages.

The specification of transformation phases with VDM models provides clear direction, dependencies, and objectives for distributed transformation projects (see Chapter 9). This level of detail requires participation of all levels of leadership.

Capability Matrix

The development and management of shared capabilities requires a separation of shared capabilities from line of business capabilities. This new matrix organization requires new organizational disciplines and technical support. Top management must ensure that the cost of services are properly computed and allocated to the consumers of the services, and that the capability units are allowed appropriate overhead to properly maintain and improve their services.

This represents a new way of thinking about budgeting, accountability, cost allocation, and management of levels of service. This also clarifies the potential for outsourcing of commodity capabilities.

Sense and Respond Directory

The sense and respond directory is central to awareness and responses to events and circumstances that may represent threats or opportunities. Top management must ensure that responsibility has been defined for follow-up on the various categories of circumstances, and that follow-up on recent posts is timely and appropriate.

Risk Management

Comprehensive risk identification, mitigation, and assessment is an important challenge. Risk management tends to focus on obvious risks and those receiving significant attention in the business community. Risk management will become a key consideration of investors since the issue is risk to their investments.

The agile enterprise should compile and maintain a risk management catalog of risks, mitigations, and levels of risk for the business as usual, as well as threats, initiatives, and external circumstances that bring new risks. These risk entries should be collected from leaders across the enterprise that are familiar with the risks of their operations. Activities driven by the sense and respond directory should adjust or add risks as appropriate.

Incentives

Top management must manage incentives and performance measures to ensure that capability managers achieve an appropriate balance of knowledge worker efforts between productivity in their primary jobs and empowerment to innovate and exchange knowledge in interest groups. Support for collaboration with CMMN technology will be important for tracking and recognizing employee contributions to interorganizational collaborations.

Technology Leadership

Technology is a critical element of enterprise success and a continuing source of change. Top management must drive the adoption of current technology and replace or transform legacy systems. Legacy systems require continued support of obsolete technology, represent a barrier to BCM and CBA, and increase the cost and delay of improvements.

The emphasis must be on transition to a technical infrastructure consistent with the agile enterprise, the automation of collaborations, and the integration of shared capabilities.

Technology Advances

In addition, top management must be sensitive to continued advances and the implications to enterprise products and services. The evolution of the following technologies should be given close attention for potential threats and opportunities.

Mobile Computing

The impact of mobile computing with smart phones and tablets is still evolving. Inexpensive and often free applications establish a user's relationship with a particular enterprise providing very personalized services with GPS location and associated sensors worn by the user.

Case Management

Case management is still a very untapped technology since applications have only recently emerged. The development of good CMMN models is still a primitive art. This will have a major impact on knowledge work including customer service, strategic planning, crisis management, claims investigation, and health care, particularly in hospital settings. It should also support management collaborations at all levels.

Analytics

Analytics has surged as a result of concurrent, distributed processing technology based on Hadoop (http://hadoop.apache.org/). The potential of such high-speed analytical processing is still emerging. Analyses that in the past were too expensive or time consuming have suddenly become feasible. The technology will be applied to complex engineering analysis, DNA analysis, and economic models if it has not already.

Cloud

Cloud computing is gaining momentum. Eventually, cloud computing, communications, and data storage services will be accepted as global utility services, and traditional information systems operations will be reduced to key competencies that provide particular value to the enterprise. The efficiency, scalability, reliability, and security of cloud services will exceed the potential of the internal information systems capabilities of most enterprises.

Internet of Things

The Internet of Things (IoT) involves connecting all sorts of things to the Internet including appliances, various forms of sensors, vehicles, and traffic systems. The growth of the Internet of Things will eventually blur the separation of business information systems and the systems of products and services. Consumers of products and services will be closely linked to the provider of the products and services through personal devices as well as devices in their homes, businesses, vehicles, communities, and other systems.

Value Delivery Maturity

Top management must have a plan and report progress toward becoming an agile enterprise. The plan and progress can be based on the value delivery maturity model included in Appendix A. The maturity model defines criteria, in business and technical dimensions, for five levels of maturity depicted in Fig. 11.3. The leadership of the enterprise should evaluate their current level of maturity, refine the maturity model to be more specific to the particular enterprise, develop a timetable with objectives, and start the transition.

An enterprise-specific maturity model will provide the basis for development of a transformation plan and the specification of objectives for monitoring progress.

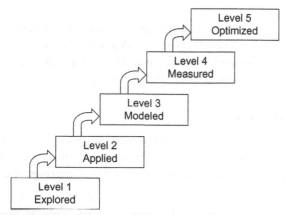

■ **FIG. 11.3** Value delivery maturity model stages.

Reorganization

Strategic planning and transformation must extend to major reorganizations described in the following sections. These are more than adaptation of the enterprise, but may involve major design changes. In addition to the considerations discussed in the following section, VDM models must be applied to define stages of transformation to implement these reorganizations.

Outsourcing

Outsourcing can provide substantial cost reduction through economies of scale, and can relieve management of managing and maintaining special capabilities that provide no competitive advantage. At the same time, there may be many dependencies between the outsourced capabilities and the rest of the enterprise, the interfaces should be based on industry standards to avoid lock-in, and the integration should be consistent with the rest of the information technology infrastructure. The governing board should review plans for outsourcing to consider the costs and risks of implementation and the long-term costs and risks.

Mergers and Acquisitions

Enterprises under consideration for merger or acquisition should be modeled with VDML for comparison to the parent organization VDM model. Particular attention should be given to any value stream or capability that is expected to bring a competitive advantage by integration and/or consolidation with existing capabilities. Consideration must go beyond performance to evaluation of practices and incentives to evaluate cultural compatibility.

Divestiture

Divestiture can involve major disruption of important dependencies and controls. VDM modeling can clarify the dependencies and support configuration of the separated business entities. Resolution of the many, less formal collaborations may be critical to an orderly transition.

Industry Leadership

Top management must make industry leadership a priority. Industry leadership means defining the future rather than chasing the future. Success at industry leadership is a strong indicator that top management is doing the right thing.

Industry leadership is discussed further in the next major section of this chapter.

Capability Management

Management of capability services is quite different from management of a traditional organization in a silo-oriented enterprise. This includes LOB management of LOB-specific capabilities. Services are designed to respond to requests through a well-defined interface while the implementation of the service is hidden from the consumer. Service level specifications define performance requirements. Value contributions define the impact on one or more value streams. The cost of the service must be billed to the consumer, including the cost of any services it uses so that alternatives, such as outsourcing, redundant services, or benchmarks can be properly evaluated.

Business leaders must create a culture where knowledge workers are inspired to be creative and collaborate. This requires incentives for both the knowledge workers and their managers. Knowledge workers should be encouraged to participate in interest groups to share experiences and develop new business solutions.

Employee Empowerment

Employees typically represent a tremendous, untapped resource for innovation and process improvement. Employees understand how their part of the business actually works and see the opportunities for improvements. They also see the marketplace and the products they produce from a different perspective.

Capability managers have knowledge workers who understand the details of the services and are the primary problem solvers and improvers. Leadership of knowledge workers is different from managing employees who simply perform prescribed activities.

Unfortunately, employees are often discouraged from contributing their personal insights and inherent capabilities beyond their formal roles because it is "not their job," and their leaders want them to focus on doing their assigned work. Leaders must develop a culture where the work gets done but employees go above and beyond their formal roles to contribute their full potential to implement leading practices and deliver exceptional value. This requires development of appropriate performance measures and incentives at all levels.

In the agile enterprise, the knowledge workers, in particular, are important resources for insight, innovation, and adaptation that improves the service and may bring ideas and solutions that go beyond the scope of their service unit. Knowledge workers should be inspired to contribute to the success of the enterprise. They must be given the latitude to innovate and collaborate to improve the enterprise.

Capability Unit Management

Management of a capability unit involves meeting the expectations of both the management hierarchy and the expectations of the consumers of the capability services. In addition, the capability unit will be a consumer of other services.

The capability manger is responsible for the implementation design of the services within the requirements of the VDM model. In addition the functionality must be maintained for many if not all the technical service interfaces described for a service unit in Chapter 3.

The capability manager is also responsible for accountability and control of processes and business records through appropriate access and update validation and authorization mechanisms, and through electronic signatures on actions involving control of assets or sensitive data.

Resource Management

Resources must be managed for optimal performance and utilization. This includes balancing workloads by appropriate assignment of personnel to roles considering their skills and the delivery of values to one or more value streams.

VDM Model

The capability manager must be constantly aware of the implications of the capability services to the supported value streams. The VDM model defines this context, and it defines the contexts of supporting services and their potential impact on value stream contributions. This context is important for optimization as well as problem solving.

Master Data Management

Each capability unit has master data associated with its operation. That data, along with master data of other capability units, represents the current state and relevant history of the operation of the enterprise. In some cases, the use of this data may be primarily for accountability and support for performance evaluation and improvement. In other cases the data represents essential records such as customer orders, shipments, agreements, and supplier contracts.

The master data must be protected, maintained, and made available where needed. This includes management of access authorization, integrity control, and acceptance of appropriate updates. The capability manager also must ensure that processes enforce relevant regulations, policies, and controls to prevent errors, fraud, embezzlement, or disclosure of confidential data. This should extend to ensuring appropriate controls are applied when the master data is authorized for use in another organization.

Sense and Respond

The capability manager is responsible for posting relevant circumstances or events to the sense and respond directory, and should receive sense and respond notices on topics that may affect the performance of the capability or could exacerbate a risk calling for additional mitigation.

Risk Management

The capability manager is responsible for reporting the potential for unfortunate events that could affect the performance of the capability, for mitigating the risk to the extent it can reasonably be mitigated within the scope of the capability unit, and for collaboration on broader scope mitigation.

The enterprise risk management unit should provide a framework for reporting risks that identifies generic or global risks that are not unique to the particular capability but could have distinct consequences in terms of losses.

Collaboration and Innovation Support

Capability managers must allow for knowledge workers to participate in collaborations and initiatives for development of innovations, sharing of knowledge, and problem solving that may improve the enterprise or contribute to industry leadership as discussed further, in the following section.

In some cases this may mean providing leadership in the promotion of an innovation, or funding to support knowledge worker participation or an interest group collaboration.

Regulation and Policy Compliance

The capability manager is responsible for compliance with regulations and policies in the operation and management of the capability services. The regulations and policies directory defines compliance requirements. While compliance may be implemented by actions of other capabilities in the associated value streams or services that are engaged by the capability manager's operations, the capability manager should ensure that these actions ensure compliance. Some capabilities may be provided by ad hoc methods, and CMMN-based tools should support activities with guidance for participants to comply with regulations and policies.

Knowledge Workers

Knowledge workers do work that requires analysis, planning, and decision-making as opposed to performance of prescriptive processes. Knowledge workers provide different levels of leadership depending on their training and experience as well as the problem at hand. They must be inspired to contribute to the success of the enterprise beyond the scope of their formal responsibilities. They should be encouraged to share their knowledge and experience in collaborations, emails, web discussions, and posting of documents. They should view these efforts as contributing to their career development and advancement. They should also envision their role as contributing to the continuous adaptation of the enterprise.

VDM Models

VDM models provide an understanding of the operation of the business so knowledge workers can understand how their capabilities impact the big picture and explore potential improvements to optimize the value to the enterprise.

Knowledge workers will also be key sources of knowledge to develop details of the VDM models, plans for transformation, and measurement of value contributions of their capability unit.

Encapsulation

Capability units are *encapsulated*, that means their consumers see their interfaces but not their implementation. Encapsulation empowers knowledge workers and capability managers to identify, plan, develop, and implement innovations and operating improvements within the scope of the capability unit and their budget.

Collaboration

Knowledge workers should represent their capability unit in collaborations for planning and problem solving related to the knowledge worker's area of expertise.

A knowledge worker should also participate in one or more interest groups where knowledge, experience, and ideas can be shared and discussed. This includes meetings (typically on-line so participants need not be colocated), email exchanges, and web-based discussions (see Chapter 6). Mechanisms must be established to provide incentives and recognition for participation.

Collaborations on particular topics or initiatives should be supported by case management automation (eg, CMMN implementation) that assists in planning, coordination, and record-keeping.

Innovation

Knowledge workers are primary sources of product or process innovations because they are most knowledgeable about the details and should be aware of the market and competitive products. They should explore their ideas in collaboration with other leaders and members of interest groups.

Sense and Respond

Knowledge workers have the opportunity to observe events and circumstances that may not have come to the attention of other business leaders. They should feel obligated to post these circumstances to the sense and respond directory if they are not already posted. They should also post interest group initiatives to ensure appropriate people are aware and for potential coordination with other initiatives.

Knowledge workers may also be responders to alerts for initial analysis of circumstances related to their area of expertise to either resolve the concern or initiate further action.

Transformation

Knowledge workers will have primary responsibility for defining, planning, and coordinating specific changes to their capability unit required for enterprise transformation.

Industry Standards

As with innovation, knowledge workers should be primary candidates for representation of the enterprise in industry standards efforts, discussed in the next section.

INDUSTRY LEADERSHIP

In this section, we will consider the path to industry leadership in four dimensions: (1) agility, strategic planning, and transformation, (2) industry advances, (3) regulations, and (4) standards.

Agility, Strategic Planning, and Transformation

In order to lead, you must be agile. It is not enough to have good ideas, you must implement them. Agility is needed, not only for continuous improvement but for strategic change.

Strategic planning and transformation are essential components of agility. Again, it is not enough to have good ideas, but it must be possible to implement those ideas in a timely and reliable fashion.

Consequently, the first step in taking the lead is to pursue value delivery maturity (Appendix A). Full realization could take a decade, although progress toward maturity may also demonstrate industry leadership capability in the near term. The potential speed of realization of maturity will depend somewhat on the enterprise and the industry. Some capabilities may be encapsulations of legacy systems where there is not a critical need for transformation. Some capabilities might be outsourced to take advantage of provider economies of scale. The consistent information systems infrastructure will be essential.

An enterprise should focus on maturity of mainstream business operations first and extend the architecture and technology to supporting services later, but obsolete support services may adversely affect the capabilities that interact with them, and will increase the cost and complexity of maintaining those interfaces.

Although the maturity model focuses on mainstream business operations, the agile enterprise should continue to expand the scope of the transformation to include all aspects of the business and exploit continued advances in technology.

Industry Advances

The enterprise must impress the industry with innovative ideas or the ability to achieve and maintain competitive advantage. It is not enough to implement best practices; it must implement better practices. Engaging the creative talents of business leaders and knowledge workers from throughout the enterprise is fertile ground for industry leadership, assuming the creativity reaches strategic planning or participation in development of regulations or standards, discussed later.

Industry advances must be driven by increased value to customers. In some cases these are new or changed markets, but customer value is one goal that all members of an industry can agree upon. This extends to the realization of value to business partners who are essential to the future success of a business. A new business endeavor may involve new business partners that must also be successful for the new business to succeed.

An enterprise cannot be the industry leader if it does not achieve value for itself, its customers, and its business partners.

Regulations

Regulations are often viewed as requirements imposed by governments for values that increase costs but not revenue. That applies to products and services as well as operating methods. However, in a broader context, regulations represent values that will not be realized in a purely competitive environment. The enterprise that, unilaterally, implements all the safety and integrity protections and precautions may be a good citizen but may also be at a substantial competitive disadvantage.

Regulations raise the costs of all competitors and benefit many customers or other citizens who are otherwise unable to obtain the benefits at reasonable cost. For example, if airbags were offered as an option on automobiles, the cost of the option would be much higher because the option would only be produced on some vehicles. In addition, many people who did not choose to go without airbags (passengers or nonowner drivers) would suffer severe injuries as a result. Air bag regulations ultimately save lives at lower cost than if the purchase were an individual choice.

So, in a way, regulations enable enterprises to do the right thing without the risk of competitive disadvantage. Stockholders are increasingly aware of the good (or bad) citizenship of the enterprise.

Business leaders should view regulations as potential benefits. An enterprise that takes the initiative to develop benefits to customers and employees should propose regulations that demonstrate good citizenship and also enable the enterprise to benefit from readiness when regulations take effect. Regulations may also reduce liability.

Of course, this works in the context of a national market, but what about competition in international markets where the lack of similar regulations creates a competitive disadvantage? First, most enterprises are not "citizens" of one country, they are citizens of the world. When a new regulation requires a product improvement in the world's greatest marketplace (the United States), foreign competitors are going to comply even if their governments do not demand it. They will also want their government to adopt similar regulations so that they do not suffer competitive disadvantage against local competitors. In the long term, there is a global benefit.

Similar dynamics can drive improvements in business practices that benefit stockholders. Stockholders will be sensitive to risks of misconduct or losses, particularly if discussion of regulations exposes these practices. Public corporations compete for investors in a global marketplace. Again, national regulations can exclude noncompliant enterprises from the national market, providing an incentive for them to advocate for regulations in other countries to level the playing field. The enterprise that takes the lead can also benefit from a reputation for quality and integrity.

The marketplace can also drive improvements in internal business practices for the benefit of employees. If poor business practices are visible to the public, then better employees will leave and better prospective employees will apply elsewhere. This will not be as effective in foreign markets, but enterprises that respect their employees will have an advantage with customers and stockholders.

Standards

In this book we have described the synergy between business and technology to achieve an agile enterprise. We have discussed a number of industry standards for systems that support the design and operation of the agile enterprise. There are standards for the information infrastructure to support the integration, security, and accessibility of systems and services. We described standards for modeling information systems and for modeling the design of the business. These standards have enabled development of today's agile enterprise.

However, the evolution continues. There will be new advances in technology that continue to change the marketplace and advances in the design and management of the enterprise. The technology solutions can be solved by each enterprise, but it would be preferable to resolve technical issues in a standard way so that the enterprise does not create new solutions that become a legacy burden down the road or limit the ability to switch to more advanced products from other vendors. The preference is to implement industry standards so that when future products provide better solutions or a lower cost, the enterprise is not faced with another expensive and time-consuming transformation.

The agile enterprise should be a leader in the development of new information technology standards. Much of the pain of developing and maintaining information systems as well as the continuing adoption of advancing technology is a result of incompatibility of new solutions. Large suppliers of the technology thrive on bringing proprietary solutions to market in order to capture an emerging market, lock customers into their products, and create a barrier to entry of competing products. The solution is for users of the technology to provide the leadership needed to define the market, exploit advances in technology, and optimize business solutions—to drive the technology rather than letting the technology drive business change. So the goal is to use and develop industry standards so that investments in transformation are built on a durable foundation.

The same principles apply to standards for products and services. Some, large corporations can benefit from creation of de facto standards—the standards they create for their products. However, in today's world, it is becoming increasingly difficult for a large corporation to develop a new product that sets the standard when smaller companies can more quickly develop a standard and deliver more specialized products, capturing an early market. Here is where Clayton Christensen's (2016) *disruptive innovation* can apply for the creation of new markets. Christensen's disruptive innovation introduces a revolutionary product that does not necessarily meet the demands of the traditional, sophisticated customers, but satisfies the need of customers who cannot afford the sophisticated solution to create a new market. It then grows into a solution that takes over the traditional market.

Development of standards is driven by market demand. Much of the work of developing a standard will be done by the companies that will implement the products that comply with the standard. These companies will not invest in that effort unless they see a business threat or opportunity. The perception of a market for new solutions must come from needs or demands of potential customers.

Larger suppliers will tend to develop solutions behind closed doors and attempt to capture the market with proprietary solutions that become de facto standards. Smaller suppliers need a standard to create a market for their efforts, and are unlikely to invest in development of a standard unless they believe the standard will be accepted by the industry. At the same time, smaller suppliers are more agile and will support early adopters and continued improvements while being compatible in the long term.

It is important for potential customers to participate in the investment so that (1) both large and small suppliers perceive and participate in a market opportunity, (2) the solution actually solves the business problem, and (3) the potential customer can be prepared to take advantage of the solution, potentially as an early adopter.

The agile enterprise should also participate in development of industry standards where they are relevant to the enterprise products or services. Leadership in development of standards can create a market, and can position the leader to be the early market leader.

NEXT GENERATION STANDARDS

In this section we provide insights on desirable standards that will enable the next generation agile enterprise. Many of these build upon the capabilities provided by VDML.

Agile enterprise business leaders should consider playing a leadership role in the development of these advances of the technology. Participation can provide insights for alignment of current initiatives and position the enterprise as an early adopter to exploit the advances.

These proposed advances, described in the following section, would benefit from participation of expected users of the technology to establish the market potential, define priorities, and guide the efforts with an understanding of business requirements.

- Strategic planning and transformation
- Business architecture support
- Data directory service
- Role-based authorization
- Sense and respond directory
- Risk modeling
- Regulations and policies management
- Multiple vocabulary facility
- Performance monitoring
- Management dashboards
- CMMN resource management
- CMMN project management
- VDML simulation
- Culture modeling

Strategic Planning and Transformation

Strategic planning and transformation involve analysis of alternative business models with VDML and development of a detailed to-be model along with transformation phase models. VDML represents value contributions and value propositions for analysis of the impact of changes on multiple value streams. The transition from the current business model to the to-be model requires analysis to define stable, intermediate states as phases of transformation. These will depend on an understanding of the changes and their dependencies. In Chapter 9 we described a framework for business transformation based on phases of transformation specified with VDML scenarios.

Transformation modeling should build on VDML to provide mechanisms to identify the specific changes from one phase to the next, identify the dependencies between changes, and assess the consequential effects of the changes that may suggest the need for additional change or refinements to the phases. The changes become the requirements for activities in the transformation plan, and deliverable flows represent transformation dependencies.

This basic transformation plan then must be refined to elaborate the activities required for the design changes, such as training and information systems development, and to define milestones that represent objectives of particular interest to the management. As phases are completed, VDML scenarios will provide target measurements for evaluation of actual performance.

Business Architecture Support

The current displays of VDML models were defined to support general requirements for creation and viewing of a VDML model with the expectation that additional displays would be developed based on user experience and practices.

VDML currently supports detailed modeling to support the work of business architects. A concern of business architects is to present more abstract artifacts of the intended business design for top management. Additional VDML display specifications should provide the needed artifacts. Business architects will then develop the abstract artifacts to capture management requirements and expand the VDML design detail to validate the approach and provide details needed for clear requirements and for transformation planning detail.

At this writing, there is work in OMG (Object Management Group) to define requirements for business architect artifacts.

Data Directory Service

The purpose of a data directory is to identify the master source of specific data along with replicas of that data in the distributed database environment. However, there is a need for more than a simple directory since the databases may not be implemented with a consistent data model, particularly if they are legacy or enterprise application (commercial software product) databases.

In general, other systems will need access to data from master databases. They may access that data ad hoc, or they may maintain a copy for future use.

A copy will become out of date, so there is a need to receive updates when there are changes to the master database. This was discussed in Chapter 6.

A solution is for the data directory to provide a data access service based on specifications of specific database views. Business item definitions in the VDM can be the basis for definition of these views. A view is data retrieved or updated as a record that includes elements coming from multiple database tables.

The data directory could receive requests for specific views to be retrieved from a master database and, if required, it could request an update to each view when the content changes. This then provides a consistent form of exchange for the data that is independent of the database implementation.

Role-Based Authorization

In Chapter 7 we described a spreadsheet approach to specification of access authorization based on roles. A computer-based model could make this easier to develop and manage with a more effective user interface and an automated link to information infrastructure access control facilities.

Roles in the model should be consistent with the roles in the current VDM, and the role authorization model also should be linked to the business process models and access control systems for improved efficiency, reliability, and timeliness of updates.

Sense and Respond Directory

The concept of a sense and respond directory has been discussed in Chapter 9. The goal is to be prepared for observations, events, circumstances, or disasters—internal or external—that require attention. The directory provides a taxonomy of circumstances for classification of an observation, event, circumstance, or disaster, and identification of the person(s) and/or processes that will receive notice to take some action.

The resulting action should lead to a disposition. There may be multiple initiatives representing different perspectives. Status and progress of each initiative should be tracked in the directory. The directory should facilitate consolidation or coordination of efforts if the same or related circumstances arise. Initiatives of interest groups or other collaborations should also be captured and tracked for potential consolidation or coordination.

The directory might be defined as a specialization of CMMN where a directory entry is case data and ad hoc participants in the case contribute to the resolution. This supports status tracking, events to initiate action, alerts to participants, as well as planning and coordination of the effort.

This facility might also be linked to the current VDM model such that the classification of circumstances includes affected business capabilities and notification to the organization responsible for each capability.

Risk Modeling

A risk management catalog is needed to capture information about risks. There are many sources of risk to be evaluated, and there are relationships between risks and the consequences of risk that call for modeling these interactions and dependencies. The risk model should generate a net assessment to provide an enterprise risk profile for top management, the governing board, and other stakeholders to evaluate.

Risk assessment is a fundamental requirement for effective governance. Risk management develops and manages the catalog and implements measures for mitigation. Risk assessment reviews the catalog for complete and appropriate identification and mitigation of risks, and consideration of the risks exceed the enterprise level of tolerance.

Risks associated with business operations and information systems represent a major issue. Security risks, in particular, have increased as a result of the connectivity of business systems to the Internet. These were discussed in Chapter 7. In addition, concerns have increased regarding other risks as a result of internationalization of business operations and markets.

The design of the agile enterprise provides a framework (VDM modeling) for identification of operational and information systems risks, as well as analysis of the propagation of effects and interactions of disruptive circumstances.

Current work in OMG is focused on operational risk. This may be a foundation for development of a full spectrum, risk modeling capability.

Business leaders must decide when actions or initiatives offer sufficient benefit to offset the risks. Changes in technology, business practices, or other factors, both within or outside the enterprise, can increase existing risks and may require additional mitigation.

A discipline and computer-based risk modeling capability are needed to more effectively determine an enterprise risk profile.

Regulations and Policies Management

A regulations and policies directory should capture all information relevant to the identification and interpretation of regulations in the context of the business. The database should include the policies that support regulatory compliance as well as other policies, including the purpose of each policy, rules expressing the policy and identification of the VDM activity(s) where the policy must be applied.

Note that there has been work in some jurisdictions to express regulations in a formal language to remove ambiguities. Formal expression could help identify overlaps and inconsistencies between regulations, particularly regulations from different jurisdictions. However, it is still necessary to interpret the regulation as it applies to a particular business and define an appropriate policy for enforcement.

The specification of policies and their application to the business could also benefit from the capability of the multiple vocabulary facility.

Multiple Vocabulary Facility

At this writing, OMG has initiated development of a *Multiple Vocabulary Facility* specification. The purpose of this specification is to define a standard way of extending OMG modeling languages to enable different users to interact using their own, particular natural language or vernacular. This is important, particularly for enterprises with operations in multiple countries, and would enable modeling tools to be more suitable for use in non-English-speaking countries.

VDML has highlighted the need for this capability since VDM will touch many people throughout an enterprise, potentially in different countries. They could each view a shared model expressed in terms from their own natural language.

As currently envisioned, a term and a definition will be expressed in alternative user languages for each concept in the modeling language and each concept defined by a user in creating a model. A term in the user's language will be used in the displays and user inputs to identify the appropriate model element, and the user may access the associated definition, expressed in the preferred language, to clarify the meaning of the term in the context of the model. A set of terms and definitions might also be defined for a vernacular where special terms are used in a particular industry or profession.

The standard will enable the development and sharing of concept definitions and terms by industry and professional groups.

Performance Monitoring

Performance monitoring should be integrated with VDM to provide a model-based context for consideration of performance. Measurements of contributions of individual capability method activities are aggregated to feed value propositions, so users can see performance from a customer perspective, and then dive into the detail to see where the positive and negative values are coming from. The measurements must be captured in the measurements database discussed in Chapter 6. The monitoring service should also support triggers for selective monitoring of performance or exceptions.

If the operational processes are automated, then the automated processes can generate notices, and value measurements may be computed based on product configuration, duration, and the action performed. If the processes are not driven by business process automation, then measurement reporting will require sensors of various forms or manual data entry to capture and communicate events and measurements. Information on the context of the measurements (business metadata), at least time stamp and source, should also be available with the measurements.

Management Dashboards

Management dashboards typically provide monitoring of key process variables. Dashboards should be developed as a general monitoring capability based on web technology where managers at all levels can determine what they want to monitor and how they want it displayed.

The primary source of dashboard variables should be the measurements database, discussed earlier and in Chapter 6. A user should also be able to set alert criteria to trigger an action when a particular threshold or combination of variables occurs.

A dashboard should enable the user to examine the metadata and detail behind measurements and browse the VDM model to understand the context and explore dependencies.

CMMN Resource Management

CMMN supports the collaboration and coordination of a group of people working together to accomplish a shared purpose. Each case will involve the same roles but a different combination of personnel and activities in different sequences. A number of active cases may require participants with similar qualifications drawn from a shared pool. Some personnel will be qualified for multiple roles. A mechanism is needed to manage the allocation of resources to optimize the utilization of scarce qualifications and observe operating priorities.

CMMN Project Management

A case may start with a typical sequence of activities and dependencies that can be adapted and dynamically refined as the case evolves. In addition, when the situation changes, some sequences of activities may be repeated for rework or corrective action. These characteristics are capabilities needed in project management, particularly adapting to evolving plans and modeling rework. A CMMN project could start with a complete (tentative) plan, knowing that it will probably change as the project evolves.

The adaptation to CMMN for project management would require the resource management capability described above with some extension. CMMN could define an enhanced project management modeling capability for dynamic resource/workload balancing and rework management that could also support planning and evaluation of the cost of project changes and rework. With CMMN, all work is part of the record even though some of the work is redone or abandoned as a result of defects or changes in requirements or design.

VDML Simulation

During the development of VDML, the representations of activities, stores, deliverable flows, and collaborations were refined for compatibility with potential support for simulation.

The VDML and companion SMM (Structured Metrics Metamodel) accommodate statistical measures so variances in measurements can be represented statistically for Monte Carlo simulation and analysis of variances. This requires an enhanced form of implementation to display the measurements and perform statistical computations.

Discrete event simulation would represent the flow of individual deliverables and key characteristics to represent variations in workloads and resource consumption. This is important for capacity planning, identification of bottlenecks, and analysis of value contributions including time and cost. This would require a significant enhancement of the VDML specification.

Business dynamics (or system dynamics) is a mathematical modeling technique for simulation of system behavior over time in terms of *stocks* and *flows* of items. The flows define the rates at which stocks are depleted or filled.

For example, Sturman reports a system dynamics model of the impact of leasing on the North American new and used vehicle market developed by General Motors (Sturman, J. Business Dynamics: Systems Thinking and Modeling for a Complex World, McGraw-Hill/Irwin, 2000). System dynamics could be useful for analysis of flows in a VDM model.

Business dynamics could be an important approach to analysis of risks of both the propagation of effects of internal disruptions and the instability of the global economy arising from the interdependencies of businesses and markets. VDML represents the stocks (stores) and flows (deliverable flows) to support business dynamics. Further analysis is required to determine the best way to support system dynamics.

Culture Modeling

Culture is a collection of intangible, informal forces, and ideas that influence how and why people collaborate for a shared purpose. It includes the interests, beliefs, experiences, and patterns of work that extend beyond any formally defined roles and responsibilities of the participants.

The agile enterprise provides the context for a culture of individual initiative, dedication, and collaboration that drives an exceptional enterprise. The culture must embrace change as an opportunity rather than a threat. Individuals should be inspired to participation in the delivery of new values to the world.

In Appendix B, we discuss a preliminary conceptual model of culture. This illustrates the multiple dimensions of culture, and the impact of culture on productivity, creativity, and inspiration to go beyond the formal requirements of business activities.

This model is a potential extension to VDML, aligning to collaborations, capabilities, roles, activities, deliverables, and organizations. The agile enterprise architecture, supported by VDML, enables the creativity and initiative of the knowledge workers and leaders of the service units to improve the service unit contribution to its value streams. Additional incentives and supports should encourage individuals to contribute to a broader range of improvements to products, services, or business operations.

In the future, effective development of a culture of inspired participation will be essential for an enterprise to be an industry leader.

MOVING FORWARD

The agile enterprise, as envisioned in this book, is not a finished work. It will continue to evolve as suggested by the changes to leadership roles and the next generation standards outlined in the previous section. BCM, CBA, and VDM are emerging disciplines that call for development of new skills, insights, and methods. Corresponding changes to business culture are on the frontier. Risk management is a major hurdle for informed investors and other stakeholders. These are not issues to be addressed by top management alone, but are issues for leaders at all levels as well as academic leaders who are instilling new ways of thinking in the next generation of business leaders.

A

The Value Delivery Maturity Model

VALUE DELIVERY MATURITY MODEL

Transformation to the agile enterprise is a major, long-term undertaking. It is not just a reorganization but has a pervasive effect on the structure and management of the enterprise. More books will be written about planning and managing transformation as well as the technology to support the transformation and implement the capabilities. Here, we provide insight into the phases of transformation and the dimensions of change.

Enterprise agility is a moving target. There have been significant changes just in the past 8 years since the previous edition of this book, and there will be more changes in the future, building on the advances described here.

The Value Delivery Maturity Model, discussed here, is based on the SOA Maturity Model that was developed by EDS and Oracle in 2007 based on the Capability Maturity Model Integration (CMMI) model for software development from the Software Engineering Institute and Carnegie Mellon University. An overview of the SOA Maturity Model was presented in the first edition of this book.

Since then, there have been considerable advances in business modeling and design that have a significant impact on both expectations for the maturity levels and the agile enterprise objective. Consequently, we discuss here a revised maturity model where SOA is no longer the primary objective. The Value Delivery Maturity Model is depicted in Fig. A.1.

The general framework of the model is much the same with dimensions of both business and IT perspectives, but it leads to a more advanced degree of agility. As with other maturity models, it provides criteria for assessment of (1) the readiness of an organization to accept and manage the associated disciplines and (2) the degree to which the necessary business architecture, organizational structure, and supporting technology are in place.

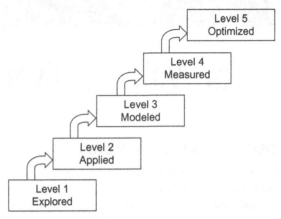

■ **FIG. A.1** Value delivery maturity model.

The model defines a progression of criteria to assess the degree to which an enterprise has realized the potential optimum of agility and value delivery. There are many paths to the future that are well beyond the scope of this book. The Value Delivery Maturity Model provides guidance for planning the enterprise transformation and a basis for objective evaluation of progress. Each enterprise must develop more detail appropriate to their current capabilities, nature of their business, and their readiness for change. The changes driven by the Maturity Model must be reconciled with business changes driven by strategic planning and transformation plans.

The Value Delivery Maturity Model aligns progress on both business transformation and IT support. It is the business perspective that sets this maturity model apart and provides a foundation for consideration of transformation in this book. A maturity assessment based on this model identifies the maturity level of an enterprise and the issues that should be addressed to progress to the next level. Each level builds on the capabilities of the levels beneath it. Just as the construction of a building must start with the foundation, progression to value delivery maturity and enterprise optimization must progress up the levels of the maturity model. An enterprise should first evaluate which level fits their current business and then should focus on the changes that are needed to get to the next level.

Investments in enterprise capabilities will be needed to support the primary objectives of each level. These investments increase some costs in the near term. At the same time, the transformation plan should achieve incremental improvements through projects that each realizes business value along the way.

Each of these levels is assessed from two perspectives: business with five dimensions and technology with six dimensions.

Maturity Levels

An enterprise achieves a maturity level when it has substantially met the criteria identified for that level. Though some of the criteria of higher levels may also be achieved when maturity is assessed, the overall capability of the enterprise is still limited by those criteria that have not yet been met for the higher level of maturity. Return on investment is lower for transformations undertaken at lower levels of maturity, but the risks are higher if an undertaking is too ambitious for the next level of maturity. Each of the maturity levels is outlined here.

Explored

- This is the current "status quo" level typical of many enterprises.
- The business organizations have participated in some form of capability mapping for identification of critical capabilities for improvements.
- There may have been consideration of consolidation of duplicated capabilities.
- The business side of the enterprise has focused on BPM and process improvement.
- Many business processes are embedded in application programs.
- The IT organization has implemented some applications or application components as shared services and has implemented some web services for customers or suppliers.
- The IT organization is aware of BPM and has installed and applied one or more BPMS (Business Process Management System) to support BPM.
- Top management may support implementation of a proof-of-concept, capability consolidation.
- Information technology projects are owned and funded by each line of business and/or functional area.

Applied

- Top management is committed to CBA, BCM, and VDM, as evidenced by funding centers of expertise.
- Top management is participating in modeling and analysis of value streams of product lines or lines of business and business model canvases (Osterwalder) or business model cubes (Lindgren) supported by VDML.

- A limited-scope VDM capability team has been established and has successfully modeled a product line value stream or larger portion of the business from an executive business model perspective and a detailed, value stream perspective.
- A BCM team has been established for alignment of business processes with VDM collaborations and application of adaptive case management for knowledge workers.
- IT infrastructure has been established to support integration of shared capability services and to support adaptive case management (eg, CMMN).
- The initial value stream models include at least cost and duration value measurements supporting a customer value proposition.
- Top management is involved in review of the capability taxonomy and performance measurements along with identification and funding of selected shared capability services.
- At least one shared service unit has been implemented with a well-defined interface and level of service agreement. It is engaged in two or more contexts (eg, lines of business).

Modeled

- There is an executive-level roadmap for the agile enterprise.
- The customer value propositions and value streams of all lines of business have been modeled for value delivery, and multiple shared capability services are implemented and managed by a matrix organization.
- There is a service integration and performance measurement infrastructure in place.
- There is a system of governance to manage the value delivery model and to plan and manage strategic transformation of the organization.
- Priorities and funding for IT budgets and transformation initiatives are managed at an enterprise-level.
- Service costs are captured, and a charge-back mechanism has been defined to support billing of the full cost of services to service consumers.
- Data exchange for shared services is consistent with an enterprise logical data model and a master data management plan.
- Capability units have been established and funded as implementation of CBA, BCM, and VDM.
- Capability units have been implemented as service units.

Measured

- Capability units and value streams are monitored and measured for cost, timeliness, and quality as well as key values of customer interest.
- The cost, quality, timeliness, and other relevant values of each value stream are used to identify and assign priorities to improvements needed in specific capabilities.
- The value contributions of shared services to value streams can be reported and analyzed.
- Information technology services are aligned with CBA.
- The organization structure reflects alignment of goals, incentives, and economies of scale in the management of capability units.
- Value measurements are captured for statistical representation of performance for specific products or product mixes to support VDM analysis.
- Service performance is continuously monitored and evaluated against formal service level agreements.
- Disruptive events, both internal and external, are captured and directed to appropriate capability organizations for resolution.
- VDM is used for operational risk analysis and mitigation.
- An analytics capability unit captures big data from relevant sources and supports analysis for correlations, trends, and significant events.

Optimized

- The governance structure ensures that the enterprise is doing the right thing and doing it well.
- Rules are defined and implemented for regulation and policy compliance, and application of the rules is measured and reported.
- The organization has a continuous change culture that strives for excellence and welcomes the opportunity to innovate.
- VDM is used to validate strategies and to plan and measure business transformation.
- Governance is supported by risk assessment, tracking of key objectives, monitoring of performance measurements and reporting of compliance with policies.
- Value propositions are the basis for investment in capability development and improvement.
- Internal interest group collaborations are formed, funded, and supported with social networking technology.
- Formal processes are defined for identification, evaluation, and funding of innovations.

- There is rapid response to disruptive events through business processes based on comprehensive risk management and an understanding of the enterprise ecosystem.
- VDM is linked to current operating measurements and is the context for executive dashboard measurements.
- New business opportunities are analyzed by reconfiguring relationships between existing capabilities and identification of required capability services or new capabilities.
- Capability service managers work to continuously improve their services based on needs of service users and enterprise values.

Business Dimensions

Each of the maturity levels is evaluated, from a business perspective in five dimensions and the technology perspective in six dimensions. The following points briefly describe the achievements of the business dimensions at the Optimized maturity level.

Processes

- Business processes are modeled and measured.
- Case management (CMMN) is applied to recurring, adaptive collaborations.
- Processes and applications are aligned with capability methods of the value delivery model and have well-defined service interfaces and level of service specifications.
- Sense and respond processes respond to threats, opportunities, and innovations to drive change.
- A BCM center of expertise clarifies and improves collaborations based on VDM modeling and value contribution priorities.

Organization

- The business organization is a matrix of line of business organizations and shared capability providers.
- Shared capability providers are organized for management of shared resources, methods, and incentives.
- Collaborations that involve significant effort or are essential to business operation are reflected in the VDM and are supported with appropriate funding and technology.

Governance

- Governance involves enterprise-level planning, priority setting, accountability, and control.

- Top management and the board of directors have visibility of performance and value contributions of capability services along with the impact of policies on operations.
- Transformations are driven and measured by phases defined with versions of the value delivery model.
- Regulations are analyzed and translated into operating policies.
- Effects of policy compliance are traced to affected activities and measured.
- Strategic planning is a continuing collaboration that drives evolving, enterprise-level transformation planning, and assessment.

Capability Portfolio Management

- A portfolio of sharable capabilities is managed to support multiple value streams, optimized from an enterprise perspective.
- Value delivery models are developed and maintained to support customer value propositions with some application to administrative support value streams (eg, accounting, human resource management, purchasing, and information technology).
- Capabilities are defined in a taxonomy and associated with the organizations that define (own) them and provide them.
- Performance of capability services is measured against service level agreements.
- The value contributions of each capability can be traced to their impact on customer and overall business value propositions.
- Value delivery models are used to evaluate strategies and to plan phased business transformations.

Finance

- Significant investments in development or improvement of capabilities are based on the value delivery model and value-based priorities.
- The cost of each capability service is measured and recovered by a billing mechanism for assessment of the full cost of each service rendered, including the cost of capability services used indirectly.
- Market share, profitability, and market segment value propositions are analyzed using VDM for potential improvements.

Technology Dimensions

The following sections outline the achievements of the six technology dimensions at the Optimized level of maturity. It is important that improvements in technology keep pace with the improvements in the business to ensure appropriate support.

Infrastructure

- Infrastructure provides a reliable messaging and integration infrastructure with single sign-on and role-based access control.
- Networking and security mechanisms are integrated with the public cloud(s).
- Applications with workloads that are seasonal or affected by growth or decline in business are deployed to cloud computing assuming relevant security, and regulatory compliance concerns are resolved.
- Access authorization is role based.
- Business process automation, adaptive case management, internal alarms, event notification, and complex event processing are supported by the infrastructure.
- Support is provided for capture of "big data" and analytics.
- Infrastructure includes a Data Directory, a Sense and Respond Directory, a Risk Management Catalog, a Regulation and Policy Directory, interest group supports, knowledge management services, and dashboard support.

Architecture

- The technology architecture supports composition of business solutions based on CBA.
- Capability methods with defined roles and activities are supported by model-based, repeatable business processes, or adaptive case management.
- Consistent mechanisms are defined for security controls and administration that put appropriate business leaders in charge.
- Technical facilities are defined for big data capture, monitoring, analysis, and detection of disruptive events.
- Technical standards and compliant product selections support interoperability and economies of scale in IT development and operations.
- Consistent mechanisms, audits, and controls are implemented for security and disaster recovery.

Data

- Capability interfaces and master data interfaces are compliant with an enterprise logical data model.
- Master data owner organizations are responsible and in control of the accessibility, security, and integrity of master data records.
- Business meta-data describes the provenance and quality of master data, event notices, and business intelligence data.

- Data networking supports reliable messaging, message transformation, and event publish and subscribe.
- Value measurements are captured from operating activities and communicated to the measurements service for monitoring performance.
- A data directory defines the sources and users of master data.
- Big data is captured, monitored for trends and critical events, and processed for analytics.
- Complex event processing reconciles redundant, related, and consequential events.

Governance

- A value delivery model reflects the current state of the business.
- Management dashboards provide manager control of individualized reporting on selected performance measurements and objectives in the context of the VDM model.
- Technology strategy and investments are driven by technology advances and enterprise-level analysis of business impact based on the value delivery model.
- Industry standards compliance is a key business factor in systems design and product selections. Industry standards are formally adopted and periodically reviewed for relevance.
- Security policies and measures are well defined and implemented along with procedures for timely response to threats or violations.
- A sense and respond directory captures and tracks resolution of events with business-changing implications.
- Business rules are integrated into business processes for policy enforcement and decision support.

Organization

- The IT organization is aligned with IT capabilities and provides services through well-defined interfaces with level of service agreements.
- An IT architecture capability is responsible for defining and applying architectural patterns and technical standards.
- Initiatives for IT development or maintenance are engaged and coordinated through collaborations for each initiative with representatives from relevant IT and business activities.
- IT application development and maintenance services are provided by members from technical specialty capability organization units.

Operations

- IT operations processes are organized as value streams that engage services developed by BCM.
- Performance of IT services and business applications is measured and reported against formal service level agreements.
- Big data capture, processing, and analytics support is a distinct capability with associated services.
- Coordination and management of cloud computing services is a distinct IT capability with associated services.
- There is a distinct capability with associated services for management of the network for exchange of data including exchanges with customers and business partners.
- IT security policy compliance, monitoring, configuration management, threat analysis, and breach response are managed by a distinct group of IT capabilities.
- Potential effects of service outages on value streams drives preparedness and appropriate response priority.

A Conceptual Model of Business Culture

Culture is a collection of intangible, informal forces, and ideas that influence how and why people collaborate for a shared purpose. It includes the interests, beliefs, experiences, and patterns of work that extend beyond any formally defined roles and responsibilities of the participants.

The challenge is that culture is complex because it involves individual values, personal relationships, and personal motivation. Fig. B.1 is a preliminary concept diagram for culture.

When employees are expected to function as automatons, following prescribed processes, their personal interests and individual values and experiences are not only irrelevant but may be a distraction.

However, today's workforce consists increasingly of knowledge workers, and the quality and efficiency of their work depends on their individual capabilities, their attitudes about the nature and quality of their work, and how they collaborate with others. Culture is important.

The two key elements of this diagram are the *participant* and *activities*. The participant fills a role in which he/she performs activities. The role and the activities are elements of a business practice. The participant provides capabilities that enable the activities. The participant interests determine the relevance of incentives that enhance motivation that drives the participant's activities. The activities consume and produce work products with values that potentially reinforce the participant's motivation, fulfill the purpose of incentives, and satisfy business objectives. The objectives support the goal(s) of the collaboration in which the participant is working with others for a shared purpose. The incentives must also promote the goals of the collaboration. The participant may have roles in other collaborations that may influence the participant's interests. The strength and consistency of these relationships will influence the performance of the participant, along with collaborations (including personal relationships) with other participants and with other persons both inside and outside the enterprise.

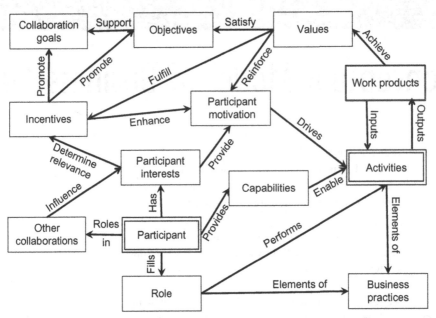

■ **FIG. B.1** Preliminary concept diagram for culture.

This diagram is a starting point for discussion. It addresses only the motivation of one person in a complex network of relationships and collaborations with others. If nothing else, a model might help a manager focus on opportunities to improve the harmony and motivation of employees to enhance their productivity, initiative, and job satisfaction.

Glossary

Activity Work contributed to a collaboration by a participant in a Role of the collaboration. A role may be filled by an actor or another collaboration and a role may contribute to multiple activities in the same collaboration (Value Delivery Modeling Language, VDML).

Activity network A network of activities and stores that are linked by deliverable flows in a collaboration (VDML).

Actor An individual (indivisible) participant, which might be human (a person) or nonhuman (eg, a software agent or machine) (VDML).

Adaptive case management (adaptive process) A form of process automation where the state of the problem domain (the case) and the expertise of participants is the basis for planning and evolving a process to deliver a result. It fosters and supports collaboration among the participants as opposed to simple performance of prescribed, complementary tasks. CMMN (Case Management Model and Notation) is the OMG (Object Management Group) standard that supports modeling components, case file, and guidance to support the collaboration.

Agile enterprise An agile enterprise is capable of recognizing and adapting quickly to changing business threats and opportunities. Agile is a relative term, and the threshold for agility evolves over time.

Analytics Technology for analysis of large volumes of data to identify patterns or events using distributed, concurrent computing resources.

Asynchronous exchange The exchange of messages or other deliverables between parties where a sender does not wait for a response. The receiver is expected to accept and process the input at a later time. This is typical of exchanges between business entities or operations that operate independently and are not expected to be immediately available to process input.

Attribute An attribute is information attached to any element in the form of a name-value pair (VDML).

Authentication A process by which the identity of a subject (eg, person or system) is validated.

Authorization A process by which a subject (eg, person or system) is given authority to perform an action or access a resource, or the process by which access authority is determined.

Backtracking A mechanism in logic programming, or in the application of diagnostic rules, where the search for a solution has reached an unsuccessful result down one path and is able to back up and proceed down another branch of the search.

Backward chaining A search strategy where a condition is evaluated by reference to supporting facts or conditions so that success is achieved by finding a set of supporting facts or conditions that are true. The strategy is to assume the truth of a statement and attempt to substantiate it by finding supporting facts. This mode is typically applied to diagnostic or proof problems (eg, theorem proving).

BCM (business collaboration management) A discipline that is an extension of BPM to include all forms of collaboration, their relationships, modeling, and automation.

BMM (business motivation model) A specification of OMG that provides a framework for strategic planning.

BPM (business process management) A management discipline for defining, continuously improving, and optimizing business processes.

BPMM (business process maturity model) An OMG specification of criteria for assessing the maturity of an enterprise with respect to business process management. The five maturity levels are derived from CMMI (capability maturity model integration) from Carnegie Mellon University. BPMM corresponds to the five levels but with a business process management focus.

BPMN (business process model and notation) An OMG specification of graphical elements and metamodel for modeling business processes. BPMN 2.0 (Business Process Model and Notation).

Business dynamics A technique for modeling dynamic, real-world systems using the abstract concepts of "stocks" and "flows." The model reflects behavior of the system over time based on accumulation or depletion of units in stocks as a result of flows in and out of the system and its stocks mediated by control functions and parameters.

Business item A business item is anything that can be acquired or created, that conveys information, obligation, or other forms of value and that can be conveyed from a provider to a recipient. For example, it includes parts, products, units of fluids, orders, emails, notices, contracts, currency, assignments, devices, property, and other resources (VDML).

Business metadata Data about data that describe aspects of interest to business people such as the source, precision, timeliness, and reliability of the data. Distinguished from technical metadata that describes the definitions, structure, and relationships of data elements as in a database or exchange of records.

Business model canvas A graphical framework representing key aspects of a business developed by Alexander Osterwalder.

Business model cube A graphical framework of key aspects of a business developed by Peter Lindgren.

Business network In VDML, a collaboration of business entities involving asynchronous exchanges of deliverables for a shared business endeavor.

BPMS (business process management system) An information system that automates the execution of business processes.

Business process An orderly execution of activities to achieve a desired business result in response to a request or event. A process defines what work is to be done, who does the work, when the work is done in relation to events, and the activities of others.

Business rule A declarative expression of business intent. There are a variety of types of business rules. See also enterprise rule, production rule, diagnostic rule, event rule, qualification rule, and data integrity rule.

Capability The ability to perform a particular type of work typically involving people, processes, resources, facilities, skills, knowledge, and motivation that can be applied to produce a desired result.

Capability map A diagram that depicts a taxonomy of enterprise capabilities for management review. A capability *heat* map highlights the capability(s) that require particular attention.

Capability method A collaboration specification that defines the activities, deliverable flows, business items, capability requirements, and roles that deliver a capability and associated value contributions. For each application of the capability method, within a scenario or in multiple scenarios, there may be distinct measurements of performance and value contributions, and role assignments suitable to the application context. A capability method does not own resources but receives them from other sources in the course of performing its activities (VDML).

Capability method consumer In VDML, an organization, a collaboration or an activity within a collaboration that engages a capability method

Capability method owner In VDML, an organization unit that defines and maintains a capability method specification.

Capability method provider In VDML, an organization unit that offers the application of a capability as a capability method.

Capability offer A VDML model element that represents the availability of a capability service from a particular organization unit. It usually identifies an associated capability method.

Capability unit An organization unit at a conceptual modeling level that provides a service or group of services for application of a specified capability.

Case management A process in which activities are defined as the process unfolds based on the state of the case and the expertise of the participants. Also described as an adaptive process. A case management model defines tasks, stages, and process fragments as well as a case file structure to be applied as required in the particular case.

CA (certification authority) A trusted service that issues signed digital certificates that include the identity of the certificate owner and the owner's public key. The certificate provides the basis for authentication, encryption, and nonrepudiation. A CA maintains a certificate revocation list (CRL) for those certificates that have been compromised (eg, the corresponding private key has been exposed).

CBA (capability-based architecture) A business design architecture that focuses on business capabilities as sharable components that may be integrated into multiple value streams to deliver business products or services.

CEP (complex event processing) Processing of event notices that identifies relationships and duplications between separate events and infers the occurrence of other events.

Channel A linkage or mechanism between business entities to execute a deliverable flow, such as email, face-to-face conversation, SOAP, REST, physical transportation, postal service, telephone, fax, and FTP (VDML).

Choreography A specification (that may be expressed in BPMN) of the interactions between two or more participants to achieve mutual benefit. Choreography is not executed by a controlling entity but describes the agreed-upon, collaborative behavior of the participants.

Class For a logical data model, a computational representation of the attributes of similar entities and their relationships to other entities. A specialized class may be defined to inherit and extend the specification of an existing class.

Collaboration A collection of participants working together for a shared purpose or interest.

Cooperative process A process that occurs between two or more relatively independent business entities where compliance with the prescribed process depends on the actions of the participants and is not driven by a shared process management system.

CMDB (configuration management database) A facility for management of hardware, software, and application components and their relationships in a data-processing center.

Community A loose collaboration of participants with similar characteristics or interests (VDML).

Competency A capability that is key to the competitive advantage of an enterprise and thus will not be outsourced.

COTS (commercial off-the-shelf software) Refers to a commercially available software product in contrast to a custom application developed by or for an enterprise.

CWM (common warehouse metamodel) An OMG specification for representation and transformation of data in different formats. Originally intended for specification of data transformations from various sources to feed a data warehouse. It has also been applied to enterprise information integration (EII). It is expected to be superseded by IMM (Information Management Metamodel), a pending specification from OMG.

Dashboard Typically, a management dashboard provides a user with an interactive interface for configuration of a display of status information and measurements, typically in graphical form, that is a representation of the current state of the business.

Data directory A directory that identifies the master-data source of enterprise data.

Data integrity rule A rule that constrains the structure or element content of data to prevent invalid entries or changes.

Delegation context A VDML model element that represents delegation by an activity to request execution of a collaboration (capability method). A delegation context also defines the delegations of activity inputs and/or outputs to/from collaboration inputs and/or outputs and may define assignments of roles within the collaboration (VDML).

Deliverable A business item (as it is conveyed from a source activity, store, or collaboration to a destination activity, store, or collaboration (VDML).

Deliverable flow The transfer of a deliverable from a provider (or producer) to a recipient (or consumer) (VDML).

Diagnostic rule A rule used in the diagnosis of a problem, typically a logic programming rule or a rule executed by a backward-chaining inference engine.

Disruptive event An event that indicates the occurrence of a change that has a disruptive effect on an enterprise or an industry and may require an adaptation in the way the enterprise operates or in the products and services it delivers.

DMA (data management architecture) A pattern of the relationships of data storage facilities, their management, content and coordination for consistent and reliable representation of business records, and the state of the enterprise.

EAI (enterprise application integration) Technology for the integration of applications and services based on store-and-forward delivery of messages typically through a hub-and-spoke message broker.

ECA (event condition action) rule A rule that is activated by the occurrence of an event (ie is, a change of state) and will perform a defined action if its conditional expression evaluates to true.

EDI (electronic data interchange) A collection of standards for the exchange of business records between enterprise applications as well as between enterprises. Established in early exchanges, primarily in transfer of files.

ELDM (enterprise logical data model) A conceptual data model of the data of the enterprise independent of the particular technologies used for storage and communication of the data.

ESB (enterprise services bus) Technology for the integration of services over the Internet or the Intranet.

Event listener An element in a CMMN (Case Management Model and Notation) model that becomes active when a specified change occurs in the case management file (the state of the case).

Event notice A message or record that communicates the occurrence of an event. In a publish-and-subscribe environment, an event notice is published by a system that observes or causes an event. The event notice is communicated by an event broker to subscribers who have submitted requests to receive events that meet certain qualifications as specified in their subscriptions.

Event rule A condition that is of interest as an event when it becomes true. The condition associated with a database trigger that generates an event notice when the condition becomes true.

Forward chaining A rules execution mode where the condition expressions of rules are evaluated against a model of the problem domain, a rule is selected from among those that have true conditions, and the action of that rule is executed, typically causing the model of the problem domain to change. The change potentially changes the set of rules with true conditions, and another rule is selected from the set and executed. The execution chains forward as it drives the evaluation of selected rules and cumulative changes to the domain model. This mode is typically applied to configuration and planning problems.

Gateway A diamond-shaped graphical symbol in BPMN that indicates a convergence or divergence of process flow. There are several icons that may appear in the gateway graphic that further define the action to be taken.

Governance The set of responsibilities and practices exercised by the board of directors and executive management with the goal of providing strategic direction, ensuring that objectives are achieved, ascertaining that risks are managed appropriately and verifying that the organization's resources are used responsibility (Information Systems Audit and Control Foundation, 2001).

HTML (Hyper Text Markup Language) A character-based language designed for specification of displays for Internet browsers, and for input and communication of data submitted through web page displays.

HTTP (Hyper Text Transfer Protocol) An internet protocol designed for the exchange of HTML in support of the World Wide Web.

HTTPS (Hyper Text Transfer Protocol Secure) An extension of HTTP designed for secure (encrypted) exchange of HTML data on the world wide web.

Hybrid cloud A computing configuration where the cloud service consumer combines public and private cloud services such as retaining the management of data and user interfaces in a private cloud while off-loading the operation of applications to the public cloud.

IETF (Internet engineering task force) An international standards organization focused on the technical standards and protocols of the Internet.

Industry framework A best practices model that represents the business processes and potentially an information model and other aspects that are characteristic of enterprises in a particular industry. eTOM is an industry framework.

Inheritance In information or object modeling, a relationship between classes by which one class may incorporate (inherit) the characteristics of another and extend the specification to address a more specialized category of entities represented by the inheriting class.

Intangible deliverable Deliverable that represents something that is unpaid or non-contractual that makes things work smoothly or efficiently (as opposed to Tangible) (VDML and ValueNet works).

Interface specification For a service unit, it is the specification of message types or requests that will be recognized, the restrictions on the interactions, and the nature of the result returned.

Internet of Things (IoT) An emerging set of technologies and protocols by which all sorts of devices, sensors, and computers are connected to the Internet for various purposes resulting in very large volumes of Internet activity and significant implications to the capabilities and services of enterprises and their products.

Knowledge worker A worker who functions with minimal supervision, performs tasks, and participates in collaborations based on his or her knowledge and experience. This is in contrast to a worker who performs repetitive, defined activities with minimal discretion.

Lane In BPMN, a segment of a pool. The pool represents a business entity performing activities in a process. The lane defines a responsibility within the entity that is responsible for performing the activities drawn within the lane.

Level of service agreement A specification of the expected performance to be provided based on recipient requirements and provider capabilities.

Library A collection of elements representing relatively stable concepts that are defined for reference in models (VDML).

Line of business The product or group of similar products produced by an enterprise generally associated with business activities engaged in developing, marketing, producing, and supporting the product.

Logical data model (LDM) A data model expressed at a level of abstraction suitable for discussions that are independent of particular technologies or media used to store, communicate, or process the data. See also enterprise logical data model (ELDM).

Loose coupling A form of integration where the interdependence of participants is minimized to promote autonomy. Typically, this is accomplished by store-and-forward message exchanges with no shared resources and with minimal interactions that might require synchronization of their activities.

Master data management Management of the data storage facilities that represent the single version of the truth about the state of the enterprise. Master data is not limited to stable, reference data. Different data bases and organizations may be responsible for segments of the enterprise master data.

Measure A method that is applied to characterize an attribute of something by assigning a comparable quantification or qualification (popularized version of definition in SMM/VDML).

Measurement The value that results from applying a measure (popularized version of definition in SMM/VDML).

Metadata Data that describe data. A database schema is metadata. A blank paper form with identified fields expresses metadata. Business metadata generally defines the source, reliability, and/or accuracy of the data.

Metamodel A specification of a modeling language. A MOF metamodel specifies the concepts and relationships for modeling a particular problem domain.

Model-driven architecture (MDA) An OMG strategy for design of solutions using models supported by the ability to transform models and exchange them between different modeling environments.

MOF (meta object facility) An OMG specification for the elements that represent the concepts of a modeling language for expression of models, storage of models, and exchange of models. MOF is used for specification of modeling languages.

Multiple vocabulary facility A pending OMG specification to provide a common facility for an MOF-based modeling language implementation to express inputs and outputs in terminology from alternative natural languages.

Nonrepudiation A principle regarding assertions or agreements that prevents a party from denying their assertion or agreement. For a record or electronic document, the content can be reliably attributed to its submitter and cannot be repudiated. Potentially achieved through the use of an electronic signature.

Notification broker A facility for distribution of (event) notices to subscribers based on their expressions of interest and qualifying (ie, filter) rules.

OAGi (Open Application Group, Incorporated) An international standards organization focused on specifications for data exchanged between enterprise applications.

OASIS (organization for advancement of structured information systems) An international standards organization with primary contributions related to the application of XML.

OMG (Object Management Group) An international standards organization focused on information systems interoperability and modeling standards.

Organization An administrative or functional structure normally interpreted as a network of Organization Units at a higher level in an organizational hierarchy (VDML).

Organization Unit (or OrgUnit) A management/administrative collaboration, with responsibility for defined resources, including a collaborations that occur in the typical organization hierarchy, such as business units and departments (and also the company itself), as well as less formal organizational collaboration such as a committee, project, or task force that is responsible for a defined set of resources (VDML).

Outsourcing The practice of contracting for an external organization to own and operate a segment of the enterprise business. Outsourcing of information systems, accounting, and human resource management services are examples.

Participant Anyone or anything that can fill a role in a collaboration. Participants can be actors (human or automatons) or collaborations or roles of actors or collaborations. They may be named in the model, or dynamically determined in runtime (VDML).

PIM (platform independent model) In the OMG model-driven architecture (MDA) strategy, a model of a solution that is independent of particular implementation technology and thus is focused on modeling the solution rather than the implementation.

PKI (public key infrastructure) The services and facilities associated with the use of public key encryption along with digital certificates for identification and authentication.

Planning percentage In VDML a specification of the expected percentage of units of production that will be output from an associated port.

Policy A statement of intent to influence or determine decisions, actions, or other matters. For business, a policy is a statement of business practice intent which may be expressed more precisely as business rules. For XACML security access control, a policy is a set of access control rules. For WS-Policy, a policy is a service specification that expresses capabilities and requirements that are the basis for forming a collaborative relationship.

Pool In VDML, a store that contains reusable resource, that is, resource that is returned to the pool after having been used so that it is again available for use. In BPMN, a stand-alone box that expresses the boundaries of a business entity around a business process model. Business processes are confined by the pool boundaries except that messages may be exchanged with other pools (ie, business entities).

Port A connection for input or output of an activity, store, or collaboration that defines the unit of production share of the input/output and the value contributions (output) of the associated activity/store/collaboration (VDML).

Portal A point of access to enterprise capabilities and services, usually designed to address the interests of a particular community such as employees, stockholders, customers, or suppliers. Often associated with a collection of web pages but potentially extending to other services such as a call center.

Practice An accepted way to handle specific types of work (VDML).

Private cloud A computing and communication configuration that provides the technology and fundamental benefits of a public cloud, but it is owned and operated by the consumer organization. Consequently the scope of the benefits is limited and the consumer organization retains responsibility and control for the management and operation of the services.

Process A sequence or flow of Activities in an organization with the objective of carrying out work (BPMN). VDML does not represent process, per se, but represents a process abstraction with a network of activities and flows that represent dependencies and statistical characteristics of a process.

Process instance A single execution of a process specification. A process instance is often distinguished by the identifier of the request that initiated the execution, for example, a customer order number.

Production rule A rule managed by a rules engine that performs forward chaining. The execution of the rules produces a result such as a product configuration or a travel plan. See also forward chaining.

PSM (platform-specific model) In the OMG MDA strategy, a model of a solution that is tailored for implementation in a particular technology. A PSM may be the result of a transformation of a PIM and be the basis for generating application code for execution.

Public cloud A service offered as a computing utility in a configuration where multiple service consumers share computing facilities of a cloud network. The consolidation of services improves economy of scale, facilitates immediate scalability of resource consumption, and minimizes consumer burden of management of computing services technology and operations.

Publish and subscribe An integration approach where sources of notices register with a broker and publish notices to the broker as conditions occur. An entity interested in notices subscribes with the broker, defining selection criteria for the notices of interest and the qualified notices are forwarded by the broker as they occur.

Qualification rule A rule that expresses the condition under which a participant is qualified for an action or a role.

RBAC (role-based access control) An approach to access control specification where access authorization is specified for roles, and roles are assigned to people. This enables separation of responsibility between control of resources and authorization of people.

Regulations and policies directory A proposed database and associated service that captures and supports analysis and tracking of regulations, their transformation to policies, and the applications of the policies in the operation of the business.

Reliable messaging A message exchange protocol where message senders are assured that each message will be delivered once and only once.

Resource Anything that is "used" or "consumed" in the production of a deliverable (VDML).

Rete algorithm An algorithm developed by Charles Forgy of Carnegie Mellon University for processing production (forward chaining) rules where the rule conditions are linked to the model of the problem domain (working storage) through a network so that changes in the domain model propagate to the affected rules.

Role An expected behavior pattern or capability profile associated with a participant in a collaboration. The link of a collaboration participant to the activities that participant is expected to perform (VDML).

Risk management catalog A proposed database as associated service to capture information about risks including the potential impact, mitigation, and interrelationships for analysis and consideration in planning and decision-making.

Risk profile A potential representation of the risks associated with an enterprise and the potential severity of impact of an unfortunate occurrence. Realization of a risk profile depends on the development of appropriate disciplines and models to accurately and comprehensively assess enterprise risks.

Rules engine A software application/product that evaluates and executes rules according to a defined algorithm.

SAML (Security Attribute Markup Language) An OASIS specification for the exchange of participant credentials and authorizations for access control.

SBVR (semantics of business vocabulary and rules) An OMG specification for a language that combines a structured representation of rules, with a capture of semantics and the ability to express the concepts and rules in alternative vocabularies.

Scenario A scenario defines a consistent business use case and set of measurements of a value delivery model by specifying a, possibly recursive, analysis context for nested collaborations in scope of that use case. The analysis contexts allow a collaboration to be used as a subcollaboration by more than one activity, each of which sets its particular delegation context and measurements (VDML).

Semantic A specification of meaning. In language, the meanings of words or expressions. In modeling, semantics are the meanings of the modeling elements.

Sense and respond directory A proposed database and associated service to capture events, circumstances, innovations that represent potential enterprise threats or opportunities for subsequent analysis and appropriate action. The status of responses can be tracked, and initiatives can be consolidated where similar and compatible circumstances or initiatives are identified.

Separation of duties A principle of accountability and control whereby actions by a person who could have a conflict of interest are approved or validated by a person with independent duties and interests.

Sequence flow In BPMN, an arrow that specifies the order of execution or evaluation of flow elements such as gateways and activities.

Service A mechanism to apply one or more capabilities, where the access is provided using a prescribed interface and is exercised consistent with constraints and policies as specified by the service description and service level agreement.

Service consumer A business entity that uses a service—a service user.

Service interface A specification of the inputs and outputs of a service.

Service registry A database or directory, accessible at runtime, that provides information on the current versions and locations of services. The registry supports selection of alternative services and provides support for management of IT functions of service units at runtime.

Service unit An organization unit that has operational responsibility for providing services associated with the application of a particular business capability. The operational corollary of a capability unit.

Service unit group An organization unit that is responsible for the management of two or more service units that have similar resources, technologies, and/or practices that will enable economies of scale.

SID (shared information data) An ELDM for the telecommunications industry developed by the TeleManagement Forum (TMF).

Single sign-on An information technology industry infrastructure capability that enables a user to log on to a network environment once and subsequently access a number of different systems based on the single authentication. There are various strategies. Digital certificates and public-key encryption are recommended for single sign-on.

SOA (service-oriented architecture) An information systems architecture in which components are implemented as sharable services for economies of scale and rapid reconfiguration of information systems solutions.

Store Represents a container of a business item pending action by one or more recipients. A shared store provides a buffered interface between collaborations where a source delivers a business item to the store and the recipient (typically the store owner) retrieves the business item when ready. A store may have many business item providers and/or many business item recipients (VDML).

Subscribe The action of submitting a request to receive notices. A publisher publishes notices that are delivered to subscribers.

Synchronous exchange A mode of exchange of information or deliverables where a sender depends upon a timely response to a delivery. The processes of the participants are "synchronized" by virtue of the requirement to wait for a response.

Tangible Deliverable that represents something that is contracted, mandated, or expected by the recipient and which may generate revenue (as opposed to Intangible) (VDML).

Task An activity within a business process that is performed by a human. There is no further specification of the operation of a task.

TMF (TeleManagement Forum) An international standards organization that focuses on standards for the telecommunications industry.

UN/CEFACT (United Nations Center for Trade Facilitation and Electronic Business) A standards organization within the United Nations that deals with specifications for electronic commerce.

UML (Unified Modeling Language) The OMG specification for an object-oriented, application analysis and design language. The general nature of UML has resulted in its use for a number of system design applications outside object-oriented programming where the modeling elements are given different semantics as required by the particular modeling domain (described as a UML profile).

Value A measurable factor of benefit, of interest to a recipient, in association with a business item. A value may be desirable or undesirable (negative measurement) such as a cost or defect rate, or desirable (positive measurement) such as a feature or performance characteristic (VDML).

Value chain Set of stages that an organization carries out to create value for its customers. Concept originated by Michael Porter in 1985.

Value contribution A measurable effect of an activity that contributes to the level of satisfaction of one or more values in a value proposition (VDML).

Value delivery management A discipline for analysis, design, management, and transformation of the enterprise design at a conceptual/business leader level of abstraction employing the VDML. The model incorporates BCM and CBM with optimization based on value streams that deliver value to customers or other stakeholders. It supports multiple scenarios for business analysis and design based on evaluation of performance and stakeholder satisfaction. Values are created by activities and interactions of people and organizations using business capabilities (VDML).

Value delivery maturity model A framework of objectives for assessment of progress toward implementation of an agile enterprise based on the levels of business and technical design described in this book. The basic concept of the five levels is based on the CMMI developed at Carnegie Mellon University for assessment of information systems development and maintenance maturity.

Value network A technique originated by Verna Allee in which actual or intended business operations are modeled as a set of roles and interactions in which participants engage in both tangible and intangible exchanges to achieve economic or social good.

Value proposition Expression of the values contributed by the associated value stream and offered to a recipient in terms of the recipient's level of satisfaction.

Value stream The network of activities that includes resources, value contributions, and capabilities converges to the delivery of a product or service and a value proposition for the representative customer who may be the ultimate customer or an internal end user of the result (VDML).

VDML Value Delivery Modeling Language specification of OMG.

Virtual enterprise An relationship among two or more independent business entities to cooperate and contribute for their mutual benefit in the conduct of a business as a shared endeavor.

Virtual private cloud A computing and communications configuration where multiple consumers of a cloud computing service share computing and communications facilities, but each is logically isolated in their own virtual computing environment. This provides similar but less robust benefits to use of a public cloud service.

W3C (World Wide Web Consortium) An international standards organization that focuses on languages and protocols for communications over the Internet.

WfMC (Workflow management coalition) An international standards organization focused on the development of standards related to workflow management, which includes business process management technology.

Workflow Business processes that move work through sequences of activities in predefined paths. Workflow often implies business processes that are focused on human activities where the performance of activities is driven by the movement of a business transaction or work order to various persons or work stations. Most BPMS implement this process model with additional features.

WS-Federation (Web Services Federation) A specification of OASIS for the federation of identification and authentication among independently managed security domains.

WS-Policy (Web Services Policy) An XML-based language of W3C for specification of the requirements and capabilities of a web services participant as a basis for establishing compatibility for an exchange.

WS-Security (Web Services Security) A specification from OASIS that defines message structure and elements for secure message exchanges.

XACML (XML Access Control Markup Language) An OASIS specification for expression of access control/authorization policies regarding access to a specified resource (eg, data or operation).

XMI (XML Metadata Interchange) An OMG standard for the expression of a MOF-based model in XML for exchange between implementations of the same modeling language.

XML (eXtensible Markup Language) A language defined by W3C. XML is a character-based data format that uses name tags to identify data elements that are variable in length and form a nested hierarchy. XML is, for the most part, technology independent so that senders and receivers may use different technologies, and the structure provides flexibility enabling recipients to ignore elements in which they have no interest. A number of related technologies have been built on XML including parsing techniques, electronic signatures, specification of XML documents using XML, and so on.

XML Schema An XML-based language from W3C that is used to specify the structure of XML documents.

XML Signature A W3C specification for electronic signatures in XML documents.

References

Allee, V., 2003. The Future of Knowledge: Increasing Prosperity Through Value Networks. Butterworth-Heinemann, Boston, MA.

Allee, V., 2008. Value network analysis and value conversion of tangible and intangible assets. J. Intellect. Cap. 9 (1), 5–24. Available from: http://www.vernaallee.com/images/VAA-VNAandValueConversionJIT.pdf.

Allee, V., 2011. Value networks and the true nature of collaboration. ValueNet Works. Available from: http://www.valuenetworksandcollaboration.com.

BMM, 2010. Business Motivation Model, Version 1.1: OMG Document Number: ptc/2010-05-01. Available from: http://www.omg.org/spec/BMM/1.1.

BPMM, 2008. Business Process Maturity Model, Version 1.0. Object Management Group. Available from: http://www.omg.org/spec/BPMM/1.0/PDF/.

BPMN, 2011. Business Process Model and Notation, Version 2.0. Object Management Group. Available from: http://www.omg.org/spec/BPMN/2.0/.

CMMN, 2014. Case Management Model and Notation, version 1.0. Object Management Group. Release Date: May 2014, http://www.omg.org/spec/CMMN/1.0.

Christenson, C., 2016. The Innovators Dilemma—When Technologies Cause Great Firms to Fail. Harvard Business Review Press, Boston, MA.

Collins, J., Porras, J., 1996. Building your company's vision. Harvard Business Review, September–October.

Cummins, F.A., 2009. Building the Agile Enterprise With SOA, BPM and MBM. Morgan Kaufmann, Burlington, MA.

Cummins, F., 2011. A Knowledge Worker Cockpit. Available from: http://fredacummins.blogspot.com/2011/07/knowledge-worker-cockpit.html.

Cummins, F., 2013. A Model Based Management Dashboard. Available from: https://www.cutter.com/offer/model-based-management-dashboard.

Cummins, F.A., de Man, H., Analysis of the Relationships Between VDML and BPMN, OMG Document Number bmi/2013-22-01. Available at: http://www.omg.org/cgi-bin/doc?bmi/2013-11-01.

Cummins, F.A., de Man, H., 2013. VDML Support for the Business Architecture Guild BizArch Viewpoint: OMG Document Number bmi/2013-11-02. Available from: http://www.omg.org/cgi-bin/doc?bmi/2013-11-02.

CWM, http://www.omg.org/technology/documents/modeling_spec_catalog.htm#CWM.

Daft, R.L., 2016. Organization Theory and Design, 12th ed. CENGAGE Learning, Boston, MA.

DMN (Decision Model and Notation), Version 1.0, OMG Document Number dtc/15-11-51, http://www.omg.org/spec/DMN/.

Drucker, P., 2002. Managing in the Next Society. Truman Talley Books, St. Martin's Griffin, New York.

eTOM, http://www.tmforum.org/browse.aspx?catID=1648.

Ferraiolo, D.F., Kuhn, R., Chandramouli, R., 2003. Role Based Access Control. Artech House, Boston, MA.

Frankel, D.S., 2003. Model Driven Architecture. John Wiley & Sons, New York.

Harmon, P., 2007. Business Process Change: A Guide for Business Managers and BPM and Six Sigma Professionals. Morgan Kaufmann, Burlington, MA.

Harmon, P., Tregear, R., 2015. Questioning BPM. Meghan-Kiffer Press.

Hruby, P., Kiehn, J., Scheller, C., 2006. Model-Driven Design Using Business Patterns. Springer-Verlag, Germany.

HTML, http://www.w3.org/html/.

HTTP, http://www.w3.org/Protocols/.

IBM, Component Business Modeling, http://www.haifa.ibm.com/projects/software/cbm/index.html.

Inmon, W., O'Neil, B., Fryman, L., 2008. Business Metadata: Capturing Enterprise Knowledge. Morgan Kaufmann, New York.

ITIL, 2011. Service Design, ITIL Version 3. Available from: http://www.best-management-practice.com/Publications-Library/IT-Service-Management-ITIL/ITIL-2011-Edition/Service-Design/.

Johnson, M.W., Christensen, C.M., Kagermann, H., 2010. Reinventing Your Business Model: Harvard Business Review on Business Model Innovation. Harvard Business School, Boston, MA.

Lindgren, P., Jørgensen, R., Li, M.-S., Taran, Y., Saghaug, K.F., 2011. Towards a new generation of business model innovation model. In: Presented at the 12th International CINet Conference: Practicing Innovation in Times of Discontinuity, Aarhus, Denmark, 10–13 September 2011.

McComb, D., 2004. Semantics in Business Systems. Morgan Kaufmann, New York.

MOF, 2013. Meta Object Facility, Version 2.4.1: OMG Document Number: formal/2013-06-01. Available from: http://www.omg.org/spec/MOF/2.4.1.

OASIS, 2006. SOA-RM, Reference Model for Service Oriented Architecture 1.0. Available from: http://docs.oasis-open.org/soa-rm/v1.0/soa-rm.html.

OASIS, 2009. WS-ReliableMessaging, 1.2. Available from: http://docs.oasis-open.org/ws-rx/wsrm/200702/wsrm-1.2-spec-os.pdf.

Osterwalder, A., 2004. The Business Model Ontology—A Proposition in a Design Science Approach. University of Lausanne, Lausanne. Available from: http://www.hec.unil.ch/aosterwa/PhD/Osterwalder_PhD_BM_Ontology.pdf. Thesis.

Osterwalder, A., Pigneur, Y., 2010. Business Model Generation: A Handbook for Visionaries, Game Changers, and Challengers. John Wiley & Sons, Hoboken, NJ.

PKI Wikipedia, https://en.wikipedia.org/wiki/Public_key_infrastructure.

Porter, M.E., 1985. Competitive Advantage: Creating and Sustaining Superior Performance. The Free Press, New York.

Prahalad, C.K., Hamel, G., 1990. The Core Competence of the Corporation. Harvard Business Review, Boston, MA.

SAML, http://www.oasis-open.org/specs/index.php#samlv2.0.

SBVR, http://www.omg.org/technology/documents/br_pm_spec_catalog.htm#sbvr.

SMM, 2015. Structured Metrics Metamodel, Version 1.1: OMG Document Number: ptc/2015-02-02. Available from: http://www.omg.org/spec/SMM/1.1.

SoaML, 2012. SOA Modeling Language, Version 1.0. Available from: http://www.omg.org/spec/SoaML/1.0/.

Stabell, C.B., Fjeldstad, O.D., 1998. Configuring value for competitive advantage: on chains, shops and networks. Strateg. Manag. J. 19 (5), 413–417. Available from: http://www.agbuscenter.ifas.ufl.edu/5188/miscellaneous/configuring_value.pdf.

Sterman, J.D., 2000. Business Dynamics: Systems Thinking and Modeling for a Complex World. McGraw-Hill, New York.

Teece, D.J., Pisano, G., Shuen, A., 1997. Dynamic capabilities and strategic management. Strateg. Manag. J. 18 (7), 509–533.

Thompson, J.D., 1967. Organizations in Action. McGraw-Hill, New York.

UML, 2013. Unified Modeling Language, Version 2.4.1: OMG Document Number: formal/2011-08-06. Available from: http://www.omg.org/spec/UML/2.4.1.

VDML, 2015. Value Driven Modeling Language, Version 1.0, October, 2015, OMG Document Number formal/2015-10-05. Available from: http://www.omg.org/spec/VDML/1.0/.

Whittle, R., Myrick, C.B., 2005. Enterprise Business Architecture: The Formal Link Between Strategy and Results. CRC Press, Boca Raton, Florida.

Wikipedia, Value Chain, http://en.wikipedia.org/wiki/Value_chain.

WS-BaseNotification, http://docs.oasis-open.org/wsn/wsn-ws_base_notification-1.3-spec-os.htm.

WS-BrokeredNotification, http://www.oasis-open.org/specs/index.php#wsnv1.3.

WS-Notification, http://docs.oasis-open.org/wsn/wsn-ws_base_notification-1.3-spec-os.htm.

X.509 v3, IETF RFC 5280. https://tools.ietf.org/html/rfc5280.

STANDARDS

WS-Federation, http://xml.coverpages.org/ni2007-03-20-a.html.

WS-Notification, http://www.oasis-open.org/specs/index.php#wsnv1.3.

WS-Policy, http://www.w3.org/2002/ws/policy/.

WS-Security, http://www.oasis-open.org/specs/index.php#wssv1.1.

X.509v3, http://www.ietf.org/rfc/rfc2459.txt?number=2459.

XACML, http://www.oasis-open.org/committees/tc_home.php?wg_abbrev=xacml.

XMI, http://www.omg.org/technology/documents/modeling_spec_catalog.htm#XMI.

XML, http://www.w3.org/XML/.

XML Schema, http://www.w3.org/XML/Schema.

XML Signature, http://www.w3.org/Signature/.

XPDL, http://www.wfmc.org/standards/docs.htm#XPDL_Spec_Final.

XSLT, https://www.w3.org/TR/xslt20/.

Index

Note: Page numbers followed by *f* indicate figures, and *t* indicate tables.

Printed in the United States
By Bookmasters